Muscle and Mayhem
The Saginaw Kid and the Fistic World of the 1890s

Lauren D. Chouinard

Cover photo courtesy of Don Scott

© 2013 Lauren D. Chouinard
All Rights Reserved.

No part of this publication may be reproduced, stored in a retrieval system, or transmitted, in any form or by any means, electronic, mechanical, photocopying, recording, or otherwise, without the written permission of the author.

First published by Dog Ear Publishing
4010 W. 86th Street, Ste H
Indianapolis, IN 46268
www.dogearpublishing.net

ISBN: 978-1-4575-1840-9

This book is printed on acid-free paper.

Printed in the United States of America

CONTENTS

Dedication v
Acknowledgements vii
Preface ix
Introduction 1
1. Mom's Story..4
2. Flesh and Blood: Cousin Confirmation 12
3. The Lavigne Beginnings 16
4. The Making of a Young Pugilist 31
5. The Early Lightweights..46
6. The Featherweight Champ and the West Coast Tour 55
7. Fugitive in the Midwest...67
8. Griffo and the Gatling Guns...73
9. Go East Young Man...79
10. From Rules to Rings: Boxing's Metamorphosis 87
11. The Tragedy of the American Title 96
12. Battling to the Top 107
13. "The Greatest I Ever Saw" 121
14. Prelude to an Englishman 133
15. The Schoolboy Goes to London......................................141
16. The Battle of the Burge for the Best in the World.........152
17. Boxing's Quest for Legality and Legitimacy..................158
18. Non-Title Interludes 166
19. The Original Kid 178
20. 1897—Suitors Abound..184

21.	He Seeketh the Demon Again	197
22.	Twenty-Six Rounds with Wilmington Jack	211
23.	Two More Go the Distance	226
24.	The Gathering Dark	239
25.	Reign's End	252
26.	Three Strikes and You're Out	262
27.	The Long Drought	271
28.	Into the Ring at Last	282
29.	Hard Times on the Comeback Trail	288
30.	From the Asylum to Paris	298
31.	Kid Palooka	305
32.	El Último Título En México	312
33.	Not Yet Dead	318
34.	Decline and Revival in Detroit	327
35.	The Long Count	339

Postscript – The First Lightweight Champion of the World 352
Appendix A – 1890s Words and Phrases 357
Appendix B – George "Kid" Lavigne's Professional Fight Record .. 360
Appendix C – Kid Lavigne's Physical Measurements 368
Appendix D – Lavigne Family History 369
Chapter Notes 371
Bibliography 403
Index 407

Dedicated to my mother, Eleanor Emma Lavigne,
the greatest little sports fan of the 20th century
1913-1999

HOOKS A KINGFISH

King Levinsky, now training at Hollywood in the World's Fair grounds for his battle with Jack Sharkey here September 15, called a new sparring partner into the ring yesterday and was hooked by a right to the chin. The Maxwell st. heavyweight now regards Miss Eleanor O'Connor as a knockout in several respects.

Eleanor Lavigne (O'Connor) in the ring with heavyweight contender King "Kingfish" Levinsky at the Chicago Century of Progress Exposition in 1933. She was a 20-year-old budding talent in Chicago's theatrical scene of the day and donned the gloves for a promotional shot with King.

ACKNOWLEDGEMENTS

It was my mother who gave me the boxing bug as a 10-year-old boy. She is the reason this book was written. My wife Carrie put up with my constant ramblings about old-time boxing for two and a half years. I'm sure there were times when she thought I was channeling spirits from the 1890s. She is relieved that the long march is over. And I would be remiss if I didn't mention my faithful little companion Trinket. She is an eight pound Chihuahua, terrier mix. She was at my side, literally, every day while I was immersed in researching, writing and editing. She knew that treats and long walks would be her reward.

Boxing historian Bill Schutte was the original collector of all things Kid Lavigne. It was his archive that was sold to Harry Shaffer from whom I purchased a copy. Many thanks to Bill, who through Harry, provided me with a trove of articles. Harry, who recently passed away, provided many pictures, additional articles, and conversation that could only be found in a person who truly loved the early years of the sport. He will be missed by many in the boxing historian community.

At one point early in my research I needed to find someone who knew their way around Saginaw and Bay City Michigan and the area's early boxing scene. I lucked out finding Jack Tany, president of the Saginaw County Sports Hall of Fame. Jack, a life-long resident of the area is an enthusiastic fan of Kid Lavigne. He and I traded dozens of e-mails and phone calls over a two year period. He encouraged me at every corner and bend, providing me with names, pictures, and information that were invaluable in my research. Jack authored the book, *Glory: The History of Saginaw County Sports*. Through various channels I was also fortunate to find John Cuthbertson, also a lifelong resident of the area, and a man with deep ties to the early Saginaw boxing community. John too is a fellow author and his latest book, *Coming to Scratch or Down for the Count*, chronicles the early Michigan fight game. I can't thank these two men enough for keeping me going on the project.

Joining the International Boxing Research Organization (IBRO) provided me with a depth of resources. IBRO's director, Dan Cuoco, was always there when I had a question and if he couldn't answer it he'd find someone who could. Every IBRO member I talked to or traded e-mails with went out of their way to assist and encourage me. What a great organization.

Many others contributed including Sandy Schwan, curator of the Castle Museum in Saginaw, Kelly Ferchau, Stacy McNally (great, great, granddaughter in-law of the Kid's first opponent, Morris McNally), Chris Applin, Chris Holubowicz, and additional staff from the Hoyt Library in Saginaw, Ron Bloomfield, Fred Welsh and additional staff from the Bay County Historical Society, William Mays of the *Police Gazette*, Dr. Louis Moore of Grand Valley State, and all the staff at the American French Genealogical Society and the *Saginaw News*.

Additional libraries consulted and whose staff provided assistance include the Rockford, Illinois Public Library, Michigan State University Library, Illinois State University Library, the Eugene Public Library and the University of Oregon Knight Library.

The list also includes the assistance of several authors, researchers, boxing historians and others including Colleen Aycock, Bob Caico, Tracy Callis, Doug Cavanaugh, Don Coleman, Jeffrey Cuthbertson, Suzanne Desort, David Doss, Andrew Fruman, Tony Gee, Craig Hamilton, Debra Hutsell, Jeremy Kilar, Jean Lamarre, Christine Lewis, Clay Moyle, Kelly Nicholson, Joe Page, Lowell Plaugher, Bill Pollock, Thomas Scharf, Donald Scott, Mike Silver, Tony Triem, Jahongir Usmanov, and Sergie Yurchenko.

Special thanks to Bob Winkleman of Evergreen Film Service in Eugene, Oregon for his painstaking work on preparing the pictures that went into this book. And a final nod to a couple of other cousins I found in Saginaw, Penny and Matt Hopper.

PREFACE

I am not a boxer. I've never had any interest in stepping into a ring. I'm too slow and while my only experiences of getting hit were the result of 12 years of playing rugby, I'm fairly certain I never had what it takes to go toe-to-toe in a squared circle. I am, however, a huge fan of the fistic arts. I grew up in the racially-ravaged 1960s inner city of Chicago's south side, just a few blocks from the home of Muhammad Ali, then Cassius Clay. I spent a lot of time as a kid trying to keep from getting my ass kicked, stabbed or shot. I made a science out of evading danger, while protecting and preserving my physical well-being. I suppose my love of boxing may have been a way to live vicariously in a world of violence where I would have been an active and lone participant against a single opponent.

I got the boxing bug from two people: my mother and Mr. Vesely. My mother was a sports fanatic, including boxing, football, baseball, basketball, tennis and hockey. I learned at an early age that we had boxing royalty in the family tree. My mother was a second cousin of George "Kid" Lavigne, lightweight champion of the world from 1896-1899. Mr. Vesely was the dad of one of my best friends, Keith. Mr. V was an ex-middleweight having fought while in the Marines. Several Friday nights each year Mr. V would take Keith, me and another best bud, Art, to the American legion hall in the neighborhood to watch fight films, eat fried chicken and drink Cokes. And we watched a lot of film of fighters from bygone eras. There was Jess Willard vs. Jack Johnson, Willard vs. Jack Dempsey, Dempsey vs. Tunney, Tony Zale fights, Rocky Graziano and Marciano, Two-Ton Tony Galento, Max Baer, Joe Louis, Jake LaMotta, and on and on.

Every so often a fighter of some renown would drift into the hall for a visit. I was shocked to see former heavyweight champion Ezzard Charles one night hobble in on double canes, slurring his speech. He was in the early stages of Lou Gehrig's disease which would take his life a few years later. That same evening we watched the Jersey Joe Walcott/Rocky Marciano classic. I still remember that seminal scene in the 13th round. Marciano appeared soundly beaten at that point but midway through the round they both threw vicious right hooks. Marciano's landed a millisecond before Walcott's. It was one of those highlights shown over and over in slow motion and immortalized in brutal still photos with Walcott's face slowly and mercilessly contorting to a shape unknown. Walcott was knocked cold—very cold—as it was many minutes before he was revived. Maybe that fight and the barely-functional former champ that graced us with his presence that evening were the images that disabused me of any notion of getting into a ring to slug it out with another man. Even so, I was fascinated with the skill, power, speed, cunning, and most of all, the endurance of punishment and pain that I watched in bout after bout.

I am not a boxer nor am I an expert on the sport. But, I just may be the world's foremost authority on Kid Lavigne. Many years ago I was visiting my brother Gene in the small rural town of Burns, Oregon. Burns is out in the wastelands of eastern Oregon's high desert in one of the most sparsely populated counties in the lower 48. He was working for the Bureau of Land Management and I was tagging along for a day while he drove south toward the Steens Mountains to check on a herd of wild horses. Along for the ride was a wildlife biologist who happened to be the world's foremost authority on Sandhill Cranes, a large bird native to that area. I was fascinated that someone could be labeled as "the world's foremost authority" on anything. As I began working on this book, I realized that if a subject was obscure and off the beaten path one could, with a few painstaking years of research and writing, become more knowledgeable about the subject than anyone else on the planet. That notion intrigued me. The story of Kid Lavigne is just such a subject, having been touched on by many but thoroughly researched and reported on by no one. Until now.

I am not a boxer, nor an expert on boxing, nor am I a boxing historian. Being an authority on one boxer hardly qualifies me to include myself in this behind-the-scenes breed of folks who dedicate a chunk of their lives to uncovering and preserving histories of ring characters large and small. The historians fascinate me nearly as much as the boxers themselves. Simply put, without them and their vast collective resources this book would not have become a reality.

I had been thinking of writing a book about my cousin for several years. When I began to do the research I found that George "Kid"

Lavigne, aka the "Saginaw Kid," was much more than a world champion. The more I read and the deeper I went I began to realize this was a book about one of the greatest fighters of all time. Lavigne was both enigmatic and typical of the fighters of his day. "Going the distance" in the early days of the Marquess of Queensberry era meant fights could last for hours. Lasting for hours was a specialty of Lavigne's.

His fights were marked by a swarming fury that often continued gaining momentum with the approach of the 20th round. His stamina and capacity to absorb punishment were seldom equaled in any age of boxing. The Kid was first and foremost a body puncher. He deployed his formidable talent through a suffocating attack designed to overwhelm and incapacitate his opponent. Submission was often the cumulative effect of many rounds of crushing body blows that set up a final smash to the chin that ended it. There was simply no quit in him. He was in a word, "relentless." He was also typical of his day as he lived fast, fought hard, drank too much, attempted a failed comeback, and died fairly young after squandering a fortune. History, from the early fight game to modern times, is replete with examples of fighters who typified this latter set of traits.

It's not often one gets the opportunity and privilege of writing the first book on a historically significant character and in my case also a blood relative. I tried my best to leave no stone unturned in splicing together a story from fragmented parts and perspectives. I wanted the Kid to be larger than life. At the same time I needed to check any temptation to overstate events. As it turned out, without any help from a relative at the keyboard, he was not only larger than life but also inclined to some of the seamier behaviors of a common man. While I'm proud to call a former champion my cousin, I am not proud that he was arrested multiple times, roughed up his wife, and drank like a sailor. I had envisioned a book of 200 pages but given the recounting of the many stories of the good, the bad, and the ugly of the Kid's life and times, the final product ballooned to over 400 pages. No regrets. And to Mom and the Kid, I'm sure there's a library in heaven. . . . Hope you enjoy the read.

INTRODUCTION

I've read a fair number of books about boxing, impressed by some and disappointed by others. In writing *Muscle and Mayhem* I attempted to sift through all the best traits of those books, discarding things that I felt detracted from the works and adding elements that I felt were left out.

The book begins with a brief story of my mother who gave me the boxing bug. It then establishes my family's genealogically-certain connection to George "Kid" Lavigne. In doing so it traces the Lavigne lineage from France, to Quebec and on to Bay City and Saginaw Michigan. Through a description of the rough and tumble logging environment of 1880s eastern Michigan, the stage is set for the young pugilist's debut in 1886.

As the Kid's career is forged the chapters depict a chronology of his fights, championships, hell-raising, arrests, infirmities, comebacks, dissipation and death. The chronology is broken by three interludes designed to give some background to those unfamiliar with this part of boxing's history and to anchor this romp through early fistiana. It is capped by a postscript that attempts to answer a nagging question.

Chapter 5—"The Early Lightweights," helps place the Kid within the historical context of the beginnings of the lightweight division. Chapter 10—"From Rules to Rings: Boxing's Metamorphosis," identifies and examines the framework as well as the physical details of the changes which ushered in the modern era of pugilism. Chapter 17—"Boxing's Quest for Legality and Legitimacy," depicts boxing's climb through a social and legal jungle to daylight. And finally the Postscript—"The First Lightweight Champion of the World," attempts to settle the question once and for all: Who was the first lightweight champion of the world under the Marquess of Queensberry rules? In between these four ring-posts, so to speak, is a blow-by-blow of the

Kid's life and career from his birth in Bay City, Michigan in 1869, to his death in Detroit in 1928.

Having no film footage to view and no living person to interview who saw him fight, the discovery of who he fought, how he fared in the ring, and how he lived outside it came largely from modern-day boxing record sources as well as newspapers and periodicals of this bygone era. This is a work of non-fiction but anytime one is relying on 100-year-old sources the line between non-fiction and fiction gets blurry. I found that many writers of the time were prone to exaggeration of events. As the late Harry Shaffer of Antiquities of the Prize Ring so aptly put it, "Reading the description of a fight by two or three different sports writers, you begin to wonder if they all watched the same bout." I found it was necessary to sift through several versions of a fight, note where testimony was in conflict or agreement, weigh the evidence carefully, and extract the most logical and consistent account of what happened.

The book makes liberal use of quoted material which begs recounting word-for-word, highlighting the colorful expression of the time and transporting the reader back to the days of bowler hats and horse-drawn trolley cars. Far too often books on boxing simply identify which newspapers, periodicals, and books were used in the production of a work without connecting material to specific sources and dates. In *Muscle and Mayhem* every quote can be traced back to its original source through a detailed notes section.

Spending better than two years immersed in the late 19th and early 20th centuries I grew fascinated with the vernacular of the day. My grandfather, born in 1874 just five years after Kid Lavigne, often called me a "scalawag" as a young boy or one of my sister's boyfriends a "bold stump." His vocabulary was peppered with these antiquated terms. I came across so many of these words in my research that I have included Appendix A, titled, "1890s Words and Phrases," because quite frankly, I had no idea what some of these expressions meant.

Through research I discovered bouts that Kid Lavigne had that did not exist in the ring records kept by Cyber Boxing Zone, Box Rec, or Fights Rec. I also found a few bouts in those records that should have been attributed to other fighters. Kid Lavigne's updated ring record with notations is included as Appendix B. I was lucky enough to find a complete set of physical measurements for the Kid in an 1897 *San Francisco Examiner* article and have included those as Appendix C. For those interested in the Lavigne family and its genealogy I included the Kid's ancestry all the way back through Canada to France in Appendix D. And lastly, I am often disappointed in historical works on boxing that skimp on pictures. To that end I have included 88 photos of Lavigne, those he fought, a few fight venues of the time, and programs and posters as well.

This is a book about George Lavigne's life and career, a biography in part, yet it is much more. It is about history and sport as well: the history of an age of boxing teetering on the edge of legality and legitimacy, and the fledging sport of pugilism as it struggled to transform itself from brutal spectacle to mainstream attraction. And finally it is about history on a different level that explores the genealogical context of a personal quest to link two families over four centuries and connect the lives of two cousins across a span of well over 100 years.

CHAPTER 1

Mom's Story

Eleanor Emma LaVigne was not yet three years old on January 23, 1916. It was a typically cold windy day on the south side of Chicago. Her mother, Agnes "Nellie" O'Connor, had died that morning at the age of 29 leaving her husband, Henry Edward LaVigne, to care for her and her three siblings. Later in the week the funeral took place. As bad as losing their young mother had to be for Eleanor and the other children, things were about to get much worse. Henry was nowhere to be found the day of the funeral. With the exception of one unverifiable alleged siting in California in the mid-1920s, Henry Edward LaVigne dropped off the map and was never seen or heard from again.

Eleanor died in 1999 after having six children in the 1930s, 40s and 50s. I was the last of the brood born in 1952. Mom and I had a common bond . . . we loved sports. She and her brothers and sisters were raised by the O'Connor and LaVigne aunts and uncles. When Mom was a teenager she was shipped off to St. Catherine Girls Academy in Springfield, Kentucky. This is where her passion for sports had its beginnings. She was the captain of the basketball team and at all of 5 feet 2 and 1/2 inches played center. No matter, she was tough, competitive and scrappy. She knew her sports and her sports figures as well. She was 15 when she wrote in her diary on January 22, 1929: "Tex Rickard's dead. Isn't it awful?" Tex of course was the legendary fight promoter of heavyweight champ Jack Dempsey. And again as a 17-year-old on April 1, 1931: "The Lord certainly got in a neat April fool on Notre Dame. Knute Rockne was killed yesterday when the plane he was riding in, and which had first taken the air, exploded. He was on his way to a football conference in California.

Terrible—too horrible to believe!! Tex Rickard—Miller Huggins—Knute Rockne—will Dempsey be next?" Or yet another on May 16, 1931: "Derby Day—and did we lose!! Pittsburgher came in seventh. Oh well, the Sox won today 3-0."

She met my father, Laurence Chouinard, when they were both employed at the 1933 Century of Progress World's Fair in Chicago. My father was not a great lover of sports but he did attend Notre Dame from 1929 to 1933. The "Fighting Irish" were a powerhouse of college football in the late 1920s under Knute Rockne. That did not go unnoticed by Mom. Over the years she rooted for Notre Dame, the Chicago Bears, Blackhawks, Bulls, and of course her beloved White Sox. A heavy smoker since the age of 14, she had two heart attacks in her late 40s and was told by her cardiologist not to watch or listen to sporting events as it was just too hard on her heart. To this very day, when I'm yelling at the TV during an Oregon Duck football game and my heart is pounding with excitement I think of her and wonder if I'll blow a gasket following that passion I'm sure I got from her.

One of her sports passions was atypical for most women of the time, or of any time for that matter; she was a huge fan of boxing. I learned why as a 10-year-old boy when she told me her cousin had been the lightweight champion of the world from 1896 to 1899, one George "Kid" LaVigne. Now that was hard to believe even coming from my own mother. I was pretty excited when I found a copy of the *World Almanac and Book of Facts* in a local bookstore and paged to the sports section on boxing records. There he was, Kid LaVigne, a.k.a. the "Saginaw Kid," the first lightweight champion of the world. I was ecstatic! I used my meager allowance to buy a copy of the book just so I could show all my friends. I was related to a world champion! The intrigue didn't stop there. She told me that not only was she related but that her father, the disappearing scoundrel Henry LaVigne, had been one of the Kid's sparring partners.

This wasn't the only time Mom told me a boxing story that seemed hard to believe. When I was a teenager she told me that her father (actually the uncle who raised her) took her to the scene of a Jack Dempsey fight in Benton Harbor, Michigan. As the story goes she was seven years old at the time and while they didn't go into the fight arena they hung around outside. They waited patiently after the fight concluded in hopes of catching a glimpse of the "Manassas Mauler" as he and his entourage left the arena. To their surprise, Dempsey was about to walk right by them when he stopped, reached in his pocket and pulled out a penny. He patted Mom on the head and gave her a big smile as well as the penny.

I sort of brushed it off as the fantasy of a young girl and didn't think much about it until one day in 1999. I had just picked up a new book about Dempsey by Roger Kahn titled, *A Flame of Pure Fire: Jack Dempsey and the Roaring 20s*. And there it was—Dempsey fought Billy Miske on September 6, 1920 in Benton Harbor, Michigan. I called Mom and began the conversation excitedly with, "Billy Miske . . . it was Billy Miske!" Of course it had been 33 years since last we talked about her childhood brush with Dempsey and an additional 46 years before that when it supposedly happened so she kept repeating, "What are you talking about?" I said, "The Dempsey penny story . . . it was Dempsey's first defense of his world heavyweight title against Billy Miske in Benton Harbor. It was 1920. You were born in 1913 and you told me you were seven at the time. It all adds up. Dempsey knocked him out in the third round. It really happened didn't it?" "Well of course it did," she said, almost a little miffed that I had doubted her all these years. "I'm your mother," she continued in a charmingly indignant tone. "I wouldn't make that up." We had a good chuckle together. Mom died later that year finally succumbing to the estimated 750,000 cigarettes smoked in her lifetime. The Chicago sports scene lost one of its most ardent fans.

In 1985 I drove from my home in Eugene, Oregon to Salt Lake City to spend a week backpacking in the Wasatch and Uinta mountain ranges east of the city. Just out of curiosity, I visited the Church of the Latter Day Saints Genealogical Library in downtown Salt Lake. I thought that as long as I was in Salt Lake I should take a few hours and finally answer the question of whatever became of her dad, Henry LaVigne. It was something I really wanted to do for my mom before she left us.

While I never asked her directly, I sensed from our conversations about her father that she was deeply disappointed and ashamed of him for leaving the family in the manner that he did. But I also got another, unspoken hit from those conversations. She was intrigued by the roguishness of his behavior at such a critical juncture and by nagging thoughts of what may have happened to him. Since she was just a toddler when he left she had almost no memories of him other that those told to her by her grandparents and aunts and uncles. It was unfinished and I felt I could provide some answers for her and for me.

I began by searching census records for the 1920s, 30s, 40s, 50s and 60s. While I found a few Henry LaVignes, none of them had the right birth year of 1882. I tried military records on an assumption that he may have enlisted to fight in World War I as a way to give his life a positive direction after committing such a heinous act. Or absent the pangs of conscience perhaps he may have seen it as a way of disappearing in the ranks of the military. No luck there either. I tried the Social Security Index which began keeping records in 1937. Henry would have been 55 that year and most likely still in the workforce at that time. Nothing.

After returning from Salt Lake City, I made some assumptions about which states he might have moved to, most of them in the surrounding states to Illinois in the upper Midwest. I also threw California into the mix based on the phantom sighting I was told about that supposedly happened in the mid-1920s. I contacted the Vital Records Offices of each of the states and asked for death records over a span of five decades between 1920 and 1970. Again, no Henry LaVigne matches with his birth year. Mom had mentioned, proudly, that not only was he a stable-mate of Kid LaVigne's but he was also a Teamster. The Teamsters were founded in Chicago in 1903. A Teamster in say, 1915, may have driven a real "team" as in a horse drawn wagon or an early motorized truck. I contacted a couple Teamster locals on the south and west sides of Chicago and asked if they kept records that far back. They said their records for that period were sketchy and I hit yet another dead end.

After a few years of searching other possible leads, I gave up. Mom told me that, back in the day, it was very easy and more common than one would imagine to simply change your name, move to a new location, and assume a new identity. You could effectively vanish from a past life. Perhaps that is what became of Henry. Each year more and more vital and cemetery records are being added to a mountain of data that is searchable over the internet. Every few years I see what's available and mine it in hopes of finding a fresh lead. I still hold on to a fantasy of standing in front of his grave someday and whispering, "Found him Mom."

Having failed in my quest to find Henry I turned my energy to uncovering the full story of this other Lavigne, George Henry, the lightweight boxing champion of the world. There would be no shortage of leads this time and the first lead came from, you guessed it, Mom. I remembered that she had been in contact with a boxing historian who was a professor at the University of Wisconsin at Whitewater. His name was Bill Schutte. Bill had a special interest in the pre-1920 boxing era. A few years after Mom died in 1999 I was going through a box of family ancestor photos and memorabilia. I came across a letter from Bill to my mom dated September 24, 1987. It reads:

> Dear Ms. Chouinard,
> I read in The Ring Magazine that you were inquiring about the ring career of Kid Lavigne, your second cousin. I am a specialist in early American boxing history and I have a large collection of old newspaper, magazine and gazette clippings on Lavigne's life and ring career. (A few sample copies enclosed).
> If you would like copies of early clippings on Kid Lavigne I can supply hundreds of them. All I ask in return would be information on the Lavigne family, copies of family photographs, marriage licenses, documents, information on his descendants, etc. Anything you might have along the genealogical line is what is of interest to me. I have been collecting early boxing history for about 35 years now and have amassed a large collection of fight-related material on Kid Lavigne but it is the family-related material that is more difficult to come by.
> If you have anything that you would be willing to share with me, please let me know.
> Sincerely,
> Bill Schutte

So Mom had written an inquiry to *The Ring Magazine*, the preeminent boxing periodical since 1922, sometime presumably in 1987 looking for history on her famous second cousin. Dan Cuoco, president of the International Boxing Research Organization (IBRO), helped me locate my mother's query in the "Ask the Answerman" section of the October 1987 issue. It read:

> "I have long sought information about George Lavigne, a la 'The Saginaw Kid.' The boxing maven of Chicago, Ben Bentley, suggested that I try The Ring. After reading Joyce Carol Oates' article in the March issue where she takes us back to 265 B.C., I decided what the heck. That's even before my time, so I'm giving it a try. He would be my second cousin, and my kids have always bugged me to find out something about him. You know how we all love to touch a celebrity.
> Eleanor La Vigne Chouinard – Lansing, Illinois

Phil Marder, managing editor, replied with a couple paragraphs giving the highlights of Lavigne's career, the date of his death and that he was inducted into *The Ring* hall of fame in 1959. Phil didn't give Mom any additional leads, so had not Bill Schutte contacted her, the 23-year chain of events that led to my writing of the Kid's biography would not have happened. Thanks Bill.

As it was now 2010 I wondered if Bill was still alive and if so did he still have the "several hundred" early clippings on Kid Lavigne. I made an assumption that if Bill told my mother in 1987 that he had been collecting boxing material for 35 years he might have been in his 60s at the time. That would make him at least in his mid-to-late 80s in 2010. I figured I would need a bit of luck to find him alive. After some on-line white pages sleuthing I found someone I assumed to be him. I called and left a message.

It was my lucky day. He called back and turned out to be in his mid-60s. He explained why he was so much younger than my calculation had predicted. He was seven years old when he began collecting boxing history! I asked Bill if he still had the clippings on Kid Lavigne. He said he did not. A crush of disappointment overwhelmed me. My heart caught in my throat for an instant only to be released by his next words: "I sold my Kid Lavigne archive to another boxing historian, Harry Shaffer, in Columbus, Ohio." "Do you think Harry would sell me a copy of the archive?" I asked. "Oh sure," Bill responded. "He has a business and a website, 'Antiquities of the Prize Ring,' and sells all kinds of boxing memorabilia."

After a great conversation with Bill I then called Harry Shaffer. I explained to Harry what I was after and he said, "Sure, I have a chronologically organized archive that spans from 1885 to 1928 with 173 pages of material in it." Harry had the mother lode! Henry Lavigne had proven to be an unknown who was virtually untraceable. Not so with George. He was famous and I would soon have a paper trail 43 years long and growing. Harry quoted me a discounted price for the materials as I was a relative of Lavigne. He also sold me a photo archive of 10 photos along with the rights for publication.

I had now spoken with three boxing historians; a subset of the boxing culture that I hardly knew existed. I joined IBRO immediately. Over a two year period Harry Shaffer and I stayed connected by e-mail and phone. He'd send me articles and we'd have long phone conversations about details of Lavigne's career and the boxing world of well over a century ago. Harry was a treasure-trove of information and he never tired of sharing his encyclopedic knowledge and resources. Unfortunately, over the two years that he and I had become chummy Harry was growing progressively ill. Harry died on June 7, 2012.

While I was a late addition to the IBRO family I knew by now what a loss he was to the boxing historian community.

Largely as a result of finding Bill Schutte and my relationship with Harry Shaffer I was off and running. The more I read about Lavigne, the story that unfolded became more intriguing. But, there was still a piece of unfinished business. I wanted to write the story in part from the perspective of a blood relative. I couldn't do that without answering the question of just "how" I was related. This would take another level of investigation and inquiry as I had very little information to establish the genealogical connection except my mom's assertion that she and the Kid were second cousins. I had no indication of who the common ancestor was and now that Mom had passed, no way of grilling her for more specifics, if indeed she had any.

CHAPTER 2

Flesh and Blood: Cousin Confirmation

One morning while having coffee with my kayaking buddies one of them asked how the book on Kid Lavigne was coming. I was telling them how I was struggling to connect the genealogy when Tim said, "So you said he's your cousin right?" I knew from the way he asked the question and from the look on his face that he was struggling to connect the concept of "cousin" between two people who were born 83 years apart. Many of us think of our cousins in the context of the children of our aunts and uncles. Our cousins are usually people roughly our own age. Many people use the term cousin loosely, giving it a definition of any relative with whom one shares a common ancestor that is otherwise not described as a brother, sister, aunt, uncle, or other person in one's own line of descent. The term *blood relative*, which underscores the existence of a genetic link, is often used synonymously. In my case, my mother's cousin was also my cousin but that falls far short of explaining distinctions.

The distinction is explained through a somewhat complex system of degrees and removes. The degree (first, second, third cousin, etc.) indicates one less than the least number of generations between either of the cousins and the nearest common ancestor. Take the example of hypothetical cousin #1 whose ancestor is his/her great grandparent. The same ancestor of cousin #1 is also cousin #2's great, great, great grandparent. The cousin in this scenario with the least number of generations between them is cousin #1. There's the cousin, his parents, and his grandparents, which equals three generations. To get the degree you subtract one from three and you end up with two, which makes them second cousins.

What Tim was tripping over was how I could be a cousin of a person who lived so long ago. That is explained further by the concept of *removes*. The *remove* (once removed, twice removed, etc.) indicates the number of generations, if any, separating the two cousins from one another. In my case, there are four generations separating us so I am four times removed . . . but still cousins. Non-genealogical usage often eliminates the degrees and removes, and refers to people with common ancestors as *cousins* or *distant cousins*. Also, the terms *second cousin* and *first cousin once removed* are often incorrectly used interchangeably.[1] Even after reading this stuff on degrees and removes it still was hard to conceptualize. I found a cousin chart, also called a table of consanguinity. For my fairly linear brain this was a big help. It is a type of X and Y axis chart starting with grandparent and going down to great, great, great, great, great grandparent on one axis. The other axis is the same. All one has to do is determine the relationship of both people to the common ancestor and where the chart lines cross is the answer both for degree and removes. Nothing could be simpler, except I didn't know who the common ancestor was.

As anyone who has dabbled in genealogical research will attest a good story becomes so much better when the main character is a flesh and blood relative. I remembered how I felt as a boy when Mom told me about our family being related to a world champion boxer. I am just as excited at 60 but also more cautious and skeptical, a product of several decades spent rubbing elbows with humanity. Mom had always said we were second cousins to Kid Lavigne but she never talked about how many times *removed* we were. Forget the removal for now—I needed in my heart to be sure we were related and although I didn't doubt my mom's veracity, I allowed for the possibility that someone had sold her a bill of goods way back when and she proudly and innocently passed it along.

So the search for "cousinship" became the search for a common ancestor. I got an on-line membership to Ancestry.com and began to do the research, focusing on the Montreal area of Quebec where both lines of the family were purported to be from. A few problems quickly popped up. Both George "Kid" Lavigne's father and my mother's grandfather were named Jean Baptiste. I learned later that Jean Baptiste was the most common first name for boys in 19th century Quebec. So common that when I found my mother's great grandfather his name was also Jean Baptiste. And, her grandfather was the second Jean Baptiste of the children in the family as the first Jean Baptiste died at age seven months.

While I could not imagine using the name of my deceased child on the next born, it was not uncommon in the days of large Catholic families with high rates of infant mortality. Not to be outdone, Kid Lavigne's dad also named one of the Kid's brothers after himself, Jean Baptiste. This was getting confusing . . . could his father and Mom's grandfather be the same person? Because Kid Lavigne was famous someone else had already done his pedigree which I quickly got access to and found that Mom's grandfather and the Kid's father, although sharing the same name were two different people. Even so, I continued to hope they were two related people.

The farther you push back into the early 1800s and into the 1700s the harder it is to find Canadian genealogical records. Canada did a census in 1851 and every ten years thereafter for the rest of the century. Before 1851 censuses were done less frequently and only on head of households so one must rely mainly on church records, handwritten in French. I knew those two years of high school French would be useful someday and I retained just enough over the years to muddle my way through the records of baptisms, marriages and deaths. I kept running into a vacuum in the early 1800s. I had Kid Lavigne's lineage back to the 1620s in France but there were blank spots on the map on my side of the family beyond my great, great grandfather Jean Baptiste. After months of research; a few hours here, a few there, I gave up and resolved to pay a professional researcher to get the proof of ancestry I needed. Then one day while Googling some ancestry websites I found a wonderful resource.

It is called the American French Genealogical Society or AFGS for short, located in Woonsocket, Rhode Island. I learned on their website that they provide a research service using a group of volunteers charging a nominal amount for specific searches. They had something called a "five-generation pedigree chart" that I thought would be just what I needed to put the nail in the ancestral coffin. For AFGS members they charged $35 for the five-generation research.

Since some of what you find on private pedigree charts contains inaccurate information I decided that I would do both my lineage and Kid Lavigne's to double check the accuracy of the lineage chart I already had on him. All that is required is that you have enough information such as date of birth, place of birth, marriage date, etc., on the primary person and his/her parents. So on one chart I requested a search for the Kid's ancestors and on the other I requested a search for the ancestors of my great grandfather Jean Baptiste Lavigne who was roughly the Kid's contemporary. It was my way of triangulating back to an unknown target. I sent it off in the mail and was prepared to wait several months for the results.

Three weeks later the results came. I nervously attacked the envelope and pulled out the contents, quickly scanning the handwritten charts each with 31 names going back five generations. I looked at Kid Lavigne's chart first noting that the lineage was a perfect match of the one I already had in my possession. I noticed a star scribbled above the name of Joseph Lavigne. I then looked at the chart for my great grandfather and again noticed the star drawn above the name Joseph Lavigne. Here was the final evidence that I had hoped to find.

Kid Lavigne and I were related beyond a shadow of a doubt. I rushed into the other room to tell my wife who had patiently listened to my ramblings for months about ancestral details and frustrating dead ends. "I found it!" I said over and over. "I found the common ancestor. It's Joseph Marie Lavigne born in 1755 in Montreal. He married Angelique Ranger in 1774 and died young at 44 in 1799." One of his son's was Jacques, Kid Lavigne's grandfather and another was, of course, another Jean Baptiste, my great, great, great, great grandfather.

So Kid Lavigne's great grandfather Joseph was my great, great, great, great, great grandfather Joseph. Now all that was left to do was to check Mom's accuracy of whether or not we were second cousins and figure out how many times removed I was from the Kid. I went to my chart of consanguinity. Moving down one axis I found "Great Grandfather." Moving across the other axis I found "Great (times five) Grandfather." In the column where they met, it said "2nd cousins, four times removed." What had been very murky and uncertain for many years was now crystal clear and of course, Mom was right as always, second cousins we were.

CHAPTER 3

The Lavigne Beginnings

Way back, the first Lavigne of the Kid Lavigne/Eleanor Lavigne lineage to come to the New World was Andre Poutre dit Lavigne. Andre was our common ancestor's, Joseph Poudrette dit Lavigne's, great grandfather. The name, phonetically pronounced *lah vehn*, en Francaise, with a breathy exhale and nasally silent "n," means vine or vineyard. A few hundred years later when the Lavignes emigrated from Canada to the United States the pronunciation changed to an Anglicized *la veen* and was often misspelled, Lavene, Lavine, and Levine. Throughout the genealogical record of the family name it was written both Lavigne and LaVigne. My mother's teenage diary given to her by her uncle Eugene Lavigne as a Christmas present in 1929 was signed by him with the upper case "V" version of the name. George "Kid" Lavigne on the other hand, changed to the lower case "v" as he became a more popular public figure, always signing his letters and correspondence with a small "v."

But what about this addition of the prefix-like "Poutre dit" or "Poudrette dit" to the Lavigne surname. In some areas of France, second surnames were adopted in order to distinguish between different branches of the same family, especially when the families remained in the same town for generations. These alias surnames can often be found preceded by the word "dit," pronounced "dee," which literally means, "said." Sometimes an individual even adopted the dit name as the family name, and dropped the original surname as most probably happened with George Lavigne and my grandfather, Henry Lavigne, as no mention is made in baptismal or census records of Poudtre, Poutre, Poudrette, Poudret or any other offshoot spelling of the name associated with either of them.

An educated guess would be that when George "Kid" Lavigne was born in 1869, his father, Jean Baptiste, and the family had been in the U.S. for only a year and they dropped the Poudrette name as Lavigne may have appeared shorter, and therefore easier to write and pronounce as they worked to assimilate in their new surroundings. The same is probably true of my grandfather, Henry Lavigne, who was born in Quebec in 1882 but moved with the family to the U.S. in 1887 where his father, also Jean Baptiste, dropped the Poudrette name as well. As with all waves of immigration to the U.S. in the 19th and early 20th centuries, families found it easier to fit in if their names appeared less "foreign."

Imagine my surprise when doing research for this book and finding that the surname "Lavigne" might have been an add-on and not the original surname of Kid Lavigne or my mother, Eleanor Lavigne. While the majority of the original surnames were patronymic (from the father's side) or matronymic (from the mother's side), it is possible that the "dit Lavigne" add-on was of matronymic origins, perhaps to distinguish between different branches of the Poutre family. However, it was also common for surnames and alias or dit surnames to be derived by occupational description. The best guess in the case of the Poutre dit Lavigne name was that Poutre was the original surname and to distinguish between different lines of the family one ancestor, who happened to be a vintner by trade, took on Lavigne, translated "the vine," as his secondary "dit" identifier.

Across the Atlantic to New France

The following passage gives the historical context of the Lavigne beginnings in North America. It was written by Lucile LeBlanc Constentino. "By the mid 1600's the French in New France (Canada) had developed very strong commercial ties with the Algonquin and Huron Indians in the fur trade. So when the Iroquois waged war on the Algonquin and Huron, as they had for many years, even before the Europeans arrived in North America, the French went to the aid of their commercial partners. By doing so, the French earned the hatred of the Iroquois. Prodded on by the English, who also wanted the French out of North America, the Iroquois began raiding French villages and slaughtering the people. To respond, the French began to form military units under militia Captain Pierre Boucher. However, this wasn't enough so Governor Davaugour dispatched Pierre Boucher to France to seek help from King Louis XIV.

Carignan Regiment Soldiers –
Courtesy of The Company of Military Historians

"At that time, there was a regiment of seasoned soldiers in France known as the *Carignan Regiment*. It had been formed as a private army in 1644 by Thomas François de Savoie, Prince de Carignan. This was an army for hire, made up of hand-picked volunteers. The standards were very high and these men had to be big and strong physically with a strong fighting spirit. In the hire of the King of France, this regiment had just returned from a successful engagement against the Turks. Rather than demobilize the regiment, the King determined to send it to New France to help the colonists. The Regiment was placed under the command of Henri de Chapelas, Sieur de Salières and was therefore renamed the *Carignan-Salières Regiment*.

"In 1662, the Marquis Alexandre de Prousille de Tracy was named Lt. General of North and South America by Louis XIV. He was ordered to wipe out the Iroquois in New France. This was to be accomplished by the Carignan Regiment. In April of 1665, he left for New France, arriving in Québec on June 30. Over the next three months the rest of the Regiment—officers and soldiers—arrived from France 1,200 strong."[1] Andre Poutre Lavigne, a 19-year-old farmer and shoemaker from Flanders, France was one of those soldiers. He joined the Saurel Company of the Carignan-Solieries Regiment. His company and three others sailed from LaRochelle, France on May 13 for a three-month voyage on the ship La Paix (the Peace) bound for Quebec. The ship's Captain Guillon dropped anchor in the harbor of Quebec City on August 19, 1665.

"Over the next two years, the Regiment manned garrisons and launched attacks on the Iroquois. By the end of this period, their task was accomplished. The countryside became peaceful for a time. About 800 of these soldiers went back to France. The remaining 400 stayed. The officers were encouraged to stay with promises of fiefs (land containing many square miles). Their troops were promised concessions of large tracts of land in these same fiefs. They could farm and start a new life in the New World."[2] Also to their great benefit was a program sponsored by the French government to supply the new colonists with wives. The men looked forward to the arrival of the "Fille du Roi."

The "Fille du Roi," translated as the "King's Daughters", were single women who agreed to travel to the new French colonies in North America and marry a soldier or settler. The program was aimed at increasing the number of women in New France as women were woefully outnumbered by men, most of whom were voyageurs, soldiers, and farmers. They made contracts of marriage with the men who had originally settled the New World and usually married within a few days or weeks of the contract signing. Often the women broke the contracts, only to remake them or make new contracts with other men.

These were young women who had been selected by their parish priests to go to the colony as prospective brides. They were given a dowry of 50 dollars for marrying a soldier or farmer—versus 100 dollars for marrying an officer—a supply of household items, and free passage aboard ship with the expenses picked up by the French royal treasury. In exchange, the women were required to marry soldiers or settlers and begin raising families. These young women had fifteen days in which to choose a mate, after which time those who remained unmarried would be returned to France.[3] Who knew the concept of "speed dating" had its origins in 17th century Quebec!

Andre decided to stay. He returned to farming and married Jeanne Burel, a King's Daughter, on November 3, 1667. Andre Poutre Lavigne, the farmer-turned-soldier was part of the first emigration of the Lavigne clan in 1665 from France to Quebec City. Andre's grandson, also Andre, named for his grandfather, moved westward to Montreal 100 years later. And in another 100 years, the second emigration took place when Jean Baptiste, Kid Lavigne's father and another descendant in a long line of farmers, pulled up his Canadian roots.

Farming was not a rich occupation unless you owned a great deal of land which Jean Baptiste did not. As a young man Jean Baptiste, one of twelve children, moved to the rural hamlet of St. Polycarpe, a small village on the banks of the Delisle River about 40 miles southwest of Montreal. There he met Marie Agnes Dufort, who went by

Agnes, marrying her on February 20, 1860. Exactly nine months to the day later, on November 20 they had their first child, a boy whom they named Jean Baptiste. As was far too often the case in rural 19th century life, the baby died before his first birthday. They had a second child, Joseph Procul born in August of 1862. He died 11 months later. Undaunted and typical of a time when a Catholic woman bearing many children was common place, they tried again and on August 1, 1864, they had their third child, Joseph Guillaume, "William." William survived and two years later in August of 1866 they had another child, this time a girl, Marie Louise, who also died an infant. Jean Baptiste and Agnes would go on to bear a total of twelve children. Only six would survive.

The Call of the Woods

I was looking forward to summer between my freshman and sophomore years at Illinois State University but was struggling to get a job lined up near my home on Chicago's south side. On a whim I called my brother Gene living in Roseburg, Oregon. He was a forester working for the Bureau of Land Management. I asked if there were any summer jobs he knew of out his way for an unskilled college kid. He said, "Sure, I can get you a job working in the woods." "Great. What kind of job?" I replied. "Settin' chokers," he responded. "What's a choker?" I said. "Never mind, can you get out here as soon as your semester is done?" "Sure, I'll load up my van and be out there by early June." "One more thing," he said, "you might want to cut your hair." Still not understanding just quite why, I cut my shoulder-length hair and piled into my "hippie" van with red, white and blue, American flag curtains and purple shag carpet for the long drive west.

After 2,000 miles on the road I pulled into a gas station near Crater Lake National Park just a few hours east of Roseburg. An old gas station attendant wandered out, looked at my license plates and said, "Illinois, huh," sounding the s like a z. "Yup," I said proudly. "Well, whatcha doin' out here?" he said in a folksy tone. "I'm going to spend the summer working in the woods," I replied. "Doing what in the woods?" said he. I puffed up my chest a bit, straightened my spine to get every inch of my 6' 3" frame into my response and said, "Settin' chokers," as if I was an expert on whatever the hell a choker was.

Now the old fella's eyes narrowed a bit and his voice softened when he said, "How did you get that job?" "My brother works for the BLM and he got it for me," I said. He got just a bit closer and in a very respectful but concerned tone he said, "Son, does your brother like you?" I responded with a nervous chuckle as if I was in on the joke. I brushed it off and went on my way with the nagging choker question in the back of my mind. To me it didn't matter what a choker was, I was going to be a "logger" for the summer and that sounded pretty romantic and was perhaps the coolest summer job of all for an inner-city kid.

Settting chokers, it turned out, was one of the most physical and dangerous jobs on the planet. It meant wrapping large cables around logs scattered across steep hillsides deep in the Coastal Range of southern Oregon. The logs were then dragged up the hill by incredibly powerful machines and loaded on what else, log trucks, for transport to sawmills. It meant getting up at 3:30 a.m. driving 30 minutes to a place where crew members were picked up by a truck called a "crummy" and then another hour on dust-choked, two-track roads to the site of the day's work. We worked 10 hour days, with one short break for lunch. It was hot, dirty, and extremely exhausting work.

My first day on the job, my brother dropped me off at the site. I looked like a logger, although way too clean, with my spiked boots called "corks," red suspenders, and hardhat. The crew boss told me to go down the hill and join the group of men 700 feet down the ravine. I watched on my way down as this group of guys, looking like ants they were so far down there, scampered across mountains of brush and logs pulling 30-feet long, inch-thick cables which they attached to the logs. They'd then run to safety—and I mean run—while the massive machine at the top of the hill called a "yarder" began to reel in the even larger cable from which the chokers, and now the choked logs, were hanging. The yarder would rip and tear these massive logs loose from their nest and if you weren't far enough away by then, the log you were standing on was likely to move as well sending us all hopping and jumping to safety. The logs would continue crashing and plowing their way upslope, digging deep grooves and obliterating all small foliage and ground cover on what was once a forest floor. It was an awesome display of power and destruction that blew me away and nearly got me killed several times over the course of two long summers.

I reached the group and after introductions we awaited the empty chokers to return after depositing their catch on the landing. During this couple-minute interlude my four crew-mates were unusually quiet as if my presence had put a damper on their normal chit-chat. When the choker rigging returned, I heard three loud toots then a short pause followed by a single toot that came from a train-type whistle on the yarder at the top of the hill. These toots are loud enough that they can be heard miles away in the mountains. I had no idea what the tooting meant until a hand reached out and grabbed me, forcefully yanking me backward. A split second later the monster line, called the "haul-back," slammed violently down on the very place I had been standing. It would have killed me if I had still been standing there. I jumped from the noise and the near miss. The crew boss, known as the "hook-tender" simply barked, "Hey kid . . . three and one, that means slack the haul-back. Never stand under the haul-back."

19-year-old author at a logging site in the Coastal Range of southwestern Oregon, 1972

"OK," I thought. Now I knew four things. First, they communicated with the yarder operator by a series of toots activated by an electronic device worn on a waist belt of the man called the "riggin' slinger." Two, that three toots followed by one toot meant you damn well better be standing clear of the haul-back. Three, there was no safety manual provided. Pay close attention and do as they do or you may be maimed for life if not worse. And four, I needed to quickly learn the glossary of logging terms as if my life depended on it . . . because it did!

It turned out to be the hardest job I had ever had. To give you some perspective, I was 19 and had just finished a season of playing rugby. I was very fit and very strong. After the first two weeks on the job I was dying. It was intense physical work in 90 degree heat with no shade at a few thousand feet of elevation skittering up and downhill over a haystack of downed timber and brush all day long. It wasn't until the third week that I started to get acclimated to the environment and learned how to finesse the choker rather than overcoming it with brute force, which was wearing me out.

After long days in the woods I would retire to a small camping trailer on my brother's driveway that I called home. I had no energy for any activity other than getting horizontal and reading. My interest in history, which was my major at Illinois State, made me intrigued about the past of the industry in which I now toiled for the summer. I picked up a book by Stuart Holbrook first published in 1938 called *Holy Old Mackinaw*. I was captivated by a promotional paragraph on the back cover that read: "A 300 year history: 1620-1920—This is a robust, roistering saga of the logger, hewing a path across the nation. He felled the forest, sent it rushing down mighty rivers; drinking, lusting and leaving a path of sunlight, and farms, towns, and cities, to flower in his wake."[4]

I would fall asleep dreaming of the heroic romance of it all, only to be awakened by the manic squawking of my alarm clock at what felt like the middle of the night—because it was—to do it all over again. Only I was too young to drink, too tired to lust, and our modern river of transport was a network of two-track logging roads not mighty rivers. Logging had come a long way from the early days. It started with the white pine forests of Maine and after cutting a swath of daylight across the Great Lake states it finished in the Douglas fir and Redwood timber of Washington, Oregon and California.

I was fascinated by the larger-than-life, Bunyonesque description in *Holy Old Mackinaw* of a bawdy culture of men and the towns that sprouted to meet the demands for timber and the needs of the loggers. One evening I was a few pages into a chapter titled, "Big Doings Along the Saginaw," that being the Saginaw River in east-central Michigan. A paragraph noted, "native talent budded among the piles of sawdust." And a bit later, "George Lavigne who worked in a sawmill and boxed on Saturday nights was on the way to having his picture on the front cover of the *Police Gazette* as the Saginaw Kid, the lightweight champion of the world (1893-1899). The Kid had plenty to practice on in Saginaw of the 1880s."[5] I bolted out of the trailer and into my brother's house to tell him I found mention of our famous cousin in a book on logging.

Logging had been the life blood of the lake states beginning in about 1840 when the white pine forests of New England played out. The "first migration" of loggers to the lake states hit its peak in the 1850s and was still going strong through the 1860s. As the American Civil War ended many Canadians saw great opportunity in the logging boom south of the border. That boom peaked in 1882 and lasted until about 1900 when the "second migration" took place to the western states. I suppose I was technically a member of the second migration even though I went west to log 70 years after the beginning of it when the western logging boom was long over and the wood products industry as it was now known was reeling from decline, shuttering towns and forcing painful changes on the entire region.

The opportunity I seized that summer had a connection to the one that faced Kid Lavigne's father, Jean Baptiste Lavigne, over a chasm of 100 years and two very different centuries. Both were based on the harvesting of trees for market. I was on the extraction end moving logs to sawmills. He was on the product development end turning logs into boards. I needed a summer job and as part of that second migration, found it on the West Coast working for Huffman and Wright Logging Company out of Riddle, Oregon on what is known as a "high lead" logging crew. Jean Baptiste needed a new beginning for his nascent family and as part of the first migration, albeit from the northern flank, found it across the U.S. border working for one of the dozens of sawmills operating along the Saginaw River as it coursed its way through Bay City to Lake Huron.

Southwest to Michigan

Jean Baptiste, his wife Agnes, and their four year old son William moved from St. Polycarpe, Quebec to Bay City, Michigan in 1868 a few miles down-river from the city of Saginaw. They boarded a train, the Grand Trunk Railroad, for the first leg of the journey. Since 1860 the Grand Trunk Railroad Company had linked central Quebec with its western terminus at Sarnia, Ontario. From Sarnia they took a ferry across the St. Clair River to the town of Port Huron, Michigan. From there they purchased a wagon and loaded all their worldly belongings on it for the final 110 miles to the lower Saginaw valley. This was the route for many French Canadians who would comprise the largest ethnic influx to the Saginaw Valley from the post-Civil War years to the decline of the logging boom in the 1890s.[6]

The name "Saginaw" has two possible derivations, both of Native American origin. The *Bay City Logbook* states that it was derived from an Ottawa term "Sag-a-nah" that meant "where the river flows out" and probably referred to the outflow of the Saginaw River into Lake Huron. The 1937 Centennial Edition of the *Bay City Times* told of a different derivation. It reads, "O-sauk-e-non, an Indian name meaning 'the land of the Sauks' is the word from which the Saginaw Valley derives its name."[7] This was common belief that had its beginnings with explorer Samuel de Champlain in 1632 when he mistakenly put the Sauks on his map as being located in the Saginaw Valley. It wasn't until 1966 when historian Francis Wakefield sorted out the discrepancy.[8]

"Lower Saginaw" as it was known in the 1860s was now a bustling community called Bay City. Just four miles from Saginaw Bay, it had been a Native American trading post until it was platted as a town in 1837. In 1865 it became a city and in 1868 it had nearly 7,000 residents. To the Lavignes, Bay City looked like the big city, having come from their tiny settlement in Quebec of a few hundred residents. The French Canadian immigrants settled primarily in two areas of Bay City; on the west side of the river in what was called Banks, and on the east side in Dolsenville—an area north of Woodside Avenue—also called "Frenchtown." Upon their arrival they found a residence just south of Woodside on Jefferson in the Pittsville section of town, so named for its proximity to the Pitts and Cranage sawmill. A few years later they moved to Frenchtown on the northeast corner of Dunbar and Hart streets.

Bay City, Michigan in 1868. Note the Pitts and Cranage mill in the upper right corner on the river and the steeple of St. Joseph's in the upper center of the photo, where the Lavignes attended church. - Courtesy of Bay County Historical Society

Jean Baptiste immediately went to work in a sawmill. While difficult to substantiate, the mill he worked for was most likely the Pitts and Cranage mill as it was on the bend in the river just a few blocks from the Lavigne residence on Jefferson and later it was accessible by horse-drawn streetcar from their second home in Frenchtown. Many of the mill owners constructed housing for the mill workers, a boarding house for singles, and a company store to meet their needs. Company houses could be purchased for as little as $200. Early maps show what appears to be company housing in the area the Lavigne's lived, although again, it cannot be proven as to whether they lived in a company house or rented a private dwelling. John's wife Agnes was known to have worked in a boarding house and it was quite possibly one built by Pitts and Cranage. John and Agnes would have their fifth child on December 6, 1869 a son named George Henry Lavigne.

Life in an Early Logging Town

Like the towns and villages that sprouted around the lumber camps and sawmills of New England before it and the far west after it, Bay City and Saginaw shared various characteristics with them all. As described in Holy Old Mackinaw, "Saginaw City of the 1850s and well beyond was a town of the new frontier. Life was more expansive, the tempo faster. They had steam sawmills here of a size and speed never dreamed of in Maine. Logging was done on a titanic scale to feed the mills. Ten miles above Saginaw City the Flint, Shiawasse, Cass, and Tittabawasee rivers united to form the Saginaw; and along the banks of them all, and miles deep on both sides, was bigger and, men said, better white pine than was ever seen in the East. Here, sure enough, was more timber than could be cut in a thousand years."[9] Truth be told, it lasted only fifty years. By 1900 there was so much "daylight in the swamp" as the loggers were fond of saying, that it hastened the second migration to the far west.

Twelve miles down-river, just a few miles from Saginaw Bay on Lake Huron was another sawmill town, Bay City. It, like Saginaw, was growing rapidly as were the number of sawmills. Saginaw County had 2,600 residents in 1850. By 1884 it was nearly 75,000. Bay County to the north had less than 2,500 residents in 1850 and grew to over 40,000 by 1884. The year 1884 was also significant because it represented the peak output of the eastern Michigan lumber era. Saginaw had grown to have 74 sawmills by that time and Bay City had 38 more. Mills arose on every parcel of land along the river between the two towns and "one could almost but not quite walk the dozen miles on the tops of the piles of lumber."[10] That year, those 114 Saginaw River mills produced over one billion board feet of lumber.

Lumber towns were tough places. They resembled the cattle towns of the old west in the manner that young men, working outside the towns for long stretches of time, would finally get some time off and head to civilization for a quick clean-up and a bender of booze, gambling, and women. The scene was the same, only the occupation and geography were different. Cowboys on the range and loggers in the camps had much in common. They were rough-hewn, hard-working, heavy-drinking, lust-filled men. The loggers lived in camps, most of them sleeping in crude cabins and "shanty" structures that would make a rustic cabin look like a five star hotel.

When I worked in the woods 100 years later in the southern Oregon forests some things still remained the same. The loggers who did the extremely dangerous work of clearing the forest held an air of superiority, of additional manliness, over those that worked processing the logs in a sawmill. Each had its benefits and downsides. Working in the woods paid more, was more hazardous, and embraced the raw elements of nature which suited the rugged logging types quite well. Working in a sawmill, while still very hard work, paid less unless it was a skilled position, and was less dangerous. It also had the benefit of home cooked meals, heated sleeping arrangements and the enjoyment of a rugged semblance of town life to break the monotony of long days inhaling saw dust amid the din of the screeching, steam-powered mill saws. When a millworker settled into an occasional hot bath in town, the farthest thing from his mind was his brethren in a soggy, cold logging camp, bunking close together with his many filthy, reeking co-workers.

The following description is taken from the *Making of America*, Library of Congress Collection. It gives a detailed overview from an 1868 account of the lumbering life:

> From the opening of the season in April or May to the close in November the stir of industry is incessant. But the summer life of the river depends upon the winter life of the forest. Year by year, as the wood is cut off, the lumberman has to go farther in from the main stream, and the log has a longer journey to make before it gets to the mill. The first party of woodmen usually go out in November, as soon as the ground begins to freeze; they select a place for their camp as nearly as possible in the center of the "lot" which they are to work upon, taking care to get a dry soil, in the neighborhood of some spring or brook; they build a log-house, and cut a road to the nearest stream, on which the logs must be floated down. The log-houses are large enough to accommodate from twenty to fifty persons. In

the center a raised fireplace is built, directly under the apex of the roof, and the only chimney is a tunnel above this fireplace.

The work of wood-cutting begins as soon as the road is finished and the ground becomes hard enough to haul the logs—usually early in December—and it is continued until the streams break up in the spring. The daily wood-chopping begins with the early morning, and is kept up so long as there is light. In the evenings the woodmen sit around their fire, play cards, smoke their pipes, tell stories, and sometimes get up rude dances. There is very little drinking among them during the season of work in the woods. Settlers are not allowed upon the premises, and the men have usually no money to buy liquor. They are paid by the day, and supplied with suitable food by their employers. Pork and beans, dried fish, bread, and tea are the most approved articles of diet. Coffee is not generally provided, and the delicacies consist chiefly in the wild game which the woodmen themselves may chance to catch. There is plenty of this to be had, if there were time to take it; for the woods are still full of squirrels, rabbits, coons, deer, and black bears, whose flesh is not unpalatable: the streams, too, are full of fish. But the men are too busy in their craft to do much fishing or hunting, and are content with their simple, but nourishing, regular fare.

In addition to their "nourishment," they get, on an average, about a dollar a day for their labor. The whole gain of a lumberman, in his winter's work, is about a hundred dollars, which a new suit of clothes and a few weeks of sport in the spring generally exhaust. The life of lumbermen is like that of sailors, and very few lay up the fruits of their toil. In character, the men are quite as good as the average of those who lead a roving life. A large number of them work in the mills in the summer season; some go on farther west; and others go home to their friends in Canada or Maine. Comparatively few of the wood-choppers are Germans or Irishmen, though there are parties of both these races. They are gregarious in their habits. In cutting trees they go in pairs, and very few of them are willing to live in separate huts or away from the camp. They sleep along the sloping side of the house, with their feet inwards, toward the central fire, which is kept burning during the night. They dispense with prayers and preaching, and make little account of Sunday. A few have books, but the taste for reading is not general; mending clothes and sharpening axes, with such amusements as we have mentioned, fill the spare time.

Their occupation is healthy and cheerful. The stock of medicines rarely needs to be replenished, and there is not much for a physician to do in their strong-armed company. A gang of forty men, it is estimated, will cut, in the course of the winter, three million feet of lumber, the product of about five hundred acres, and draw it to the streams. Only the trunks of the trees are saved for lumber. These are sawed into logs of twelve, fourteen, or sixteen feet in length, according to their diameter and the width of the stream down which they are to be floated. It needs some art to launch them properly, and to place them so that they will float freely when the ice breaks up in the spring. A few inches of snow upon the ground greatly assisted the lumber operations, by enabling the men to substitute sledges for the drag with its heavy weight and its friction.[11]

Winter logging circa 1880 – Courtesy of the Public Libraries of Saginaw

These hearty souls were known as "Shanty Boys." Once the logs were "skidded" across the frozen ground from the woods they were stacked in piles known as "rollways" along the river's edge or in holding ponds. With the coming of the spring thaw, they would cut them loose into the river for the ride to the mills downstream.[12] Sawmills began operating as soon as the spring thaw allowed the first logs to appear from upstream. In this part of Michigan it meant sometime in May. In a good year they would still be turning logs into boards through the end of October when the supply of logs petered out.

During these early years in Michigan the Lavigne's were doing well. They would reside in Bay City for twelve years surrounded by a tight knit French Canadian community and attending St. Joseph's Catholic Church. With Jean Baptiste working in the mill and wife Agnes supplementing the family income through her work in a boarding house they lived comfortably. The move from Canada had been a good one.

CHAPTER 4

The Making of a Young Pugilist

I had been randomly calling Lavignes from the white pages of Bay City and Saginaw hoping to find a relative of the Kid's that had information about his early life and career in the area. A pattern was developing in the responses I was getting. Several people assumed they were related but were unsure exactly how and knew little of his life other than the highlights that had been printed over the years in the local papers. I had a theory that in every family there are one or two relatives who take an intense interest in their heritage, avidly researching and collecting any and all documents, stories, pictures and other memorabilia about their ancestors. I just had to find one of them. But try as I might, I never did, however, one afternoon nearing the end of a conversation with a Lavigne relative the man said, "you need to talk to John Cuthbertson . . . I think he's writing a book about Michigan boxers and he lives in Saginaw."

One of the things I learned in my research was that almost everyone I talked to had at least one little tidbit, one little lead that made an otherwise friendly but uninformative chat very worthwhile. John Cuthbertson was one of those leads. He wasn't related to Kid Lavigne but he was related to the early Saginaw boxing scene. When we connected by phone the next day we were both very excited that we'd found each other. John was working on a book about Michigan boxers, due to be published in late 2012 titled, *Coming to Scratch or Down For the Count*, in which he planned to include a piece on Kid Lavigne. By this time in my research I was sitting on an archive of over 400 pages of material on Lavigne so I could be of great help to John. On the flip side, John had boxing roots in the Saginaw area that went back to the turn of the 20th century. As John so aptly put it: "Remember, I go back 77 years and the people I knew went back another 70 years beyond that."

John, a retired school principal, is the son of Jim Cuthbertson, the rugged middle weight champion of northern Michigan whose career spanned 1910-1919. After getting injured in World War I, Jim went on to become a promoter of many great Michigan boxers of the era. As it turned out, John was one of the last folks left in the area who had connections to the early days of the Saginaw fight scene. He told me a tale of a man named Billy St. Mary, a promoter in the early days of legal boxing in Michigan just after the end of World War I. St. Mary left a "steamer trunk" full of boxing memorabilia, pictures, old programs, posters, etc., with John's dad Jim. John told me over the phone, "I've got pictures and stuff from the early days that no one has." He sent me a photocopy of one such picture. It shows Kid Lavigne and a couple of other "toughs" standing in front of the Michigan House hotel in Saginaw circa 1887. Lavigne and another man are holding axe handles. Their job was to secure the premises from rowdy loggers that came to town hell bent on a bender. I wondered what else he had from the trunk regarding Lavigne. It had me thinking buried treasure! Now I was excited.

George Lavigne (leaning against post) and enforcement crew at the Michigan House - Courtesy of John Cuthbertson

The Move to Melbourne

Opportunity knocked again for Jean Baptiste, Agnes and the family when word spread of a new mill being constructed a few miles to the south of Bay City. Henry A. Batchelor, a native of Port Huron, 100 miles to the southeast, formed a partnership with David Whitney Jr. of Detroit, a famous lumberman who owned a large body of white pine timber along the tributaries of the Titabawassee River. At one time Whitney owned by far the largest timber acreage ever possessed by any individual in the state of Michigan.[1] In 1877 the partners bought a site eight miles north of Saginaw at a settlement known as Melbourne and erected a mill which was completed in early 1879.

This wasn't the first sawmill at Melbourne. In 1864 another early lumber baron and world traveler, Wellington Burt, built a sawmill at the site he named after his favorite Australian city. The Whitney and Batchelor mill operated at Melbourne until it burned to the ground in 1894 and was not rebuilt. During its time the Whitney and Batchelor mill reached an annual capacity of 30 million board feet, quite high for that time period. As with most mills of that era along the Saginaw River it also operated a salt works. Many mills also made barrels to ship the salt. The mills would use scrap lumber to boil away brine water and recover the salt residue. The Whitney and Bachelor mill produced 80,000 barrels of salt annually.[2]

In the fall of 1880 Jean Baptiste pulled up stakes in Bay City and moved the family to Melbourne taking a job as a machinist in the newly opened mill. The wage for an experienced laborer in the mill was $1.60 per day. A machinist was considered a skilled position and was paid more than the general laborers. Agnes, having learned the ropes by working in a boarding house in Bay City soon opened her own boarding house in Melbourne. Many mill owners in company towns such as Melbourne built standard two or three story railroad boardinghouses, 30 x 80 feet, to house their workers. The going rate for room and board was $5 to $6 per week. When the communities became well established the lumbermen sold or leased them as few saw them as profitable.[3] It's possible that John and Agnes owned or leased the boarding house she managed there. That same year the newest addition to the family was born, a baby girl, Agnes, named after her mother. George turned eleven in December.

As the story goes, young George was "raised" in a mill. Those mills were most likely the Pitts and Cranage mill in Bay City and the Whitney and Batchelor mill in Melbourne. Some of the early lumber settlements lacked school buildings and in those places home schooling was prevalent. George attended the old Second Ward School in Bay City until he was ten.[4] However, when the family moved to Melbourne George discontinued his formal education. According to the 1880 Federal Census, eleven-year-old George was not enrolled in school so it is a safe bet that he was being home schooled by Agnes. When not cracking the books he delivered papers and helped his mom doing chores at the boarding house.

It was typical at the time for women to supplement the family income by taking on boarders or to seek employment in boardinghouses. As noted by the *Bay Journal*, "The lumbering boom brought an army of transient workers to the city creating a huge demand for boarding houses."[5] It was also typical that boys began working in sawmills in their early teens. George was no exception. His father died in 1882 although no cause of death was found in either the cemetery record or State of Michigan death records. This left Agnes and the children to make due. George would have been a few months shy of 13 and he no doubt began working at the Whitney and Batchelor mill as his father had. Children were paid 50 cents per day and were an attractive alternative to hiring men as it cut the mill owners' expenses.[6] Sources indicate that he eventually worked his way up to the skilled position of "cooper," building barrels from wooden staves and metal bands.

His older brother Billy was working in East Saginaw as a bell hop at the posh Bancroft Hotel on the corner of Genesee and Washington.

Bancroft Hotel circa 1880, corner of Genesee and Washington
- Courtesy of the Public Libraries of Saginaw

It was the finest hotel of its time north of Detroit. Bell hops were noted for their knowledge of the "goings on" in town and Billy had "heard stories about the small ring a barber had set up in a room next to his shop to teach boys how to box."[7] Billy's curiosity probably got the best of him and he paid a visit to the shop just two blocks east of the Bancroft on Tuscola. He would be captivated by what he saw. And it would change his life and the life of the Lavigne family forever.

Enter the Black Barber

Charles A. C. Smith was a large, muscular, and handsome black man. In the same decade that brought the Lavigne family south from Canada, the Smith family came north from Macon, Georgia to better opportunities in the Saginaw Valley. While the Civil War had just ended and with it came freedom for the black population, oppression of blacks was nevertheless rampant in the pre-industrial, agrarian south. Seeking a new beginning at war's end, C. A. C., as he was known, and his mother moved north to the Saginaw area to lessen, although not entirely escape, the typical treatment of black people in late 1860s America. One having moved south and the other north, landing just a few short miles from each other, the futures of the Lavigne and Smith families would soon intertwine.

Charles would become an accomplished heavyweight boxer. His fight record is incomplete with various sources in conflict on how many fights he had in his career, possibly as many as 225, and the dates they took place. One source reported that he may have fought, and lost to, Jack Johnson in 1906, while pointing out that the bout is unlikely as Smith would have been at least 46 at the time. One thing that is not in dispute is an appraisal of Smith's abilities by his manager Bill Muldoon who called him, "a great fighter, a terrific hitter, and clever boxer."[8] Muldoon was a good judge of sporting talent and is widely recognized as the first American and world heavyweight Greco-Roman wrestling champion. He also trained boxing greats John L. Sullivan, Kid McCoy, and Jack Dempsey, the "Nonpareil." Many years later he became the chair of the New York State Athletic Commission.[9] Given this assessment by Muldoon and a record that is littered with early round knockouts of his foes it is easy to understand how Smith got his ring name, "The Black Thunderbolt."

Smith fought the Canadian heavyweight champion, Jack Stewart the "Scotch Giant," at Port Huron, Michigan in a gloved contest in February 1883. At this point in the transition from bare-knuckle to gloved era, gloves were skin tight "riding gloves" with no padding. As told by the *National Police Gazette,* "Sporting men of Port Huron had paid Stewart to come on and knock Smith out. Smith fought him to a standstill in three rounds and he [Stewart] left the stage. Robert Wright, the wrestler from Detroit induced Stewart to come back, and in the next round Smith knocked him out."[10]

Smith had his shot at a title slip away when a scheduled bout in May that year against the reigning "Colored Heavyweight Champion" of America, George Godfrey, fell through as Godfrey "got sick" at the last minute. It may be more accurate to conclude that Godfrey refused to fight Smith for fear of losing his title. Godfrey, whose ring name was "Old Chocolate," stood 5 feet 11 inches and weighed 175 pounds. He may have had second thoughts after seeing Smith in person upon his arrival in Boston for the fight. Smith whom the *Police Gazette* called the "Colored Hercules" stood 6 feet tall and weighed about 200 pounds. The *Gazette* described Smith as "a powerful athlete and possessed of great muscular development. He trains daily and is always in condition."

Several times in the early 1880s Smith challenged the great "Boston Strong Boy," John L. Sullivan, to no avail as Sullivan repeatedly ducked prominent black heavyweights throughout his career. After his knockout of the Canadian champion, Smith had a falling-out with his backers. Richard K. Fox, owner of the *Police Gazette,* stepped in. The *Police Gazette* was the leading "sporting" magazine of the time and was the organization that bestowed various championship belts on fighters included those on the "colored" fighters. Fox, being a boxing aficionado recognized Smith's talent and became his financial backer. Fox

C. A. C. Smith, heavyweight fighter and Saginaw barber - Courtesy of Antiquities of the Prize Ring

and Smith challenged all-comers to stay four rounds with Smith for $100 at Albany, New York in June 1883. They got no takers.

Smith was then matched against the former, and first, colored heavyweight champion, Professor Charles Hadley. "Hadley was to receive $100 if he stood up and boxed Smith 4 three-minute rounds. Hadley only boxed three rounds when he stopped." The turning point in Smith's career would happen later that year when in August, he was knocked out in two rounds in a rematch with Jack Stewart. He never quite recovered from the stunning defeat and the rest of his ring career was marred by enough losses to remove him from the picture as a contender.

Smith had been engaged as a barber in Port Huron for several years owning a first class establishment before selling out to move to Albany, New York to focus on his boxing.[11] After his defeat at the hands of Jack Stewart he moved back to Saginaw and opened a new shop on Tuscola Street. A first glance it may seem unlikely that a black man would be proprietor in a day when many blacks were getting their first taste of freedom, but it was not unusual in early lumber towns. As told by historian Jeremy Kilar in *Michigan's Lumbertowns*, "the rough and tumble environment of the lumber towns often permitted financial success regardless of origin or race. Many of the service trades that catered to the shanty boy such as barbering and restaurants were owned by or employed black pioneers. There were 32 black barbers in the Saginaws."[12] But only one with the fistic skills of C.A.C.

Smith had two sources of income both involving skillful use of his hands. His primary source of income was barbering while also making money in the ring as well, where by one account he had been boxing since 1869. Although purses in those days were meager, and less than meager for black fighters, he may have been able to save enough to purchase his barbering equipment and pay his rent to get started. With his barber shop showing success he opened his boxing school just before Christmas in 1883.[13] The man, his ring, and his skills would play a pivotal role in the development of another fighter-to-be, the young pugilist George Lavigne.

Billy Lavigne soon began taking lessons from Smith and was developing rapidly under his tutelage. While he never developed into a heavy hitter he was a "clever boxer," often characterized as being far more "scientific" in the ring than his brother George would ever become. Billy was good enough to lose a close decision in 12 rounds to Harry Gilmore in 1890. Harry was one of the early lightweight greats having claimed the Canadian lightweight title and taken arguably one of the greatest fighters of all-time, lightweight champion Jack McAuliffe, into the 28th round of a title fight before being knocked out.

Billy fought often between 1887 and 1892. He was hailed as the lightweight champion of Michigan and often defeated heavier men. In March of 1891 he accepted the challenge of a black New Orleans heavyweight, John Lewis, who had been knocking fighters out from middleweights to heavies. Billy's science befuddled his much larger antagonist and he stopped Lewis in the fifth round.[14] Three years later Billy's corner threw in the towel in the fifth round after he was beaten badly by another very good lightweight, Bobby Dobbs.

Dobbs was one of several unsung black fighters of the era. At the time of his fight with Billy, Dobbs had fought 45 times with 32 wins, seven draws and five losses. Of the 32 wins, 30 were by knockout. Several accounts of the time say that Billy had "brittle" hands which became a serious boxing limitation. However, according to George it was Billy's work in a bathhouse in his mid-twenties at what would have been the height of his boxing career that gave him "soft" hands. Given the gloves of the day with minimal padding, those hands would not stand up to the repetitive pounding of the early era fight game. Billy's loss to Dobbs marked the end of his career as a fighter but his contribution to the ring as a manager, trainer, and promoter would continue until 1907.

Mitts on the Mite

In a 1927 *Los Angeles Times* column George would tell the story of his first go-round with gloves when he was 14 years old. "One day Billy came home with a mysterious looking bundle under his arm, and opened it to show me a set of boxing gloves, the first I had ever seen. He kept those gloves hidden from me, but one fearfully cold day, between Christmas and New Year's, I came across them. I brought the mitts out to what we called the men's room, where the boarders hung their clothes and washed their faces. There were three neighbor boys of my own age who used to come over to help with my work, and I asked one of them to put the gloves on with me. While we were boxing, three big French-Canadians who boarded with us came in and started to laugh at our efforts. These giant fellows had been drinking. I told the kid who was boxing with me to let one of the big Frenchmen take his place. All of them accepted my challenge, one after another, and in ten minutes I had the three wise-crackers stretched flat on the floor. My mother, hearing the racket, came out, gave me a licking and took the gloves away."[15]

"It was from his mother that the Kid inherited his fighting sense," recalled the *Saginaw News* many years later. "Agnes was a small, wiry woman, and brooked no nonsense among the some 60 boarders in her house. She kept a set of rolling pins handy and any mill-hand who tried to start a fight in the Lavigne household nursed a bump on the noggin for days afterwards."[16]

Billy would learn tricks from the big "colored" professionals and would come home and practice them on George. "George learned fast," wrote sportswriter Larry Gustin, "too fast for Billy, who found it harder and harder to dodge his brother's vicious blows."[17] They would do their sparring and training in a barn near their home. Before long George had a nifty bag of fistic skills to compliment his short but powerful frame. "Nature handed me a remarkable body," he would later write. "Although under 5 feet 4 inches tall, I had a giant's shoulders and arms, and fast legs. I had the strength of a man twice my weight, even in a country of strong men. I also had wonderful endurance and speed."[18] Many early boxing writers concluded that it was George's work as a "cooper" building barrels at the sawmill and loading salt on barges that contributed to his powerful physique.

George started fighting as a teenager in local taverns in bare-knuckle contests against other lumbermen before beginning his professional career.[19] After six long, cold months in the woods, the "shanty boys," as the lumberjacks of the day were called, would come to town arriving in April and May. The transition is described in the *Bay City Logbook:* "The 'ticket to hell' is what the shanty boy called it, and it was often a ticket to Bay City [or Saginaw]. When the northern logging camps closed down in the spring the hands were paid off. They wandered out of the woods, purchased a train ticket at a small, byway rail station and set out for one of the booming lumbertowns."[20]

With their earnings for the winter in hand, usually about $100, the first stops were a bath and a new set of clothes, followed by the beginning of a bender in the nearest saloon. And one didn't need to go far as there was no short supply of saloons in the Saginaws. In the early 1880s there were more than 200 "thirst parlors" in East Saginaw and Saginaw City which together boasted a population of just over 20,000 inhabitants. That's one saloon for every 100 residents. The shanty boys would spend the next 10 to 14 days in an orgy of drinking, "whoring," and of course, fighting before their earnings ran out

> **The Cooper Shop Crew Takes Time Off**
>
> is cooper shop picture, showing the crew of the cooperage shop at the H. A. Batchellor mill at Melbourne, is made especially notable by the fact it includes a man who later won great fame for himself and for Saginaw. This notable, holding a partly finished barrel (fourth from the left), was none other than George (Kid) Lavigne, who became lightweight boxing champion of the world. But here's a list of those in the picture: Standing: Henry Bunton, Lottie Bunton, Tim Shuerette, George (Kid) Lavigne, Jim Ellis, an unknown; sitting: Jack Withey, Cherley Ellis, Tony O'Brien, Joe Deauvid; in the window: Mike O'Brien, Oscar Marceaux, Frank Lavigne.

Grainy photo of George Lavigne standing fourth from left holding an unfinished barrel at Whitney and Batchelor mill. George's brother Frank is in the white shirt in the window on right. - *The Saginaw News*. Copyright 1934. All rights reserved. Reprinted with permission.

and they were forced to look for work in the sawmills or return to the farms that many of them depended on for their grubstake in the summer months.[21]

And the shanty boys loved to mix it up. As described in a short biography of Kid Lavigne in the 1946 publication, *Michigan's Old Inn*, "The lumberjack did not fight because he was angry but because he loved to fight. Every logging camp had its champion and any camp would bet its last dollar that its champion could put the boots to the other camp's favorite. The Marshall or police officer just stood by and acted as a referee. No one of course thought of interfering."[22] The fighting and generally raucous behavior was condoned by the city fathers of Saginaw. As told in Holy Old Mackinaw, "They advised their police to humor the Red Sash Brigade." The Red Sash Brigade was so called because the prevalent ethnicity of the lumberjacks was

French Canadian who wore fringed sashes of red wool around their waists. "So long as a logger did not leap through a window or commit murder in the first degree, they were to be left alone. Saginaw nights might be made hideous by the howls of men released a few days from the savage forest, and of course there would be mayhem on Water and Potter streets, but it was all good clean fun, and citizens might go to bed in security if not in quiet."[23]

Looking East from the Genesee Avenue Bridge circa 1880
- Courtesy of the Public Libraries of Saginaw

The "Kid" Is Born

George was small but was always itching and ready for a good scrap. He got plenty of action and meager supplements to his sawmill wages by challenging and knocking out often larger opponents who were the kings of their lumber camps. But clouting inebriated lumberjacks could only go so far to develop his budding boxing skills. It was time for a step up in competition. One day Billy came home and told George he had arranged a real fight with one of C. A. C.'s rising stars. He was a fellow by the name of Morris McNally who would become one of the top featherweights in the state. "They think McNally is the goods," chuckled Billy, "but what you'll do to him will be plenty and then some." "Gosh, I hope your right," George answered trying to look confident.[24]

The fight was held in the old Saginaw Auditorium on September 7, 1886. George was just a few months shy of his 17th birthday. It was billed as an "exhibition" as prizefighting was illegal. Labeling a fight as an exhibition was just one of several ways used at the time to skirt the laws. It also helped that local authorities took a very lax stance on enforcement. They were to fight six rounds at 120 pounds. The day before his first professional fight George was still a bit in doubt when he asked Billy if he didn't think McNally knew too much for a "green youngster like me." "Say kid," Billy would respond, "you can beat any man in the world at your weight. No one can hurt you the way you can sock."

Billy's comments would ring true for many years to come. His confidence in his tough younger brother was well warranted as George "murdered" McNally knocking him out in the first round. McNally was well respected by the local fight community and they were "dismayed that their champion should be vanquished with such ease by a boy."[25] The Saginaw promoters wanted revenge so four days later they brought in Billy White, a more experienced 130-pound fighter from another town. Young George was flattered. As was his way throughout his career, he didn't balk at the fact he was on the lighter end of a ten-pound weight disparity and was facing a far savvier fighter. George "pickled" White in a first round knockout.

A ringsider that evening was a journeyman by the name of Pikie Johnson. Johnson was well known nationally having dropped a close decision earlier that summer to American featherweight champion, Tommy Warren. "When Pikie saw me knock White kicking, he stood up at the ringside and challenged me, offering to stop me in eight rounds or forfeit [the purse]," Lavigne later recounted. "Happy days," exclaimed brother Billy, as he accepted on George's behalf. "Kid you're made now. This fight will get you known all over the country."[26] And that is how George Lavigne became the "Saginaw Kid" as the moniker used by his brother that night stuck. He was the original "Kid" of the prizefight ring, the name many fighters have adopted since.[27] George was only 16, had the face of a cherub, and looked like a kid. He was a shy and humble blue-eyed youngster outside the ring. But in the ring, his opponents would meet a relentless, aggressive, hard-hitting madman. The fight with Johnson would not occur for another 18 months but in the meantime the Kid had work to do.

He won his next three bouts against Billy Roberts, Bob Ralph, and Jimmy Priest as he had the first two, by early round knockouts. C. A. C. took the boy-wonder under his wing and began instructing George in the finer art of the boxing craft. He tutored George on the orthodox style of boxing that would be the trademark of many a good Michigan fighter to pass through the doors of his school. The style was marked by jabbing with the left hand while using the right hand for serious punching. Smith would go on to develop several good fighters during Saginaw's boxing heyday which hit its zenith in the 1890s. In addition to Billy and George Lavigne, Smith taught Bob Cherry, Pete Major, Ollie Freeman and others. Many of his early pupils went on to teach others employing the same style that Smith had taught them.

The Kid, while never touted as a great "boxer" was developing into a magnificent "fighter." He was quick on his feet and possessed "a fast left jab, a powerful right hand, and indomitable courage. He was one of the first boxers to employ the short right hook, his blows travelling no more than a few inches. Seldom did he essay a long swing," wrote an unknown old-timer that saw him in action.[28] And of that fearsome right hand a *Saginaw News* reporter wrote, "Not a nifty boxer, he was adequate. But he had a right hand punch with the stunning authority of a mallet, and he never gave up—never."[29]

Late in the fall he won two more bouts against Red Elliot and Jack Cherry although not by knockout as he was fighting progressively more experienced opponents. He finished those four months of his first year as a professional with seven wins and no losses with five early-round knockouts. The local fight talent now avoided Lavigne and as a result he fought but once in 1887, a three-round, return match with Red Elliott. The *Saginaw News* misidentified the Kid as Charles and didn't report the outcome of the set-to.[30]

With no fights on the horizon Lavigne would begin a pattern of behavior involving alcohol and the police that would stick with him for nearly three decades. In late June, George was arrested in what would be the first of many arrests; the last one happening in 1916. "Police Court—Daniel McAllister and Ephraim Anderson couldn't pay $3 for having indulged in too much beer and were consigned to the cooler for six days," noted the *Saginaw Evening News*. "George Flicken, George Levine [Lavigne], and Thomas Kain had the necessary $3 and paid."[31]

In February 1888 he met Dan Connors in Saginaw. There is a story—a bit of Lavigne lore—that may have its origins in this bout. The tale has the referee center stage with Lavigne playing the "straight man" of the comedy. According to a 1911 story in the *Mansfield News*, the Kid was engaged in a bout in Saginaw when in the sixth round, "Lavigne landed a swing on the man's jaw, the latter promptly going to the carpet. It was a clean knockout, and Lavigne went to his corner wearing the smile of a victor. When the beaten man was floored the referee walked to the ropes, leaned against them and reflectively chewed gum, making no effort to count out the loser. Finally the man on the floor revived, got on his feet and wobbled to his corner, where his handlers set to work on him. He had been on the floor 30 seconds, but when he had been sponged and invigorated, the referee called time for the seventh round. 'But,' yelled Lavigne, 'he was knocked out. Why didn't you count?' 'Count what?' asked the official. 'Why, count 10, and if he didn't get up he's licked.' 'Oh, well,' said the referee, 'I'll remember that next time. Go on with the fight.'"

Lavigne protested but the referee told him he would not get the purse if he didn't continue with the fight. The Kid resumed the battle and promptly connected on the jaw and down went his man again. "The referee was up to snuff on this occasion, and standing over the fallen boxer began to tick off the seconds like a town clock. At six the fighter struggled up and would have got on his feet, but the referee pushed him back and said, 'Hold on, there! I haven't counted to 10 yet.' And the official held the poor fellow down until he had counted him out."[32] While it can't be certain that it happened in this fight, it is the only bout fitting the description of being in Saginaw, and getting a win by knockout in the middle rounds. According to a contemporary news story he knocked Connors cold in the fifth round. Close enough to the sixth round as told in this humorous tale.

It was time to square off with Pikie Johnson and the match was arranged for March 2, 1888. The fight was to be held at Bordwell's Opera House "which had a fare of booze, vice and 'girlie' stage shows in East Saginaw. Prizefights were held on the stage there in the lumber heyday."[33] It was a haven for lumberjacks "who liked their entertainment raw and their fights bloody."[34] As the fight date neared, Johnson told Lavigne he would "take it easy on him and stop the fight in eight rounds."[35] "When Pikie and I fought each other in Bordwell's Opera House," Lavigne wrote, "the place was packed. All of Saginaw was there. But the best the wise ones allowed me was to stay the limit with a man of Pikie Johnson's class. Well Pikie showed me plenty of gloves and gave me a boxing lesson, but he didn't stop me. I almost stopped him, and he was lucky to be on his feet at the finish."[36] The Kid had Johnson staggering in the fourth and while he couldn't put him away, he was an easy winner in eight rounds, although it was officially recorded a draw in the absence of a knockout.

The victory over Johnson propelled Lavigne to the national stage, although it made it progressively harder to find fights at the local level as Lavigne's reputation as a hard hitting mauler preceded him. After his triumph over Pikie he fought two more bouts in 1888 both in

Bordwell's Opera House circa 1888 - Courtesy of the Public Libraries of Saginaw

Manistee on the other side of the state. In June he fought an unknown opponent, knocking him cold in three rounds. In September he defeated Jack Menton in 12 rounds. The young pugilist was on his way but he needed a step up in competition to test his mettle. He would soon get all he could handle.

CHAPTER 5

The Early Lightweights

In the beginning there were heavyweights. No matter how tough or skilled a smaller man may have been, if he met a man 50 pounds heavier, the result seldom varied. In early 1700s England, public interest in the noble art centered on "brawn and weight, muscle and punch, blood and guts, rather than speed and skill."[1] Then slowly a shift took place as boxing enthusiasts began to appreciate the smaller fellows who nimbly slashed and dashed about the ring with speed and cunning. In a nod to the lighter men, the "Father of Modern Boxing," Jack Broughton, created the first lightweight division in 1738, defining it as any man who weighed less than 160 pounds.

When the London Prize Ring rules superseded the Broughton rules in 1838 the lightweight range was set at 130-150 pounds. By the time the Marquess of Queensberry rules were developed in 1867 and were in widespread use in America in the late 1880s, the limit was set at 133 pounds. In the 1880s and 1890s three more divisions were added. It wasn't until 1909 that the National Sporting Club of London defined eight weight classes which were universally adopted the following year. The lightweight limit was then set at 135 pounds where it stands today. The number of weight divisions has grown over the years to 17.

Rulers of the "Raw Uns"

As with all things boxing, it is a matter of debate as to who was the first lightweight champion. Boxing historians Herbert G.

Goldman and the late, Nat Fleischer, haggle back to 1795 on whether it was Caleb Baldwin. After that a series of names are prominent including Jack Randall, Dick Curtiss, and Barney Aaron. Johnny Moneghan was the first to claim the English lightweight title in 1850. Moneghan, a Kid Lavigne-sized lightweight at 5 feet 4 inches and 124 pounds, came to America and in 1855 he claimed the American lightweight title after knocking out "Little" Jimmy Hart in the 45th round. Had he been widely recognized as the English champion, rather than self-anointed, he might have been considered the first lightweight boxing champion of the world.

He held the title on and off over the next two years trading honors with Hart until he was knocked out by "Young" Barney Aaron in the 80th round of their championship bout in 1857. Aaron was a chip off the old block so to speak as his father, also Barney, was a famous English lightweight bare-knuckler under the Broughton rules from 1819 to 1834. "Young" Barney, the first Jewish fighter to win a ring championship in America, won his title under the revised London Prize Ring rules which had recently been modified in 1853. Aaron lost the title in 1858 on a foul to Patrick "Scotty" Brannagan in a match that went 10 rounds in only 15 minutes.[2] The deposed champion went the next seven years without a match as no fighter dared challenge him.

Aaron finally put a standing challenge for a match in the *New York Clipper* and it was answered by Sam Collyer. In the 1866 bout Collyer prevailed in the 47th round thwarting Aaron's attempt to regain the title. The brutal contest lasted over two hours and both men were taken away on stretchers. Aaron returned serve, defeating Collyer in 1867 in a 67-round battle. This was another punishing affair with the *Baltimore Sun* reporting, "The left side of Collyer's face is beaten almost to a jelly and his left eye is completely closed up."[3] Aaron played the "drop game" to avoid too much damage. This entailed falling to the ring surface when in trouble thereby ending the round and stopping the carnage.

Collyer reclaimed the title later that year after Aaron retired. In August 1868 he fought Billy Edwards and lost the title on a 34th round technical knockout of this 1 hour and 14 minute bare-knuckle affair. "At the end of the mill it was said that both men were badly bruised, the friends of Collyer being compelled to carry him out, he being greatly exhausted."[4]

At this point boxing in England and America was in a transition period between the London Prize Ring rules and the Marquess of Queensberry rules. Most of the fights were still bare-knuckle matches with gloved bouts slowly gaining favor. When gloves were used in the late London rules and early Queensberry days, they were anything from skin tight "riding" gloves, also called "hard gloves," to those called "soft gloves" lined with up to two ounces of curled horse hair.

Edwards was born in England, as were many of the early lightweight champions, coming to America in 1865 and working as a boilermaker in New York. He held the title from 1868 to 1872, rebuffing another challenge along the way from Collyer in 1870, earning a technical knockout in the 41st round. He would fight Collyer a third time in a match that aptly illustrated the colorful circumstances of many a bout of the time.

A tip was given to the sporting world that the fighting expedition would depart at midnight on an open sand barge from along the river in Pittsburgh. The spectators would be towed to the scene of the fight several miles down the river. Keeping the time and location of the fight under wraps was essential for outwitting the police. "About fifteen hundred devotees gathered to embark," wrote Alexander Johnston in *Ten and Out*. "Many of them did not have tickets and lacked money to pay for them. Tom Allen, the heavyweight champion, and Red Leary took tickets at the gang-plank, and any man who did not have the proper ticket or money was simply pushed over into the water. When the barge was stuffed to suffocation the ropes were cast off. But the unfortunates who were left on the bank did not propose to stand their marooning in any tame manner. Nearby was a pile of cobble-stones, and the roughs on the bank seized these and hurled them after the departing 'fancy,' accompanied with imprecations and wishes of lots of luck, all of it bad."[5]

The group was towed down river for the rest of the night and when day dawned they disembarked, hiked about a mile back from the river, and pitched a ring. It was so hot that the spectators took to the cover of trees watching the fight from a distance of over 100 feet.

Billy Edwards circa 1870

Johnston continued, "Just as the men were squaring off for the beginning of the fight, some spectator lit a cigar and threw the match away. The little piece of wood was still burning, and caught a clump of dried grass. This flared up, and suddenly there was a loud report and a column of fire shot up into the air twenty feet or more. The careless sport had lighted a natural gas well, which burned all through the fight to the discomfort of both fighters and onlookers."

The fight was not nearly as exciting as the attendant circumstances with Edwards getting the best of it. Collyer quit after 10 rounds claiming that Edwards committed a foul by rubbing his palms in balsam fir pitch to help keep his hands tightly closed. The referee didn't buy it and awarded the fight to Edwards.

In 1871 Edwards fought a 95-round marathon with Tim Collins. This was still in the days of the London Prize Ring rules which called for a round lasting until one or both men were knocked down after which each man could be aided to his corner. Following a 30-second rest the men would be required to "toe the scratch line" within eight seconds or be deemed the loser of the contest. In the early days of boxing a line was scratched out on the ground in the center of the ring. When time was called for the beginning of the next round, each fighter must toe the scratch line signaling his readiness to continue or his opponent would be awarded the victory. Given this knockdown rule, a round may end in five seconds or go on for many minutes. This fight went on for a mere 2 and 1/2 hours and with darkness approaching and honors even, it was stopped, to be resumed the next day, but both combatants were subsequently arrested. Two days later they were sentenced to one year in prison for illegal prizefighting.

Edwards lost the championship to Arthur Chambers in September 1872. Chambers began fighting in England in 1864, losing only once before coming to America in 1871. He is not to be confused with English sportsman, John Graham Chambers, author of the Queensberry rules. Arthur was also Lavigne-sized at 5 feet 3 inches and just over 120 pounds. He met Edwards in a bitterly fought battle at Waldpole Island in Canada. In the 26th round they

Arthur Chambers circa 1877
- Courtesy of Cyber Boxing Zone

went into a clinch and Chambers protested to the referee that Edwards had bitten him. "Sure enough, teeth marks showed on Chambers' side, and the referee gave him the fight on a foul," noted Alexander Johnston. "As a matter of fact, one of Chambers' seconds had bitten him before he went up for the round. In such sportsman-like tricks the old bare-knuckle ring abounded."[6]

Chambers held the title until he was forced to retire for nearly two years in 1877 having had the middle finger on his left hand amputated. When he returned he engaged "Professor" John Clark at Chippewa Falls, Ontario, Canada in March 1879 in what many consider to be the first great lightweight championship battle. The bout was fought under London rules in a 20-foot ring covered with straw and sawdust from a barn nearby. The fighters were bare-knuckled except for Chambers who wore one glove made of sheepskin and horsehide to protect the amputated finger on his left hand.[7]

Chambers won by technical knockout after 2 hours and 23 minutes when Clark's seconds threw up the sponge in the 136th round. He had taken almost every round and Clark was so badly punished in the end that it was thought he might die. It was touted as the longest fight between international opponents in boxing history when measured by number of rounds. The international claim is an awkward distinction; true, Chambers was born in England and Clark in Ireland, but both had been living in America since 1871 and were essentially American fighters at the time. This was the last American lightweight championship bout to be fought under the London Prize Ring rules.

The Queensberry Champions

Arthur Chambers continued to fight but only in exhibition bouts, letting the American lightweight title become vacant. Another English transplant, Charlie Norton, then challenged George Fulljames in 1881. When Fulljames declined, Norton boldly, and without foundation, claimed the American title. Few acknowledged his claim and for all intents and purposes the title continued to remain vacant until 1884. It was in September of 1883 that a remarkable fighter, John Edward Kelly, began his fistic career in the U. S. with his sights set on the title.

Kelly, born in Ireland soon took his mother's last name, Dempsey. At some point he added "Nonpareil," forever after to be known as Jack Dempsey the "Nonpareil" (without peer). Dempsey has often been lauded as one of the greatest pound-for-pound fighters to step in a ring and one of the top three welterweights of all time. He lost only three fights in his career: one against George LaBlanche

Jack Dempsey, the "Nonpareil" -
Courtesy of Cyber Boxing Zone

from an illegal punch and two against greats Bob Fitzsimmons and Tommy Ryan when he was well past his prime. Dempsey held the middleweight title from 1886 to 1891 when Fitzsimmons succeeded him.

Some sources claim that Dempsey was the lightweight champion in 1882 but the major record databases and newspaper accounts all show his career starting in September 1883. In March 1884 he fought Bill Dacey in what was billed as the lightweight championship of New York but both men were over the lightweight limit of the time. It wasn't until November 6, 1884 that he allegedly gained the American lightweight title by defeating Tom Ferguson in four rounds in New York under Queensberry rules. Newspaper reports located for this bout did not include the fighters' weights so it's possible Dempsey wasn't under the lightweight limit for this one either.

Further clues appear just two weeks later when Dempsey fought Billy Frazier. Frazier, a legitimate 133 pounder, peeled off his gloves after four rounds and quit, uttering, "He's too big for me, I've got to give up."[8] Ten days hence Dempsey, weighing in at 149 pounds, fought Mike Malone. While several sources claim Dempsey briefly held the American lightweight title before vacating it to move up in weight, on careful examination it appears he never did. In December he issued a challenge to fight any man in the world at 140 pounds, leaving no doubt he would dabble with the lightweights no more.

The title had now remained vacant since 1879 when one of the greatest fighters of all time, amateur lightweight champion Jack McAuliffe, began his professional career in 1885. McAuliffe's first claim to the American title came very early in his professional career when he defeated Jack Hopper in January 1886. In October of 1886 McAuliffe defeated Billy Frazier and claimed both the American and world lightweight titles. He again asserted his claim to the world title after defeating Canadian Harry Gilmore in January 1887 with a 28th round knockout. In what was his greatest challenge of all he met English lightweight champion Jem Carney in November 1887 for what was to be the undisputed world lightweight title.

McAuliffe and Jack Dempsey were good friends having been workmates in a New York cooperage and over the years they acted as seconds for each other's matches. Dempsey, now middleweight champion, was in McAuliffe's corner for the match with Carney to be held under Queensberry rules with skin-tight gloves. Dempsey was concerned with McAuliffe's level of conditioning and instructed him to finish it quickly. He went out fast forcing the fighting but Carney was very tough and weathered the storm. When Carney took the lead McAuliffe would clinch and stifle Carney's effective in-fighting. Carney grew weary of this tactic. "In his anxiety to do some real damage, he began fouling McAuliffe, hitting low and butting in the clinches," wrote Alexander Johnston.

Despite Dempsey's protestations the referee paid no attention to him. "This went on for a couple of rounds and after the twelfth canto had passed, Dempsey, who was long on trickery, hid McAuliffe's shoulder under a towel and bit it until the blood came," continued Johnston. "McAuliffe, as the 13th round began, rushed from his corner, pulled Carney's head down on his shoulder and yelled, 'He's biting me!' The referee dragged the two men apart, looked at the teeth marks, and then called Carney aside. Gravely he opened his mouth to examine his teeth, presumably to see if any pieces of American cuticle were still clinging to them, but alas, Carney was entirely devoid of front teeth!"[9]

Jem Carney circa 1887
- Courtesy of Tony Gee

Carney was a fierce fighter having once killed a man in the ring. He chased McAuliffe around the ring and by the 40th round McAuliffe was tiring badly. The fight continued for hour after hour. "At the end of the 68th McAuliffe wanted to quit badly, and from that time to the finish Carney everlastingly pounded him," reported the *Newark Daily Advocate*.[10] In the 74th round, with McAuliffe nearly out on his feet the men fell into a ring post which gave way. McAuliffe's backers, who had entered the ring twice before to save their man from certain defeat, stormed the ring and the referee called the fight a draw after nearly five hours of combat.

Partly as a result of the draw with Carney, McAuliffe's claim to the world title is highly disputable and is examined at length in the postscript of this book. As he continued to take on and defeat all comers, his claim to the American lightweight title was rock solid. He remained undefeated for the rest of his career, save for a couple of very dubious decisions, one of only nine professional boxers ever to accomplish the feat.

McAuliffe was a second in the corner of John L. Sullivan for his championship fight with "Gentleman" Jim Corbett in September, 1892. After watching Corbett chop Sullivan to pieces, and getting some sage advice from the "Boston Strong Boy" after his loss, McAuliffe vowed that he would retire. Although he came out of retirement twice, he no longer defended his title and it laid vacant until George the "Saginaw Kid" Lavigne began to whip every lightweight in the division. Some sources show Kid Lavigne as the American champion as of 1893 with the news of McAuliffe's retirement.

While Lavigne was undefeated and widely recognized as the best of the lightweights of the early 1890s, he had no legitimate claim to the title until in 1894 he knocked out the lightweight champion of the South, Andy Bowen. Lavigne strengthened his case when he defeated the "Barbados Demon," Joe Walcott, in what to this day is recognized as one of the most savage and gamely contested battles in ring history. The Kid went on to win the world title in London by defeating the English Champion Dick "Iron Man" Burge in 1896. He lost the title in 1899 to Frank Erne.

Bobby Dobbs - Courtesy of BoxRec

Aside from this lineage of men who held, or at least claimed to hold, the American and world lightweight titles before the turn of the century, there were a few other lightweights who deserve recognition when discussing the best of the pre-1900 Queensberry era. Some of them are discussed in later chapters. They include the incredibly talented black fighter, Bobby Dobbs, who it was said had fought as many as 1,000 bouts, and the English champion Jem Carney, who should have held the world lightweight title had he not been robbed of a 74th round knockout of Jack McAuliffe.

Others on the list include English lightweight champ, Dick Burge, although Burge always weighed a few pounds in excess of the lightweight limit, and the incomparably deceptive Australian, Young Griffo. Griffo, had he backed off the booze and trained for his fights, might have ruled the featherweight and lightweight divisions for many years. Saving perhaps the best for last, the honors go to the "Old Master," Joe Gans, whose dominance straddled the last decade of the 19th and first decade of 20th centuries. His style of fighting marked a departure from the old stand-and-fight brawlers to the more modern boxers who employed feints, counterpunching, and movement. Many historians rate him as one of the top two lightweights of all time.

Arguably, at no other time in the history of boxing has the division seen so many skilled little men as those who put up their dukes in the early Queensberry era. But as far as the sheer number of talented, game, and crafty fighters goes, the 1890s may be lauded as "the decade of the lightweights."

CHAPTER 6

The Featherweight Champ and the West Coast Tour

While brother Billy was supportive of the Kid's rise in the local fight circles, he was conflicted as to whether he should encourage him to continue. He knew the fight game promised a hard and painful living and few made it to the top where the money and fame made it all worthwhile. "Billy tried to discourage young George from a fistic career," wrote a *Saginaw News* reporter, "but George persisted, so Billy arranged a match with [George] Siddons, a top-notcher, hoping and expecting that Siddons would beat the idea out of George's head."[1] At least that is the tale as local legend would have it, however, the real story is that Billy knew early on that George was championship material and encouraged him to take on all comers on his way to the top.

George Siddons, born Ambrose Smith, claimed to be the featherweight champion of the Northwest at the time. His only losses were to top drawer featherweights, Ike Weir and Tommy Warren. This fight would define Lavigne.

Back-to-Back Marathons

Billy Lavigne recalled the difficulty he had pulling off this fight. It was to be "under the guise of a friendly bout for points, but the fact of their being matched with a side bet with small gloves leaked out . . . interest increased to such an extent that we were all threatened with arrest to keep the peace." It was common in those days to keep the fight venue a secret until the last minute so as not to alert the local

George Siddons
- Courtesy of Thomas Scharf

police who may arrive and shut it down.

It was finally settled that the bout would be staged at Old Man Putnam's roadhouse near Swan Creek on March 1, 1889, out back in a large barn. The dancehall in the roadhouse was secured on the pretense of a cock fight. "The next obstacle to remove was the sheriff of that county," Billy continued, "which we did by a phony message, calling him out of the county until the mill was over." Ticket holders were simply told to follow the Gratiot Road to Swan Creek. There a man was stationed to check their tickets and direct them to the roadhouse.

The price of admission was three dollars and the barn was packed to capacity even though half the folks who bought tickets didn't show because they didn't know where the fight was to be held. The fight took place in the middle of the dance floor and with no ropes available a line of spectators formed the ring. The men wore two-ounce gloves and would fight for a side bet of $100 and share 75% of the gate receipts. The bout started just before midnight.

Siddons, clearly the better boxer, mauled the Kid for 40 rounds cutting his face badly. At one point in the fight some of the spectators pleaded with Lavigne to stop but he simply muttered "No" through mangled lips. "But the Kid, with his indomitable courage, wouldn't quit," wrote the *Saginaw News*. "As the fight wore on Lavigne turned the tide of battle his way and was giving Siddons a beating."[2] There was blood all over the ring and all over both fighters. "Neither would quit, though they scarcely could hold their arms up. The bloodletting finally ended in a draw after 77 bruising rounds."[3] It was stopped after five hours and eight minutes—the longest fight on record at the time under the Marquess of Queensberry gloved rules. "Word had come that the sheriff was on his way out to stop it," continued the *News*. "That was the unwritten law in those days; the officers knew about the fights but they stayed away until daybreak; the fights had to be fought at night; if they lasted until the next day as many of them did, the law was sure to arrive on the scene."[4]

"I looked more like a baboon than a human when I left the ring," Lavigne recalled years later.[5] Lavigne's face was so swollen after the fight that he said he could not see for three days. But just ten days after the fight, the indefatigable Lavigne would win a four-round bout against little known Butch Kinney at the Palace Theatre in Manistee, Michigan. Clearly the Kid was a man who loved to fight. "The bout was fought under strict police restrictions. The police at the last moment forbade a knockout and the fight was a rather tame affair," noted author John Schuch.[6] He fought another short bout as part of a benefit for local featherweight, Sam Purdy on April 16th. It was one of five bouts on the card which included a mill between Billy Lavigne and Purdy. The Kid fought local boy, Billy Bushy, for a four-round exhibition in which no decision was given.

At the Kid's insistence a rematch was made with Siddons. Just 56 days after the 77-round mauling they gave each other the two fighters would meet again at Al Carroll's Roadhouse at Reed's Lake, Grand Rapids, Michigan. It was to be a "finish-fight" meaning there would be no set number of rounds agreed to. The fight would continue until one man was knocked out or couldn't toe the scratch line after a round. The purse was to be $100 a side for the featherweight championship of Michigan.

The battle began at 1:30 a.m. "At dawn we were still at it," wrote Lavigne. "Street car drivers and conductors began coming up to watch the struggle, and as we were afraid of the police, we decided to call it a draw."[7] The fight went 55 rounds and in the words of a *Boston Herald* reporter, "both men were severely punished."[8] The Kid scored two knockdowns; one in the third round and one late in the fight. Siddons had decidedly the worst of it this time often tempting the Kid to foul him. "He continually dropped on his knees, hoping Lavine [sic] would hit him, and many times he sank down to avoid punishment," wrote the *Saginaw Evening News*. "He was constantly jeered by the spectators for his way of fighting, and the crowd was decidedly on Lavine's [sic] side before the close."[9]

Again in Lavigne's own words, "The battle was fought with gloves that originally weighed two ounces, but the [horse] hair had been removed. I leave it to the reader to picture Siddons and me at the finish."[10] "Although it was officially ruled a draw," wrote columnist Stephen Schroeder, "Siddons admitted he was beaten and his backers paid off those who had bet on the Kid."[11] The "newspaper decision" came to the same conclusion that Siddons had. Newspaper decisions, also called "popular verdicts" by the sportswriters in attendance, were common during a time when prizefighting was illegal in most states and fights were often prearranged to a conclusion of a "draw" or a "no-decision" when no knockout occurred. With the admission of defeat by Siddons, the Kid claimed his first title.

Big Doings in Frisco

After absorbing great punishment in the Michigan title fight, the Kid would enter the ring again just 17 days later, his face and body still sporting signs of the trauma from the second marathon with Siddons. He ventured to what surely must have seemed like the "big city" when he fought his first bout in Detroit, defeating Billy O'Brien in a short, four-rounder on May 12, 1889. The newly crowned featherweight champion of Michigan would find himself in a boxing lull just as his career appeared to be taking flight. He fought once more in 1889, a December, four-round exhibition match with Billy Bushy again. He would scratch out three short bouts in Saginaw between March and May, 1890: a win over his first foe, Morris McNally, now a Saginaw fireman, a draw with Billy Boucher, and an exhibition against Jack O'Brien, all three-round affairs.

The Kid would not fight again for another six months. He was a bit of a rowdy when not focused on his next fight and got into trouble again outside the ring. His second arrest came in mid-August, 1890. "George Lavigne was arraigned yesterday before Justice Simoneau charged with assault and battery on Gilbert Derno," wrote the *Saginaw Evening News*, "the alleged assault being committed on board the *Handy Boy* on Saginaw River in Zilwaukie Township. He pleaded not guilty and the case was adjourned until Friday morning at 9 o'clock, the defendant giving bonds in the sum of $100 for his appearance."[12]

He was next matched to fight Sam Eaton on November 12, 1890 in La France Hall at West Bay City for a 15-round "spar." About 250 spectators were on hand, most having made the half hour train ride from Saginaw to the public hall built on the second floor of Fred La France's livery stable. Eaton was the taller of the two men and his superior reach gave him a decided advantage. "Every round showed Eaton was a clever man," noted the *Saginaw Evening News*. "He is nicely scienced and is a great foot man. He is very cool, got good wind, and uses good headwork. He lacks the power to punish however."[13]

While this was a fairly even fight over the first five rounds it was to end there. The victory went to Lavigne on a technical knockout when at the end of the fifth Eaton said he broke his hand and could not continue. Injured and broken hands were not uncommon particularly when fighters removed much of the padding from two ounce gloves that were already of little protection. There were few checks and balances to ensure adherence to standards of glove weights. When a sparsely padded hand collided with full force against the skull of an opponent, the skull sometimes got the better of the exchange.

The lull continued and it would be another 11 months until his next fight. In Lavigne's words, "No other matches being in sight, I went to work in a cooper shop at Ludington [Michigan] but brother Billy was determined to keep me fighting. He was always telling me I could lick anyone in the world. Boxing promoters out on the Pacific Coast got word of me, and offered me a match at San Francisco with Joe Soto. That was in 1891. Soto was then the featherweight sensation of the Coast. He had just licked the mighty Tommy Danforth and his victory made him Pacific Coast Champion."[14]

The Danforth fight had gone 55 rounds before Soto knocked Tommy out. Why Lavigne took a cooper job in Ludington about 145 miles away on the shores of Lake Michigan is unknown, particularly when he was no so well-known and hailed as a champ in his home towns of Bay City and Saginaw. One would think that cooper jobs were plentiful locally. It's possible that he simply liked the area and wanted a change of pace, having fought two early career bouts in Manistee in 1888 and 1889, a few miles north of Ludington.

Billy accepted the San Francisco offer. While Billy had gotten the Kid this far with the help of C. A. C. Smith, the San Francisco trip would be a step up to the big time. In a wise business move he and George brought on Joe Courtmarsh to function as the Kid's first professional manager and trainer although Billy would continue to assist in both roles. They quickly arranged for a tune-up bout the month before the Soto fight. The Kid was matched against Jimmy Lewis in San Francisco for a four-round bout on October 15, 1891 which he won handily. Lavigne was duly impressed with the boxing scene in California. "It was a revelation to me to see the nice big rings in San Francisco with their padded floors. Prizefighting was very popular in the West. In Frisco great fighters could be seen on almost any corner, men of the class of John L. Sullivan, Peter Jackson, Jim Corbett, Jack Dempsey [the Nonpareil], Joe Choynski, Bob Fitzsimmons, or Jim Hall."[15]

The event of the evening at the Pacific Athletic Club in San Francisco on November 20, 1891 was a finish-bout between the Saginaw Kid and Joe Soto. The purse was $600 with the loser getting

$100. The referee was the great light heavyweight of the turn of the century, Joe Choynski. The fighters weighed 124 pounds, just two shy of the featherweight limit at the time. Although Soto was a formidable opponent for the Kid and a local favorite, word of Lavigne's growing legacy had reached the West Coast and the betting was 2-to-1 in the Kid's favor. "On toeing the scratch for the first round," the *San Francisco Chronicle* reported, "Lavigne looked the more muscular and the better trained."[16]

The Bay area papers reported that attendance was slim for the monthly boxing card at the Athletic Club, however for Lavigne, who to this point in his career had fought in small venues, crowd size was a matter of perspective. "Soto and I met before an enormous crowd. He was a flashy and popular boxer. We fought a bloody battle. In the early rounds as usual, I took a pasting. But I kept everlastingly on top of Soto."[17] The fight started with Soto as the aggressor, darting in and out, landing, and then slipping away. Soto was also a fencing master and put his thrusting and parrying skills to good use against the Kid. Lavigne kept trying to work his man into a corner but Soto was very fleet of foot and continually escaped. "Finding that Lavigne's blows were easily avoided, Soto commenced to act the monkey," reported the *San Francisco Morning Call*. "He pranced and stamped and tried to disturb his opponent's equanimity, by imitating the sounds of a man sawing wood. Lavigne looked serious and attended to business. And as the fight progressed, Soto discarded levity."[18]

By the 12th round Soto was still dodging in and out and Lavigne continued the chase, throwing the harder punches but having trouble landing them on his shifty opponent. Soto employed another tactic that as boxing progressed through the years, would be ruled a knockdown. As told by the *San Francisco Chronicle*: "In the 13th Lavigne seemed to get angry, and going in for slugging, landed a heavy left on the neck, staggering Soto to the ropes, and rushing at him to finish him. Soto dropped to the floor and repeated these dubious tactics several times as the Michigan man chased him around the ring, Soto winding up grabbing him by the legs. The crowd hissed and the referee warned him."[19] In the 14th, Soto was peppering Lavigne but got caught by one of the Kid's vaunted right hands on the chin and was nearly dropped again. At the start of the 16th Lavigne came at his man with relentless pressure without regard for any counter Soto could muster. Between dropping to the canvas without being hit and being put to the canvas by the Kid's onslaught, Soto was down half a dozen times and was "severely punished."

The fight was getting to that place where the Kid excelled. The longer the fight went, the more he began to take charge and wear his man out. "In the 20th Soto fared badly," wrote the *Chronicle*, "He claimed to be hit below the belt, and was knocked down three times, getting to the floor with suspicious quickness each time. Toward the finish he scored a lucky shot on Lavigne's jaw that staggered him, after missing several LaBlanche swings."[20]

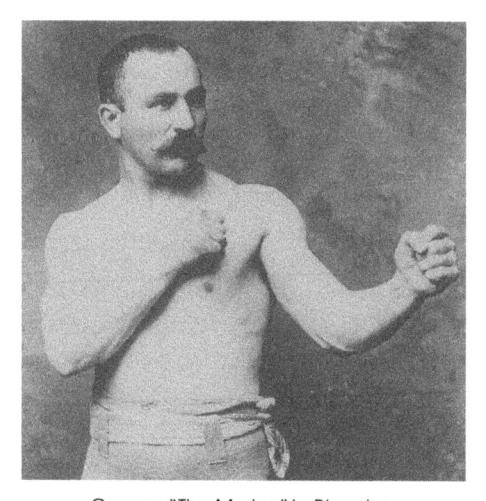

George "The Marine" LaBlanche
- Courtesy of Cyber Boxing Zone

The LaBlanche swing was an illegal punch made famous by middleweight boxer George LaBlanche in 1889. He was fighting the undefeated Jack Dempsey (the Nonpareil, not the famous heavyweight of later years) in San Francisco. Although ten pounds lighter, Dempsey was slaughtering LaBlanche but in the 32nd round LaBlanche threw a weak left hand and as it missed Dempsey he continued to spin his body around 360 degrees, connecting with the back of his right fist or his forearm to the head of Dempsey. The blow, with the centrifugal force of the spin behind it, cold-cocked Dempsey and the referee had no choice but to award the bout to LaBlanche. It was later ruled an illegal punch. While LaBlanche claimed the middleweight title, it was ruled that he scaled 161 pounds at the weigh-in, clearly over the middleweight limit. Dempsey kept his middleweight crown.

Soto's use of an illegal punch was simply an addition to the other questionable tactics he employed throughout the bout. Soto's methods didn't matter to Lavigne as he recalled, "About the 25th round I felt the Coast Champion begin to weaken."[21] From then on the Kid kept forcing the fight. And the finish as described by the *Chronicle*, "When time was called for the 31st round Choynski held up his hand and announced that Soto gave up, as his hands were disabled. Lavigne was accordingly declared the winner."[22]

After the fight a doctor confirmed that Soto's hands were very swollen although no bones were broken. "The maddest man in that house was Lavigne," wrote sports journalist Tad Dorgan who was attending his first professional fight that evening. "He stood in his corner stamping his feet and muttering to himself. The win was all right but he wanted the knockout. He had taken his [punishment] and he wanted to give Soto what was coming to him."[23]

The Sullivan Prophecy

So far, the San Francisco trip had been profitable and again, career defining. The Kid was now known to a greater audience outside his home state. He stayed in San Francisco through March of 1892. The legendary heavyweight John L. Sullivan had recently returned from Australia where he had been involved in a theater production. The Pacific Club threw a benefit for him in early 1892 with several fights on the card including a four round exhibition between Lavigne and the "Saint Paul Terror," Danny Needham. Needham was a long distance warrior of the class of Lavigne. He had fought battles of 27, 29, 43, 76 and 100 rounds in his early career, the last going six hours and 38 minutes. And in the 100-rounder he broke his hand in the fifth frame fighting the other 95 rounds with one hand to a draw. There were perhaps never two fighters with the unparalleled stamina and grit of Lavigne and Needham in the ring at the same time. It's unfortunate for the record books that this bout was only four rounds and an exhibition at that. Had these two come together for a fight to the finish, it may have gone down as the longest fight in the annals of Queensberry boxing.

While training for the Soto fight the Kid would meet his future manager, Sam Fitzpatrick, in Danny Needham's saloon in Oakland. Fitzpatrick, who would later become manager of the great heavyweight Jack Johnson, would be instrumental in guiding Lavigne to the world championship five years later. But before leaving San Francisco the Kid would get the greatest compliment of his life from the most famous pugilist of all time, John L. Sullivan. In his own words, "Sullivan was a warm friend of Billy Harrison, manager of the [Pacific Athletic] Club and through Harrison I met

Charles Rochette
- Courtesy of Cyber Boxing Zone

Sullivan. The champion saw me box Needham and watched me fight with Soto. One day he said to Harrison in my presence, 'This kid is going to be the next lightweight champion.'"[24] But for now, more rungs on the ladder awaited Lavigne.

It would be a few more months before Lavigne would be the main event on a fight card. On March 17, 1892 he would fight San Franciscan Charles Rochette at the Pacific Athletic Club in the preliminary bout to a bantamweight contest between a black boxer, Deacon Jones, and the "Australian Butterfly," Harry Dally. The Jones/Dally fight ended in a draw after 66 rounds when both fighters were too worn out to continue.

The Lavigne/Rochette bout was scheduled for 10 rounds. The *San Francisco Chronicle* noted, "Lavigne had great strength and this was sufficient to wear out Rochette. Lavigne showed himself to be a hard hitter and but for quick ducking, Rochette would have received some terrible swinging blows. Lavigne would rush in with his head down and try for in-fighting, while Rochette's effort was to keep him off. Rochette tired himself by running about too much, and this together with the hot work in the last few rounds, was too much for him to stand against the work of his stronger and plucky opponent."[25] The Kid had his man groggy at the end of the fight but could not score the knockout. He was given the decision but it was "not the victory he had expected to achieve over the local man."

Lavigne's West Coast tour headed north when Portland, Oregon promoters offered him an engagement with a favorite of the Northwest, Harry Jones, who hailed from Spokane, Washington. The Kid went into training at a racetrack near Portland. Family news from Saginaw would shake him five days before the fight when he and brother Billy got word that their younger brother, John, had died in Saginaw of peritonitis at age 20. The Lavigne brothers were no strangers to deaths in the family, having lost their father and several siblings along the way. And now this. "It was a shock to me and I quit training," the Kid remembered.[26]

The match was scheduled to take place May 25, 1892 at the Pastime Athletic Club. The referee for the bout was the great middleweight champion, Jack Dempsey the "Nonpareil." The *Portland Oregonian* reported that both men were evenly matched in size, weight, and hitting power. The fighters had one opponent in common in George Siddons whom Jones had lost to on a foul in the 33rd round. While betting was heavy prior to the bout with Lavigne as the favorite, the *Oregonian* noted, "No smoking, and positively no betting is a rule of the Pastime Club, which will be enforced tonight."[27] This was indicative of a time when wagering on boxing was rampant while not being legal or officially condoned by the "athletic club" that sponsored the fight.

The Kid started the fight as he did many of them, rushing at his opponent and bullying him about the ring, landing heavy punches. In the second round Lavigne knocked Jones down with a left hook. He staggered Jones with a right that landed squarely on his right eye, but Jones rallied and fought back although his punches "lacked steam." Jones was groggy at the end of the fourth round, the *Oregonian* reported, "Lavigne looked as fresh as when he entered the ring. In the seventh Lavigne landed on the face and body with his right and left, but Jones made no effort to return. A heavy left on the jaw sent him to the floor. When he arose Lavigne planted two straight lefts on his chin, sending him down again. Jones was groggy when time was called for the eighth and Lavigne had everything his own way. He jabbed Jones on the neck with his left and lodged his right on the jugular, knocking him down."[28] Jones remained on the canvas and was counted out, only to immediately get to his feet attempting to reenter the fray. Referee Dempsey stopped him. In the Kid's words, "I knocked Jones cold in the eighth." Per the *Oregonian*, "Jones was badly used up. Lavigne did not show any signs of punishment."

The First Battle of the Burge

After the Portland win, Lavigne returned to Saginaw at the end of May to console his mother and grieve with family. He got one more opportunity to display his fistic prowess on the West Coast when a match was arranged for him to fight Jim "Iron Bark" Burge at the Pacific Athletic Club in San Francisco on August 10, 1892. Burge hailed from Sydney, Australia and was fighting his first bout outside his home country. He is not to be confused with the Brit, Dick "Iron Man" Burge, whom Lavigne would meet in London for the world championship four years later. Jim Burge had only three defeats in 21 bouts and had six contests of 29 rounds or more with one that went 50 rounds to a draw. He had claimed the Australian lightweight title in 1890 only to lose it 10 months later. It was to be Lavigne's 23rd fight with no defeats. This had the makings of a long-distance slugfest.

Aside from being small men, Burge at 5 feet 1 inch and Lavigne at 5 feet 3 and 1/2 inches, the two were kindred spirits in another way . . . they both loved to fight. A couple of quotes illustrate their predisposition. According to the *San Francisco Chronicle*, "He [Burge] fully verified his Australian reputation. He is the kind of man who

Jim "Iron Bark" Burge

impresses people with the idea that if there was no money in fighting he would fight for pleasure."[29] In 1919, Robert Edgren recalled a conversation with Lavigne's first manager, Joe Courtmarsh, about the Kid's love for a "scrap." In Courtmarsh's words, "Fight was the Kid's middle name. He'd fight anyone I matched him with and he never even asked me who he was going to fight next. I had to keep him busy fighting all the time to keep him contented. Fighting was an amusement. He loved any kind of roughhouse. Why, the only way I could get along with him was by being ready to scrap at any moment. If we were walking down the street in the winter he'd jump on me the instant he saw I wasn't watching and roll me in a snowdrift. If I got him down it tickled him just as long as there was a scrap."[30]

The Lavigne/Burge bout, a finish-fight, was the main event of the evening for a purse of $1,250. The preliminary bout had been marred by several LaBlanche punches and it took intervention by the local police to restore order in the middle of the bout. The referee for the main event, Mike Sullivan, declared that the man who used the LaBlanche swing would lose the fight. The *Chronicle* made unusually descriptive comments about the physical appearances and abilities of both fighters when they noted, "Lavigne showed up with healthy looking skin and not an ounce too much or too little on his bones. His legs looked like a pair of tongs and he used them with an agility that surprised the spectators and later in the fight caused them to advise him to go on a race track." And of his opponent, "Burge is the queerest looking individual ever seen in the ring. He possesses short, thin legs which he uses in a jerky sort of way. His left shoulder is a large knob of bone covered with flesh, which he uses to shield his head against drives from his opponent's right. He keeps the shoulder squirming around in its socket, and when he sees the right coming his head drops down behind it and the other man's fist collides with the shield."[31]

The fight began with Burge coming out the aggressor but every time he landed a hard body blow "his head shot back as if it had springs from the instant return he got from Lavigne's left on his mouth," the *Chronicle* reported. "The nob on Burge's shoulder worked viciously as he closed in and tried to land his right," the *Chronicle* continued, "but Lavigne had the art of ducking down to a fine point and the effort failed. Lavigne is a great general. He depends on his legs to a great extent. They carry him all around the ring away from his opponent. Very shifty is he—one of those men the other fellow seldom knows where to find, and whose locality is generally announced by a blow."[32]

While the spectators may have been impressed with Lavigne's ability to evade and slip his aggressive attacker, this was not the style that Lavigne was noted for. He was the indefatigable mauler of any opponent he faced, the consummate front-door, pressure pugilist. Something had changed and it wouldn't be known until after the fight was concluded. Lavigne was content with stopping his retreat long enough to get in a few good left hand wallops then dance away. The *Chronicle* would claim, "Lavigne is a foul fighter. His favorite trick was to butt in the stomach with his shoulder after ducking. Burge stood this for a while and then started in to do it himself. From that time on each man shouldered the other whenever he had a chance."[33] By the 15th round the fouls were getting rougher. At one point Burge ducked under a Lavigne right hand and came up underneath him so that Lavigne was on top of Burge's back. Burge promptly threw the Kid over his head to the canvas. Later Lavigne tried an illegal La Blanche swing that missed. He was warned by the referee and did not do it again.

"From the 33rd to the 41st round the fight assumed much the aspect of a walking match," lamented the *Chronicle*. "Lavigne, owing to the injury received early in the fight, being unable to press matters, and Burge showing no desire to do so." Lavigne, it would be learned after the fight, had broken his right hand in the fifth round, quite possibly by a hard collision with the bony protuberance of Burge's shoulder shield. "In the 50th round," the *Chronicle* continued, "there being no apparent prospect of either man winning, the police authorities interfered, and referee Sullivan was compelled to declare the fight a draw."[34] It was the end of a five-fight, 10-month West Coast tour.

CHAPTER 7

Fugitive in the Midwest

Lavigne headed back to Saginaw with a few thousand dollars in his pockets and a growing reputation. For perspective, $1,000 in 1892 would be the equivalent of $25,000 today. This was a tidy sum for the son of poor French-Canadian immigrants when a decent wage in a mill-town of the time was much less than $1,000 a year. The Kid would spend three months healing his hand before climbing back into the ring to resume his undefeated career.

Mauling a Middleweight

Back in the comfortable surroundings of his home town the Kid's next opponent was Detroit native, Martin Shaughnessy. Looking at the historical record it's hard to tell how good of a fighter Shaughnessy was at the time. According to his record from *BoxRec.com* he had only four professional bouts, all losses, with Lavigne being his last. But when one looks at who he fought the battles paint a different picture. Three years prior to his bout with Lavigne, Shaughnessy had faced Tommy Ryan twice. Ryan, whose given name was Joseph Youngs, would later become a leading candidate for greatest welterweight of all time followed by greatest middleweight of all time, as he was world champion in both weight classes. Ryan reflected on his early career in a series of articles published in 1911 in the *Syracuse Herald* when he said, "I was immediately matched with the best lightweight of whom Detroit could boast at that time — Martin Shaughnessy. Shaughnessy was a figure in the boxing world; I was almost an absolute unknown. Few people

Tommy Ryan - Courtesy of BoxRec

thought that I stood even a chance with the experienced man."[1] Clearly Ryan knew something of Shaughnessy's record that history failed to record.

Shaughnessy was knocked out in the 23rd round of the first fight and in the 48th round of the second fight just six weeks later. The first fight was an odd affair with Ryan knocking Shaughnessy for a 10-count in the 13th round. "The referee told me that I had won the fight fair and square," Ryan recalled, "and advised me to leave the ring. The fans had not taken the defeat of their idol any too well and everybody seemed to want another bout. I had no particular objection for Shaughnessy now had no terror for me. I knew in my heart that I was his master. I was feeling too good to take his [the referee's] advice in the face of the taunts of Shaughnessy's friends. Tossing the coat I had wrapped about my shoulders to my seconds I announced that I was going to fight the Detroiter again and would surely knock him out so decisively that there would be no come back. I was mad 'clear through.'"

At the beginning of the 14th round, or first round of the second half of the fight, Shaughnessy caught Ryan with a hard right breaking his nose and sending him down face-first on the wooden boards of the ring surface. There was no canvas and thus no padding. Ryan, dazed, got back to his feet at the count of eight and managed to survive the round. In the 23rd Ryan landed two hard uppercuts. "When he went down it was to stay for many minutes," Ryan finished, "There was no question about the second knockout."[2]

The second fight, in which both men were knocked down several times, went on for nearly three hours. According to Ryan, "We were both pretty well battered up, but my opponent seemed to be even more tired than I was and that gave me courage. When the forty-seventh round arrived, we were both near that stage of physical exhaustion which is best known as 'all in.' I managed to get my tired legs into action and Shaughnessy seemed dazed in trying to find me. After a hard left to the body Shaughnessy's guard dropped and I waded in with a right hook to the point of the jaw and the bout was over."[3]

So the Shaughnessy Lavigne was to meet at the Washington Avenue rink in Bay City belied his winless record. It could be said that Shaughnessy had taken the great Tommy Ryan to the 23rd and the 48th before succumbing but that would easily be an overstatement as Ryan was still a neophyte in the ring at the time, although a very skilled one at that. The Shaughnessy that Lavigne would meet in front of an audience of 400 was not a featherweight either, as Lavigne in his early career fought mainly at the featherweight standard. Lavigne would weigh 122 pounds for the match on November 21, 1892. According to the *Bay City Times-Press*, Shaughnessy "was fully 20 pounds heavier than his opponent".[4] The *Saginaw Evening News* gave his exact weight as 145 pounds, two weight classes above Lavigne's.[5] The fight, scheduled for 10 rounds was a one-sided affair with Shaughnessy down once in the seventh round, three times in the eighth, and KOed in the ninth. It would not be the last time he defeated a larger man. The little fellow was a power hitter.

In anticipation of the Kid's next fight a benefit was held for him at the Park rink in Saginaw on January 30, 1893. Two hundred people watched an assortment of entertainment including bag punching, boxing, and club swinging. Club swinging was an element of calisthenics developed in Australia which became quite popular during the Victorian age in the U.S. Billy Lavigne fought an exhibition with Will Skimmins while George sparred with John Hayes for three or four rounds.[6]

Boxing Brothers

Billy and George Lavigne weren't the only boxing brothers of the 1880s and 90s. Billy and Eddie Myer were also sibling pugilists in the lightweight class who made a few headlines in that era. Billy Myer, whose ring name was the "Streator Cyclone" was the older brother and fought many of the big name lightweights of the time with great success including two KO wins over Harry Gilmore and a 64-round draw against the undefeated lightweight champion, Jack McAuliffe. He and his brother Eddie called Streator, Illinois home. It was a small, hardscrabble farming community about 70 miles southwest of Chicago. Younger brother Eddie was in Billy's corner for nearly all of his fights learning from a master. It was now time for Eddie to step into the spotlight and he signed for a finish-fight with the Saginaw Kid on February 12, 1893. The bout would be for a side bet of $1,000 and a purse of $1,500, winner-take-all.

Both fighters were being trained by their older brothers. The *Milwaukee Evening Wisconsin* reported several days before the fight, "Arrangements have been made that will bring the featherweights together in a well-lighted and warmed hall."[7] This is flat, windy, central Illinois farm country and the note that it would be a "warmed hall" was an essential detail for the fighters and spectators in the frigid dead of February. "About twenty-five Milwaukee sports left this afternoon for Chicago," the *Evening* continued the day of the fight, "where they will join the delegation of sports of that city who will leave by special train for the scene of the Myer-Lavigne battle, which takes place somewhere near Streator, Illinois." Obfuscation of location was again the order of the day. When the train arrived at Streator the Chief of Police refused to allow the bout to go on. Undaunted, the train ran down the track another 30 miles to the tiny farming community of Dana, Illinois.

Billy Lavigne tells the story: "When the train arrived about 3 a.m. and the crowd surged off the cars, we were met with the most peculiar sensation I ever experienced. It seemed that someone had either telephoned or telegraphed the town marshal of Dana, and he in turn had made the round of the village, calling forth a general riot alarm, and every fire and church bell in the town was pealing forth a call for the citizens to stop the mill. The crowd, not daunted, proceeded down the street to an old abandoned skating rink, where an entrance was forced, and the ring pitched in the middle of the floor. All the kerosene lamps that could be had in town were brought forth to furnish light and within the space of half an hour's time the battle was on, with a strong cordon of door keepers to keep the marshal of the town at bay and to prevent him from interfering with the proceedings."[8] The abandoned rink of course was not heated and the combatants fought in sub-freezing temperatures.

In the early going of the fight it was the upstart Myer who was getting the best of it, "nearly closing the left eye of the man from the Sawdust City," noted the *Police Gazette*. Myer injured his right hand on Lavigne's head in the third round forcing him to lead with his left. The fight was a back-and-forth affair with both fighters receiving "hard punishment." "In the twenty-second and closing round," the *Gazette* continued, "Eddie got home in the eye and received a hard right in the neck in return. George landed twice in the stomach. Myer touched up his opponent's nose again and avoided a swing. Several rapid blows were exchanged. Then, while the men were in Myer's corner, Lavigne landed heavily on the chin and neck. A terrible punch over the heart, and the Streator man went to the floor and was counted out."[9] Lavigne's powerful body blows had claimed yet another victim.

The early morning fight in an out-of-the-way location kept additional authorities from arriving in time to stop the bout. A local newspaper reported, "The Sheriff and six deputies started in sleighs to stop the fight but failed to reach Dana until after the fighters returned to Streator. The officers said they are going to prosecute the backers and seconds." Two days later the *Milwaukee Evening Wisconsin* printed a few short lines on the illegal fight when they noted, "Warrants have been issued for the arrest of Eddie Myer and George Lavigne for their prizefight Sunday morning at Dana, Ill." The law finally caught up to Lavigne three months later when he was arrested in Chicago in early July. Lavigne was forced to pay $250 to the La Salle County court in order to gain his freedom to return to Saginaw.[10] Lavigne would later sue the county court after claiming that he could not be extradited back to Illinois and that the $250 he paid amounted to extortion.

Lightweight Champion of Michigan

Lavigne, being a fugitive from the Illinois law, stayed close to home, fighting his next bout on March 29, 1893 at the Auditorium in Detroit against native Billy Gaffney. It was billed as a match for the lightweight championship of Michigan. Local authorities, fifteen-strong, were present for the bout. "Sergeant Noble of the Detroit police had positively forbidden more than scientific sparring," noted the *Chicago Tribune*, "and that in case of a knockout all concerned would be placed under arrest. This sounded the death-knell of knockout fights in Detroit."[11] The referee stepped from the ring as none would be needed under the circumstances.

The talk of police interference had an impact on attendance and only 700 people attended which made for a purse of about $600. The fighters, both weighing 127 pounds, climbed into the ring at 9:20 p.m. and after lacing up six-ounce gloves—large for the early 90s—time was called to begin round one. The Kid held back from his normal seek-and-destroy routine, playing more for Gaffney's face with solid jabs, perhaps figuring his body blows would be less effective with the big mufflers on. Gaffney was handicapped early in the bout when he broke his hand landing a hard left on Lavigne's head. The

Kid led throughout, starting the blood flowing from Gaffney's nose in the third round, which continued to bleed freely throughout the bout.

The remainder of the fight was all Lavigne's. "There was a lack of steam in Gaffney's blows," noted the *Detroit Free Press*.[12] Gaffney was reportedly cautious with an injured mitt and was afraid to extend himself because of the police declaration. The bout went the scheduled ten rounds with the result left to the perspective of those who watched. "The contest showed conclusively that Lavigne is the better man of the two," continued the *Free Press*. Gaffney had been advised not to take on a talent of the caliber of Lavigne. Opinions varied as to what would have been the outcome if not for Gaffney's injury and the police presence. Some thought Lavigne would have prevailed in three rounds while others thought Gaffney would have done better.

The Kid fought twice more in 1893. In April he bested an unknown, Charley Mitchell, in a four-round, no-decision contest in the small town of Ludington, Michigan. He was clearly having trouble getting quality bouts as his reputation grew as an indestructible, hard-hitting fighter. In August a benefit was scheduled for the Kid at the Park Rink in Saginaw in which several exhibitions bouts were contested. In front of a crowd of 600 people, Billy Lavigne fought two, three-round matches and the Kid fought a three-round exhibition against "Mysterious" Billy Smith.[13] Smith would become close friends with the Kid and would figure prominently in the Kid's downfall six years later.

CHAPTER 8

Griffo and the Gatling Guns

At last, the Kid was to get a shot at a growing ring legend who would be favored to defeat him. Albert Griffiths was the lightweight champion of Australia and had arrived in June of 1893 seeking to test his considerable boxing skills against American talent. Lavigne would never face a more experienced fighter at any stage of his storied career than Young Griffo, the Australian "Will O' the Wisp," as he was known. Griffo and Lavigne both had their first professional bouts in 1886. The upcoming fight with Griffo scheduled for September 4, 1893 would be Lavigne's 29th fight. It would be Griffo's 162nd fight on his way to an astounding career total of 262 bouts scattered over 25 years. While many of Griffo's bouts were four-rounders, he was very capable of going into the late rounds having gone over 40 rounds four times prior to coming to the U.S.

The fight was to take place at the Columbian Athletic Club in Roby, Indiana, a town just over the Illinois border near East Chicago. It was to be a finish-fight. The *Milwaukee Evening Wisconsin* reported two days before the fight, "With all his [Griffo's] cleverness he will have no cinch in the coming battle, as Lavigne, who is the champion featherweight of the Northwest, is clever, game, and has the reputation of being the hardest-hitting little man in the business. He is a terrific swinger, but unlike most fighters that rely on swinging blows, he is a great judge of distance and throws very few of his blows away. He has defeated numberless good men in his class and he never yet met his match."[1]

The *Tacoma Daily News* in 1916 wrote of Griffo's astounding fistic talents: "Not known as much of a puncher, but his skill was uncanny. He had wonderful headwork, almost impenetrable defense, dazzling feints, and rapid two-handed methods of attack. The cleverest boxers and hardest punchers were made to look ridiculous when exchanging swats with him."[2] Griffo would indeed make Lavigne look ridiculous but not in September 1893 at Roby.

On the evening of the fight a bizarre scene unfolded. The Columbian Athletic Club arena had been completed in June of 1893 with a capacity of 18,000 "sports," as sporting men of the day were known. Politics were at play at this venue, named for the 400th anniversary of Columbus' voyage to the New World. It was felt that it had such money making potential that nothing over the border in Chicago could equal it. A short piece in the *Illustrated Police News* examined another complication, "The trouble seems to be that Indiana objects to being made the 'dark and bloody ground' of a fighting club projected and directed from Chicago or New Orleans."[3]

Young Griffo (Albert Griffiths) - Courtesy of Cyber Boxing Zone

Indiana Governor Matthews was determined that there would be no more fights at Roby and called out the Indiana Militia. As recalled by the *Milwaukee Evening Wisconsin*, "Last night 700 soldier boys were sleeping within a stone's throw of the big pine building, and a Gatling gun was planted on the boardwalk in front of the arena with its muzzle directed to the main entrance. A military camp has been established, pickets are out, and the commanding officer says in answer to all questions: 'There will be no more prizefights at Roby.'" Lavigne and Griffo were in the ring and waiting for the time-keeper's gong when officials called off the two scheduled bouts.

Several hundred of Lavigne's Saginaw supporters made the 350 mile journey to Roby and were not pleased with the program's cancellation at the last minute. Griffo was perhaps the most disappointed of all as this was to be his first fight outside his home country and it was expected to be a great one. In the Kid's words, "Griffo and I stayed around Roby two weeks hoping for an opportunity to meet, but in the end we had to give it up. I went back to Saginaw and opened a saloon. Griffo got busy at Chicago with his dazzling science and became a boxing sensation at the old Battery B Armory. He made monkeys of such crafty ringsters as Tommy White, Ike Weir, Solly Smith, and Johnny Van Heest. There were times when those experienced boxers would be swinging at the air with Griffo behind them."[4]

No evidence was found as to a saloon owned by the Kid in early 1890's Saginaw but with over 200 saloons in town that record may have been lost in the shuffle of time. It was the first of several business ventures in which the Kid would be involved throughout his career. Lavigne talked of his hope for a bout with Griffo when he recalled, "I had a strong itch to try my fists against such a marvel, but it was not to be for several months."[5] He would not fight again until February of 1894 when the battle with Griffo was finally to happen.

In the meantime Griffo stayed busy fighting seven times. He suffered his first loss in his 163rd bout when he was knocked out in the first round by the featherweight champion of the Pacific Coast, Solly Smith, in a "private fight." These fights were often private gatherings of wealthy patrons at one of their estates. Many never made it into the record books as official bouts. Little is known about this fight but boxing historian Tracy Callis' description of Smith in his Cyber Boxing Zone record may hold a clue. Per Callis, "He was very strong but a little slow—a hard hitter who relied on a heavy right hand punch; that blow was described as being like 'the kick of a mule.'"[6] Perhaps Griffo entered the ring in a state of inebriation and got careless early; the mule kicked and he was put to sleep by Solly's thundering right hand. A month later Griffo would fight Smith again to a six-round draw.

The fight with Young Griffo was finally rescheduled for February 10, 1894 at Chicago's Second Regiment Armory. "Griffo is doing a little training," the *Milwaukee Evening Wisconsin* noted the day before the fight, "something unusual for him."[7] Griffo was well known for his lack of training and his penchant for the bottle. The *Tacoma Daily News* was quite clear on both points when it reported, "He had a dislike of training and was deemed lazy. There were times he got drunk before a match."[8] Lavigne later recalled that prior to his bout with Griffo his opponent had "drunk a lot of beer just before entering the ring."

The Griffo fight was an eight round contest with five-ounce gloves, refereed by one of the most respected officials of the era, George Siler. The *Chicago Tribune* printed a summary of the bout in which it reported, "Young Griffo had a close call from defeat at the Lake Front Armory last night in his eight-round go with George Lavigne. In the first two rounds Griffo kept Lavigne in his own corner, but in the sharp rallies that followed in rapid succession the Michigan lad secured almost an even break. When Griffo closed with him he would stand and punch and landed quite as often as the Australian. The third round was just as fast and in the fourth round both men tired. That caused no surprise, as the work had been remarkably fast. If Griffo has a chance to win it was in this round. Lavigne was dead tired, but Griffo was no better and the round was uneventful. From that time on Lavigne was much the stronger of the two. Griffo began to break ground, and Lavigne, following him, fought wildly at times, his left hand particularly going high over the alien's head, but he landed at times and several stiff punches over the heart did the Australian no good."[9] The fight was ruled a draw and the *Tribune* concluded, "On last night's showing, Griffo would have his hands full winning from Lavigne in a finish-fight."

As was often the case for Lavigne he looked back on his fights with a certain amount of lighthearted amazement. "Griffo's science was a revelation," he said. "I had never seen such speed with hands, feet and head. For the first two rounds I thought all Griffo's seconds were in the ring helping him. 'For the love of Mike,' I said to my brother Billy between rounds, 'how many hands has this fellow got?' In the fourth I decided to cut loose biff-bang with everything I had, shooting in all directions hoping some haymaker might connect. A wild wallop caught Griffo in the kitchen. And just as soon as I eased off a bit to blow, there he was right back at me with his left stuck in my face."[10] He would fight Griffo again a year and a half later in a longer battle scheduled for 20 rounds. Never would the Kid face a fighter with more "science" in the ring.

Letting Smith Stay

Solly Smith, born Soloman Garcia Smith, the man who KOed Griffo a few months prior would be the Kid's next opponent on March 7, 1894. Smith and Lavigne had two common opponents both having fought Soto and Siddons. The Smith-Siddons bout went long distance to a 56-round draw, one round longer than the Kid's shortest bout with Siddons. As described by Lavigne, Smith was one of the great featherweights of the 1890s and was a rugged, fast man, and a "terrible" hitter. The fight was to be eight rounds at Arbeiter Hall in Saginaw. The fighters agreed to a prearranged draw if neither was knocked out.

Arbeiter Hall, Saginaw – Courtesy of the Historical Society of Saginaw County

There was an unusual circumstance that preceded the fight and had a bearing on its outcome. "Solly put me in an awkward hole before the fight. He told me he was in no condition and asked me not to knock him out. It made it rather bad for me, especially in my home town, but I gave him my word I wouldn't try to stop him. I let Smith stay the eight rounds, but I hit him hard enough to give him a black eye and he got sore about that. It hurt me with my friends in Saginaw, but it taught me a lesson, and I made no promises to anyone afterward."[11]

Smith weighed 123 pounds for the contest and Lavigne 127. The combatants wore five-ounce gloves. While Lavigne did let Smith stay and due to the prearrangement the fight was ruled a draw, the newspaper reports all favored Lavigne with the *Police Gazette* commenting,

"Smith was groggy in the eighth and had a badly swollen eye. Lavigne showed up far superior to Smith in every respect and should another contest take place, there would be plenty of Saginaw money to back Lavigne who is a great deal better pugilist than many credit him with being."[12] The two would fight again in New York a year later.

At the end of April, Billy Lavigne, age 29, would be the first of the Lavigne clan to tie the knot. He married Bertha Christine Dewey on April 30, 1894 at Saginaw. The Kid was a long way off from the altar with his career in full swing and his mind on the next opponent.

Solly Smith - Courtesy of BoxRec

CHAPTER 9

Go East Young Man

With all his fights taking place in the Midwest and the West Coast, the Kid had never fought a bout east of Michigan but that would soon change. He agreed to fight Dick O'Brien in Boston on May 25, 1894.[1] Young Griffo was due to fight Johnny Griffin in late April and Billy Murphy in early May, two of the top featherweights at the time. Both fights were to take place in Boston as well. Lavigne left for the east coast a month prior to his bout with O'Brien to get settled in to a pre-bout training routine and to attend Griffo's two fights. Bemused and fascinated by Griffo's talents in the ring and knowing he wanted another shot at the wily Australian, watching him in action would help him study his gifted ring tactics. It would also give him a needed change of pace from the grueling monotony of daily training. The Kid was the consummate fight fan continuing to stay active as a spectator and commentator during his career and long after his last go in the ring. Little did the Kid know that a dangerous brush with fate awaited his early arrival in Boston.

A Close Call

On May 18th in a Court Street saloon, the Kid was approached by a local struggling welterweight by the name of Jerry Sullivan. Sullivan's nickname was "Horsebite." He asked to borrow fifty cents from the Kid. One of the Kid's fatal flaws was that he was generous to the point that he squandered several fortunes throughout his career. He was willing to help Sullivan and pulled out a quarter. Apparently a quarter was not enough and Sullivan pulled out a pocket knife and made several slashes at Lavigne cutting him slightly on the cheek.[2] The *Police Gazette*, which specialized in reporting events of sport, crime and sex, covered two of their bases in one story when they noted, "George Lavigne, the 'Saginaw Kid,' had a close call in Boston recently. Sullivan, the welterweight, tried to borrow money from the Saginaw boxer, and because he did not give him the full sum asked for, repaid his liberality by slashing Lavigne's throat and cheek with a knife."[3] The Kid went to the hospital where his three cuts were dressed but refused to press charges. Luckily the damage was superficial and he would carry out his promise to meet O'Brien on May 25th.

O'Brien was a few fights into the beginning of his career as a successful middleweight when he met the Kid for a six-round bout. Dick would later fight, and lose to, the Barbados Demon, Joe Walcott, four times. Most of his early and mid-career losses were to a who's-who of the welter and middleweight ranks including Walcott, Tommy Ryan, Mysterious Billy Smith, Jimmy Handler, Kid McCoy, and the English great, Dick Burge. This was another no-decision affair. Outweighed by at least 20 pounds, Lavigne nevertheless got the best of an inexperienced O'Brien. At least that is what Lavigne recalled years later and what was shown in "Lavigne's Complete Ring Record" in a *Detroit Times* story of 1928, however, no newspaper record of the bout was found to support these two sources.

Working his way toward New York the Kid had another engagement lined up at Providence, Rhode Island to fight Stanton Abbott, the notable English lightweight in a scheduled four-round, no-decision bout on June 4th. The contest as planned never came off because there was not enough money in the house to pay the men for coming together. Instead, Abbott fought Jack Slavin and Lavigne found an able substitute in Billy Hennessey. Lavigne would again be fighting a man 20 pounds heavier as Hennessey was a solid middleweight. "Lavigne made a good showing against Hennessey of Boston, a much heavier man," noted the *Police Gazette*, "There were about 100 spectators and 20 policemen."[4]

There was a distinct pattern evolving here; many of the lightweight fighters were unwilling to step in the ring with Lavigne due to his growing reputation, therefore he had to reach up in weight to find willing opponents. The combination of his speed and hitting power served him well when giving away so many pounds to the larger lads. His manager at this point in his career was Joe Lewis who was struggling to get the Kid any matches, even reaching down in weight to the feathers. He was focused on a rematch with Young Griffo. Lewis and Lavigne were asked to step aside and wait their turn clearing the way for Griffo to fight fellow antipodean and former featherweight champion of the world, "Torpedo" Billy Murphy after which they would get the winner. Instead, when Griffo defeated Murphy he and his manager bypassed the Kid to fight George Dixon.[5] Frustrated, Lavigne arrived in New York, ended his relationship with Lewis, and sought out Sam Fitzpatrick to manage his affairs.

While in New York the Kid and Young Griffo were approached by a famous inventor who wanted to capture a boxing match on his newest marvel, the kinetograph. The kinetograph used celluloid film invented just a few years before in 1889 by George Eastman, later of Eastman/Kodak fame. Thomas A. Edison had built a studio that had a retractable roof and could be rotated on tracks to capture the best available sunlight to film subjects on his prototype motion picture camera. His fanciful name for the studio was "Black Maria," as it was covered with tar paper on the inside. In 1891 Edison made one of his first films now called simply, *Men Boxing*.[6] It was a little more than five seconds of film showing two of his employees sparring with large white boxing gloves.

In June of 1894 Edison and his partners were looking for the real thing . . . a true pugilistic contest. "The inventor's friends then made an arrangement with Kid Lavigne and Young Griffo, both featherweights," noted the *Boston Herald*, "but when they saw the 12-foot ring in which they were expected to do the desired knocking-out, they rebelled and refused to fight, notwithstanding the liberal offers made them."[7] Had that mock fight been filmed and survived the test of time it would have allowed future fight fans a glimpse of two of the great sluggers and dancers of the 1890s. Instead, Edison found Mike "The Fashion Plate" Leonard, a decent New York lightweight, and little known Mike Cushing to be the first to star in a boxing motion picture film. Leonard put Cushing to sleep in the sixth round to the great excitement of Edison and his backers.

Color Was No Barrier

As noted earlier, the Kid never ducked another fighter and welcomed competition regardless of race. He had already fought two fighters of Mexican descent in Joe Soto and Solly Smith. His next bout, arranged by his new manager would be against a black fighter and "colored" featherweight champion of Australia, Jerry Marshall. Marshall had fought his countryman Griffo twice, losing once on points after a 25-round contest was stopped by police in the 12th round, and losing a second time a few months later in early 1893 on a fourth-round disqualification. Marshall was making his first tour to the east coast.

The fight, to be refereed by Dominick McCaffrey, was scheduled for 10 rounds and a purse of $1,500 at the Seaside Athletic Club of Coney Island on September 17, 1894. "Although the Brooklyn police authorities had issued a manifesto that there should be no knock-outs or slugging, the announcement did not keep away the "sporting men," noted the *New York Times* as the fight drew spectators from cities within 500 miles of New York.[8] As with many sporting clubs of the time betting was officially prohibited in the club, however, the "sports" privately bet $50s and $100s on the contest.

The police were on hand for all four bouts on the fight card. Inspector Reilly stopped the first bout just short of a knockout in the second round. He stopped the second bout in the sixth when the contestants "abandoned science" and began slugging wildly, and stopped the third bout, which featured Young Griffo overwhelming Eddie Loeber, before the end of the first round. The Lavigne-Marshall bout was the last bout of the evening and the principles, each weighing in at 126 pounds, awaited the gong at a bit past 10 p.m.[9]

George "Kid" Lavigne 1894
- Courtesy of Antiquities of the Prize Ring

The *New York Times* gave a wonderfully descriptive accounting of the physical attributes of the fighters. "Marshall is a shrewd looking Negro, a trifle taller than Lavigne, and to reach of arm he also had the advantage. His countenance is thin, stern and forbidding. His eyes are deeply set in his head, under projecting and beetling brows, with high, prominent cheek bones, so that it must be a very difficult task to close his optics. His face appeared to be nearly all skin and bone, and presents an appearance of toughness, which gives the idea that he could stand a very considerable amount of pounding without serious detriment.

"Lavigne did not seem to be so severely trained as his opponent. He was a trifle shorter of stature, but more robustly built, a splendidly made man with a form of perfect symmetry, indicating great energy and physical power. As they stood there on guard, erect and defiant, their flesh glowing in the strong light, Lavigne like polished bronze, and Marshall like polished ebony, a murmur of admiration ran through the crowd. Marshall looked stern and vindictive, while Lavigne, the great little Michigan boxer, looked smiling and confident, and gave assurances of a determination to do all in his power to carry off the coveted honors and the purse which was the bone of contention."[10]

The first round was an even one with both fighters showing considerable skills. The *Times* praised both fighters saying of Lavigne, "He was nimble as a mountain goat on his feet, while he would cleverly stop the Australian's straight left-hand leads and counters and cross-counters with wonderful quickness." And of Marshall, "[He] fully confirmed the high opinion entertained of him as a boxer, showing himself to be a very clever two-handed fighter and a punishing hitter."[11]

The *Philadelphia Item* gave a round-by-round commentary saying Lavigne was the aggressor and at the end of the third, "was hitting like a piledriver." As Lavigne pressed the action in the fourth, he "laughed at Marshall's futile effort to get back." By round eight, "Marshall realized that he was up against certain defeat unless he could change the tide of battle." With Marshall desperately trying to carry the remainder of the fight to Lavigne, he continued to be out-slugged. "The bell rang just after Lavigne had landed a sockdolager on Jerry's back." The 10th and final round was all Lavigne with a series of powerful rights to the body and a few left uppercuts. While the fight was clearly a victory for Lavigne neither fighter sustained extensive punishment which kept Inspector Reilly in his seat, allowing the bout to reach a natural conclusion.[12] "[Referee] McCaffrey said he had nothing against Marshall's color," noted the *Boston Daily Globe*, "but he had to declare Lavigne the winner, a popular decision."[13]

The Kid and the Lad

In Jerry Marshall's next bout on Christmas Day, 1894 he would give a karmic gift to Lavigne in a "pay-it-forward" bit of fate when he bested Lavigne's slasher, Jerry "Horsebite" Sullivan, in six rounds. Lavigne's record was now 21 wins, 4 no-decisions, and 7 draws. After his victory over Marshall the Kid increased his pressure on Young

Griffo for a rematch of their February 1894 bout. "I have waited many months for another opportunity to meet him since our draw in Chicago," the Kid said. "Now my patience is exhausted. I will post $1,000 tomorrow, the next day, or a week hence, if Griffo desires it, to fight him at any weight, the contest must be to a finish, with any size gloves for $5,000 a side and a purse, if any club agrees to one. The size of the latter will make no difference to me. In the event of no purse being offered, I am satisfied to meet him in private with skin tight gloves for the stakes."[14] The Kid would have preferred to fight Griffo with riding gloves. He knew just how slippery Griffo was and that he would land very few solid punches in the match. With no padding in the gloves it would only take one shot to put the little imp to sleep.

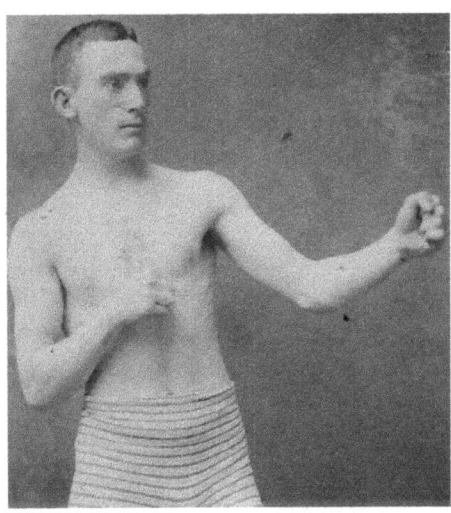

Lavigne would stay in the East for one more bout on October 29th at the Coney Island Casino in Brooklyn in a go against Johnny T. Griffin, from Braintree, Massachusetts, aptly nicknamed "the Braintree Lad". The Kid and the Lad were both born in 1869 and both started their careers as teenagers, Lavigne at 16 and Griffin at 17, no doubt the origin of their youthful monikers. Lavigne was familiar with Griffin having seen him fight Young Griffo to a six- round draw in Boston earlier that year. While Lavigne had stayed busy, it would be Griffin's first fight since his match with Griffo.

Johnny T. Griffin, "The Braintree Lad"
- Courtesy of Cyber Boxing Zone

Although Griffin's record was spotty with a number of losses, he had fought some of the best in the featherweight class in Tommy Danforth, the "Belfast Spider" Ike Weir, Solly Smith and "Torpedo" Billy Murphy. He would later fight two bouts with the exceptional world champion featherweight, George Dixon, losing 20- and 25- round decisions on points. Tracy Callis in Griffin's Cyber Boxing Zone record described Griffin as "a red-headed boxer who carried a stiff right hand punch and a good left hand too; He hit with straight, hard blows; Johnny was often described as having all the qualities that make up a great fighter—clever, active, scientific, game, strong, and a terrific hitter."[15] All the same qualities Lavigne possessed as well. There was no doubt the Kid respected Griffin's abilities and considered him a worthy and dangerous opponent.

The record is muddled as to the intended length of this fight although the *Associated Press* wire report indicated it was to be a 15-round bout. Tim Hurst, a well-known baseball umpire of the time, was the referee. The contestants agreed on a weight of 124 pounds but at 6:00 p.m. on the evening of the fight Lavigne weighed 127 pounds. It was after 10:00 p.m. by the time the two camps agreed to proceed in light of the three pound disparity. Had Griffin been the one that was overweight it would have mattered little to Lavigne. The fight, for a purse of $1,500, was well attended. In a derogatory comment indicative of the social stratification of the times, a local paper reported, "The effect of the popular prices was particularly noticeable in the bleacheries [sic], which were well filled with the lower types of sports. In all there were about 3,500 persons present."[16]

As Lavigne told it, "I then proceeded to give Mr. Johnny Griffin one of the most artistic trimmings that I ever handed any fighter."[17] The *Milwaukee Evening's* headline summarized the fight well when it flashed, "The 'Braintree Lad' Meets His Master in the 'Kid' from Saginaw." On the detail of the fight the *Evening* reported, "The fighting during the first four rounds was terrific, the 'Braintree Lad' doing the rushing. He was soon obliged to resort to defensive tactics, however, as the 'Kid' took kindly to fast work. Griffin was groggy at the end of the fourth." From then on it was Lavigne dictating the fight, his strength continually overwhelming Griffin's cleverness as he rushed him to the ropes "punishing him severely."

In the seventh round Griffin's eyes were nearly closed, yet he gamely fought on. In the 10th round Lavigne staggered Griffin again with a left and a right to the jaw and in the 11th Griffin's blows caused a trickle of blood to flow from the Kid's nose. In the 14th with Griffin looking weary Lavigne again rushed him to the ropes and sent the Lad to the floor with a crashing right hand. The 15th would last only ten seconds. "At the call of the 15th round," the *Evening* continued, "Lavigne bounded out of his corner intent on mischief. Griffin had just reached the center when Lavigne let drive his left. It caught his man squarely on the mouth and staggered him. Before he recovered, the westerner landed his right on the jaw, knocking his plucky antagonist down. Griffin struggled to his feet and was anxious to continue but Inspector McKelvy interfered and refused to proceed further. The referee declared Lavigne the winner amid a storm of applause."[18]

Griffin, with bloodied and swollen face, complained after the fight that he had been weakened by working to get down to 124 pounds. Sounding a bit the sore loser, he complained that Lavigne had not kept his promise to "make weight." Griffin later told the Kid he was deaf in one ear from the beating he had been handed.[19]

CHAPTER 10

From Rules to Rings: Boxing's Metamorphosis

A fight is just a fight until there are rules. When boxing had a rebirth in England in the early 1700s after lying dormant for a period of 1,200 years there were virtually no rules. If the term "boxing" can loosely be defined as a contest between two people using fists to strike one another, then what was called "prizefighting" at the time was not boxing. In the days of James Figg, the first champion of England, prizefighting was a brutal, and not infrequently fatal, contest between two men that more closely resembled the gladiatorial savagery of the distant past.

In Figg's time as undisputed champion from 1719 to 1730, his somewhat rule-less form of prizefighting featured no rounds and no rest. "Fighters were allowed to trip an opponent, grasp his head and batter it against a corner post, hold him by this hair with one hand and punch him into insensibility with the other, gouge ears and eyes and twist the nose, and toss a rival with a cross-buttock," wrote Frank Butler in *A History of Boxing in Britain*. "Elbows, fingers and thumbs were frequently used, as were blows below the belt."[1] Even biting and "spiking" were not taboo. Spiking referred to the use of one's shoes which were fitted with spikes to get purchase on the turf of the ring. Figg possessed little ring science and according to Butler, "If his methods of fighting were subject to the criticism of the present day, he would be more of a slaughterer than a neat and finished pugilist."[2]

Rules of the Game

Jack Broughton circa 1743
- Courtesy of Cyber Boxing Zone

It was into this world of unrestrained combat that a modicum of order was soon to be introduced. It would come through a set of simple yet crude rules. Rules overlay fairness, and to a certain extent, predictability and respectability, on what is otherwise violent mayhem. Rules also protect the wellbeing of the combatants and the financial interests of those wagering on the outcome. It was a combination of all of the above that motivated English bare-knuckle champion, father of modern boxing, and Figg pupil, Jack Broughton, to lay down the first set of organized rules in 1743.

Just two years prior, Broughton's challenger, George Stevenson, died several days after a 35-minute set-to in which Broughton leveled him with the hardest blow of the contest. Broughton, despondent over the outcome, declared he would never fight again. He did return to the ring and the unfortunate event was the catalyst that drove him, along with a small group of like-minded sports, to develop the rules. Broughton had erected an amphitheater in 1742 near Marylebone Fields for instruction in the art of self-defense and the promotion of prizefighting. The new rules were developed for use in his amphitheater but were soon widely adopted.

By any current standard, save those of the burgeoning modern day mixed martial arts sport, the Broughton rules were still fairly primitive as they continued to allow most of the non-boxing tactics such as head butting, kicking, gouging, biting, elbowing, kneeing and throwing your opponent to the turf. This form of fighting was still not yet boxing. But the Broughton Rules marked the beginning of a metamorphosis that would take nearly 150 years to change an ancient, chaotic fighting ritual into the modern sport of boxing. In summary, the rules called for a one-yard chalked square to be drawn in the center of the ring to which, after being thrown or knocked to the turf, the fighter's seconds would assist him to "toe the scratch" within 30 seconds or be deemed a beaten man. The seven rules also specified how the seconds and two umpires should conduct themselves and how the prize money was to be divided. Lastly, in an attempt to eliminate a bit of the savagery of the past, no man could hit his adversary when he was down; grab him by the "ham, the breeches, or any part below the waist."[3]

After a fallout with his benefactor, the Duke of Cumberland, legislation was enacted which closed Broughton's Academy. "Cumberland even caused Parliament to declare prizefights illegal, and many of the English gentry, or 'fancy' as they were called, withdrew their support for the game."[4] Boxing was under a cloud and in time the sport became outlawed. English gamblers began to adapt horseracing concepts to prizefighting by separating fighters into light, middle, and heavyweight classes and over the next 90 years a new set of rules began to coalesce.

In 1838 the British Pugilistic Association developed a set of 23 rules which built upon the Broughton rules. They were later revised in 1853 to a total of 29 rules which became known as the London Prize Ring rules. Many significant changes were involved including: the ring would now be a 24 foot square with posts and ropes; a referee was to be appointed to resolve disputes between the two umpires; spikes in boots were not to exceed 3/8 inches in length; in addition to a 30 second rest between rounds, the fighters had eight seconds to toe the scratch line without the aid of their seconds; a man could not throw himself to the ground to effect the end of a round; fouls now included head butting, striking a man while down, striking a man below the waist, gouging, tearing the flesh with fingers, nails, or biting, as well as kicking, strangulation, or the use of hard substances in the hands such as stones or sticks.[5]

From the standpoint of safety and respectability, the London rules were a major improvement. Under these new rules prizefighting more clearly resembled sport yet with the continued allowance of wrestling throws and the use of elbows for striking an opponent, its transformation fell short of what we now call boxing. This final evolution would come in 1867 as the result of collaboration between two men, one a commoner of notable athletic skill and the other a member of the aristocracy whose father had been an amateur pugilist.

It was in 1865 that John Graham Chambers proposed a new set of rules. Chambers was an elite oarsman at Cambridge and also founded the Amateur Sporting Club in 1866. He met John Sholto

Douglas, the eighth Marquess of Queensberry, at Cambridge where the two shared an interest in boxing. Chambers drafted the rules and the Marquess provided his considerable patronage toward their adoption. As a result of Douglas' sponsorship, the new rules, first published in 1867, were called the Marquess of Queensberry Rules Governing Contests of Endurance. They were originally intended for amateurs but in a few short years they were being used by professional prizefighters as well.

Unlike the London Prize Ring rules before them which moved the sport of combat further along toward its ultimate pugilistic progeny, the Queensberry rules finished the metamorphosis, ushering in the modern era of boxing. It was now solely fistic in nature. Gone were the elbow smashes and the body throws. A round was no longer over when one man was knocked to the ring surface. He was given a count of ten to get back on his feet and resume fighting or lose the match. The rounds were now timed to last three minutes with one minute of rest in between. And in perhaps the most profound change of all, gloves were required.

Although the Queensberry rules were in widespread use in America by the late 1880s, many of the fighters of the transition period continued to engage in both styles of fighting. There was also cross-over between the London and Queensberry rules with some matches being fought under London rules but with the addition of gloves.

Early Mufflers and the End of Tights

Jack Broughton not only ushered in the era of rules but he also made another significant contribution to modern boxing: he invented the boxing glove. As the story goes he got the idea from studying the hand wraps or "cestus" on a statue of a Greek boxer. A cestus was a battle glove made of leather and filled with iron plates or fitted with blades or spikes. Broughton's design objective was defensive rather than offensive, creating a padded surface to reduce injury to the hand and to the surface it would strike. His early "mufflers" were only used for sparring, training and instruction.

When Chambers drafted the Queensberry rules he wasn't very specific as to the type of glove to be used writing, "The gloves to be fair-sized boxing gloves of the best quality, and new." This was open to broad interpretation and often fighters used nothing more than a skin-tight pair of leather riding or driving gloves. In a 1911 column in the *Syracuse Times* on the subject of early Queensberry gloves, the great bruising middleweight, Tommy Ryan wrote, "Right here I want to tell my readers that the boxing glove of those days and the glove of today are entirely different things, though known by the same name. The boxing glove of 1885 was a skin-tight leather glove that was devised more for the protection of the hand of the boxer wearing it than for the protection of the man upon whom it was to be used."[6] These skin-tight gloves were often made of cured and hardened leather and with no padding added were referred to as "hard gloves."

Gradually the use of gloves padded with two ounces of curled horse hair became the mitt of choice in the early 1890s but often the fighters would remove much of the horse hair. By the late 1890s many of the bouts were fought with four- and five-ounce gloves. Even a five-ounce glove is light by today's standards. Nowadays, weight class determines the size of boxing gloves, from eight ounces (generally at 137 – 147 pounds and below) to ten ounces (over 137 – 147 pounds).[7]

NONE BETTER AT ANY PRICE!

POLICE GAZETTE

Boxing Gloves,

Made from the finest kid and curled hair, they are used by all noted Professionals and Amateurs.

CHAMPION BOXING GLOVES
　　Made in 3, 4, 5, 6 and 8 ounce weights. Price, per set of four, $7.50

EXHIBITION BOXING GLOVES
　　Made in 6 and 8 ounce weights. Price, per set of four, $6.00.

AMATEUR GLOVES
　　Made in 6 and 8 ounce weights. Price, per set of four, $4.00.

Address all orders to

RICHARD K. FOX, Publisher,
Franklin Square, － **New York.**

Newspaper advertisement for boxing gloves, 1894 – Courtesy of the *Police Gazette*

The padded glove had an unintended consequence. It was thought that padding would reduce injuries to the hands of fighters as the small bones of the hand were no match for the thickness of a skull. While it accomplished this outcome it failed to reduce injury to the faces and heads of combatants. The reason was simple; bare-knuckle fighters didn't target the head as much with hard swinging blows as they knew a broken hand may result. "Gloves protected fighters' hands more than their heads, added weight to each punch, and allowed men to throw innumerable blows to such hard-but-vulnerable spots as the temples and jaw," wrote Elliot J. Gorn in *The Manly Art: Bare-Knuckle Prize Fighting in America.* "In bare-knuckle fighting, punches tended to be straight and cutting. A man who threw many hooks or roundhouse-style shots to the side or back of his opponent's head risked breaking his fingers. But with gloves, boxers would use these more dangerous punches with impunity."[8]

Boxing trunks, while not as critical to the outcome of a match as were boxing gloves, nonetheless have their own history. Throughout boxing's resurgence in the late 1800s fighters always wore full-length tights. The origins of the long, loose fitting shorts worn by today's boxers can be traced to a lightweight bout on March 21, 1890 in San Francisco. The match was a finish-fight between champion Jack McAuliffe and Jimmy Carroll and was billed as being for the lightweight championship of the world. As told by Kid Lavigne, "McAuliffe was finding the going hard. Carroll had everything—speed, skill, punch, stamina, a cool head, and a quick eye. McAuliffe's legs were dying under him. Jack Dempsey, the original Nonpareil, was McAuliffe's chief second. After the 25th round Dempsey whipped out a knife and cut off McAuliffe's tights just below the hips. A short time later, Jim Corbett introduced the short trunks fighters now wear in the ring."[9] Dempsey's innovative action between rounds may have helped as McAuliffe won the fight when he knocked Carroll out in the 47th round.

Rounds

Boxing in the new Queensberry era with the addition of gloves, three-minute rounds, and the 10-second, get-up-or-lose rule, was still a very violent sport. Gorn also points out, "The new ten-second knockout rule further encouraged clubbing blows, because it was much easier to punch a man into ten seconds than into thirty seconds [the London rules allotment] of unconsciousness."[10] As Gorn so aptly put it, "In a word, boxing might look a bit less brutal but became more dangerous."

Another thing that increased the damage done to the fighters was the number and length of rounds fought. Under London rules the average round lasted less than a minute and a half and often just a few seconds. Doing the math, a lengthy fight of 60 rounds including 30 seconds rest plus eight seconds allowance to toe the scratch between rounds may clock-in at about two hours and eight minutes. Under Queensberry rules, that same fight with three-minute rounds and one-minute rest in between would last four hours! Ninety minutes of actual fighting time under London rules and a whopping three hours under Queensberry rules. It is quite fitting that they were called the Queensberry Rules Governing Contests of Endurance.

Under both London and Queensberry rules there were no set number of rounds. The longest match fought under Queensberry rules was 110 between Andy Bowen and "Texas Jack" Burke in 1893. It lasted seven hours and nineteen minutes. One of the longest bare-knuckle matches was 185 rounds between Mike Madden and Bill Hays in 1849. It lasted six hours and three minutes. These were termed "finish-fights" for obvious reasons. By the late 1890s less finish-fights were being contested. By then the maximum number of rounds fought was usually 20 or 25. Changing the number of rounds fought altered the dynamics of a fight. Longer bouts favored fighters who were endowed with great stamina and who were game enough to take punishment over the long haul. Such a fighter was Kid Lavigne, who over the course of his career fought bouts of 77, 55, 50, 30, 25, 24, 22, and four times, 20 rounds. In the boxing world of today, championship bouts are 12 rounds; a mere warm-up for the pugilists of the past.

The Circle Is Squared

In almost any dictionary definition of the word "ring," it is described as circular. Why is it then that a boxing ring is a square? The concept of a fighting ring goes back to the days of the gladiators where the arena in the amphitheater tended to be circular in shape. Throughout history, when a hand-to-hand challenge was to be settled, spectators formed a circle, or ring, around the two combatants. When boxing resurfaced in England in the early 1700s, a crude ring was employed. "When an Englishman of this period wanted to battle or argue out a point, he drew a ring on the ground around himself and invited his opponent to fight it out and 'may the best man win,'" wrote John Grombach in *The Saga of Sock*.[11]

The circular ring posed a problem. When a fighter was knocked into the sea of spectators crowded around the ring, the observers may get in a few licks of their own on the opponent of the man they were betting on. Over time, ropes and stakes separated combatants from spectators. Finally, with the adoption of the first set of London rules in 1838 the circle was squared: "That the ring shall be made on turf, and shall be four-and-twenty feet square, formed of eight stakes and ropes, the latter extending in double lines, the uppermost line being four feet from the ground, and the lower two feet from the ground."[12] The last rule in both the 1838 and the revised, 1853 versions, allowed for fights to take place on the stage provided the rest of the rules were adhered to as nearly as possible.

The squared circle had another advantage; the rules called for designated areas in opposite corners for the seconds and bottle holders. Unlike in modern times these "cornermen" were inside the ring. In the old days when fighters stood toe-to-toe in the center of the ring to pummel each other, additional persons inside the ring were hardly in the way, particularly as the ring was 24-feet square, whereas today's rings are 18-feet to 20-feet square.

As things progressed by Queensberry rule, no one other than the fighters was allowed in the ring during a round. Being inside the ring facilitated better control of the fighters allowing the referee to separate them from clinches and more clearly monitor the match for fouls. This changed in America, where by the 1890s the referee was routinely inside the ring. England was a bit slower to adopt this practice as it wasn't until 1907 that celebrated referee, Eugene Corri, officiated a match in the National Sporting Club of London from inside the ring.

Throughout the early days of the 1880s and 1890s, fights were held in a wide variety and type of locale. As prizefighting was illegal at the time in most states in America fight organizers had to stay one step ahead of the law. Fights would be held in barns and stables, on barges in the river, in fields, opera houses, theaters, dancehalls, and even private residences. In the 1890s a few states enacted laws allowing for quasi-legal "sparring exhibitions" to be held in bona fide athletic clubs. As a result, athletic clubs began to proliferate and boxing had found a new and more respectable home.

It had been several decades since the great lightweight champion of the 1880's, Jack McAuliffe, had donned a glove when he described to Nat Fleischer, with a bit of disdain, just how much the game had evolved. "The game has changed, from finish-fights to limited-round bouts, with beautifully illuminated arenas, padded posts, silk covered ropes, luxury unlimited. I wonder how the chaps who box under such aesthetic circumstances would feel if they went out into the cold, gray early morning to crawl through a plowed field on to a bit of frozen turf, and slug away, maybe in rain or snow, until one of 'em went down for keeps? There'd be maybe, one hundred, or perhaps fifty spectators, and they wouldn't know whether they'd get ten bucks or a hundred! Also, there'd be the chance of taking an awful beating and finish up with a police raid, to be followed by a jail term. If there was anything of a quitter in a man, it would show then."[13]

In the early 1890s the latest in ring technology was developed. According to the *Milwaukee Evening Wisconsin*, "The outfit is known as a stakeless ring, so constructed that the posts which support the corners are removed from the arena far enough to be out of the way of a fall. A contestant in going down or against the ropes cannot strike the posts. The felt carpet is three-quarters of an inch thick and protects the man from a hard fall on the floor."[14]

In this era of boxing no mouth guards were used. No rigid cups were worn to protect from low blows. No vaseline was used to reduce facial cuts though the petroleum product had been in general use since 1872. And the mandatory eight-count, which would dramatically increase safety for vulnerable fighters, was not to come into widespread use until the early 1950s. Even so, times were changing with a growing emphasis on making the sport safer for contestants and more appealing to a broader audience. Padding under the canvas of the ring, or lack thereof, would play a prominent role in a tragic outcome of one of the Kid's fights just a few years later.

CHAPTER 11

The Tragedy of the American Title

"Having demonstrated my superiority as a pugilist over Jerry Marshall and Johnny Griffin, I want to continue to climb the prize ring ladder until I reach the top," declared Lavigne to the *Police Gazette* on November 17, 1894, one week before signing articles to fight Andy Bowen in New Orleans.[1] Newspapers began to buzz with the announcement. "Kid Lavigne has the hardest job on his hands that he has yet tackled," opined the *Milwaukee Evening Wisconsin*. "When he meets Andy Bowen at New Orleans on December 14 he will find him one of the toughest customers he ever met. The Saginaw lad is also giving away considerable in weight. Bowen is the cleverer of the two and Lavigne will have to depend upon getting in a 'right swing' in order to land the purse."[2]

The Kid's fighting weight had been in the featherweight range to this point in his career with one exception, that being his 50-round contest against Jim "Iron Bark" Burge in 1892 when he weighed nearly 137 pounds. Although he never feared fighting heavier opponents, he

Andy Bowen, "The Louisiana Tornado"
- Courtesy of Cyber Boxing Zone

wisely added some weight to take on a very tough and strong Bowen, thus erasing an advantage conferred upon Bowen by the newsmen. While Bowen wasn't very "scientific" he was as durable as they come and could give and take with the best of them. Like Lavigne, he was also noted for his incredible stamina, having fought several fights of over twenty rounds, a few over 40, and two over 80. The year before his fight with Lavigne, Bowen fought the longest bout on record under the Marquess of Queensberry rules when after 7 hours and 19 minutes his bout with Texas Jack Burke was called a draw at the end of 110 rounds. The following month he won a 5 hour and 35 minute, 85-round decision from another skilled, long distance warrior, Jack Everhardt.

A Vacant Title

The bout was billed for the American Lightweight Title. The title had been vacant since the legendary Jack McAuliffe, the so called "Napoleon of the Prize Ring," last defended it. The passing of a championship torch generally happened in one of three ways: a fighter retired undefeated—the rarest of the three—he was dethroned in defeat, or he vacated the title when he outgrew the weight and pursued his future in a higher weight class. The first two would happen in one night, two years prior on the evening of September 7, 1892 in the Crescent City.

It was at the fistic carnival promoted by the Olympic Club of New Orleans that John L. Sullivan faced "Gentleman" Jim Corbett in defense of his heavyweight crown. Two nights before in the first night of a three-night tripleheader, McAuliffe defended his lightweight title decisively when he knocked out the "Streator Cyclone," Billy Myer in the 15th round. McAuliffe was a second for his close friend Sullivan for his bout with Corbett. This would be the last heavyweight championship fight for Sullivan. It ended badly for the storied champ. He was past his prime, too fond of drink, and not in top shape for the battle. Sullivan was knocked out in the 21st round.

In *Ten-And Out!* Alexander Johnston recalls the story of the passing of the two great champions. "As McAuliffe tells it now, he was sitting with Sullivan after the latter's defeat. The old champion was just a weary old man, and he turned to McAuliffe and said, 'Everyone gets his sometime. Do what I'm telling you now, Jack, and retire with the glory of a world's championship and avoid the disgrace of a knockout.' 'And', says McAuliffe, 'I made up my mind that night, sitting alone there with John L. in his room. I quit fighting and retired.'"[3] It may seem odd that McAuliffe saw Sullivan as a "weary old man." Sullivan was just 34 years of age, however, given the average life expectancy of a man born in 1858 was a scant 40 years, and add to that the wear, tear, and brutality of countless bare-knuckle and gloved matches as well as the toll of years of hard drinking, it's a wonder Sullivan didn't look old long before 1892. He retired in defeat and McAuliffe, only 26 years of age and undefeated, retired as well, although only from defense of his title as he fought a few more bouts after his announcement.

Lavigne was the heir-apparent having actively sought out, fought, and defeated the best that would try him from feathers to middleweights from coast-to-coast. McAuliffe fought a couple of bouts while "retired" going 10 rounds with Young Griffo in August of 1894. It was yet another show of fistic mastery by Griffo, fighting the man who was considered to be one of the most scientific boxers of all time. McAuliffe rushed in only to find Griffo no longer there. Nat Fleisher in *Jack McAuliffe: Napoleon of the Prize Ring* saw the fight this way: "Jack missed as often as Griffo scored, and the champion was red in the face and decidedly flustered as the fight progressed. It was therefore a stunning surprise when Referee Moore declared McAuliffe the winner. The cheers of McAuliffe's partisans were quite drowned out by a storm of boos and hisses from indignant spectators who believed the visiting boxer had been cheated out of a victory."[4] McAuliffe's marvelous ring abilities were eroding and later in 1894 he again vowed to retire, as Fleischer intoned, "before the Goddess of Victory quit him for keeps!"

The Louisiana Tornado

Lavigne would be the visiting boxer in New Orleans as Andy Bowen was a native of the festive city and fought just once outside the south in his 27-fight career. He lost only two bouts prior to meeting Lavigne and they were lengthy affairs of 21 and 48 rounds. The "Louisiana Tornado," as Bowen was known, was recognized by the *Police Gazette* as the lightweight champion of the South in an era when regional championship claims were in abundance. In Lavigne's words, "Bowen was a terror to the lightweights and most of them were side-stepping him."[5] Suspicion had it that he was a mulatto, a person of mixed white and black heritage. He vehemently denied this, passing for a white fellow of Irish and Spanish bloodlines. Melissa Haley in *Storm of Blows* noted that his denial was accepted by the boxing community for "to fight or witness bouts in the sanctioned, upper-class athletic clubs of

New Orleans, which usually adhered to segregation policies soon to be institutionalized, one would have to be white."[6]

The athletic clubs were the corner stone of the New Orleans fight scene. In March of 1890 the New Orleans city council, under considerable pressure from influential supporters including Captain Bat Galvin of the police department, permitted all regularly chartered athletic clubs to stage gloved contests. Opponents felt it was a slight-of-hand. To these reformers, it was a false distinction to legalize "prizefighting" by simply labeling it as a "gloved contest," or an "exhibition of sparring." With boxing's new approval of the city council, athletic clubs sprang up across the city. Soon it brought New Orleans to the forefront of the American prizefighting scene in the early 1890s.[7] After several high-profile contests including the "Carnival of Champions" triple-main-event in September of 1892, the stage was set for a bout that would change the course of New Orleans boxing history. After the city's climb to the summit of the boxing world it would be knocked from its pugilistic pinnacle by the result of the match between their home town favorite and the little brute from Saginaw.

Bowen toed the line at 133 pounds and Lavigne at 135. The 25-round fight was for a purse of $3,000 with $2,500 to the winner and $500 to the loser. Both fighters were in top shape for the contest. Bowen, under the tutelage of Jack Dempsey (the Nonpareil), had been honed to fine fighting shape with a deep, broad chest and heavily muscled shoulders. The *New Orleans Picayune* described Lavigne's legs as "marked by long sinewy muscles that had

"Kid" Lavigne
- Courtesy of Antiquities of the Prize Ring

the appearance of bands of steel."[8] Expectations were high from the 2,500 spectators on hand at the Auditorium Athletic Club, most having come to cheer on their popular hometown fighter. With John Duffy serving as referee, the bout started at about 10 p.m.

Round one found Lavigne taking the fight to Bowen with both fighters getting in some good blows. In the Kid's words, "Poor Andy wasn't able to use much science against me. I set too fast a pace. From the first tap of the bell I was on top of him without a second's pause."[9] By the fourth round Bowen was already showing signs of punishment on his head and face. He slipped to the floor trying to land while rushing at Lavigne. "As Bowen got up from his fall he rushed at Lavigne with his head lowered," the *Picayune* reported. "The Saginaw man stepped to one side and uppercut him savagely with his left on the face. The visitor sent Bowen to his corner groggy at the close of the round with a hard right hand drive on the neck."[10] At this early point in the fight it was obvious to the spectators that the Louisiana man was clearly outclassed.

The middle rounds were all Lavigne, chasing his man, driving him to the ropes and landing hard punches often. Bowen's left eye was battered and closing. His face was bruised and his lips terribly swollen. He was saved by the gong in several rounds. "At the end of the 9th Bowen had bellows to mend while Lavigne was seemingly as fresh as when he began," noted the *Chicago Tribune*.[11] At some point in the fight the canvas on the floor of the ring peeled back in one of the corners laying bare the cypress boards. Prior to the fight Bowen had insisted that all padding be removed from under the canvas as he felt it would slow him down against Lavigne who was known to be quick on his feet.[12] The bare corner must not have caused the fighters any difficulty of footwork during the fight for the referee did not find cause to delay the bout in order to repair it. It was an ominous prelude for what was to come later.

Of the 14th round Lavigne recalled, "I was anxious to end the slaughter but Bowen doggedly kept his feet. As we started up for the 14th round, Jim Hall [one of the Kid's seconds] yelled, 'Walk him into a corner and saw into him. Get this damned thing over.'"[13] By the 17th round Bowen was weakened and groggy and taking savage punishment from Lavigne on his body and head. He went down to the canvas; partly slip, partly as a result of the blows reigning down on him. He stayed for a count of six arising only to be pummeled again by the relentless Kid. At the beginning of the 18th round Bowen's "mouth was opened while his eyes were a wild, frightened look," noted the *Picayune*. "Bowen was staggered to the ropes by an onslaught of his powerful foe. While there in a helpless condition and trying to clinch, Lavigne planted his left over the heart, and crossing savagely with the right landed a terrific blow on the angle of the jaw. Bowen fell back like a felled tree and his head struck the floor heavily."[14] It was the corner with the bare cypress wood. No canvas, no padding. "The dull thud was heard all over the auditorium," Lavigne recalled. "'Oh,' I heard many men exclaim, 'Oh, my God.'"[15] He lay motionless with his head underneath the ropes as Referee Duffy counted him out.

From Bad to Worse

"Bowen's seconds ran quickly to his side and raised the unconscious pugilist to his knees and feet, and bore him to his corner," wrote the *Washington Post*, "while the roar of the great throng proclaiming the coming of a new star was still ringing through the building."[16] "Five minutes later I walked over to Bowen's corner to shake hands but he was still out," the Kid added. "I went to my dressing room, put on my street clothes, and then two policemen came and took me in a patrol wagon to the jail."[17]

His seconds worked on Bowen for nearly 10 minutes after which he was carried to his dressing room where three doctors administered to him. The doctors appeared doubtful as to whether Bowen would recover. "There was great excitement in the man's room with the fear that he was about to die entertained by all present," noted the *Chicago Tribune*. "Dr. Hannan, who has had much practice at conditions of this kind said Bowen was evidently suffering from concussion of the brain. One of the bad symptoms was that the pupils of the eyes were different colors and a spell of vomiting again caused the man's friends much alarm."[18] It was then that Sergeant McCabe of the New Orleans police placed Lavigne and his party under arrest. "Lavigne and his seconds and timekeeper including pugilist Jim Hall, Sam Fitzpatrick, Martin Murphy and George Considine, and also referee John Duffy, were at once placed under arrest," reported the *New York Times*.[19]

"No one seemed to anticipate that Bowen might die," wrote Melissa Haly in *Storm of Blows*. "His fall was compared to Jim Hall's the previous year, from which the fighter recovered. It was recollected that the Australian Young Griffo was once unconscious for four hours following a bout. Bowen showed signs of life in his dressing room; his hands continued to work as if fending off opponents or delivering blows and this was seen as a 'favorable omen.' He vomited up undigested peas. The doctors administered whiskey, which raised his pulse rate from thirty-two to seventy. An ambulance was summoned, but fears that hospital admittance might create negative publicity for the sport kept him from there. In one report, Bowen was passed through a hospital on his way home; in another, the unconscious pugilist was dispatched straight to his house on Thalia Street; in both, his wife, Mathilde, waited anxiously."[20]

"The doctors remained with Bowen to the end," noted the *Post*, "with his wife also standing by his bedside. Just as the hands of the clock were creeping around to seven Mrs. Bowen leaned over the bed. 'Oh Andy, say something to me,' she said and her ears were strained to catch the word. Andy shivered and groaned, his frame shook, and then without ever having come back to consciousness after Lavigne had landed, he breathed his last."[21]

The Auditorium Athletic Club, New Orleans – Courtesy of Antiquities of the Prize Ring

Lavigne and his party spent the night in a holding cell at the Tenth Precinct Station. At just past seven the next morning word was received that Bowen had died. Lavigne, who had slept little that night, was greatly shocked when he heard of Bowen's death and expressed profound sympathy for Bowen's wife. The group sent their condolences to Mathilde Bowen via telegram. At nine they were taken to the Third Precinct Station where the Kid was charged with murder and the others were held as accessories. Lavigne was arraigned in court and held on $10,000 bail. The rest of his entourage were held on $5,000 bail. The Kid sent a telegram to his brother Billy that read: "Dear

Brother – I am in a little trouble. Don't worry. Take care of mother. Things will come out all right. 'Brother George'"[22]

The Inquest

The local coroner, assisted by two doctors and a jury of five men performed an autopsy and inquest into Bowen's death at one o'clock that afternoon. "Coroner Lawrason after the inquest said that the death of Bowen was probably caused by his head striking the hard floor" reported the *New York Times*, "for if it had been caused by the blow, his neck would have been broken."[23] Mathilde Bowen was satisfied that Andy's death was simply a boxing fatality. Lavigne paid Bowen's funeral expenses. The charges against him and the members of his party were formally dismissed two weeks later on December 27th.

The funeral was held at the Bowen residence. Sam Fitzpatrick and the Kid arrived to pay their respects. When Mathilde Bowen heard they had arrived she went immediately to greet them. "The meeting was quite pathetic," noted the *Times-Picayune*, "and both the widow and the conqueror were deeply affected. The two shook hands and Mrs. Bowen sobbingly said: 'Mr. Lavigne, I do not blame you for this unfortunate ending of the contest but it has broken my heart. I feel that none regret it more than you.' Lavigne could hardly reply and tears sprang to his eyes. He walked slowly to the head of the coffin and peered intently through the glass lid at the face of his unfortunate rival... He gazed at Bowen's features for about five minutes. 'Too bad. Poor Andy. I did not think the affair would end this way,' and with another long look at Bowen's face he left the mourning widow and mother at the side of the casket and quietly moved out of the crowd and joined Fitzpatrick, Jim Hall and his brother in the rear room where he wept bitterly."[24]

There are a few curious contradictions regarding Bowen's death that bear illuminating. First, several sources reported that Bowen had demanded the removal of the felt padding underneath the canvas, yet after the fight, one of his seconds, Billy Layton, said he had complained about the ring because it had no felt under the canvas, but that Bowen replied that it was all right and he would fight anyway. Second, the coroner correctly concluded that Bowen died from "concussion of the brain." However, he then deduced that it had to be caused by his head hitting the bare wood floor because if it had been caused by a Lavigne blow Bowen's neck would have been broken.

That is not consistent with the medical science of the day. While they clearly did not know what we know today of concussive head trauma, the symptoms of brain hemorrhage were well known at the time. They had to assume that repeated blows to the head and hitting one's head once on an unpadded wooden surface could be of equal gravity in causing the brain to swell. At the time of the knockout Bowen had been taking a severe beating for several rounds with the *Picayune* noting his eyes had a "wild, frightened look" at the beginning of the final round. It's quite possible that he was beginning to exhibit signs of brain trauma before he was knocked out.

Perhaps the coroner was looking for a way to absolve Lavigne and his camp and in doing so limit the damage to the future of prizefighting in New Orleans which was teetering on the verge of being shut down by the state of Louisiana. The fight had been fought under the permit of Mayor Fitzpatrick who had attended the contest and was one of the most concerned watchers at Bowen's side, naturally anxious that there should not be a fatal conclusion. Some, like the *New Orleans Daily Item*, blamed Referee Duffy for not stopping a contest dominated by Lavigne when it opined, "The referee and not the other principal is the person responsible to God and man for Andy Bowen's death."[25] Duffy agreed in part with the *Daily Item* that the bout should have been stopped earlier, but he believed that Bowen's corner had that responsibility.

The power to stop fights conferred upon referees in modern boxing was rarely exercised in the brutal age of 1890s pugilism. Beyond the debate, most people blamed the unpadded floor for Bowen's death, which also shifted blame to the Auditorium Athletic Club. The manager of the club, Captain Frank Williams, while not admitting complicity gave this statement to the *Picayune*: "In my opinion the outlook for a continuance of the pugilistic sport in the state of Louisiana is blue."[26] And the *Picayune* clearly showed its anti-boxing bias when it wrote, "The killing of Andrew Bowen in a prizefight in this city Friday night should sound the death knell here of that bloody brutality misnamed 'sport.' The fistic carnival is over. It ended in a murder."[27] These were prescient statements by Captain Williams and the *Picayune*. The Louisiana Attorney General intervened with a knockout blow of its own and the Bowen tragedy became the last legal prizefight in New Orleans in the 19th century.[28]

The Bowen fight had been billed as a turning point for the lightweight class. It was well attended by some of the best known fighters and "sports" in the country. Per the *Post*, "It was a fight that meant a great deal for the future life, if he had lived, of Bowen, for McAuliffe's star is on the decline and Bowen was one of three or four lightweights of celebrity who were anxious to get into the shoes of the peerless lightweight champion. Lavigne was equally ambitious and it required no stretch of the imagination yesterday, to anticipate a very fierce and interesting fight with a decisive ending. Bowen was licked from the beginning."[29] Gentleman Jim Corbett attended the fight and later remarked in an article published in the *Chicago Tribune* that Lavigne was the best 125 pound man living, with the *Tribune* adding, "And last night's battle would seem to stamp him as a fairly good man at 130."[30]

Such an epic battle to the literal end for one of the contestants might appear on its surface to be fed by snarling dislike and bitter contention between the principals. But that was not the case. Lavigne recounted his cordial and lighthearted dialogue with Bowen as the two came together to do battle: "My brother Bill had made Andy's acquaintance and they got to be warm friends. As we stepped to the center of the ring and shook hands, I said, 'Andy, my brother Bill sends his regards to you.' Andy responded, 'Good, and how is old Bill coming on?' 'Fine [I said], and how are you Andy?' 'Oh, I am fit all right, and are you able to take care of yourself tonight George?' 'Oh, I am able to sit up while my bed is being made.' Bowen laughed that chuckling laugh which made him famous. 'Well,' Bowen said, 'Here is the case of the best man wins.'"[31] The best man did win but he claimed the American lightweight title under the terrible cloud of death. Lavigne gave his $2,500 winnings to Bowen's widow. "I attended Bowen's funeral and there I met his mother," Lavigne recalled. "It was an ordeal I would hate to go through again. No one outside Bowen's family mourned his death more than I. The awful event will never leave my mind."[32]

"The Kid was despondent and thought seriously about quitting the ring," wrote Larry Gustin. "After brooding for months he decided against it . . . he had to continue fighting. It was in his blood. The inactivity was driving him mad."[33] Lavigne decided to ease his way back into the ring and organized a benefit for Andy Bowen's widow at the Saginaw Armory on February 4, 1895. The Kid's brother Billy acted as master of ceremonies. As part of the evening's entertainment Billy donned the gloves in a three-round exhibition with George Campbell and "showed his old-time skill and cleverness, and although he met in Campbell a foeman well able to take care of himself, he made it very interesting for him and the audience cheered them both insistently." The evening concluded with three rounds between the Kid and Eddie Myer. "The Kid merely toyed with his old antagonist whom he bested at Streator, Illinois about two years ago," recorded the *Saginaw Evening News*. "George looked the picture of physical strength and both men gave a lively exhibition. A snug sum of $250 was realized for Andy Bowen's widow, which doubtless would have been larger were it not for the severity of the weather, which kept a number away that would otherwise have been present."[34]

CHAPTER 12

Battling to the Top

The Bowen benefit in February helped the Kid begin to refocus on the ultimate goal of his fistic career . . . a shot at the world title. By this time he was widely recognized as the American champion. One source concluded that he laid claim to the American lightweight title as early as 1891 when he scored a technical knockout over the lightweight champion of the West Coast, Joe Soto, in San Francisco, however there is no evidence and nothing in the record to support that claim. At the time Jack McAuliffe was still actively defending his American lightweight title. His last defense came in September of 1892 when he knocked out Billy Myer in New Orleans after which he announced his retirement. Some of the early record books have Lavigne as American, and even world champion as early as 1893 due to McAuliffe's announcement.

"It was 1893 when McAuliffe actually turned over the lightweight title to Lavigne," wrote Alexander Johnston in *Ten and Out!*. "It is doubtful if there ever before had been an occasion when the handing over of a championship by a retiring champion to a claimant has met with general approval. It did in this case. Sporting men generally felt that Kid Lavigne was the logical title-holder, with Jack McAuliffe in definite retirement. With the exception of McAuliffe, young Lavigne had gone against the best lightweights that there were and had emerged with a clear claim to a battle for the title"[1] While Lavigne would have jumped at the chance to settle the question, McAuliffe was not so inclined having seen the savage fury with which the Saginaw Kid dispatched all that dared.

In mid-February 1895, Lavigne received a letter from his manager, Sam Fitzpatrick, regarding a cable from Arthur Valentine accepting an offer to fight the Kid the first week of May in New York for a purse of $3,000. Valentine was an up-and-comer having recently won the English 132 pound title. In March he would defeat Jim "Iron Bark" Burge, a common opponent of both fighters, in 20 rounds. For unknown reasons, the fight never came to fruition; however, the *Police Gazette* reported that Valentine was reluctant to come to America. A source of the *Gazette's* who had recently returned from Europe and had seen the British champion in action believed Valentine "would be fruit for any of the good men in that class on this side of the Atlantic."[2]

Still searching for his next bout, Lavigne signed to fight Jimmy Dime on April 12th in Cleveland. Dime was an impressive fighter who won his first 17 professional bouts by knockout. He would have fought 27 times by the fight date, his only loss coming to Eddie Connolly. Dime had fought two common opponents of Lavigne's besting Jerry Marshall once and drawing with Marshall and Griffo. Both Dime and Lavigne were "brisk" boxers and hard hitters and the fight was not anticipated to go the 15-round distance, but again for unknown reasons, it was not to be. There are numerous newspaper accounts of bouts throughout Lavigne's career that were scheduled but never fought.

Perhaps a bit frustrated, Lavigne decided to stay with the familiar when he signed to fight a rematch with Jerry Marshall whom he battered in a 10-round win the previous fall. The fight was to be held on April 11, 1895 at the Triangle Club in Chicago. It was agreed that if both men were on their feet at the end of the eighth round the contest would be declared a draw. "Lavigne had the better of it," noted the *Milwaukee Evening.* "It was a lively fight from the start up to the fifth round, when Marshall ducked and ran about the ring. Lavigne made what fighting there was. Marshall's excuse for not fighting was a bad right hand which was injured early in the engagement. Toward the end Lavigne became overanxious for a knockout and was exceedingly wild."[3]

Marshall lasted the eight rounds and a draw it was. "Referee Siler said he was sorry not being able to render a decision which he considered Lavigne had fairly won," added the *Detroit Free Press.* As evidenced by the Kid's late push for a knockout, the fire was back. Just after the match Lavigne was approached by Chicago Police and arrested for his fight two years previously in Dana, Illinois against Eddie Myer and charged with "complicity" in a prizefight. He later posted bail and was released. He had been arrested for the same fight 18 months previously and posted $250 bail. Knowing they would not extradite him from Saginaw, he never returned for his court date. Apparently the Chicago authorities were patient and waited for him to return on business when they nabbed him again. It would be the last time he would fight in Illinois.

The Everlasting Everhardt

Lavigne was waiting patiently for a much anticipated rematch with the master of the ring, Young Griffo. Articles were signed for a bout in New York on April 27th but it was subsequently cancelled. The Olympic Club of New Orleans offered a purse of $2,500 for a match between Lavigne and Jack Everhardt. It's possible that the Kid was still too raw to return to the city that caused him so much pain only a few months past and the match was never consummated. It's more likely that the Louisiana Attorney General stopped it before the bout had legs. But the idea of fighting Everhardt was intriguing.

Everhardt was described by Tracy Callis as "never much bigger than a lightweight but fought and hit like a man much larger; He was quick and scrappy, tough and durable—and a stiff puncher."[4] By late April, 1895 Everhardt had logged 20 bouts with his only loss being the 85-round, 5 hour and 35 minute brawl with Andy Bowen two years previously. Jack was no stranger to roughhousing either. In a 25-round draw with Scott "Bright Eyes" Collins in April of 1894 Everhardt threw Bright Eyes to the floor repeatedly and hit or kicked him while he was down. He used the illegal, LaBlanche pivot-punch as well. The two fighters were reportedly choking each other and wrestling. Local journal-

Jack Everhardt, "The Louisiana Tiger"
- Courtesy of BoxRec

ists counted between 200 and 300 fouls committed during the course of the fight. According to the *Dallas Morning News*, "The referee was so nearsighted he just did not know a foul from a side of beef."[5]

The match with the Kid was made for May 30, 1895 at the Seaside Athletic Club at Coney Island for a 20-round bout at 133 pounds. As was most often the case for Lavigne at a bit better than 5 feet 3 inches, he was shorter than his opponent who stood 5 feet 6 inches tall. What Lavigne lacked in height he made up for in his reach which was four inches longer, fingertip-to-fingertip, than his height. This would be the first of two grueling fights between these two warriors. While attendance was reported to be light that evening it was not without many notable fighters and sporting men including the featherweight champion George Dixon, Tommy Ryan, Solly Smith, Jim Daly, Jim Hall, and former Marshall of infamous Dodge City, Bat Masterson. Masterson was a prolific gambler and fight promoter. The referee was Tim Hurst who had officiated when Lavigne thrashed Johnny Griffin.

This was the third bout of the evening with the first two being stopped by police. The fighters got to work quickly with Lavigne rushing in and landing body blows. "Jack countered on the nose which soon showed pink," reported the *New Jersey Journal*. "Lavigne kept feeling it as though to assure himself that it was there. Lavigne banged on the body pretty sharply. His play was to lead, and if he landed or missed, close in and clinch with the man."[6] In the second stanza Lavigne continued to press but Everhardt skillfully faced his man and returned fire. "Both men struck with frightful force," the *Journal* continued, "and the thwack of their gloves echoed all over the house. Lavigne was making the pace very fast . . . and the house rang with applause as the gong sounded them to their corners."

By the fourth round Lavigne's left eye was badly swollen. "The punching was terribly hard and if both men had not been as strong as little bulls they could not have stood it." Lavigne was landing his left with "fearful force" almost every time he rushed in. At the end of the fourth and fifth rounds Lavigne staggered Everhardt with thundering lefts as the gong rang. At the end of the sixth, "Lavigne followed Everhardt to the ropes and got in a stunning punch on the face that sounded all over the hall."[7]

In the seventh, signs of the cumulative effect of Lavigne's body work appeared. "He had Everhardt's body as red as if it were mustard blistered," the *Journal* described. Rounds seven, eight, and nine were a steady flow of give and take with Lavigne always the aggressor. The *Journal* noted that rounds 10 through 13 "were distinguished by the

Handbill from the Seaside Athletic Club - Courtesy of Antiquities of the Prize Ring

fiercest kind of give and take fighting, with honors easy." In the 14th, Everhardt appeared unable to stop the Kid's rushes but fought on gamely taking three punches for every one he doled out. After taking a couple of crisp straight left leads from Everhardt in the 15th frame, Lavigne's nose was bothering him and appeared to be broken. In the words of the *Sporting* Review, "The Kid was much annoyed and hurt by these attentions to his nasal protuberance."[8]

In the 16th and 17th rounds Lavigne was battering Everhardt, once nearly knocking him through the ropes. Everhardt, bleeding from his right eye, was tiring and began to clinch to avoid further punishment. "The Kid seemed to be as fresh as ever," the *Journal* noted. Lavigne caught Everhardt with a hard right on the side of the head in the 19th staggering him. "There he goes," cried the spectators, but Everhardt recovered. At one point while attempting to clinch, Jack threw Lavigne to the floor and referee Hurst helped him to his feet. In the 20th and final round both fighters "were wild and weak" with Everhardt getting the best of the exchanges.

The Kid had done everything to try to knock his man out. He fought more cautiously toward the end of the round knowing he was well ahead on points and after getting walloped several times by a resurgent Everhardt. "The referee awarded the bout to Lavigne, whereupon there was much cheering and much hissing. It was a tremendous battle," concluded the *Journal*.[9] After the bout there was speculation that Everhardt employed a strategy designed to let Lavigne take the fight to him and tire himself out in doing so. In the late rounds Jack would come on strong and finish Lavigne. However, he underestimated the Kid's power and his pluck.

An Early Brush with Destiny

By this time in his career the Kid had amassed a small fortune of several thousand dollars yet he was not the wisest of money managers. He had already dabbled in the saloon business and was always on the lookout for a place to park some of his hard earned cash. One such opportunity presented itself to Lavigne by chance on a dusty road outside Saginaw while training that summer for his next bout. Lavigne and his trainers were doing road work. As his trainers became winded, one of them advised the Kid to invest his growing wealth in something solid. Being too tired to keep up with the younger, fitter Lavigne, they told him to continue and they'd wait under a shade tree for him to return. In the meantime they'd think up some investment ideas.

A while later, the Kid returned to the tree and as they headed for home he told them quite a story as recounted by writer George Franklin. "'Y'know,' he said, 'a funny thing happened after I left you guys. Around the bend I met a fellow trying to get one of them there horseless carriages started. The thing just wouldn't go. We started talking together and you know what he said? He said I should invest my money in his horseless carriage business. Hell, did he expect me to throw my money into something that he couldn't even start? He had to get a horse to haul that thing home.' One of the trainers asked, 'You get the guy's name?' 'Yep,' answered the Kid, 'said his name was Henry Ford. I told him I'd make my money the easy way—by fighting.'"[10]

Illustration by Clem Boddington – Courtesy of Antiquities of the Prize Ring

Or so the tale goes. A quick check of facts relating to Henry Ford finds that while he didn't form the Ford Motor Company until 1903 and didn't begin mass marketing the famed Model T until 1908, Henry had been a busy inventor years before that. He began working as an engineer for the Edison Illuminating Company in Detroit in 1891 and produced an early prototype of a gas powered buggy in 1892.[11] In 1893 his promotion to chief engineer gave him the money and the time to refine his early prototype into a vehicle he called a "quadricycle" in 1896. So the time frame for a chance encounter between the two men is realistic. Where the story's veracity looks suspect is in the distance between Saginaw and Detroit. It is highly unlikely that Henry Ford would travel 100 miles in a prototype that often would quit before it made it a single mile, as finicky prototypes were in the habit of doing. It's also unlikely that he would have shipped his gas buggy to the outskirts of Saginaw just to run it on a country road.

If indeed the implausible really did happen and the two famous folk did, by chance, bump into each other, it would not be the last time their paths would cross. As providence would have it, after the Kid's boxing career was over, he would end up in the employ of the Ford Motor Company. That story, verifiably true this time, will be told in a later chapter.

Fitzsimmons' Pupil

Another rising star in the lightweight ranks of the day was Jimmy Handler, a Jewish fighter from Newark, New Jersey and brother of welterweight Joe Handler. Jimmy was the better of the two boxing brothers and was under the tutelage of world middleweight champion Bob Fitzsimmons. "He was in a measure, a protégé of Bob Fitzsimmons when Bob made his home in Newark," noted the *Illustrated Police News,* "and it was thought that he had acquired so much of Fitz's style and skill in fighting that no one of his inches could cope with him."[12] In late July 1895 Lavigne came to terms with Handler for a 20-round bout at the Empire Athletic Club in New York on August 26 at 133 pounds. It was to be opening night for the newly constructed club with a seating capacity of 6,300 sports. The arena was state of the art with both gas and electric lighting and something quite progressive for the time, heavily padded ring-posts. The purse was set at $1,700. The preliminary contest matched Frank Erne and Jack Skelly in a featherweight bout. Erne, who would figure prominently in Lavigne's fistic career four years later, knocked Skelly out in the seventh.

Jimmy Handler – Courtesy of Don Scott

As the main event unfolded Lavigne, after a few moments of dancing and looking for an opening in the beginning of round one, reverted to his stock in trade, rushing his man and landing powerful body blows while taking a few in the nose in return. He would land several hard right hands over the heart throughout the fight. The rest of the round saw lively exchanges at close quarters. "Lavigne rushed matters viciously," noted the *New Jersey Journal* of the battle in round two, "but was unable to get in an effective blow, Handler guarded himself so perfectly."[13]

Round three was more of the same with Lavigne carrying the fight to his opponent. In round four, Lavigne was equally as aggressive but missed several left-hand leads. "He then tried his shoulder and knocked Handler against the ropes," continued the *Journal*. "As Handler bounded back Lavigne placed his left hard on the Newark man's body. In the next rally Lavigne smashed Handler hard over the heart and followed with a smart left on the mouth, drawing blood. Lavigne rushed Handler to the ropes and tried hard to land a knockout blow, but failed, as Handler stopped all blows cleverly. Handler's defensive work was loudly applauded."[14]

Lavigne appeared tired at the beginning of the fifth and sensing this, Handler went on the offensive landing a hard shot on the Kid's jaw. This angered and invigorated Lavigne as he then pounded Handler over the heart again followed by a right to the jaw and another left to the body forcing him to the ropes. Handler was rattled and absorbed another left shot to the heart. The *Journal* described the final moments: "The Newark man made a vicious lunge with a right for the jaw, but fell short and left a bad opening. Lavigne landed his right squarely on the jaw and knocked Fitzsimmons' protégé in a heap on the floor. After an effort that seemed to cause him considerable pain, Handler arose and pulled himself together. He looked around in a dazed sort of way. Lavigne lost no time. He brought his terrible right down on Handler's jaw with awful force and the Newark man fell like a log. Handler tried to arise but could not and rolled over. He was out to all intents and purposes and the referee promptly declared Lavigne the winner."[15] The time of the last round was 1 minute 7 seconds.

Within days, the *Police News* commented that Handler was a great disappointment to his friends who looked upon him as invincible in his class. The *News* noted, "When it came to facing Lavigne, he hadn't a look-in from start to finish. In vain did Handler's seconds warn him: 'Don't mix it with him Jimmy.' Fitzsimmons in speaking of Jimmy Handler's defeat by Kid Lavigne said: 'I am greatly surprised. I was under the impression that Handler would win in six rounds and told my friends to bet that way. Lavigne is a great little fellow and should win the lightweight championship.'"[16] Yet again Lavigne was not thought to have the "science" to win a match with a Fitzsimmons-crafted ringman like Handler. And yet again his muscle-and-mayhem style overwhelmed another ill-equipped foe.

Also from the *News*, Lavigne was said to be ready to "don the mitts with the 'Black Hurricane,' Joe Walcott. Sam Fitzpatrick his manager states that Lavigne is open to fight anybody in the world at 133 pounds, Young Griffo or Arthur Valentine preferred." While Lavigne felt ready for Walcott, the powerful black welterweight from the islands who went by other formidable nicknames including the "Barbados Demon" and the "Giant Killer," Fitzpatrick was in no rush to put his undefeated fighter in harm's way. He wanted to continue to clean out the lightweight division before stretching to fight a natural welterweight who was feared even by the heavyweights of the day.

Rematch with the Aussie Wonder

A match with Valentine would have provided the Kid with a legitimate shot at the world title as Valentine claimed the English lightweight title at the time. Jack Everhardt was also angling for a rematch and published a challenge in the *New York Illustrated News*. This "want ad" method of issuing challenges was a common practice of the time. The challenge read: "Fights Wanted – Would like to meet Kid Lavigne at 133 or any other lightweight from 133-137 for $1,000 a side; a $250 forfeit is posted at *Illustrated News* Office for Lavigne or others to cover. Address Jack Everhardt, *N.Y. Illustrated News*."[17]

Instead, the Kid preferred a match with Griffo. A contest was set for October 7, 1895 at the newly constructed clubhouse of the Active Athletic Association at Constable Hook, New Jersey. Three bouts were on the card that night; the main event being a 20-round go between Griffo and Lavigne. "At four o'clock on fight day, it was rumored that the Hudson County Authorities would not permit the fights to take place," reported the *Detroit Free Press*, "but not withstanding this, fully 4,000 persons made their way by rail and water to the club house."[18] Indeed the fights were cancelled, but unlike the fiasco in Roby, Indiana two years earlier, it would happen without the assistance of a Gatling gun and hundreds of state militia. Nonetheless, it was déjà vu and the two fighters had to wonder whether they were jinxed.

The Empire Athletic Club, having recently opened in August, jumped on the opportunity to host the bout and within a few days Griffo and Lavigne had signed articles to fight a 20-round bout there on October 12. Griffo had been very busy since his eight-round draw with Lavigne in February of 1894 fighting 29 times in the 20-month interim. Lavigne had only fought eight times in the same time span. The data was telling: everyone wanted to have a go with the marvel of Griffo who eagerly accommodated all comers but few would tempt fate with the mania of Lavigne.

Griffo was a truly enigmatic character by any standard. He was physically an odd mixture of anatomy. "The strange thing about it was that Griffo had the appearance of a destructive hitter," Lavigne recalled. "He had a huge upper body for a featherweight, a deep chest and big arms."[19] Historian Stan Weston described him as having short arms, knock knees, a constant smile and wide black eyes giving him the appearance of a good natured goblin.[20] He was indeed extremely good natured with a devil-may-care attitude toward boxing and life in general. As mentioned earlier, he abhorred training and it was often said that his only training was a haircut, a shave and a few bottles of beer before the fight. Despite this, he was so crafty in the ring and naturally endowed with a good deal of stamina that his lack of conditioning rarely cost him a decision. His one deficit as a fighter was his lack of power in either hand. Had he been a heavy hitter as his anatomy suggested, it was universally agreed that he would have been the champion of several weight divisions for many years.

A good time was always first on his mind. It was perhaps hard to figure whether he was simply enjoying life in a way that most adults had long left behind or whether he had the brain of a child tucked into a strange body with incomparable reflexes and ring instincts. And Griffo's instincts were uncanny. When Muhammad Ali first rose to prominence many of the fight pundits jumped to the conclusion that his style of slipping punches by jerking his head back would not be sustainable over the course of a bout. Of course they were wrong. Griffo had perfected the same move and a dozen others while being so quick of foot that he often ended up behind his opponents, slapping them on the back of the head as he danced away. No one could teach this. He was a master of anticipation and quick as a cat to react. It was a natural gift.

Griffo was such a strange character that he occasionally ended up in jail and mental hospitals where his sanity was questioned. On one occasion he was thrown in the clink for being drunk and disorderly in Indianapolis. "The judge ordered him examined," wrote Weston, "and the diagnosis reported an unbalanced and possibly dangerous ape."[21] Boxing manager and ring announcer, Joe Humphries heard about Griffo's incarceration and went to help him at the jail. "Griffo stuck his hands through the bars and shook hands with Humphries," continued Weston. "'Thanks for coming Matie,' he said and then, to Joe's complete amazement, he said, 'see that fly flying around the cell; bet you a fiver I can catch it between my thumb and forefinger and not hurt it.' 'It's a bet,' replied Humphries. Griffo walked around, always watching the tiny black speck. Suddenly his arm shot out. He smiled and walked back to where Joe waited. 'Watch my hand Joie.' He slowly opened his fingers and the fly quickly flew away. Humphries gave the fighter five dollars and then watched him strut back to his cot and doze off. Joe shook his head and walked out of the cell block. The guard met him in the outer office. 'Did he bet you he'd catch a fly?' asked the guard. 'I thought so. He ain't crazy. He's making more money in here than he could make working on the outside.'" It was the wily Griffo in his own little world.

Having learned from his previous eight-round draw with Griffo, the Kid knew it would be hard to win the fight without knocking his man out yet one had to catch him to dispatch him. The Australian wizard was too elusive and what he lacked in his ability to hurt the Kid he made up for in piling up points. "I insisted that the contract provide that the decision be a draw if both men were on their feet at the finish, for I expected to be outpointed," noted Lavigne.[22] In the preliminary lightweight bout between Arthur Valentine and Billy Ernst, Valentine was saved from a full knockout when referee Hurst stopped the bout late in the fifth with Valentine hanging helplessly on the ropes. It's doubtful he would have lasted that long had the Kid chosen to fight him versus Griffo.

Just after the principles had entered the ring, the crowd roared as John L. Sullivan at ringside made a short speech saying this would be the last year he would put on the gloves, however, full retirement must not have agreed with him as he continued to fight exhibition bouts up to 1909. Of the condition of the fighters the *Chicago Tribune* noted, "The lines of Griffo's body were smooth and fleshy while Lavigne's muscles stood out in knots and ridges."[23] Lavigne was a slight betting favorite.

George "Kid" Lavigne - *The Saginaw News.* Copyright 1895. All rights reserved. Reprinted with permission.

The Kid made up his mind to set a furious pace so that "even [Griffo's] curious cleverness couldn't save him." Even so, Griffo came out aggressively in the first round as well landing effectively and slipping the bull-rushing Kid. The first round went to Griffo. Near the end of the second, one of Lavigne's powerful rights got home with such force it staggered Griffo and "looked as if it would put Griffo's left eye out of plumb," added the *Tribune*. In the third Lavigne targeted Griffo's fleshy middle, "landing blow after blow till Griffo's body was red as raw meet." Griffo cut the Kid's cheek open in the fourth with a right-hand cross.

Lavigne takes us through the next couple rounds: "It would have required an adding machine to total up the number of haymakers I wasted on the air. But in the sixth round I finally connected with a solid right to his whiskers. Griffo rocked on his heels and swayed drunkenly while I tried with everything I carried to knock him over into Long Island Sound. But he dived into a clinch. Teddy Alexander, a noted turfman and trainer of fighters, who was sitting at the ringside stood up and yelled, 'Go on Kid, you got him.' Griffo, shaken down to his toes, dizzy and weak, calmly looked over his shoulder and grunted, 'In a pig's eye.' A few seconds later, the Australian was somewhat recovered and was dancing about as light as a feather. I tore after him but I simply couldn't land a kayo. His head would be right there in front of me like a punching bag. I would let fly a fast hook, but the target would vanish like a shadow. I chased him from rope-to-rope, landing on his arms, neck, shoulders, back; anywhere I could put a glove. I cornered him now and then as he grew more tired and managed to sock him some."[24]

Lavigne was getting the best of the bout through the 10th frame with Griffo doing what he could defensively to hold off his rampaging foe. For the next three rounds Griffo began to tire and clinched to avoid punishment. He did some "sharp work" in the 14th but as Lavigne kept pressing and crowding he again resorted to clinching, with the Kid working the body while in close. The late rounds of the fight were described by the *Washington Post*: "The next three innings Griffo needed wind and played for it, while Lavigne worked for his heart until the end of the 18th, when he drove the Australian into his corner and got him groggy, with a shower of blows. Still he made a game defense in the 19th against Lavigne's attack."[25] In the final round Lavigne was fighting as fresh as ever while Griffo was content to stay on the defensive and finish the round on his feet.

Referee Hurst, obliged by the contractual arrangement of the principals, called the fight a draw. In the opinion of the *Post*, "Lavigne had demonstrated his superiority clear through." The *Police Gazette* summarized the battle succinctly in three headlines: "One of the Most Scientific Boxing Events Ever Seen," "Skill Versus Strength," and "Cleverness of the Australian Offset by the Michigan Lad's Fierceness."[26] It was reported that Lavigne was grinning at the end of the fight. From Lavigne's post fight comments the source of his smile was sheer admiration. "I never saw so many gloves in my life," he said. "That fellow is just too marvelous for words. There were times when he just stood dead still in his tracks and I thought I had him and let one go that had 'finish' on it. He would jump away or block. His timing was so perfect that he would just edge over an inch or two and the blow would miss. What can you do with a fellow like that? There never has been anyone just like him."[27]

Unbeknownst to the fighters that evening, a warrant for their arrest had been issued at the request of Reverend Edward McGuffy of Newton but the deputy sheriff and other officers refused to serve it until after the fight. With the conclusion of the main event all four of the fistic participants were arrested by Sheriff Dohl, taken to Newton, and no doubt released on bail a few hours hence.[28]

CHAPTER 13

"The Greatest I Ever Saw"

The 1890s were teeming with great "little men" of fistic talent, many of whose careers continued strong into the nineteen-aughts. Fight fans of the teens and the 1920s longed for the savagery, the grit, and the skill of the lighter weight fighters who populated the last decade of the 19th century, when, as Lavigne himself later commented, "Fights were fights." There was the tail end of lightweight champion, Jack McAuliffe's career, the rise and dominance of Lavigne, and the ring wizardry of Griffo. There was also George "Little Chocolate" Dixon, the first African American to hold a world title, often called the greatest fighter of the 19th century, the mastery and speed of Joe Gans, and the unheralded domination of lesser known Bobby Dobbs, to name just a few. There was one more who earned a spot in this upper echelon. He was feared by great fighters in weight classes from light to heavy. That man was the first Joe Walcott.

Born in 1873 in Demerara, British Guiana and later moving to the island of Barbados in the West Indies, Walcott came to Boston as a cabin boy when just a teen. After working a few odd jobs he got on as an elevator operator at the American House Hotel, spending his nights around a local gym where he paid 25 cents a week to learn how to box and wrestle. At age 17 he began to earn money for thumping the competition. In late 1892 he met George Dixon who introduced Joe to his manager Tom O'Rourke. O'Rourke's concept of a "tryout" was to pit Joe against all comers awarding $50 to any man who could go the distance for four rounds. No one did.[1] O'Rourke knew he had a diamond in the rough but also a fighter with the spirit of a warrior and incredible physical strength packed onto a small frame. It was the beginning of a long and prosperous partnership.

The "tryout" turned into a steady job for Joe. While George Dixon was doing burlesque shows at the Miner's Theater on Bowery in New York, his sidekick Joe was taking on all comers at Miners' and knocking them cold, sometimes four and five in a night. Not far away in Madison Square Garden, Jack McAuliffe was offering $500 to any man weighing 133 pounds who could stay with him for three rounds. Joe saw the promotional posters for Jack's challenge plastered all over town. To Joe this looked like easy money, after all, at $50 a fight he was getting, it would take him ten fights to make $500.

Founder of *The Ring* magazine and famed boxing biographer, Nat Fleischer, recounted Joe's next move. "Walcott walked up to O'Rourke and said, 'Mister O'Rourke, I wish you'd let me off early tonight. There's a fighter calls himself McAuliffe, who says he'll give $500 to any 133-pound fighter who stays three rounds with him. I know I kin do it. I kin win dat $500, Mister O'Rourke. There's no man around who kin knock me out in three rounds, Mister O'Rourke.' O'Rourke almost dropped. He knew that Joe Walcott was speaking facts. Tom realized then as he did when the Barbados Demon became world welterweight king that it would take far more than McAuliffe possessed to put his man away in so short a time—if at all."[2] O'Rourke owed McAuliffe a big favor after Jack had come to his aid a while back when an unruly mob was trying to stop his fighter, George Dixon, from winning a bout. After the melee he had offered him $1,000 for his assistance which Jack declined. O'Rourke kept Joe from going after the $500. In McAuliffe's words, "Both Tom and I knew what would have happened had Walcott gotten into the ring with me that night. Though not yet a champion, there wasn't a man his weight who could sock as he could."[3]

The Measure of an Opponent

Of all the things written about Joe Walcott perhaps the most fascinating is the description of his physique and the unique advantages endowed by it. He was a very black, black man, his color often masking the damage an opponent was inflicting in the ring. He stood a bit over 5 feet 1 inches tall and packed 140 pounds on his short frame. Nat Fleischer described Walcott as, "A sort of sawed-off Hercules," and "an abnormally powerful puncher, his conical skull possessed the hardness of *lignum vitae*. Men who fought him were handicapped sorely . . . for all his opponents were taller, and their blows usually landed on his shoulders or on top of his granite skull. Probably more men ruined their hands on Walcott than any other scrapper of that day."[4]

And of that skull one sports writer scribed, "Blows bounced from his rounded turret of a head as if he were armor-clad." His upper body was massive with bulging muscles, a short, thick neck that seemed to all but disappear when he put his dukes up, and a wingspan from finger-tip to finger-tip six inches longer than his height. "A most powerfully constructed man, he seemed almost invulnerable from fistic punishment," noted east coast sports writer and fight manager B. H. Benton. "He was most deceiving to look at, for his small thick-set form created an impression that he would be slow. It was just the opposite. Walcott had a steam-roller action and marvelous speed and action when fighting, and he was the nemesis of all the tall middle and heavyweights, whom he used to mow down."[5]

Joe Wolcott, "The Barbados Demon" - Courtesy of BoxRec

Lavigne and Walcott had many things in common: incredible stamina, quickness, brutal hitting power with either hand, ability to absorb a great deal of punishment, and a style of fighting that gave no quarter. They both had well-earned reputations as fighters to avoid at all costs. Walcott was the first to coin the quote, "The bigger they are, the harder they fall," as an expression of his confidence when fighting bigger men which he did often. He used to say that the big fellows were made to order for him. Early and throughout his career he beat middleweights like Dick O'Brien and Dan Creedon and took out a few light-heavy and heavyweights as well. His greatest fight against a larger man was a few years after his bout with Lavigne when he knocked out prominent light heavyweight, Joe Choynski, in seven rounds. Choynski had fought some of the all-time greats in Jim Jeffries, Jim Corbett, and Bob Fitzsimmons. A year after he was defeated by Walcott he knocked out a young Jack Johnson. Another of O'Rourke's fighters was heavyweight contender, "Sailor" Tom

Sharkey, a tough, Marciano-type brawler. "I had to stop Walcott from sparring with the sailor," recalled O'Rourke, "because Joe dumped him on his ear one afternoon in the gym."[6]

In August of 1895 the *Police News* claimed Walcott's near invincibility when it stated, "Walcott now surpasses any of our welterweights, unless it be (Mysterious) Billy Smith, in the telling execution of a single blow. I do not see how he is to be beaten by any foeman who will give him hit for hit. Any man except a very big man whom he gets his right hand on to fairly and squarely isn't coming up for much more. Walcott in his dumpy, dwarf monitor build, his hardness of flesh, his power of punching and the small surface he offers for return hits, is in a class by himself—different from anything else in the field."[7]

His reputation of beating the big 'uns labeled him with the nickname, "Giant Killer." His ferocious, attacking fighting style gave him his other nickname, the "Black Demon," and also the "Barbados Demon." In Lavigne's words Joe was, "a ferocious fighter, fast, cruel, almost impossible to hurt, a terrific two-handed puncher, Walcott was one of the most formidable men at any weight that ever beat down a foe. Such a scourge was Walcott that finally it became impossible for his manager to get even the big fellows to meet him. O'Rourke had challenged Kid McCoy, Tommy Ryan and "Mysterious" Billy Smith until he got tired."[8] He was also pestering heavies Tom Sharkey and Jim Jeffries but neither wanted a go with Joe.

Out of desperation O'Rourke issued a challenge to all the lightweights with a preference of Jack McAuliffe or Kid Lavigne. He figured that with McAuliffe retired, Walcott had a legitimate claim to the lightweight title even though it had been a couple years since he had gotten down to the lightweight limit. McAuliffe ignored it. He was through risking his unsullied record. The offer was to bring Walcott in at 133 pounds when he normally fought at between 138 and 142 pounds. O'Rourke would wager $1000 to $500 that his man would stop any many at that weight in 15 rounds. "When I called Fitz's attention to it," Lavigne continued, "he snorted—'to hell with that guy—we'll let Mister Walcott alone.'"[9] Lavigne was afraid of no man at his weight and urged Fitzpatrick to make the match.

The next day Fitzpatrick and O'Rourke met in New York. "What's all this stuff about that fellow of yours doing thirty-three?" said Fitz. "No fake about that," replied O'Rourke. "Walcott can make thirty-three and be strong enough to murder all the lightweights in one night." "You must be going to cook him into condition," said Sam. "How long do you need to boil him?" "Oh, five or six weeks'll be

Manager Sam Fitzpatrick (left) and "Kid" Lavigne
- Courtesy of Antiquities of the Prize Ring

plenty," was the answer.[10] When the agreement was struck it stipulated that Walcott had to knock Lavigne out in 15 rounds or forfeit the entire purse and the fight would be awarded to the Kid. When word got out that Lavigne had been matched with the Barbados Demon, even his best friends and admirers "shook their heads in dismay." Fitzpatrick, while confident in his fighter, knew this would be the toughest battle of the Kid's career and forced him to adhere strictly to a rigorous training program. Given the Kid's taste for drink, that was no small accomplishment.

The fight was to take place at the old Empire Athletic Club at Maspeth, Long Island on December 2, 1895 for a purse of $5,000. Much was made of Walcott's reduction in weight before the bout. Many concluded that it would weaken him greatly. At the weigh-in Walcott and Lavigne both weighed within a fraction of 131 and 1/2 pounds. As to the speculation of Walcott's diminished state, the *Police Gazette* reported that Walcott "manifested no signs of any weakness and told the *Police Gazette* representative that he never felt better."[11] At the weigh-in the fighters joked about how hungry they were and afterwards went off to have a good meal. "It is a fact that never but the best of feelings existed between the two men," noted the *Detroit Free Press*.[12]

Walcott came into the bout having only lost twice in 51 fights over a six-year span; a three-round decision very early in his career to Ted Kelly in the second of two fights on the same day, and a four-round go with Mike Harris whom he knocked out in six rounds the next year. Lavigne would enter the ring undefeated in 39 fights over a 9-year career. Joe's last fight was in August when weighing 138 he knocked out one of the better middleweights of the time, Dick O'Brien, at 2:25 of the first round. O'Brien weighed 150. Lavigne had also beaten O'Brien in a six-round contest 18 months previously while outweighed by 20 pounds. The Kid was coming off his 20-round draw with Griffo in October. It had been a bout with an elusive, light hitting fighter of science who was hard to find in the ring. Yet now he would face a man who would be ever present, boring in for the kill with every rush. For Lavigne, the two opponents were polar opposites in style. It would be quite an adjustment for him.

Fight Night

The preliminary bout was scheduled to be between two lightweights that Lavigne had defeated in Jerry Marshall and Solly Smith, however, Marshall came in overweight and the bout was cancelled. Two good bantams, Casper "The Sicilian Swordfish" Leon and Joe Elms, fought a four-rounder awarded to Leon on a foul. The referee for the evening was again Tim Hurst, by now a familiar sight for Lavigne. At 9:21 p.m. Walcott climbed through the ropes accompanied by his seconds, Tom O'Rourke, George Dixon, and Joe Gordon. The Kid was loudly cheered as he ducked through the ropes a minute later with his seconds, Sam Fitzpatrick, Tommy Ryan and Ted Alexander.

"When the men stepped forward and met in the ring there was a remarkable contrast in their appearance," recorded the *Free Press*. "Walcott, although trained fine, loomed alongside as a bulldog to a fox terrier. Massive of chest and shoulders with a bullet head set down firmly between his shoulders, there appeared no dividing line between his neck and chest. He was the most magnificent muscled gladiator that ever donned a glove. Supreme confidence showed in every glance of his eye and in every movement he made. O'Rourke was equally confident of his protégé and looked for no possible chance of defeat, not even a draw. Lavigne on the other hand did not impress the spectators with his physical make-up, but there was absolutely no confidence lacking."[13] There was nary an ounce of fat on either of the men.

Years later in the 1920s Tom O'Rourke recalled, "The two men were the greatest at the weight the prize ring has ever seen or, in my estimation, ever will see. Each was at his pugilistic peak, hardened and experienced, but with the fire and snap of youth still invigorating heart and muscles. Walcott could hit harder than any middleweight. Few heavyweights ever packed as much dynamite as Joe carried in either glove. Lavigne was made of rawhide and iron, a bulldog in attack and bronco in staying power. No gamer, tougher man ever drew on a glove than the Michigan lumberjack. The present day scrappers would be pigmies in the hands of a Lavigne or a Walcott."[14]

Just prior to the beginning of the fight the ring announcer stated that Walcott desired to challenge Tommy Ryan for a fight at a future date. Ryan accepted the challenge for a match to be arranged.[15] But what else could he do in front of 5,000 onlookers. Ryan was one of the greatest middleweights of all time and at the time of Walcott's challenge was the welterweight champion of the world. He was one of Fitzpatrick's stable of fighters who often trained with Lavigne and was one of his seconds for several fights. Ryan never did fight Walcott. Perhaps after being a ringside witness to the war in the ring about to be fought he thought it prudent to continue to avoid the Demon, although that would be hard to believe knowing what a warrior Ryan was after one look at his record.

Sound the Gong

The betting was very heavy and the odds were 8-to-5 on Walcott. The two combatants shook hands at 9:30 p.m., the gong sounded, and round one began. "Walcott smiled when the fight started," wrote famed journalist Robert Edgren. "This slim, wide-shouldered white boy looked so soft a mark. He began at once to rush and tear at Lavigne with all the ferocity that gained him the name, 'Black Demon.' To Wolcott's amazement Lavigne didn't dance about and try to spar. Instead he met rush with rush. He bent to the work, even more furiously aggressive than the black."[16] The Kid refused to abandon the style that had kept him undefeated, but he was taking a pounding. He would remark later that "I had a new experience in fighting."

At one point in the first frame Walcott launched a roundhouse right that caught Lavigne on the left ear cutting it badly so that it looked like it was hanging by a thread. A clipping from Lavigne's scrapbook read, "The whole house was bewildered by the swiftness and savagery of Wolcott's attack. It seemed that Lavigne would go under in the very first round, but he clinched and for a brief second recovered sufficiently to ward off the Demon's terrific body blows."[17]

"As I walked to my corner after that fearful round I realized that I would need all my superhuman stamina and capacity to take punishment," Lavigne recalled. "'Better let him set the pace for a few rounds,' whispered Fitzpatrick anxiously. 'I don't see what else I can do,' I answered. 'He surely is doing it up grand.' 'Fight for the body,' advised Sam. That also was all I could do, for Walcott had practically no neck, and when he pulled down his bullet head under his huge shoulders, there was little target to shoot at above."[18]

Round two saw the fighters toe-to-toe raining terrific volleys of lefts and rights to body and head. Neither backed down and at the end of the round they were still at it "hammer and tongs." The crowd was going wild. "Walcott laughed as he walked to his corner," wrote B. H. Benton, "but the effort was a forced one and the crowd recognized the black demon had met a tartar in the Saginaw Kid."[19] At the beginning of the third, the Kid rushed in. Joe sidestepped and caught Lavigne with a terrific uppercut that dazed him. Fitzpatrick shouted, "Steady Kid," and Lavigne sparred cleverly until the fog was gone. The Kid spent much of the round on the defensive backing away and slipping the onslaught as best he could. When he had Walcott in a rhythm, luring him in as he backpedalled, "The Kid suddenly came to a halt, stood still, and carefully measuring, sent over a terrible right to Joe's jaw, staggering him."[20] He may have learned this bait-and-switch tactic from Young Griffo.

Walcott continued to savage the Kid in round four with left and right uppercuts but Lavigne shook his head and kept coming, knocking Walcott into the ropes with a combination of lefts and rights. Joe pounded Lavigne with a barrage of blows on "heart and wind" followed by damaging smashes to the head. "Walcott battered Lavigne from rope-to-rope in the fifth," wrote George Underwood, boxing editor of the *New York World*, "One of Joe's rights closed Lavigne's left eye completely. Near the end of the round Lavigne stirred the fans to a frenzy with a lion-hearted rally. The sixth was a repetition of the fifth, with Walcott battering Lavigne to a pulp only to have the Saginaw Kid close with a fiery burst that left no doubt of stamina and vitality being unimpaired."[21] Midway through the sixth a straight right from Lavigne put Joe's hands on the floor but he recovered quickly and continued his onslaught.

Sullivan Calls for an End

It was looking grim for the Kid. His left ear was puffed up like a "funny looking tomato." He was bleeding from the nose and his left eye was closed. Many seasoned spectators, even some who bet on Walcott, turned their heads unwilling to view what more and more looked like a slaughter. John L. Sullivan at ringside begged referee Hurst to stop the fight. "'Oh quit, John;' 'I'm all right; I'll lick him yet. I've got his nerve now only he won't show it.' 'Dat so, is it?' said Joe, and he slammed another terrific punch in. 'Yes, dat's so,' said the Kid, 'if that's the best you can do.'"[22]

Staggering back to his corner in those brutal early rounds the Kid had words with Sullivan muttered through swollen lips: "John, if that referee stops the fight I'll never talk to you again," reported the *Saginaw News*. "I'm going to lick that man."[23] The exchange with Walcott was typical of Lavigne to show no pain and with a smile on his face and a lighthearted banter, go about his business of giving and taking punishment for as long as it took to get the job done. His lack of quit could suck the will right out of an opponent.

Then the tide began to turn in the seventh. "By this time the greatest excitement prevailed," wrote B. H. Benton. "Never had such incessant and terrific fighting been witnessed and most comments were about Lavigne's remarkable show of gameness."[24] The Kid may have looked beaten but he came out fighting like a man possessed. "Lavigne took the initiative and tore into his man with a smashing body attack that seemed to slow up the colored boy."[25] With half a minute left to go in the round, Walcott landed a tremendous smash on the heart using everything he had to land the blow. "He waited for the fraction of a second," reported the *Free Press*, "expecting to see the Kid quit or drop. But that wonderful little dynamo of the ring simply smiled and said, 'Quit tickling me, Joe.'" Walcott's face took on a look of surprise and dismay. "He had shot his most formidable bolt, only to have it turned aside with a grin. He then saw for the first time a glimmering of defeat and his courage forsook him, but under the watchful eye of O'Rourke he had to fight as long as he had an ounce of strength left, and he made a gallant and despairing effort to win."[26] Lavigne would later admit that the heart blow made him "sick in his throat."

The back and forth beating continued unabated in the eighth. The Kid blocked several blows and sent Walcott to the ropes with a vicious heart punch of his own. He pounded Walcott's kidneys and began to notice Walcott weakening in the clinches. Lavigne recalled hearing John L. Sullivan bellowing, "Kill that gorilla! Kill that gorilla!" above the roar of the crowd. Sullivan thought nothing of shouting an obvious racial slur, but then this was the 1890s. The concept of racism wouldn't be born until 1907 and later become a prevalent term in the 1930s. Little constraint for such insults could be found in the culture of the last decade of the 19th century.

"Tom O'Rourke stood up in astonishment and howled for Walcott to knock me cuckoo," Lavigne wrote. "Walcott goaded to desperation, made a rally, drove me to the ropes with a wild lunge and whaled away with both hands. O'Rourke continued to snarl his commands to murder me."[27] Joe was tiring fast. "In his corner Wolcott turned to his manager Tom O'Rourke and said: 'Mista Tom, this boy

Tom O'Rourke, who made a fortune with George Dixon. Tom is one of the few survivors of the old school

Wolcott's Manager, Tom O'Rourke
- Courtesy of BoxRec

ain't human. I cain't hurt him.'"[28]

In the ninth and tenth stanzas the trend continued with Lavigne getting stronger and Walcott continuing to weaken. Even so, both sides continued to inflict heavy damage on the other man, the difference being that no one had ever fought this hard against Walcott and hurt him so badly. Tom O'Rourke would later recall, "In all my years of experience in the ring I never saw a fighter stand up under such terrific punishment as Lavigne did in the ninth round."[29] Lavigne's left ear was a repeated target of Walcott throughout the middle rounds and by the eleventh it was grotesquely swollen. Midway through the round Walcott threw a right that grazed the ear and then brought the heel of his glove back, raking the appendage. The ear burst, showering a cascade of blood over the Kid, Walcott, and several spectators at ringside. Lavigne was a gory sight, his upper body a blotchy, crimson mess.

At the end of the 11th, Walcott begged his corner to throw in the towel. He probably had concluded that the man of mayhem he faced in the ring would still be standing at the end of the 15th round and therefore the fight was lost per the prearranged agreement. Why subject himself to further infliction of damage. His corner would hear nothing of it and O'Rourke ordered him to finish the fight. And in the 12th, Walcott continued to do harm but Lavigne responded. In O'Rourke's words, "The Kid suddenly cut loose on a lion-hearted rally. He missed with a right and went to the floor but was up in a jiffy and tearing in on Walcott like a wolf. Lavigne figuratively went fighting crazy. The fury of his onslaught drove Walcott to the ropes while the crowd roared like insane men. I never saw anything like the wild rally of Lavigne's and the wild frenzy of the spectators."[30]

And now a series of events happened that while possibly true are most likely embellished by the excited sources of the time. At the end of the 13th round Walcott, weakened and rattled according to Lavigne, tried to crawl out of the ring. As the story goes, O'Rourke dragged him back into the ring and pulled a gun on him. "Stay in there, you baboon, or I'll kill you," the manager roared. "My money is lost but you're going to finish this fight or die."[31]

Early in the 14th round Walcott went down. It was a combination of blow and slip. He was up quickly without taking a count. Lavigne was all over Joe when he regained his feet keeping him off balance and recoiling. Many in the arena thought Walcott might not weather the storm but he clinched and recovered sufficiently to make it to the end of the round. He was wobbly and his seconds helped him to his stool. "When the gong rang to start the last round, Lavigne rushed across the ring and met Walcott coming out of his corner," wrote Alexander Johnston in *Ten and Out!* "He poured in a deadly fire of rights and lefts at the negro's wind. During the whole round he never gave Joe a chance to get set and started. He followed him around the ring remorselessly."[32]

Lavigne was astounded at Walcott's ability to take the beating and remain upright. "'Suffering cats,' I yelled to my corner as I piled blow on blow, 'have I got to knock down the ring post to get him on the floor?'"[33] "Although Tom O'Rourke shouted long and loud to Walcott to 'do his man,' and Dixon's cries of 'Go in, Joe, and show him the old trick,' Walcott could not get in on the Kid sufficiently hard enough to stop him." The fighting ended with Walcott against the ropes and Lavigne pumping in a fusillade of rights and lefts. Wolcott had to be carried from the ring.

The Superlatives Flow

"No such excitement was ever seen in the arena before," reported the *Police Gazette*. "Lavigne's game showing excited the admiration of friend and foe alike and when Referee Hurst's decision was announced, pandemonium was discounted, sedate-looking, cool-headed men stood upon chairs waving their hats and cheering lustily. The ring swarmed with enthusiasts all eager to shake the hand of the little champion. As the crowd filed out of the building there was only one sentiment heard on all sides, 'the greatest I ever saw.'"[34]

Much was made after the fight of just how much Walcott lost by starving himself down to get under the lightweight limit of 133 pounds. Many felt it cost him the fight as he appeared to wither in the later rounds while Lavigne was picking up steam. Lavigne himself, ever the modest and humble victor, would later remark, "I did not beat Walcott. The weight beat him."[35]

While Walcott's supporters would blame it on the weight, his own manager, Tom O'Rourke, did not agree and actually believed it was an advantage when he said: "It was popularly believed Walcott would have to weaken himself greatly by making that weight. That was a fallacy, but I was glad to have other managers and boxers think Joe would hurt himself scaling in as a lightweight. The truth of the matter, however, was that Joe was better below 135 than he was above it. This was owing to his peculiar build. He had enormous biceps and tremendous girth of chest with abnormal pectoral muscles. Whenever he took on weight it was about the chest, and it made straight punching difficult to him, the biceps rubbing against the chest mound. That was why he used round-arm rights in contests in which he was above 135. When down around the lightweight limit he had greater freedom of movement and there was no friction between arm and chest." O'Rourke continued with a bit of sarcasm: "Joe was so weak he gave Lavigne the most terrific lacing ever administered in the prize ring, and I still believe if Walcott had not suffered seriously from stomach cramps, something which bothered him in many other contests, he would have knocked Lavigne cold."[36]

The fight has been described with flowing superlatives from all the old-timers, many who witnessed it. Robert Edgren called it "the most desperate fight in the annals of the Queensberry game."[37] Alexander Johnston wrote, "The Lavigne-Walcott fight is one of the traditions of the American ring."[38] From B. H. Benton it was, "One of the most vicious prize ring duels ever given under modern rules."[39] And from O'Rourke, who would know better than anyone, "No battle was ever fraught with more desperate fighting. It was a fierce, savage give and take from the first to the final clang of the gong. There was never a moment in which each was not desperately trying to bring down the other and they fought with the speed of gamecocks and the savageness of pit bulldogs."[40]

The final word will go to George Underwood, the famed old-time New York sportswriter when he wrote in 1920: "Wherever fighting men gather and wherever fights are told of, there always is one ring combat which is uppermost in the comment. It has been more than a quarter century since Kid Lavigne and Joe Walcott met in their memorable 15-round encounter at Jim Kennedy's old Empire A. C., at Maspeth, Long Island, but the telling of the tale never will grow old. Start a fanning bee among any circle or class of ring enthusiasts, enthuse on any bout you may. There always will be some old-timer present whose eyes will light up with a reminiscent sparkle and who will declare: 'Ah, but you should have seen the Saginaw Kid and the Barbados Demon at Maspeth!'"[41] Indeed.

CHAPTER 14

Prelude to an Englishman

Any lingering doubt had been erased as to who was the top lightweight in America. Lavigne's victory over the seemingly unbeatable Walcott stunned all of fistiana. Few, other than Fitzpatrick and the Lavigne faithful, had given him a chance of winning, let alone making it through 15 rounds with all his faculties intact. He returned to Saginaw to convalesce after the brutal bout and spend time with his mother over the holidays. The memory of another mother lingered heavily in his heart. Before leaving San Francisco he penned a note to Andy Bowen's mother and enclosed a $50 gold certificate.[1] He was clearly still grieving Andy's death.

With "Lavigne fever" sweeping the continent, a benefit was arranged in his honor to be held at the Grand Central Palace in New York on January 9, 1896. Several exhibition matches were set. In the meantime, Fitzpatrick and Lavigne were negotiating with Jack Everhardt's camp for a rematch to be held in El Paso in February. For unknown reasons the bout never came together and the pairing of the two would have to wait for a date in October. Looking for a fight with a top contender, Fitz received word that Dick Burge, the English champion, had given a challenge that he would meet any "140-pound man" in the world. "Kid Lavigne is the only one who seems disposed to pick up the gage thrown down by Dick Burge to the light and welterweight divisions of America," reported the *Police Gazette*. He has authorized Richard K. Fox [proprietor of the *Gazette*] to send a cable to England in which the British champion's challenge is accepted for a fight in England, during derby week, weight to be 138 pounds at the ring side."[2]

On the day of the New York benefit 2,000 people were in attendance. Lavigne fought a four-round exhibition against Billy Woods and a second four-rounder against his stable-mate Tommy Ryan. Another interesting match was in the making behind the scenes as, unbeknownst to many, the old salt, Jack McAuliffe, was contemplating a comeback. Jack had retired once in late 1892, but kept on dabbling with exhibitions and a few non-title bouts. He retired again in late 1894, only to continue the same pattern.

A Match of Champions

Jack McAuliffe, "The Napoleon of the Prize Ring" - Courtesy of BoxRec

Throughout these semi-retired years he was very selective of whom he would fight and would never put his lightweight title on the line even though, by as early as 1893, Lavigne was widely recognized as the current American lightweight champion. Just how selective Jack was, is in evidence in this quote from Lavigne: "Dick Burge came to this country in 1892, and Boston promoters tried to match him and McAuliffe. A purse of $50,000, the largest ever bid for a fight up to that time, was offered. Burge was willing to weigh 138 but McAuliffe refused to go over 135. For the sake of three pounds, McAuliffe let a $50,000 purse go by. I hope my friends will not consider me unduly boastful when I say I would have fought John L. Sullivan for $50,000."[3] It was apparent he wanted no part of Burge even for what would be $1.2 million in today's dollars.

Since Lavigne's rise to prominence, he had been ever respectful of the undefeated champion. "He has not pressed him for a battle, or claimed the title on a forfeit," noted the *Detroit Free Press*. "Although looked upon as the champion since McAuliffe's retirement, Lavigne has refused to style himself so, holding that he could only secure it in one way—by a battle with the man who held and defended it for ten years."[4] And McAuliffe did not come looking for Lavigne either. But with Jack sniffing the comeback trail he knew one way to measure his progress would be to schedule a short dust-up with the Saginaw Kid.

The match was scheduled for March 11, 1896 at Madison Square Garden and was to be a six-round bout. Fight fans began to buzz and speculate about the match. "Defeat at the hands of the clever Western boy meant for McAuliffe an end of his career in the ring, a draw would sustain his reputation, and a favorable decision over Lavigne would place the Brooklyn boxer ahead of everything in his class," opined the *Chicago Tribune*.[5]

But Lavigne would face another challenger before he finally had his long-anticipated go with McAuliffe in the Garden. It was a fight that didn't occur in the ring. It happened in another venue in which the Kid was a regular. At Martin Dowling's saloon on Sixth Avenue in New York, Lavigne, Dowling and Solly Smith were having a few drinks when a sports writer, Dick Bell, entered the establishment and congratulated the Kid on his success in getting a match with McAuliffe. The Kid was afflicted with a Jekyll and Hyde personality. When he was sober he was the humblest and kindest of gentlemen, but when he had been drinking he could be surly, hostile, and aggressive. Bell met Mr. Hyde that afternoon when the Kid "attempted to put the lighted end of his cigar in Bell's eye. Dick's natural reaction was a wild right which rendered Lavigne unconscious for a full hour."[6]

At least that's how one source told it. Another, the *Detroit Free Press*, under the headline, "Lavigne Whipped by a Reporter," had a slightly different version when it recalled, "The Kid, however, was in an ugly mood and started in to abuse Bell in vile language. Bell threatened to thrash Lavigne if he did not stop his abuse. This had no effect and Bell landed a quick right-hander full in the boxer's face, the force of the blow sending Lavigne back a dozen feet. Lavigne came back and Bell, getting his head in chancery [in a head lock], punched him hard and often. Solly Smith and Martin Dowling parted the two and Bell left the place."[7]

Bell, possibly feeling emboldened by his conquest of the Kid, was not so fortunate when "he undertook to whip a Negro on Broadway several weeks later and was so badly cut with a razor that he died from his injuries."[8] Bell's assailant, described as an "octoroon," a person who is one eighth black, escaped his pursuers by ducking into Joe Wolcott's saloon and vanishing out the back door never to be caught. Lavigne survived this embarrassing episode, as he would several more throughout his later career, when drinking to excess summoned the behaviors of Mr. Hyde from the depths within.

The public had the general understanding that the upcoming bout would be for the lightweight championship and belt, held by McAuliffe. When learning of this, Jack was quick to disabuse the sporting world of any such notion when he asserted, "There has been no understanding that the belt was to go with the decision, and no mention was made of that trophy when the match was arranged, and it is a fact that no championship contests are ever decided in six-round bouts. I am ready to make a match for the belt, but it must be for twenty or twenty-five rounds, and be decided before the club offering the largest purse. I am in better condition than at any previous time in several years, and am satisfied that I can repay my friends for their confidence."[9] And Jack's fitness for fights was nearly always suspect. He was "notoriously unfit," wrote the *Detroit Free Press*, "but was so much better than his opponents that he pulled himself through a winner."[10]

Perhaps this formula had worked in the past but would it hold up now that he was 30 years old, and was up against a foe that the *Milwaukee Evening Wisconsin* called, "the hardest nut he ever attempted to crack." Jack hadn't been very active in the past 16 months. He fought Owen Ziegler in November of 1894 in an injury-shortened, three-round bout, breaking two small bones in his left wrist. He had sparred three short exhibitions in early 1896 against Ziegler, Jimmy Nelson, his former sparring partner, and Billy Madden, his former manager, who at 14 years his senior, did not provide McAuliffe with much of a workout. And now he would go against the man who just out-demoned Joe Wolcott.

By all accounts McAuliffe was bucking his normal trend and training hard for the contest. "Jack recognizes now that he has one more chance," reported the *Detroit Free Press*, "and as a consequence he has been working off his superfluous flesh. There is one thing certain—if Mac gives a good account of himself against Lavigne and shows that his arm is all right, he will not lack for backing for a bout of a longer duration with Lavigne. He has studied Lavigne carefully, and is of the opinion that a straight left would prove decidedly uncomfortable for the Saginaw lad, as the latter is a round-arm hitter."[11]

A war of words from the McAuliffe camp erupted a week before the contest. McAuliffe learned that the National Sporting Club of London was referring to the upcoming Lavigne-Burge match in June as being for the world lightweight championship between the American and European champions. McAuliffe was offended by the slight, as he still considered himself the rightful holder of the world and American titles, even though he had retired two years ago and

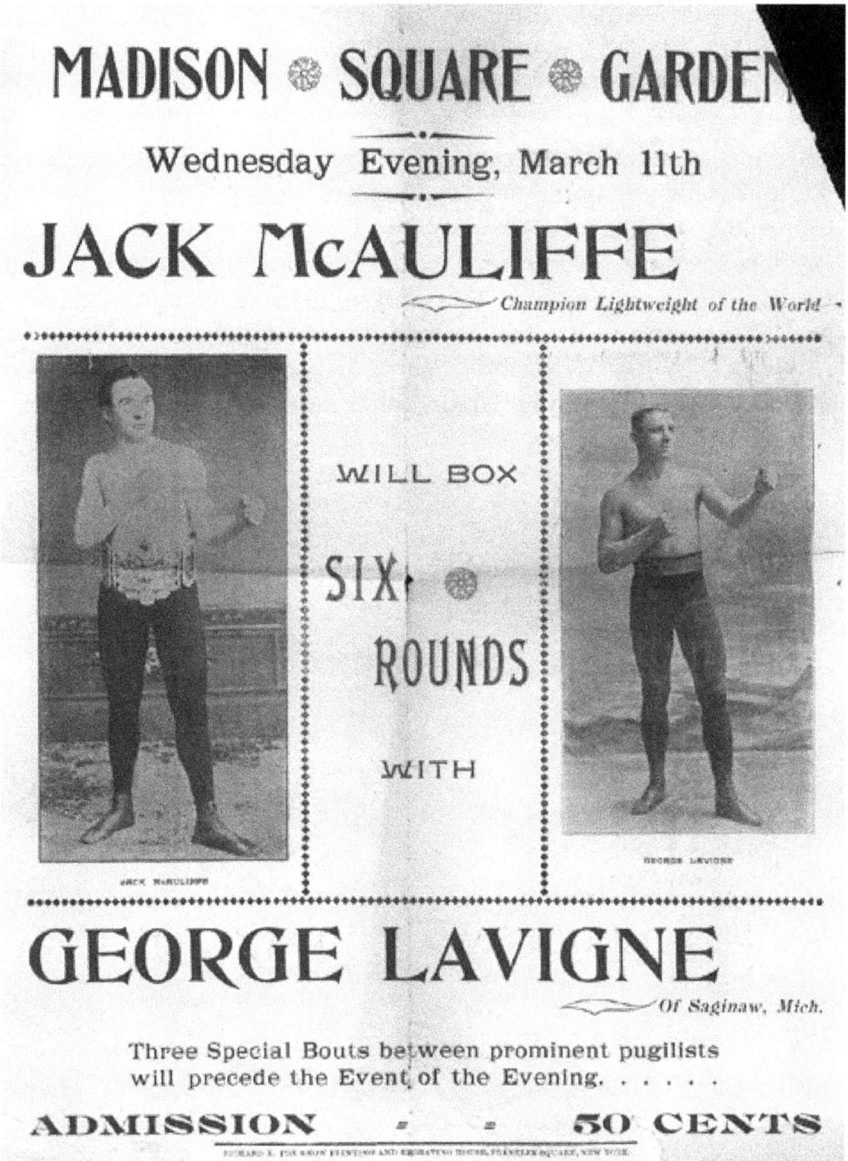

Program for the Lavigne-McAuliffe bout
- Courtesy of Bill Pollock at Champions of the Ring

had not been actively defending his titles. In a preemptive strike he challenged Lavigne to a longer fight after they finished their six-rounder the next week. Many thought it might cause the Kid to cancel the fight with Burge to meet Jack instead. Murmurs mentioned a 32-round affair to settle the American championship once and for all.

Sam Fitzpatrick stuck a fork in the controversy when he responded: "Lavigne never authorized the National Sporting Club of London to advertise him as the champion lightweight of America, and has no intention of claiming the title. Jack McAuliffe is the only real champion until someone defeats him. He [McAuliffe] says that 'Lavigne is a great man, but not a champion now.' I propose to show him that George is a better man than he is and if McAuliffe is good enough to make a draw with Lavigne in the six-round bout next Wednesday at Madison Square Garden I shall declare the fight with Dick Burge off and challenge McAuliffe for the championship. We will have a fight ten weeks after signing articles, and the winner will go to England and fight Burge or any other man in the world."[12]

Madison Square Garden circa 1896 – Courtesy of Library of Congress, Prints and Photographs Division, Detroit Publishing Company Collection.

A Short but Telling Bout

The challenge and response heightened anticipation among the 5,000 sports in the Garden the night of the match until they learned a damper had been put on the entire evening. "Inspector Brooks and Captain Pickett, who had charge of 100 policemen in the big amphitheater, had warned the management no hard fighting would be allowed," noted the *Chicago Tribune*. "The police officers also warned the fighters the first hard blow struck would be a sign for the bout to be stopped, and the arrest of the principals and all others concerned in the exhibition would follow."[13] While no arrests were made that evening, the lawmen definitely had an impact on the proceedings. In the first round of the preliminary bout as soon as the combatants began to "hit rather lively," the contest was stopped without a decision. Inspector Brooks interceded again just prior to the main event when he told the ring announcer to inform the spectators that no referee would be allowed to enter the ring and they would have to judge for themselves who was the better man.

And Brooks wasn't done asserting his authority on the evening's events. He allowed only two-minute rounds and just as the men were drawing on their gloves the Inspector demanded to have a look and determined they were too small. He required six-ounce gloves, commonly referred to back then as "pillows," before they could proceed. At about 10:30 p.m. Lavigne and McAuliffe were ready to square off after both receiving a hearty round of applause upon their entrance to the ring. McAuliffe weighed 138 with some sources claiming he was closer to 145. Lavigne was a few pounds over the lightweight limit.

The first three rounds were fairly even marked by lively exchanges between the fighters with no damage done but both getting in several rights and lefts to the body and face. Lavigne picked up the pace and the force of his blows in the fourth getting the best of Jack. He hit McAuliffe with lefts and rights to the body and face and a hard left on his jaw. "McAuliffe fell short in an attempt to land his right," recounted the *Chicago Tribune*. "Lavigne sent his right on the face which made McAuliffe turn around."[14]

In the fifth frame Lavigne again got the better of the fighting and staggered Jack with a hard left to the head. And in the sixth and final round, Lavigne worked hard to the body with lefts and rights and then worked to the face. "Lavigne had McAuliffe in 'queer street' when Inspector Brooks entered the ring and stopped the bout," the *Tribune* ended.[15] Inspector Brooks was simply doing his job and one that he had forewarned he would do. But at the same time, he had stepped in at the precise moment that kept the "Napoleon of the Prize Ring," and long-revered hometown favorite, from tasting the first defeat of his storied career.

The *Milwaukee Evening Wisconsin* summarized the results briefly when it recounted, "The police saved Jack McAuliffe's reputation last night in New York when he came near being knocked out by 'Kid' Lavigne. Mac was the heavier of the two and appeared to be in good condition, but he was not a match for the clever Michigan fighter. No decision was given, although every one present admitted that Lavigne would have won."[16] Lavigne himself recalled in his ever-respectful tone, "I had all the better of it, but Jack showed me enough to prove what a great fighter he had been."[17] Although McAuliffe continued his semi-retired pattern, fighting a few more bouts in 1896, his go with Kid Lavigne told him everything he needed to know about mounting a serious comeback. Early in 1897 he would make a formal presentation in which he passed the title to Lavigne.

CHAPTER 15

The "Schoolboy" Goes to London

Robert Edgren, the accomplished turn of the century sports journalist and political cartoonist wrote in 1919: "Lavigne had the round, smooth, smiling face of a cherub—a perfect oval of a face with light yellow hair and light blue eyes. He looked like a choir singer, or one of Raphael's youthful angels, or a Sunday school book hero of the style of literature slipped over on Sunday school children twenty years ago. But from the ears down he was all fighter. He had a strong neck, very wide and powerful shoulders, thick arms and fists like longshoremen's. He always smiled like an angel, and smiling like an angel he would fight as if he had horns, hoofs and a tail."

It was in San Francisco at the Pacific Athletic Club on March 17, 1892 that Edgren watched his first professional fight, a 10-round decision for Kid Lavigne over Charles Rochette. Looking back 27 years Edgren remembered his first impressions of Lavigne: "I'll never forget the impression of Kid Lavigne as he was in those days, cherubic oval face, cherubic smile, and his wedge shaped body, smoothly muscled, gleaming; white under the glare of the single arc light. I saw it from the gallery. I saw Lavigne feeling quite sure that my youthful and inexperienced eye had detected signs that he was a coming champion."[1]

The Iron Man of England

In 1896 the stage was being set for the unfolding of Edgren's premonition. Lavigne was undefeated over a ten-year career in the lightweight class and the only thing standing in his way of the undisputed lightweight championship of the world was England's Dick Burge.

Burge, who had acquired the title of "Iron Man," was advertising himself as the world's lightweight champion. And again from Robert Edgren: "Burge was the idol of all Great Britain. He was called lightweight champion and won the title at 140 pounds, the English weight. He had grown beyond that and had knocked out a number of middle and heavyweights. Everywhere under the Cross of St. George the name of Burge was spoken with respectful awe. No Englishman dreamed that he could be beaten."[2]

Burge was a rugged fighter and a very clever boxer with power in both fists. In the interest of Burge, the English promoters and managers had raised the lightweight limit to 138 pounds. The American lightweight standard at that time was a maximum of 133 pounds. Burge, as noted previously, offered to fight any "140 pound" man in the world. As Burge often tipped the scales at close to 150 pounds when he stepped into the ring for his lightweight bouts he was clearly a welterweight by American standards.

Dick "Iron Man" Burge - Courtesy of BoxRec

Popularity and reputation aside, Burge's record was not summarily impressive. According to *Boxing's Book of Records,* Dick's record going into the championship bout was four wins, four losses, and one draw.[3] He won the English lightweight title in 1891 in a bout with the great Jem Carney. Carney was getting the best of Burge, however, he was inexperienced in the Queensberry rules and in the 11th round he threw Burge to the turf and was disqualified. Carney, it should be remembered, was the man who was getting the best of Jack McAuliffe in the world lightweight championship match in 1887 when the crowd rushed the ring and the bout was stopped and called a draw in the 74th round. In defense of Burge, three of his losses were collected from middle and heavyweights. In his last bout before Lavigne, he was knocked out by heavyweight, Jem Smith, who weighed 178 to Burge's 144.

B. H. Benton, better known as Rob Roy, was an east coast sports writer widely acclaimed as "the greatest of all sporting writers" at the turn of the century. He also managed several fighters. He was currently on assignment in London on newspaper business. Upon hearing of Burge's offer, Benton summoned one of the top American welterweights of the time, "Mysterious" Billy Smith, to England anticipating an agreement to fight Burge. As told by Benton: "I cabled Mysterious Billy Smith to this country and he arrived in London two weeks later unheralded. I took him to Anderson's Hotel in Fleet Street, where we ran into Dick Burge, Jem Carney, and other fistic heads. The Mysterious one's appearance was a thunderbolt, and Smith announced that he had come over to accept Burge's challenge. Burge called me out to one side and said that he had no wish to fight Smith, and his challenge was more to keep up his prestige with the English sporting world, particularly racing men, and asked me not to force an issue."[4]

Smith's reputation must have preceded him across the Atlantic as Burge clearly knew Smith would prove to be a dangerous match. Smith was notorious for having a roughhouse fighting style and was disqualified 13 times over the course of his career, more than any other boxer in history. He would routinely employ such tactics as wrestling, elbowing, and even biting his opponent. On one occasion he flung an opponent to the canvas and stepped on his face. In another bout, he cold-cocked the referee who had disqualified him.

While Burge was discretely and perhaps wisely, declining the match with Smith, Dr. Aaron P. Ordway, a well-known American patron and supporter of the boxing game suggested a match with the recognized American lightweight champion, Kid Lavigne. Dr. Ordway was influential in English boxing circles as he owned the *Mirror of Life* in London. The *Mirror of Life* was the most important illustrated sporting weekly in the world featuring boxing. The *Mirror* also had exclusive rights to make all international matches held at the National Sporting Club of London. He contacted the manager of the National Sporting Club, John Flemming, with his proposition. Many astute followers of boxing at the time thought that matching the smaller, lighter Lavigne against Iron Man Burge was foolhardy; however the American fight fans had become accustomed to Lavigne dispatching bigger foes. Flemming accepted Dr. Ordway's judgment about Lavigne, and Burge reportedly did not care how small his opponent would be.[5]

On January 27, 1896, Lavigne's manager, Sam Fitzpatrick, got a cable from the *Mirror of Life* in London. The cable was an offer to match Burge against Lavigne for the world lightweight title. After negotiating the terms, the National Sporting Club put up a $3,500 purse. There was also a side bet of $2,500. Fitzpatrick accepted the final proposal provided the *Mirror of Life* sent on $500 for expenses.

After the McAuliffe bout in early March, Lavigne and Fitzpatrick tried in vain to get Jack to agree to a longer contest. "We dickered for a long time after my contest with McAuliffe for a finish-fight," said Lavigne to a *Detroit Free Press* reporter, "but as there was no chance of anything coming out of it we decided to go to London and keep the engagement which Fitzpatrick had made for me to meet Burge." "McAuliffe made a good show with me," the Kid continued. "He has fought well and may be all right for a finish, but if a man were to set a fast pace for him he might not be able to stand it all the way through."[6] The *Free Press* reporter continued to question Lavigne: "What do you think of Burge?" he asked. "I have never seen him," replied Lavigne, "but they tell me he is as big as Ryan [world welterweight champion]. We couldn't get a match on any other basis except weigh in at 138 pounds at four o'clock in the afternoon. I still feel confident of beating him. He would not fight Walcott and I beat Wolcott, so there you are."[7]

Off to Europe

On April 4, two months before the bout scheduled for June 1, Lavigne and Fitzpatrick left for Southampton, England from New York on the steamship St. Louis. The trip took six days. They would be joined later by Lavigne's youngest brother Frank, his trainer Michael "Dad" Butler and others. B. H. Benton met them at dockside and took them straight to the Victoria Hotel at Trafalgar Square, London. After registering at 11 p.m. Lavigne asked to be taken to the dining room as he was very hungry. Benton recalls: "When told that it was impossible to get anything after the night dinner hour, the Kid and his manager were initiated into the absurdities of English hotel customs. I took the visitors to a public house in Whitehall and when the proprietor knew who his guest was he ordered that the champion be served with whatever the house offered and to the limit. The champion's inner demands were satisfied with a plentiful supply of good old English roast beef, not long over from Texas, washed down with a mug of Bass Ale."[8]

The next day Lavigne and Fitzpatrick visited the *Mirror of Life* office for a reception in the morning before journeying to the National Sporting Club in Covent Garden to pay their respects to the heads of the famous fight institution. B.H. Benton recalled, "Lavigne was the cynosure of all eyes and he was scrutinized minutely. The unanimous opinion was that it was an absurdity to match such a little fellow against their pet fistic idol, the man who had defeated Jem Carney, Lachie Thompson, Harry Nickless and Tom Williams and who had also fought Jem Smith, the heavyweight champion, and Ted Pritchard, the English middleweight champion."[9] One London newspaper of the time reported that when Fitzpatrick introduced the Kid to the manager and co-founder of the National Sporting Club, John Flemming, club president, Lord Lonsdale, and other members of the Club, they were "thunderstruck." "Why", said Fleming, looking the American champion over, "this cannot possibly be Kid Lavigne!" "What's the matter with him? Doesn't he look the goods?" asked Fitzpatrick, who was puzzled. "Oh, he's so small, only a bit of a lad! I fear he is not half big enough for Burge!" declared Flemming. "Don't worry about his size," said Fitzpatrick with a grin. "I think Burge will find him big enough in the ring!"[10] Lavigne was a short lightweight of only 5 feet 3 and 1/2 inches. Burge by comparison was nearly 5 feet 8 inches in height. The Kid's appearance was also a disappointment to English boxing fans having expected a lantern-jawed individual not the mild mannered youth that the London sports prints referred to derisively as a "schoolboy."

The meeting at the National Sporting Club was recalled with even more detail by Kid Lavigne in the *Los Angeles Times* in January 1928. The Kid had written a series of 15 columns for the paper in 1927 and 1928 looking back on his ring career. In his words: "Sam had the address, and we decided to stroll over and get acquainted. After a long hike we found ourselves before what looked like a swell dwelling house. Sam rang the bell and a flunkey all covered with buttons opened the door. He took Sam's card, welcomed us in a very dignified way, and showed us into a large room. 'Mr. Flemming will be glad you're here, sir,' he told Sam, respectfully. He never glanced at me. Sam annexed a big leather armchair and I walked across the room and pulled myself up on a high stool. My legs dangled. My shoes were a foot from the floor.

"Pretty soon in came Mr. Flemming, president of the club, a fine appearing, aristocratic Englishman. 'Awfully glad to see you old chap,' he said, shaking hands with Sam. Then Mr. Flemming swept an inquiring glance around the room but I might have been a piece of furniture for all the notice he paid me. He looked disappointed. 'I'm sorry you didn't bring Mr. Lavigne along, so some of the members could see him,' he said. 'That's Kid Lavigne,' replied Fitz, jerking his head towards me. I'll never forget the look of astonishment on Mr. Flemming's face as he lamped me. And the more he lamped, the smaller I appeared to him. 'What, that little boy!' he exploded. 'You don't expect him to fight Dick Burge? Why it's preposterous!' 'That's Kid Lavigne alright,' answered Sam easily. 'He can lick two Dick Burges.' 'Oh, come, come,' said Mr. Flemming impatiently. 'This thing is a joke. You can't be serious. I can scarcely believe that little fellow really is Lavigne. But if he is, it will never do for the members to see him. You must get him away, somewhere out to the suburbs. He simply must not train here at the club. My word!' 'Well,' retorted Fitz, 'he may look small, but we think pretty well of him in our country. And we have some fairly tough geezers over there.'"[11]

"But finally I eased myself down off my high stool and walked over to the tall Englishman," the Kid continued. "'I may look small,' I said, 'but if any of the members doubt my fighting ability, let 'em bring in some hard geezer right now, even Dick Burge himself, and I'll peel off my clothes and show a sample of my stuff in the club gym.' But my spunk failed to impress Mr. Flemming." Later, on the way out to the training quarters Lavigne asked Fitzpatrick, "What kind of a bird is this Burge that I must hide out from the National Sporting Club so that the members won't know what a set-up the U.S.A. has sent over for him?" "He's a tough cockney all right," answered Fitz, "but he won't be so tough after you've massaged his bread-basket for a few rounds." Sam Fitzpatrick was prophetic.

Fitzpatrick also recalled the way they were treated, reminiscing in a *Washington Post* article of 1914: "Though they didn't greet us with brass bands and parades as they seem in the habit of doing now days in England, nevertheless they were very nice to us. Probably because they felt sorry for the Kid. I don't know. You see, they had a hard time convincing themselves that Lavigne was a fighter. He looked so small in his tight fitting sack suit, and his modesty, combined with rosy cheeks and a pair of innocent blue eyes, made him look so little and harmless that they thought I was bringing over a 'ringer' and not the champion of America at all. They laughed at the idea of the Kid beating their champion. Burge was an excellent fighter and extremely popular, and it was impossible for them to conceive of a little baby-faced boy whipping him. Everyone felt sorry for Lavigne as he walked down the aisle [the night of the fight]. They all liked him and sympathized with him."[12]

On Training and Weighty Matters

It was the first time Dick Burge, who was present at the club that morning had ever seen Lavigne. "Burge readily congratulated himself over the 'soft' thing fixed for him to attach world's champion after his name," noted Benton.[13] The American group took no issue with the weight or any other conditions of the fight and after signing the articles they left for the training headquarters arranged for them by Dr. Ordway. The selected place was the Prince of Wales Hotel in Etham, a suburb about eight miles southeast of London. Several other boxers were quartered there at the time including Australian middle weight champion, Tommy Duggan. It's possible Lavigne took advantage of Duggan's presence and sparred with the 157-pounder to prepare for the oversized lightweight he would fight in Burge.

Lavigne spent the next seven weeks in arduous preparation for the bout. In May, two weeks before the fight, the *Mirror of Life* reported on a party of English "sporting men" who paid a visit to the Lavigne training camp: "Two four-in-hand coaches were called into requisition, and the departure made from the Plough, in Mile End Road, at one o'clock on Monday afternoon. The drive was a most delightful one. The lightweight champion immediately proceeded to his afternoon's work. There was plenty of room in the large gymnasium for the party to sit and see Lavigne go through his work. His first labour was ten, three-minute rounds at the punching bag. So well and perfectly did he accomplish his task that he elicited the warmest praise and admiration from his audience. The exercise was declared as simply marvelous. Another half hour was used up in skipping rope, dumb bell, chest weight and wrist machine, when Lavigne put himself in the hands of trainer Mike Butler for rubbing and finishing up."[14]

Butler was one of the most accomplished trainers of his day. Returning from England after the championship bout he opened a school of physical culture in New York for a time. He then moved on to become the athletic director of the Chicago Athletic Association from 1897 to 1907, where he was Knute Rockne's first coach. He spent several years as the track coach for Oregon State University followed by a long stint as a coach and trainer at the University of Detroit where he ended his career in 1944.

The training session was followed by a banquet for the visitors and the Lavigne entourage. After dinner, the entire party assembled in the front yard for a group picture. It was getting dark as the visitors began their return to London leaving Lavigne, "delighted and assured that although he is in a strange country to meet the most popular champion England has had in a decade, still there are some of the natives who wish him well."[15]

The parties had agreed to fight at the English weight limit of 138 pounds; however, Burge was heavier and was having troubles making the weight. The fighters had agreed to weigh-in at 4:00 p.m. the day

Sam Fitzpatrick, "Kid" Lavigne, and Michael "Dad" Butler (Lavigne's trainer) at their training quarters in Etham, England prior to the Burge fight – Courtesy of John Cuthbertson

of the fight. On the day before the fight, the other co-founder of the National Sporting Club, A.H. Bettinson, a former amateur lightweight champion of England, told Sam Fitzpatrick that it was impossible for Burge to even get down near the required weight. "I'll fight him anyway," declared Lavigne. "Let him weigh 145." "Then in justice to you as champion of America," said Mr. Bettinson, "I will publicly announce that this fight is not for the world's championship. You should not be forced to risk losing your claim to that title." "I insist on its being for the championship," said Lavigne. "I don't care if he weighs a ton," said Lavigne laughing. "I'll lick him."[16]

Lavigne and his party were late getting to the weigh-in and Burge had already come and gone. Reports of how much Burge actually weighed are conflicting with the *Sporting Life* contending that no weight for Burge was recorded. It was admitted that he was the heavier of the two. Lavigne's official weight was given at 133 pounds. Rumor had it that Burge, shortly before the date, refused to make the weight and insisted on being allowed to weigh in at 145 pounds. According to Fitzpatrick, Burge undoubtedly weighed 150 pounds or more at the opening bell.

A. J. Liebling, one of the finest writers on boxing of the 20th century, wrote in 1951 on the hazards of giving away weight in a boxing match when he noted, "The division of boxers into weight classes is based on the premise that if two men are equally talented practitioners of the Sweet Science, then the heavier man has the decided advantage. This is true, of course, only if both men are trained down hard, since a pound of beer is of no use in a boxing match. If the difference amounts to no more than a couple of pounds, it can be offset by a number of other factors, including luck, but when it goes up to five or six or seven, it takes a lot of beating. The span between the top limit of one weight class and the next represents the margin that history has proved is almost impossible to overcome."[17] Proportionality rules here, as seven pounds in the lightweight class is much greater than it would be in the heavyweight class. Imagine what Lavigne was up against if indeed Burge weighed close to 150 or an 18 pound difference to Lavigne's 133 and a nearly five inch height difference between the fighters.

England's Hallowed Venue

The National Sporting Club was founded in 1891 as a private club for boxing matches. The club was run under very strict rules regarding both the boxers and the members. Bouts took place after dinner, before about 1,300 members and guests, and were to be fought in silence as no talking or applauding was permitted during the rounds. No smoking was allowed at the matches either. The club also followed the English tradition of the referee being outside the ring, in formal dress, shouting instructions to the fighters from a tall chair. By the rules of the club all members were entitled to admission to witness the contests. This rule was so strict that when Saginaw, Michigan lumber millionaire Clark Ring tried to get in he was barred despite a personal plea from Lavigne. When big attractions were held at the National Sporting Club all seats were reserved with the price of the seat commensurate with its location. The ring-side seats were selling for ten guineas each or $52 in American money, the equivalent of $1,300 today.

The National Sporting Club circa 1896 - Courtesy of the London Ex-Boxers Association

The night of the fight B.H. Benton, who attended the match, remarked about the crowd: "One of the most representative crowds that ever gathered to witness a prize ring affair in England gathered in the celebrated fistic emporium. Many titled Englishmen, including the Prince of Wales who could only be seen at the club on star occasions, graced the institution with their presence." No doubt the double draw of the fight and derby week brought out more of society's elite. As reported via a special cable dispatch to the *New York World* newspaper, "The twenty-round contest for the lightweight championship of the world between Kid Lavigne, the American champion, and Dick Burge, the English champion, proved so great an attraction that an hour and a half before the fight was timed to begin the theatre of the National Sporting Club, at King Street, Covent Garden, was packed to suffocation."[18]

There appears to be great disagreement among sources on how many spectators witnessed the bout. The National Sporting Club had a capacity of roughly 1,300. Several sources indicate the crowd was an intimate gathering of between 350 and 450, quite strictly open only to members of the club. However, Benton, in recalling the fight many years later said there were 1,200 who attended the match and as many as 200 of them were Americans. One plausible explanation to this discrepancy may be that the 450 counted only the elite club members who sat in the seats closest to the ring with the remainder, including club members who were English commoners as well as Americans, making up the throngs in the gallery.

At 10:30 p.m. John Flemming called for Lavigne and Burge. Lavigne was first to appear in the ring with Burge following shortly. According to the *Sporting Life* he wore "chocolate colored knee breeches and high laced boots, whilst the Tynesider had on white linen breeches and also had high boots."[19] "Tynesider" is a reference to the city of Newcastle on the Tyne River in northeast England where Burge spent most of his fighting years. Lavigne's seconds were Sam Fitzpatrick, Steve O'Donnell, the fine Australian heavyweight, and Mike Butler. In Burge's corner were Jem Carney, Funny Cook and Dan McGannon. Four-ounce gloves were used. "Butler, with true Yankee cuteness," noted the *Sportsman*, "carefully watched Burge's corner while the gloves were being adjusted, and then, satisfied that all was correct and in order, he crossed over and assisted in Lavigne's preparation."[20] "As I waited for the gloves to be tied on, I was amazed to learn that the odds on Burge, which had been three-to-one, had shifted to five- to-one," the Kid recalled. "'Pinch me,' I said to Fitz, 'how do these English figure these odds? Has Burge got a horseshoe in his glove?'"[21] Butler had seen to it that he hadn't.

A few bets were wagered with a shout while most were simply placed and accepted by the motion of a hand. In the National Sporting Club it was customary to make bets by holding up fingers to indicate the amount of the bet, thus three fingers would be 300 pounds.[22] While Lavigne stood in his corner waiting for the announcements to be made and the fight to commence, he heard one ringsider yell, "One hundred on Burge." He turned and quietly said, "I'll take that." "You're on old chap," was the sport's reply. "I like your pluck, but I don't like to take your money," the Englishman continued. "Oh that's all right," retorted Lavigne. "I'll take yours."[23]

After making an announcement that the fight was for the world lightweight title, the seconds left the ring as did the referee, well-known stock broker and famous sportsman, Jack Angle. Angle said, "Get ready," and nodded to the timekeeper who sounded the gong, calling "time." The fight was on and history was in the making.

CHAPTER 16

The Battle of the Burge for the Best in the World

Many fights start with combatants cautiously feeling each other out with light sparring and feinting. This was not one of those fights. At the clang of the bell Lavigne rushed Burge and according to Fitzpatrick "was on him like a whirlwind." "Those who expected to see Burge start off scoring with a rush were astonished when the Yankee literally went at his man like a tiger and forced him back," stated the great English sporting authority, the *London Sporting Life*. "The body blows that were sent into the Englishman were enough to disconcert a less seasoned and plucky veteran of the ring than Burge."[1] On one of the Kid's rushes, Burge deftly side-stepped while landing an uppercut and Lavigne's momentum sent him face first into a ring post. He recovered quickly and while his nose bled from the collision he was back on Burge in a flash. "When the first round ended," reported the *Washington Post*, "the betting ceased, and everyone seemed to realize that Burge had run afoul of a cyclone. Burge's admirers were simply paralyzed, and even his seconds were at a loss how to advise him."[2]

The Best Laid Plan

The advice Fitz gave the Kid in planning the most promising way to battle Burge was to use the same strategy he employed against Walcott. And it was "spot-on." Like Walcott, Burge was very powerful and skillful. He also had a weight, height and reach advantage over the Kid. The formula that worked against Walcott was threefold:

don't box him, keep unrelenting pressure on from the opening bell, and work hard for the body. "He was a better boxer than Walcott and it would never do for me to attempt to box with him," Lavigne recalled. "I would have been cut to pieces. I decided to carry the fight to Burge all the way, as I had done with Walcott."[3] The strategy shocked Walcott and was now shocking Dick Burge and his English faithful. "In that first round," Lavigne continued, "Burge caught me several terrible cracks on the head and I saw the Milky Way. I said, 'You're starting off well, Dick. I'll try to get even.' Burge laughed. A little later I sent one smoking hot into his kitchen and he bent over like a bear. 'Now it ain't goin' to be so funny,' I said."[4]

At the start of the second Burge relied heavily on his skill and science to deflect the Kid's maniacal rushes. He punished Lavigne with rights and lefts to the face. He was surprised at the Kid's speed and hitting power which caused him to fight with more caution than he otherwise may have. Lavigne was worried about getting disqualified for a foul as he and Sam were certain that the English referee would look for an excuse to call a foul and save their man from defeat at the hands of the American. In the second round the Kid clinched. "Suddenly the referee shouted, 'You're holding Mr. Lavigne; be careful; I shall not warn you again,'" recalled the *Denver Post*.[5] The Kid was forced to fight very cautiously the rest of the way. "Half-way through the third round," wrote B. H. Benton, "at a signal from Fitzpatrick, Lavigne cut loose, fought like a demon, casting all idea of cleverness to the winds. He beat down Burge's defense and administered the most severe punishment on the Briton's body."[6]

Through the fourth and fifth stanzas, Burge was getting more used to Lavigne's incessant rushes, fighting defensively as if his strategy was to tire the Kid out. If only he could hear Lavigne's words from 1928, when he said of the fight, "In those days I was tireless. The minute rest between rounds freshened me up as much as five minutes in later years. I felt that night as if I could sock like a heavyweight, as I probably could."[7] No one before Burge had succeeded in tiring the Kid out: not in a 30-rounder with Soto, a 50-rounder with another Burge, nor 55- and 77-round bouts with Siddons. A 20-rounder was a veritable stroll in the park for the Kid. All the while, Burge's midsection and chest were beginning to show severe punishment, looking red, bruised, and battered. Lavigne's strategy was mounting its intended toll.

Near the beginning of the fifth, the Kid landed a vicious right hand under Burge's heart. "Dick clinched and held on," noted Benton. "He was hurt. He would not break as the referee shouted,

'Don't hold Burge.' He had to repeat his order and got up as though to enter the ring. The referee warned Dick not to repeat his violation of his orders. Burge most of the time was cool and clever but Lavigne would not stop his fast assaults. The more Dick jabbed him the harder the Kid fought and he showed not the least sign of tiring. The sound of the gong was much welcomed by the Englishman, for he still felt that heart punch."[8]

In the sixth round Lavigne got tagged by a hard right hand from Burge that nearly toppled him. Throughout the round Burge "had so much the better of the fighting that cries of 'Bravo Dick!' were frequent," wrote the *New York World*.[9] The next three rounds were marked by steady fighting from both men. Lavigne tucked his chin to his chest and bore in without caution,

George "Kid" Lavigne - Courtesy of Antiquities of the Prize Ring

not caring how many times he got nailed by Burge, who was backpedalling and jabbing defensively. The Kid got the best of the rallies although midway through the seventh Burge caught him square on the nose. "No one ever hit me as hard on the nose," Lavigne recalled years later. "I had to guess where my corner was at the finish and I steered to it by the voice of my handlers." "I see three fighters," he told his trainer Michael 'Dad' Butler, "What shall I do?" "Hit the fellow in the middle and keep after him," was Butler's advice.[10]

The Kid Takes Control

Lavigne redoubled his efforts in the 10th. "The Kid rushed the Briton against the ropes," recalled Benton, "and then fought him all over the ring sustaining but little damage in return. Eventually the

English champion sent his right heavily to the Kid's ear and it shook him up. The Kid smiled and went after Burge in a second."[11] The next three rounds saw Lavigne gaining steadily. "In the thirteenth," recalled the Kid, "he came out evidently under instructions to do or die. He started a red hot offensive. I was feeling stronger than when the fight opened. The crowd stood up on their seats yelling like mad. I broke then for a minute and let him shoot his bolt."[12] So much for the rule of not applauding during the rounds.

The *New York World* described the effects of both fighters' damages when it reported, "[Burge's] chest and ribs had assumed a lobster hue. Lavigne's eyes were by this time swelling from the frequency of Burge's stops."[13] The *World* continued: "Lavigne started his lightening rushes in the fourteenth round with the same strength as at first and continued to land with sickening regularity upon Burge's bruised and bleeding body."[14] The Kid, noted Benton, "had punched all the strength out of the English champion."

In the 16th, Lavigne caught Burge on the side of the head with a hard blow and Dick hit the floor . . . a clean knock-down. He got up groggy; the Kid hammered away, and down went Burge again. Lavigne pounded Dick's body hard again. Burge was in desperate trouble as the gong saved him at the end of the round. At the start of the 17th Burge had barely risen from his stool when the Kid was on him pounding away on his ribs. "Lavigne's furious onslaught was ceaseless," noted the venerable English *Sportsman*, "and it was quite evident that he could stand against it little longer. About half-way through Burge went weaker than ever and Lavigne landed a right-hander on the chin, which drove his antagonist to the boards. Dick managed to scramble to his feet, but Lavigne was in waiting for him, and as the Englishman faced the music Lavigne met him with another stinging punch on the jaw, which not only made Dick renew acquaintance with the boards again, but left him limp as a rag."[15] And then came the end. "Referee Angle quietly called out, 'That's enough: he is finished,' while Burge was gamely trying to pull his paralyzed body up by the ropes."[16] The Kid was the undisputed champion of the world.

The *London Sporting Life* brusquely summarized the end without a nod to Lavigne when it wrote, "He was not technically out, but it is very certain that the next pass would have been a sleep producer . . . the greatest of certainties that has ever been known for some time was upset." The *Sportsman* was more generous with honors to the Kid when it stated, "Burge had done great things in his time, and in this, the hour of defeat, he may console himself with assurance that in Lavigne he met one of the most remarkable boxers ever seen in a ring."[17] While the English sports were gravely disappointed in the outcome they left the club sated with the experience of having witnessed one of the greatest battles in the pugilistic history of England.

A cable dispatch from London of unknown origin was later quoted by Lavigne: "After Dick's head cleared a bit, tears rolled down his cheeks, and he cried like a child. Other strong men wept with him. All England mourned the defeat of Burge but all who saw his colors lowered said that the victor was the greatest fighting machine England had seen in action."[18] Fitzpatrick later concurred when he said, "Although it was a big surprise to everyone, nevertheless they cheered Lavigne to the echo. They liked the Kid, those Englishmen, and they marveled at his victory over their idol."[19] Acceptance of the grievous loss was evidenced in many ways however. "The English in the printed record of the National Sporting Club," recalled Robert Edgren, "took to themselves a slight consolation for the defeat of their champion. Lavigne was born and bred in Michigan, but after he whipped Burge the English writers called him "the French-Canadian."[20] No nods to America there.

There was more to the prize than the claim of world's champion. A great deal of money changed hands, and some that should have, did not. The purse was split, $2,500 going to Lavigne and $1,000 to Burge. Lavigne of course earned the side bet of $2,500. Then there was the matter of the betting. As Lavigne was leaving the arena he was approached by the fellow whose wager he had taken for 100 at ringside. The gentleman shook the Kid's hand in congratulation. "And here's your wager lad, which you jolly well won," he said as he pressed money into Lavigne's hands. Looking at it Lavigne saw that it was 100 English pounds worth $500. "Here," he called. "Haven't you made a mistake?" "I made a terrible mistake in betting on Burge," was the reply.[21] Fitzpatrick had wagered the entire purse as well, assuming he was betting in dollars only to be quite surprised to find the payoff was five times the amount.

All told, if Lavigne had lost, he and Fitz would have been liable for almost $40,000 or nearly one million dollars in today's money! "Fitzpatrick, telling the story," noted Robert Edgren, "declared that he went up to the dressing room with Lavigne without a word and sat down and wiped the cold sweat from his brow for fifteen minutes while he thought over all the horrible things that might have happened to him if Lavigne had lost. After which, of course, he went down and let everybody pay him off in pounds as if it were all a matter of course."[22] Not all the debts owed American bettors were paid. B. H. Benton recalled that many English "welched" on the money they owed and that several club members and favored guests "ran out." Benton was there on newspaper business and with persistence and time he collected on his winnings.

Lavigne and Fitzpatrick stayed in London for a time basking in the Kid's triumph and painting the town. Fitz recalled that everywhere they went after the fight people followed the Kid. "One night," said Sam, "the Kid was dining in a prominent hotel and the eats he put away made one fellow's eyes stick out. He walked over to Lavigne's table and patting him on the shoulder remarked: 'My word but you eat quite a bit for such a little fellow!' Lavigne grinned; then looked up at his admirer, chirped: 'I'm not as little as I look from the outside.'"[23] The two left five weeks later for the U.S. The steamship St. Louis arrived in New York on July 13 bringing the champion and the world's lightweight championship back to America to a cheering throng of well-wishers.

CHAPTER 17

Boxing's Quest for Legality and Legitimacy

In post-Civil War America violence needed outlets. In the West it was marked often by armed conflict between cow punchers, miners, gamblers, and the law of the tin star. It was a time and a place struggling for stability and a semblance of order. In the South, racial violence was the outlet of the day for common folk and dueling for the landed gentry. In the industrialized Northeast, violence took a different form. As population density increased tension in the closely knitted patterns of daily urban life, people there grew less tolerant of violent outbreaks marked by the crack of a gunshot. "The notion grew that violence could be accepted only if it were controlled and regulated, and if it resulted in an outcome not directly harmful to society," wrote Michael T. Isenberg in *John L. Sullivan And His America*. "Instead, forms of surrogate violence, in which aggressive behavior could be acted out in a setting of rules and equity became more and more popular."[1] Prizefighting and other violent sports would fill this need.

Boxing in particular was well suited for this role. The vast majority of prizefighters of the time came from the lower orders of society, usually recent immigrants. While their sport was struggling for legitimacy, the fighters appealed widely to men of their station who filled the factories and saloons in cities across America. And the saloons played an important part in the rise of the cult of masculinity in the last two decades of the century. The saloon was the antidote to the strictly regulated efficiency of the industrial factory. Drinking and sport, particularly prizefighting, became closely connected. Where there was drinking and sport there was also gambling. It was the growing middle class in America that would seek to regulate all three of these "vices" that they considered the bane of the commoner. As boxing evolved it would not only have rules to regulate what happened within the ring but it would also be subject to laws that threatened to destroy it from without.

The Governance of Fighting

It was thought that the introduction of gloved fights would soften the resistance to prizefighting yet as Guy Deghy put it in *Noble and Manly: The History of the National Sporting Club,* "The suspicion that two men bashing each other, with or without gloves, were not engaged in a sporting contest but were fighting in good earnest and thereby committing a misdemeanor, was not easily eradicated from the official mind."[2] Boxing in England had been illegal since about 1760 just after the fall of Jack Broughton. "In fact, boxing in Britain has never been declared legal, but by 1914, partly due to its popularity, its position was secure."[3]

On the other side of the Atlantic boxing got off to a rocky start. It was introduced by British sailors during the Revolutionary War. According to Michael Isenberg, "With independence the sport was made illegal immediately, not only for its violence but also because of its British associations."[4] As of 1880, boxing in the U.S. was still illegal in all 38 states. Jeffrey T. Sammons noted in *Boxing's Legal Status*, "As the frequency of prizefights increased, various states moved beyond general and sometimes vague statutes concerning assault and enacted laws that expressly forbade fistfights . . . Boxing thus took a course of evasion by bringing a greater appearance of order to the sport through changes in rules and by relocation to more lenient environments. Matches were frequently held in remote backwaters and were not openly publicized in order that the fighters might avoid arrest; barges were also used as fight venues because they could be located in waters outside U.S. legal jurisdiction and fights could be held unimpeded."[5] In the waning years of the century a conviction for prizefighting in most states was punishable by a $1,000 fine and up to two years in prison.

But beyond the objections to violence, boxing's reputation was tainted by its associations, particularly to gambling, gangs, and the urban underworld. Despite its growing popularity under the more respectable Queensberry rules which accommodated the social and cultural needs of many Americans, forces to the contrary were at play. During the 1890s, "Purity Crusades," which were reform-minded movements of Victorian ethic, worked to ban boxing throughout the

U.S. Boxing's close connection to gambling, often referred to as a "barnacle of sport," was the nexus of corruption that would plague the game for decades to come and hinder its quest for legitimacy and ultimately, legality.

Isenberg summarized gambling's impact thusly: "The association between prizefighting and gambling was close, perhaps even necessary. Some boxers, if they had the money, bet on themselves; some became specialists in 'throwing' fights. Their 'backers' were driven primarily by the profit motive, and some were none too scrupulous in the means they used to achieve these ends. The smell of corruption produced by gambling was consonant with the sport. Indeed, it was a fine question whether the prizefight existed for the gambler or vice versa."[6] It was from this moral pit that boxing slowly clawed its way to daylight over the next 30 years.

The Rise of the Athletic Club

The dilemma was one of conflict; boxing was becoming more socially acceptable yet it was still an unlawful activity. As described by Adam J. Pollack in *John L. Sullivan: The Career of the First Gloved Heavyweight Champion*, "Boxers could be convicted criminals for engaging in their professions and simultaneously be public heroes."[7] This put tremendous pressure on local and state authorities to walk a fine line between bending to public opinion while upholding legal statutes, all the while cognizant of the economic windfall that boxing was beginning to provide their cities. As Jeffrey Sammons wrote, "State regulation became the middle ground between outright prohibition and unfettered legalization."[8] The solution from the early 1890s until after the turn of the century was two-fold: create a distinction between fighting and "gloved exhibitions of skill," also described as "sparring contests," and, sanction these exhibitions only in the confines of an athletic club adhering to strict rules.

There were four centers of boxing in the U.S. as the 1890s unfolded: New Orleans, Chicago, San Francisco, and New York. Athletic clubs were not, per se, a product of the 1890s as the first in the country was the San Francisco Olympic Club established in 1860. New York had its first in 1868, New Orleans in 1872, and the Chicago Athletic Association was formed in 1890. But the decade of the 90s saw a proliferation of clubs in major cities across America due in part to the introduction of laws in several states that allowed gloved sparring contests. It was New Orleans that led the way and became, arguably, the center of fistiana in the U.S and the world in the early part of the decade.

"To travel to this stretch of boxing history is to go south, and catch a glimpse of the sport's modern version as it struggles to emerge," noted Melissa Haley in *Storm of Blows*. "Here in New Orleans, bourgeois Victorian men preoccupied with virtue, order, and 'scientific' sport will openly adopt and attempt to legitimize an unforgiving, lower-class pastime. They will briefly succeed in shedding pugilism's seamy stigma, but the move from saloon backroom to refined athletic club to consumer spectacle will prove to be risky and tumultuous."[9] It began here with a few private athletic clubs taking up amateur boxing, then later holding professional fights with gloves under the Queensberry rules.

In early 1890 influential supporters of boxing pressured the New Orleans city council to permit sparring exhibitions. In March the council added a loophole to circumvent the 1882 statute forbidding personal combat with fists; it permitted all regularly chartered athletic clubs to hold gloved contests, noting the distinction between these contests and prizefights. The local paper, the *Times-Picayune*, claimed the distinction was deceptive and asked Governor Nichols to work with the legislature to strengthen the statute. They did strengthen the law but a few legislators sympathetic to boxing's plight were successful in codifying the loophole developed by the New Orleans city council into the state statute. Louisiana thus became the first state to legalize boxing. As a result, clubs throughout New Orleans began staging prizefights and several newly chartered clubs came into existence to host boxing events.[10]

This left the local police authorities as the sole arbiter of when a "gloved exhibition" crossed the line, becoming a prizefight. In effect they became secondary referees as they could stop a bout if they felt the fighters were slugging with intent to injure or knock the other man out. They could also stop a bout if one man was injured or on the verge of being knocked out. "However, because the law was left open to interpretation, the police had a great deal of discretion, and what action or lack of action they took often was a reflection of their own feelings about the sport or the fighters, or a result of the local political climate," wrote Adam Pollack. "They could stop the bouts and either arrest the combatants or let them go, or allow the slugging to continue until someone was knocked out and arrest them afterwards, or do nothing. In many jurisdictions, as long as the men were boxing with gloves according to the Queensberry rules, they did not offend the law against prizefighting."[11]

Legal Intervention

And so it went in New Orleans until early in 1894 when the attorney general for the state of Louisiana appealed to the state supreme court regarding a suit against the Olympic Club, the city's preeminent athletic club. The suit alleged the club was engaged in promoting and staging "prizefights," illegal under state law. Again the Olympic Club prevailed but Attorney General Cunningham would not give up, pursuing an angle regarding inadmissible testimony. His persistence paid off and the court ordered a new trial. In the meantime fate would intervene from the ring of another New Orleans athletic club.

On December 14, 1894 Kid Lavigne met Andy Bowen at the Auditorium Athletic Club for what was billed as the American lightweight title. The next morning Bowen died as a result of striking his head on the boards of the unpadded ring surface. Bowen's death had a profound effect on the Supreme Court's decision just a few months later. ". . . Justice Samuel D. McEnery, speaking for the court, ruled: 'Fighting in the arena of the [Olympic] Club . . . is prizefighting, and no other description can be given to it,'" noted Jeffrey Sammons.[12] New Orleans's stay atop the boxing world was short lived as the high court's decision effectively ended prizefighting in the state. Lavigne's bitter sweet triumph over Bowen would prove to be the last legal, professional bout held in New Orleans in the 19th century. Nearly a year went by without a match but although still technically illegal, bouts continued to be fought over the next several years in New Orleans. Boxing in the south still had a heartbeat.

Other states began to follow suit with Louisiana, allowing sparring exhibitions under Queensberry rules in bona fide athletic clubs. The state of New York was a case in point. New York had criminalized "prizefighting" in 1859, making it a misdemeanor to engage in, arrange for, or help a fighter train for a prizefight. On September 1, 1896, the Horton Law became effective in New York which expanded on the existing law in two ways. It added to the definition of misdemeanor to include public or private sparring exhibitions at which an admission fee was charged or received. But it also provided a loophole in *New York Laws*, 1896, Chapter 301, Section 458, allowing "sparring exhibitions with gloves of not less than five ounces held by an incorporated athletic association in a building leased by it for athletic purposes only for at least one year, or in a building owned and occupied by such association." Just like in New Orleans, the new law encouraged the formation of several new athletic clubs in the late 1890s.

However, also like New Orleans, New York's "legalization of boxing" was short lived when on August 31, 1900 the Lewis Law repealed the Horton Law. Ironically, it was signed into law by then Governor of New York, Teddy Roosevelt, himself an avid boxing fan and amateur boxer in his college days at Harvard. The chief objection to the Lewis Law was that it may wipe the Horton Law from the statutes. In the words of Assemblyman Lewis, namesake of the law, "If the law permitting prizefighting is to remain on our books, then in heaven's name let us place dueling also on the statute books. When you challenge a man to a duel you probably have good cause for it, but there is no good reason for prizefighting, except to pound on one another for money."[13] In fact, while "prizefighting" was illegal under the Lewis Law it did not accomplish the purging of the Horton Law from the statutes that it sought. It also left several loopholes including one that allowed boxing matches to take place only between members of private clubs. It was a small obstacle that was overcome by fighters obtaining membership, albeit temporarily, in the clubs in which they fought. The Lewis Law did have a chilling effect on New York boxing until the promoters found ways to circumvent the new law's porous provisions.

With tighter restrictions and outright prohibitions against boxing in the South, East and Midwest, the sport found a more agreeable climate in the frontier states of the West. Fewer championship bouts were fought in New York, Pennsylvania, and Illinois with many non-championship contests limited to six-round affairs. The epicenter of fistic concerns, particularly championship bouts, shifted to California and the somewhat lawless mining towns of Nevada. San Francisco was quickly becoming the boxing capital of the world.[14]

It was another famous fight that would stir a national controversy and further galvanize many against the fight game. The incomparable African American fighter, Jack Johnson, had taken the heavyweight title from Tommy Burns in 1908. Johnson completely dominated the division and arrogantly flaunted his success at every turn. He liked the company of white women, a serious taboo of the time. White America wanted him stopped and called for retired heavyweight champion, Jim Jeffries, to lace up the gloves once more and put an end to Johnson's reign.   On Independence Day, 1910, Johnson met Jeffries in Reno, Nevada for a scheduled 45 round bout, an unusually long bout at the time, and one which no other state in the union would allow.

Johnson destroyed Jeffries winning almost every round while taunting the ex-champ throughout. Jeffries' corner men stopped the bout in the 15th round. The black population of America celebrated ecstatically, while the white population turned to violence, engaging in rioting and killing. Historian Randy Roberts wrote, "Never before has a single event caused such widespread rioting. Not until the assassination of Dr. Martin Luther King, Jr., would another event elicit a similar reaction. The fight and its aftermath led reform groups to intensify their effort to push legislation that would abolish boxing."[15]

Undeterred by the backlash, the state of New York passed yet another piece of legislation designed to increase oversight while at the same time easing the way for sparring matches as opposed to prizefights. It was the Frawley Law of 1911 that created the New York State Athletic Commission, known at the time as the "Boxing Commission," the first of its kind in the U.S., placing matches under state control. The law provided for 10 round sparring contests with eight-ounce gloves. In an attempt to reduce corruption in the outcome of matches the law also deemed that any bout not won by knockout would be declared no-decision. This placed the burden on newspaper reporters to decide on the outcome of fights, referred to as "newspaper decisions," and simply shifted the possibility for corruption from boxing judges to newsmen.[16]

A mere six years later the tables were turned again, as a direct reaction to the death of middleweight Stephen "Young" McDonald in Albany on January 30, 1917. McDonald was engaged in his first professional bout and was felled by a right hand blow to the heart from William "Toddy" Hicks in the second minute of the first round. He staggered against the ropes and slumped to the canvas dying instantly while the New York State Boxing Commissioner, several state legislators, and his own father looked on from ringside. McDonald, 22, had gone against the will of his father who had forbid him to engage in the contest.[17] He was arrested on manslaughter but was cleared a week later of the charge. Governor Whitman supported the passage of the Slater bill in May to become effective on November 15, 1917 that repealed the Frawley Law and outlawed boxing again. It would remain illegal for nearly three years.

It would be a confluence of historical events that set the stage for boxing's final conquest of legality. It was around the time of Jack Dempsey's triumph over the giant, Jess Willard, in 1919 for the heavyweight championship that marked the turning point. The country was changing. The Treaty of Versailles was signed that year officially ending the war between Germany and the Allied Powers. The 18th amendment to the U.S. Constitution was ratified instituting prohibition. American women won the right to vote in 1920. Historians

James Roberts and Alexander Skutt suggested that boxing "began to shed its unsavory reputation when influential people like former president Theodore Roosevelt recommended controlled fisticuffs to promote health and fitness. This view, as well as growing public acceptance of the sport as conducted on a professional level, led to its legalization in many states."[18]

And once again it would be New York that would lead the way. In 1920 state senator James J. Walker introduced a bill to legalize professional boxing in New York. The bill called for the state to license everyone connected to the game including fighters, managers, promoters, referees, and judges, supervised by a board of three state commissioners. On April 25, 1920, Governor Alfred E. Smith signed the bill into law. "The Walker Law proved to be a critical turning point for boxing in the United States," noted Robert Rodriguez in *The Regulation of Boxing*. "It became a model for the legalization of the sport in other states, where similar legislation creating athletic commissions was passed."[19]

The long fight was over. While boxing was not universally accepted by all Americans, it had run the gantlet, being tempered with gloves and new rules, and in the end, professionalized by state athletic commissions. It had fought and slowly won the battle for legitimacy as well, for now that it was legal, boxers could take their hard earned place among other heroes in the pantheon of sport.

CHAPTER 18

Non-Title Interludes

Returning to America triumphant, the Kid was the toast of the fistic world. The best fighters in his class were clamoring to get a match with the Saginaw wonder. Jack Everhardt was waiting in the wings to challenge the Kid to a rematch upon his return from Europe. Charles McKeever, a Philadelphia welterweight, had been trying to get a bout with Lavigne for some time to no avail. McKeever finally got the nod as the Kid always preferred to match fists with someone he hadn't fought before. A deal was consummated even before Lavigne and Fitzpatrick had returned from London. It would be a six-round, non-title bout scheduled for July 20, 1896 at Madison Square Garden. Lavigne was now in a position to dictate when, where, and against whom he would risk his coveted world title. But against the men in his first three fights stateside, he would not put his title on the line as all of them were well above the 133- pound standard.

McKeever was not an unknown by any means although it was early in his career when he challenged Lavigne. He had 14 bouts under his belt having faced an impressive array of top lightweights of the time. Most notably, he defeated Owen Ziegler, Stanton Abbott, and Arthur Valentine and drew with Wilmington Jack Daly, and Jack Everhardt. But his crowning achievement was to do something only a few could claim; he defeated Young Griffo in a 20-round contest. "McKeever is not inclined to boast," wrote the *New York World*, "but he appears to believe he can outpoint the conqueror of England's greatest lightweight boxer, just as he polished off Mr. Griffo."[1] And who could argue? While McKeever didn't dominate his match with Griffo, he used the same strategy as Lavigne did against him; rushing, chasing, and pommeling every time he could catch the slippery one, round after round. In the 12th Griffo had his man in trouble but lacked the power punch that would have ended it in his favor. McKeever scored often enough to give him an edge going into the final round which he won handily by getting to Griffo's head and body repeatedly. "As it was he gave the Australian more punishment than Lavigne administered," noted the *Boston Daily Globe*, "and when referee Hurst decided in McKeever's favor there were few if any dissenting voices.[2]

There would be no referee, however, in this limited affair between Lavigne and McKeever. It was agreed, under orders from the New York police, that it would be a no-decision match with the merits of the men left to the opinions of the spectators.

Charles McKeever
- Courtesy of BoxRec

Given the effects of police oversight, the nature of the fight would prove to be more of a scientific bout, short on knock-out blows but lively in every other way. It was also short on time as the rounds, according to the *Boston Globe*, were two minutes in length.[3] There were 3,000 in attendance at the Garden when the two men entered the ring shortly past 10:00 p.m.

"The science looked on the surface to be a trifle on the side of the Philadelphian, who was heavier, taller, and longer in the reach than Lavigne," reported the *New York World*. "But a man in the top gallery's remotest corner could have picked out the fighter [Lavigne] without the aid of opera glasses."[4] That fighter did what he always did in the ring; he forced the fighting from the beginning to the end of each round, however, he did so with some reserve, knowing the authorities may stop the bout if he began throwing bombs at his opponent. Such was the nature of boxing in a time when going to jail for crossing the fine line was nearly guaranteed. The two mixed it up in the first round, both landing with regularity. "But there was not that force in the blows that was yearned for by the sports," noted the *Globe*.

In the second round it became apparent that the Kid's hitting ability was superior to McKeever's and that had he been less restricted he could have done more damage. In the third and fourth he bullied McKeever around the ring although taking some good counters in the exchanges. At the end of the fifth, "they mixed things and exchanged swings until both were blowing like grampuses."[5] In the beginning of the final round, McKeever caught the Kid with a hard body blow to which Lavigne responded with an attack and the two began to slug it out in earnest which delighted the crowd. McKeever did some excellent infighting with his fans shouting his name believing he was doing damage to the Kid. "Lavigne, however, was not hurt," wrote the *Globe*, "and laughed heartily when it was time to shake hands."[6]

One sports fan that day lamented the poor reception of the world champion in his first bout back in the states. He saw it foreshadowing the decline of the fistic arts. "Old Dooney Harris, in his day, a great fighter," wrote the *World*, "weighed up the situation with tears in his eyes. 'Here's a lad just come back from lickin' an English champion,' he sighed with a shake of the head. 'Just won a fight which was a credit to him and his country, and nobody knows or cares that he is in town. I tell you fightin's dead; more's the pity.'"[7] And for the record, Dooney Harris was far from a "great fighter" in his day. He was a heavyweight who lost his only officially recorded bout, a four round scrap with Denver Ed Smith in 1884. And yet in his early days back in 1872, Dooney was touted by the *New York Herald* as "the darkly mysterious Dooney and the savant of all pugilism."[8] But clearly Dooney was a big picture guy who saw the fight game struggling for legitimacy and survival in a time when the law was doing everything it could to shut it down.

McKeever got his brief chance to show what he had against the champ and acquitted himself well, however, in the opinion of the majority of the spectators Lavigne would have won a bout of 20 rounds.[9] McKeever would get another shot the following year. Next up was the Kid's second bout with Jack Everhardt which would also go down as one of the greatest fights of the '90s and one in which Lavigne would be tested from start to finish.

The Second Go with Everhardt

Talk of a rematch with Jack Everhardt began to surface in early August just a few weeks after Lavigne's no-decision scrap with McKeever. Since their first fight in May of 1895 where the Kid was victorious in 20 rounds, both fighters had remained busy. Lavigne fought three of his greatest fights in that span; drawing with Young Griffo, defeating Joe Wolcott in a blood bath, and knocking out the Iron Man of England, Dick Burge, for the world title. The Kid was at the zenith of his career.

Drawing of Agnes Lavigne, Billy Lavigne, Sam Fitzpatrick, and the "Kid" at training quarters in Saginaw – Courtesy of *Police Gazette*

Everhardt, a native of New Orleans now fighting out of Philadelphia, had drawn with Owen Ziegler, another tough Philadelphia lightweight, knocked out Horace Leeds, and twice fought draws with Young Griffo in 6- and 20-round bouts. Lavigne chuckled at the distinction of the "Philadelphia lightweight." "That was a joke expression of those days," the Kid later recalled. "A 'Philadelphia lightweight' differed from those of other cities in that they were really welterweights or middleweights who fought at catch-weights, but called themselves lightweights."[10] "Catch-weight" was a term used to describe a weight between two recognized weight divisions mutually agreed upon by two boxers prior to a match.

Make no mistake about it; Jack Everhardt was one of the very top lightweights, or light-welterweights, of the 1890s. He had fought 24 bouts and a few exhibitions losing only twice, once to Lavigne and once to Andy Bowen in 85 rounds. He was fast, rugged, employed an effective jab, and was a splendid defensive boxer, all qualities one would need to have a prayer against the Saginaw mauler. He knew what to expect from Lavigne. In his first go with the Kid, he may have mistakenly employed a strategy that cost him the fight. He had been determined to move and jab, letting the Kid punch himself out and then take over in the late rounds to get the win. It didn't work as the Kid had more than enough stamina to maintain his unrelenting onslaught for the full 20 rounds. The second fight was billed for 25 rounds and the question became, would Everhardt assume the extra five rounds may be what he needed to perfect that strategy or would he have learned like so many others had that the Kid was virtually indefatigable?

"Everhardt, moreover, is jealous of the Kid," noted the *Logansport (Indiana) Pharos*, "and is eager to wrest his laurels from him."[11] Having been so close before, Jack was confident he would gain the upset in the return match. "I have felt that with proper time to condition, which I did not have at that go, I can certainly win from him on points," explained Everhardt. "But if he wins this time I can have no excuses; it simply will be because he is the better man."[12]

For this fight Everhardt insisted on 138 pounds as he knew he'd have trouble getting below that. The *Milwaukee Evening Wisconsin* noted on the issue of weight: "Everhardt and Lavigne are to box at 138 pounds, a weight which seems to indicate that it is only a question of time when the Michigan man will outgrow the lightweights and flock with the welters."[13] A quick glimpse at Lavigne's recent bouts begged for a different conclusion. He was outweighed in his previous two fights with Burge and McKeever yet he continued to fight at the true lightweight standard. He seemed to be more effective fighting lightweights or welterweights with the hardened stamina of his leaner, more chiseled physique at, or just under, 133 pounds. Lavigne, in Everhardt, would yet again fight a man heavier than he, this time a real Philadelphia lightweight with southern roots.

So was it a fight for the world lightweight championship now held by Lavigne? Sources disagree on this point. The agreed upon weight limit for the contest was 138 pounds, five pounds above the American lightweight limit. Remember that just prior to Lavigne's fight with Dick Burge for the world title in June of 1896 the English had raised the lightweight limit to 138 even though the American standard remained at 133. Lavigne's record according to BoxRec and Cyber Boxing Zone identifies it as a world lightweight title bout at the 138 pound limit; however newspapers of the time and Lavigne himself disagreed. "Last night's contest was advertised as being for the 'lightweight championship of the world,'" reported the *Daily Iowa Capital*, "but the weights at which the men fought preclude any such conclusion."[14] And Lavigne agreed with the *Capital's* assessment when he wrote in 1928, "The championship was not involved, as we were fighting at 138 ringside, the lowest Everhardt could do. But it would have meant a loss of prestige to have a decision against me."[15] Indeed it would have as Lavigne was yet to taste defeat in his ten years in the roped square.

The fight was put together by Richard K. Fox, proprietor of the *Police Gazette*, and was to be held at the small, exclusive Bohemian Club in New York on October 27, 1896. The purse was $3,500 and the bout was to be the first championship match ever held at the club, if indeed it was a title match. The Bohemian Club, reported to be the American counterpart to the famed National Sporting Club in London, accommodated only 650 spectators. The promoter, Charlie Genslinger, ran it like the British version, with the ushers in hammer-tail suits and the price of seats from $10 on up to $50 at ringside. Few "dead-heads" got in to see the fight and as many as 5,000 sports waited outside for round-by-round news of the bout.[16] Betting odds were set at 10-to-7 in favor of Lavigne.

A fight of this magnitude also garnered police attention. Police Commissioner Andrews, Inspector Varley, and 25 policemen in civilian clothes were in attendance to ensure compliance with the Horton Law, which had recently become effective in the state of New York on September 1, 1896. The law created a quasi-legal allowance for boxing matches to be held under specific conditions in bona fide athletic clubs. This was the first high-profile bout to be held in the state since the law changed and the police in attendance made it clear they would "put a stop to bouts if the contestants became at all rude."[17]

Honest John Kelly was the third man in the ring. Lavigne was accompanied by Sam Fitzpatrick, Paddy Gorman and Sammy Kelly. Everhardt's seconds were Charley White, Caspar Leon, and Harry Black. Lavigne emerged first at 10:25 p.m. Everhardt kept Lavigne and the crowd waiting for ten minutes before making his way to the ring. "As they sat in their corners they seemed to be trained to the hour," stated the *Police Gazette*. "His [Everhardt's] unconcern and easy manner were in marked contrast with the appearance of Lavigne, whose face was drawn, pale and prematurely aged from constant training and whose glance shot nervously around the house. It was plain that the Kid, like a mettlesome horse, hungered at the issue and chafed at the delay. Lavigne had the wrinkles in his forehead and the troubled look of a man who is about to study an intricate problem. It is Lavigne's habitual expression in the ring, and every really great, dogged and conscientious fighter wears it."[18]

Just before the men shook hands Lavigne's party registered a bet of $5,000 to $2,500 on their man. It was 10:40 p.m. when the bell sounded to begin round one. Uncharacteristic of Lavigne, he began round one by sparring lightly, carefully measuring his man. Everhardt put his straight left in the Kid's face a few times and that was all it took; Lavigne rushed Jack and started his barrage of crushing body blows. By the end of the first round the pattern for the entire fight was set; the Kid made for the body relentlessly and Everhardt tried for the head fending off his attacker as best he could with movement and jabs. "Lavigne had the best of the round, his drives, swings, hooks and punches, being terrific in their force," noted the *Gazette*. "As the round ended the question was on everybody's lips, 'How long will Everhardt stand it?' For the next six rounds Lavigne rushed his man furiously, giving him not a moment's rest, and banging with right and left like an animated battering ram."[19]

It was not quite as one-sided in the early rounds as the *Gazette* would suggest. Everhardt was countering effectively with straight lefts to the face and while Jack was peppering the Kid, the punches were more jab-like than hard punches. "After the first few rounds," reported the *Detroit Free Press*, "he [Lavigne] said to Fitzpatrick: 'I'm all right. I can get him before it's over. I'm just waiting to finish him.'"[20] Both men bled from the mouth at the end of the second, Lavigne from a straight left and Everhardt from a left hook. In the third, Everhardt picked up the pace fighting at closer range and ending the round with a flourish of blows.

In the fourth stanza Lavigne was back on the attack the second the bell rang. "With a minute to go in the round," recalled the *New York World*, "Lavigne sent out a straight left that caught Everhardt squarely on the chin. It staggered him, and like a flash the Kid brought over a right on the jaw. Everhardt's knees wobbled, and 'It's all over' was the cry that arose from all parts of the house."[21] Two punches later, the bell saved Jack. In the fifth, Everhardt changed tactics and instead of trying occasionally to go toe-to-toe with the Kid he fought "parlor" style, keeping his distance and relying on more movement to slip punches while countering with numerous jabs. Midway through round six, Everhardt scored heavily but paid for it. "Everhardt landed a right that tore the skin from Lavigne's forehead," wrote the *Boston Daily Globe*. "The Kid was furious. He rushed in, landed a right on the head and drove both hands on the body. It was a terrific pace and they were fast at it when the bell sounded."[22]

Lavigne was trying to finish it in the seventh. He rushed his man and landed right and left on body and head four times in succession but Jack fought back landing with uppercuts. In the eighth round the Kid again staggered Everhardt with a solid right on the ear. Lavigne was fighting like a mad man and Everhardt resorted to clinching to limit the damage done. And the damage to both fighters was mounting, as in the ninth round Everhardt nearly closed the Kid's left eye with a powerful right hand. Lavigne responded with his own right to the jaw that nearly dropped Jack but he recovered quickly. Near the end of the tenth frame, Lavigne connected with a fierce left uppercut that had his man in serious trouble but before he could finish it the gong saved Jack.

"The rounds from the twelfth to the eighteenth were the best of the evening," described the *Police Gazette*, "Everhardt waking up with the aid of a little stimulant, and mixing it up so vigorously that his partisans began to think he might yet wear Lavigne out."[23] But at the close of the seventeenth Jack was showing signs of wear and extreme fatigue shuffling to his corner on wobbly legs. "He drank from a small black bottle too frequently to please his backers," continued the *Gazette*. It was well known that several pugilists of the time drank alcohol before and during fights, Young Griffo perhaps being the best example. But the effect of alcohol on an athletic contest of endurance was short lived leaving the contestant in worse shape in a few short rounds. Other concoctions were also imbibed including a stimulant potion popular in the late 1800s which included a mixture of strychnine, brandy and cocaine. Now this was a powerful additive that could boost performance for several rounds. It's quite possible that Everdhardt's small black bottle held such a substance.

As the fight moved to the 20th round, Honest John Kelly was separating the clinched fighters more often shooting a disapproving glance at Everhardt as he did. "Once more I had the satisfaction of noting an ebbing of my foe's strength," recalled Lavigne. "I felt this distinctly in the clinches. There were five more rounds to go. I was satisfied. Once more my own endurance and strength had carried me through a fearful pace, and I retained my full power."[24] This was the Kid's signature throughout his career. If a bout made it to the 20th round, he was still fighting with the same relentless fury that marked the first few rounds. No little black bottle was needed. His drive came from a place deep within.

In the 22nd round, "Lavigne put in three straight lefts and followed them with a right and a left," wrote the *Police Gazette*. "Then he crossed Everhardt viciously with his right. Everhardt reeled like a drunken man and the crowd cried: 'He's going.' But no; up he came again." The Kid threw a terrific right cross and Everhardt was tottering again, but again he stayed upright and fought gamely to the round's end. The beginning of the end came in the next round.

"'Right on top of him,' whispered Fitzpatrick as I started up for the 23rd round," Lavigne remembered. [25] Midway through the round Everhardt missed with a right and the Kid caught him with a monstrous left, spinning Jack completely around and almost flooring him. Somehow Everhardt survived and his ring skills got him to the end of the round where he was blazing away toe-to-toe with the Kid as the gong sounded. This was the most desperate time of the fight for both combatants. Everhardt was severely weakened from the pace of the fight and absorbing an unending fusillade of sledge hammer body blows. "Everhardt's body looked from the waist like a boiled lobster," reported the *New York World*.[26] Lavigne was bleeding from the mouth, the left ear that had been so badly damaged in the Walcott fight was ballooning again, and both of his eyes were nearly closed from walking into Everhardt's jabs all evening.

"'Did you see that punch?' queried Honest John Kelly of friends at the ringside in between the 23rd and 24th rounds. 'I thought it had broken poor Jack's neck. I'm not so sure of it now. That missed swing had him in a peculiarly dangerous position and Lavigne's punch landed in just such a way as to figuratively rip Everhardt's head from his shoulders.'"[27]

It was apparent at the start of the 24th round that the big left by the Kid had taken a toll on Everhardt as Jack weakly met Lavigne's rushes. Lavigne knew it too. He fired lefts and rights almost nonstop to body and head. The Kid had taken a beating getting to this point in the fight and he wanted to end it badly now. His manager sensed Lavigne's desperate impatience. "Fitzpatrick's voice cut through the bedlam of sound: 'Steady Kid. Take your time.'"[28] The end came at 1 minute and 53 seconds of the round. "Everhardt couldn't get his hands up to block or counter," noted the *Detroit Free Press*. ". . . Everhardt was out on his feet, but his fighting instinct was keeping him going. Finally, the Kid swung a pile driving right to the jaw and Everhardt toppled back into the arms of the referee. Kelly signaled to the timekeeper to ring the bell and end the fight. Everhardt's seconds made a foolish roar about Kelly ending the fight with their man on his feet but Honest John smiled grimly and snapped: 'You better have him on his feet than in a coffin.'"[29]

Bloodied and nearly blind, Lavigne had stopped the Louisiana Tiger. In the dressing room after the fight he remarked to the *Police Gazette* reporter, "'By gosh,' said Lavigne, who never swears, by the way of emphasis, 'he's the toughest game I ever went against in my life . . . And can't he take a whalloping, too, the gamest I ever saw.'"[30] After a physician attended to Lavigne's battered face, he and Fitzpatrick entered the barroom of the Bohemian Club and the Kid was cheered heartily. Jack Everhardt approached and being a good sportsman shook the Kid's hand congratulating him on the victory. The fight promoter ordered champagne for everyone. "Lavigne picked his glass up, then put it down again," wrote Jack Kofoed. "'I can't drink it Sam,' he said through his puffed and bleeding lips. 'Feed it to me.' So the faithful Fitzpatrick filled a large tablespoon with champagne and poured it down the champion's throat."[31]

Adonis Calling

Who would be next for Lavigne? Several suitors were anxious to land a bout with the champ including Charles McKeever hoping for a rematch of their shortened, six-round bout in July. Also clamoring for a contest was Philadelphian larger-than-lightweight, Owen Ziegler. "'Horace Leeds is another fellow,' says one of Kid Lavigne's friends, 'who is making a terrible bluff that he is anxious for a glove contest with Lavigne,'" noted the *Milwaukee Evening Wisconsin*. "'Yet he neither fools the public nor himself when he makes such a proposition.'"[32] Leeds had been KOed by Everhardt in the 15th round of a bout earlier in the year. He was badly battered and it took physicians more than an hour to revive him. The doctors later advised him to retire from the ring. Leeds was a defensive fighter cut out of the mold of Young Griffo. The vast majority of his bouts were four- to six-rounders, with his longest being the 15 he lasted with Everhardt. There is little doubt had he landed a fight with Lavigne, he would have been cut to pieces in short order.

By mid-November details were being drawn up for a rematch with welterweight McKeever, also of Philadelphia, at the Marlboro Athletic Club in New York on December 23, 1896. The agreed upon weight was 140 pounds to accommodate McKeever at his more natural weight. This was odd as Fitzpatrick had vowed not to let the Kid fight above the 135 to 138 range again. The night of the contest, the arena was only half full and with the purse of $2,500 in jeopardy due to limited paying spectators, the bout was scrapped at the last minute.

When the McKeever bout fell through Lavigne turned to Owen Ziegler. A six-round, non-title, no-decision contest was arranged at the Quaker City Athletic Club of Philadelphia for January 11, 1897. Ziegler had fought some of the top lightweights of the time and had shown he belonged in the ring with any of them. He defeated Stanton Abbott and drew with Jack Everhardt three times in battles of 6, 6, and 20 rounds. He fought Charles McKeever three times, winning once, drawing once and losing the final one. Perhaps his most famous fight was a go in 1894 with then lightweight champion, Jack McAuliffe. The police stopped the bout after three rounds. Reports suggested that Owen was getting the best of McAuliffe and nearly had him out in the third; however, Jack had broken two small bones in his hand in the second round.

Ziegler was a wonderfully muscled pugilist with Adonis-type good looks. Lavigne described him a bit differently when he said, "Ziegler was a chunky Dutchman with the head and shoulders of a heavyweight."[33] Reports had him at between ten and fifteen pounds heavier than the Kid and lacking the conditioning that Lavigne had. Owen's last bout was with Lavigne's last contender, Jack Everhardt. Ziegler met Everhardt in a six-round, no-decision bout in Philadelphia on January 5, 1897, just six days before he and Lavigne would mix it up. Reports from several papers indicated that Everhardt had the best of it from start to finish and nearly had his man out in the fourth round. Although it was ruled a draw most people present thought Everhardt had earned the win.

The *Boston Daily Globe* weighed in with its opinion three days before the fight when it wrote, "Kid Lavigne and Owen Ziegler will meet at Philadelphia Monday night. The club might as well give Lavigne the winner's end now."[34] This one-sided summary of the fight was given by the *Washington Post:* "Lavigne had all the best of the bout, and it looked as though he could have put the Philadelphian to sleep in the first round. Before they had sparred one minute, Lavigne feinted with his right and as Ziegler attempted to duck, the Kid brought his left around with terrific force, landing squarely on Ziegler's chin. The latter sat down suddenly, and for the next four rounds he was on Queer Street."[35]

Owen Ziegler - Courtesy of BoxRec

The round-by-round, blow-by-blow description of the fight was a variation on the *Post's* report. Ziegler landed almost as many blows as Lavigne but they were not nearly as effective. Taking a pounding, Ziegler clinched and ran particularly in the fourth round when to his surprise, the Kid rushed to Owen's corner and was on top of him at the opening bell. It was more of the same in the fifth stanza when at one point Ziegler went through the ropes with a push from the Kid. The final round was tame by comparison. "Lavigne seemed satisfied to let things rest as they were," wrote the *Philadelphia Evening Bulletin*, "and Ziegler had no fight left in him."[36]

One day before Lavigne's fight with Ziegler a small-town newspaper in the Midwest made what may have been a prophetic statement about the Kid when it wrote: "An eastern paper says it is feared by the friends of Kid Lavigne, the lightweight champion, that he will go the John L. Sullivan route."[37] Lavigne knew Sullivan well as they were personal friends. The "route" referred to by the chronicler was one of dissipation, a well-worn word of the time that described an unrestrained indulgence in alcohol, gambling and women, individually or in combination. John L.'s dissipation was accompanied by a disdain for training. The impact of the two spelled decline and disaster for even the greatest of pugilists. While it was well known that the Kid liked his drink, this was the first inkling in print that it may be getting the best of him. Fame, money, competition, adrenaline, physical abuse in the ring, and now alcohol were all conspiring to bring the Kid down. How long he could stay at the top was anyone's guess.

CHAPTER 19

The Original Kid

On January 15, 1897, while still working to resurrect the rematch with McKeever but getting no traction, Fitzpatrick signed the Kid to a 25-round contest to meet Kid McPartland at the Broadway Athletic Club in New York on February 8. This was the first and only "Kid" that Lavigne would face but it would not be the last boxer to adopt such a nickname. It would also not be the last Kid Lavigne to lace up a pair of gloves. As history demonstrates, the "kid" sobriquet was a popular one for boxers and other larger-than-life characters over several decades beginning in the late 1800s.

William H. Bonney, born Henry McCarty in New York or Indiana, was a teenage runaway. His mother and stepfather moved to Silver City, New Mexico in 1873. Shortly thereafter, his mother died and he fled to Arizona, taking his stepfather's last name and going by Kid Antrim. In a few short years he would become Billy the Kid, the most infamous outlaw the west had ever known.[1] Legend has it that Billy drifted into a saloon in Camp Grant, Arizona, tired, dusty and sporting a wispy goatee. A drunken behemoth of a blacksmith, Frank P. Cahill, whose nickname was "Windy," approached and began to taunt him, saying he looked like a little scared billy goat then called him "Billy the kid goat." Billy didn't cotton much to the smithy's harassment and blew him away. As he exited the saloon to high tail it out of there, he heard someone yell, "Stop him! String up that Billy the Kid."[2]

In 1881 a dime novel titled, "The True Life of Billy the Kid," was published. His legend continued to grow from there and young boys across America began to fantasize about being the famous young-gun. Young George Lavigne was 12 that year and his older brother Billy was

17. Five years later at the beginning of his rise to pugilistic fame, George took the nickname of "Kid Lavigne" also bestowed by another, his brother Billy Lavigne.

William Henry Bonney became the first western icon to go by "Kid." George Henry Lavigne became the first fighter of renown to go by "Kid." The next in a long line of "Kids" was Norman Selby. A well-known farmer and butcher, T. A. McCoy, in Selby's home town of Milroy, Ohio thrashed a town bully one day to the cheering delight of the townsfolk. As young Selby began to acquire a reputation for the skilled use of his fists his nickname in town became "Kid McCoy."[3] Kid McCoy began his fistic career in 1891 and went on to become an accomplished light-heavyweight whom Nat Fleischer rated as the number one all-time in that weight division. McCoy had one more claim to fame; the saying, "the real McCoy" is said to be attributed to him. Over the next 124 years there have been as many as 3,609 boxers who followed in their footsteps and added the youthful nickname to their given names.[4] There were also 17 other Lavignes who fought with the name "Kid Lavigne" between 1898 and the 1926. It appears that none of them were related to the Saginaw Kid.

William Lawrence McPartland, aka Billy "Kid" McPartland, was a New York fighter with 18 bouts under his belt when he signed to meet Lavigne. His only losses were two short, four-rounders to one of the better lightweights of the time, George "Elbows" McFadden.

McFadden would be a central figure in Kid Lavigne's career just two years later. Other than his losses to McFadden, McPartland had faced a number of obscure lower-tier lightweights with the exception of Jimmy Handler whom he defeated in ten

William "Kid" McPartland - Courtesy of Craig Hamilton, JO Sports Inc.

rounds and Owen Ziegler whom he fought to a 20-round draw. He fought Ziegler just two weeks before Lavigne faced him in his last contest. Doing a quick comparison of how Lavigne and McPartland faired against their two common opponents in Handler and Ziegler would make Lavigne the odds-on victor for the upcoming fight.

McPartland had an advantage of over five inches in height and a greater reach as well. He would need both to keep the Michigan lad from boring in on him time after time. "McPartland was first-rate in every way," claimed writer Jack Kofoed. "He had watched Lavigne in action several times, and believed that he knew how to stop the champion's merciless body blows while cutting him to ribbons with his own accomplished left hand."[5] The men weighed in at 3:00 in the afternoon, both tipping the scales slightly under the 133-pound limit. This would be Lavigne's first true defense of his world lightweight title. "After the gloves had been examined by the police," reported the *Police News*, "the battle began at 9:40 p.m."[6]

Police involvement in bouts by the late 1890s had gone beyond simply warning principals about the legal hazards of fighting too roughly and halting matches when they did. It was not uncommon, particularly in New York where the nascent Horton Law was still being interpreted match-by-match, for the police to take a more active role in confirming order and fairness from the outset. Inspecting gloves ensured that a fighter had not removed some of the padding or added a foreign object into the mix that would cause greater damage when he struck his opponent.

There was a good sized crowd of 3,500 sports on hand. The betting was focused not on who would win the contest as that seemed a foregone conclusion, but on how long McPartland, or "Mac" to his friends, could take the heat. "Many people thought that the New Yorker would not stand ten rounds before the champion," noted the *Washington Post*, "while others placed their hopes in his being able to withstand Lavigne's rushes for fifteen rounds, but outside of his backer and manager, Jack Dougherty, and a few very close friends, none could be found who would venture a bet on his going the limit."[7]

Chasing a Runner

This bout followed a path that varied little throughout. Lavigne led from start to finish, never letting up while rushing and swinging from all angles non-stop. McPartland was on the defensive nearly the entire time and when he did get in one of his lefts, he found himself literally running for his life as if he'd angered a bear. Round one was typical of many as the *Police News* wrote, "Lavigne rushed and was neatly avoided, the local boy showing lightness of foot and surprising coolness. Lavigne, however, kept up his attack, his opponent hustling around the ring to get out of the way. When the bell sounded the crowd began to buzz in conversation, and the general question was: 'How long could McPartland possibly stay?'"[8]

In the second round Lavigne knocked Mac down with a left jab in the face but he was up and back at it in an instant. "George continued his fierce rushing tactics," the *Police News* continued, "and toward the end of the round McPartland turned his back and ran away. These tactics while not particularly encouraging to those who wanted to see blood, served to nettle Lavigne considerably."[9] One of the few rounds where McPartland held his own was the third when he scored with a straight left and then twice connected with rights and lefts to Lavigne's head.

The fighting was brisk from the fourth through the seventh when Lavigne rushed his man with a fury and all McPartland could do to avoid damage was to drop to his knees. "After Mac put a left on the nose in the tenth, Lavigne forced him to the ropes and nearly finished him with a right on the jaw," reported the *Decatur Morning Herald Dispatch*. "McPartland locked twice at the close of the eleventh, but though Lavigne was doing all the work he appeared very fresh and kept up the fusillade in the twelfth."[10] It was nearly halfway through the fight and to the surprise of many; Mac was still in the game.

The 13th was fast paced with McPartland holding his own but still giving way. He tired of meeting the Kid's rushes and at one point sprinted around the edge of the ring to the amusement of the crowd. "He was advised to fight from a distance in the fourteenth, but singularly enough he forgot to keep out of range and persisted to mixing it up," noted the *New York World*. "At this game, Lavigne had not the slightest difficulty in showing his superiority."[11] In the 18th round Lavigne was swarming McPartland. Mac clinched and as the Kid was punching to the body, Mac slipped and fell against one of the ropes taking Lavigne down on top of him. "The fall was roundly denounced by the followers of McPartland," continued the *World*, "who claimed foul in such a boisterous way that fifty-odd policeman present had to raise their clubs and demand silence."[12] This incident speaks to the dichotomy of the police presence. They were there to uphold the recently enacted Horton Law but they were also "sports" at heart and quickly acted to quell the crowd when it interfered with their enjoyment of the contest.

McPartland had been instructed by his handlers to hold off for a "grand stand" finish, however, he found that nothing could slow the Michigan lad's relentless attack which forced Mac's reliance on his defensive skills to stay to the end. Typical of the last five rounds was the description of the twentieth by the *Police News*: "Lavigne again bored in, his opponent simply dodging, clinching, side-stepping, and sprinting to get out of danger."[13] Try as he might, the Kid could not put McPartland away. He had knocked his man down a few times, staggered him many times, and had him clinching for his life as the bell rang at the end of several rounds. McPartland made it to the end of the 25th frame and referee Dick Roche awarded the fight to Lavigne.

The *Philadelphia Record* searched for the positives in McPartland's efforts when it stated: "In McPartland's behalf it is only necessary to say that any pugilist who can stand up before Lavigne for 25 rounds without being knocked down or showing a single drop of blood is in a class pretty near the top. It is, of course, understood that McPartland went into the ring to stay as long as possible inside of a 24-foot ring, and though perhaps he resorted to running tactics a trifle too much, his defense was in every way legitimate and also of the cleverest nature. He was fairly outpointed but he was a long way from being disgraced."[14] Several newspaper accounts had referenced McPartland being knocked down, although apparently the knock downs were not of the caliber the *Record* determined to be noteworthy. The *Washington Post* chronicled Lavigne's frustrations when it wrote: "Lavigne seemed puzzled at times at McPartland's clever dodging and ducking, and as he afterward exclaimed, 'Mac's a clever one, but he is so awkward it is hard to get to him.'"[15]

Minutes after the bout had ended, Jack Dougherty, McPartland's manager and Fitzpatrick were making arrangements for a rematch that never came to fruition. Lavigne insisted that for a rematch to take place, McPartland would have to agree to a side bet of $2,500. The Kid later recalled: "One of the New York papers published a half-page cartoon showing McPartland riding a bicycle around the ring with me chasing him. Sam Fitzpatrick was dissatisfied with a decision victory, and was for arranging another match. But I said, 'What for? To give him another chance to run a foot race with me?'"[16] For the Kid, the first true defense of his world title was more of a lengthy training bout as he was in complete control the entire fight and was never in danger of being overwhelmed by his fleet-footed antagonist. A much shorter and much tougher fight awaited in a rematch with a vastly improved Charles McKeever.

Maybe there was another reason that McPartland ran a foot race in the ring with Lavigne. More than two years later near the close of 1899, Lavigne reflected back on a detail of this fight that was not public knowledge at the time. As reported by the *Decatur Daily Review*: "Kid Lavigne says that Kid McPartland, the New York welterweight, is the gamest man he ever met in the ring. When McPartland fought Lavigne he broke his hand in the third round, but refused to allow his seconds to throw up the sponge, and remained in the ring to the conclusion of the twenty-fifth round."[17] Kid McPartland would go on to fight many of the great lightweights of the time including multiple bouts with Owen Ziegler, Jack Everhardt, Eddie Connolly, Wilmington Jack Daly and the great master, Joe Gans. He also fought a four round draw with Joe Walcott. He ended his career in 1905 with a record of 40 wins, 15 losses and 12 draws.

CHAPTER 20

1897—Suitors Abound

Having fought seven bouts in the eight months since his first shot at Lavigne, Charles McKeever had remained very busy and had honed his skill in the ring. In the interim he had fought and beaten a very polished journeyman welterweight in Charley Johnson, and earned newspaper decisions over Wilmington Jack Daly and Jack Everhardt. He also fought a draw with Owen Ziegler. The *Philadelphia Record* reported on the day of the fight: "There is every prospect of seeing one of the most scientific bouts ever witnessed in this city . . . and he [McKeever] knows that to achieve a victory over such a phenomenal boxer as Lavigne would put him at the head of the class."[1]

Although many had anticipated a 20-round affair for the title, the bout again would be a six-round, no-decision contest to be held on March 8, 1897 at the Quaker City Athletic Club in McKeever's home town, Philadelphia. The fight would not be for Lavigne's world title as McKeever weighed in at over 140 pounds. "The Philadelphian had all the physical advantages," noted the *Boston Daily Globe*. "He was taller, heavier, had a longer reach and had more science."[2] Once again, the Kid was taking on a welterweight.

The bout commenced at shortly past 10:30 p.m. in the evening with neither man wasting time on sizing the other up. They met in the center of the ring and began exchanging blows. After some lively exchanges, "Charley got into the game," wrote the *Philadelphia Record*, "and he sent out his left and right with lightning rapidity on Lavigne's head and face, but the blows were too light to hurt."[3] A theme was quickly developing in this short fight; McKeever would land more blows in almost every round but they lacked the power of the Kid's smashes. Another local paper, the *Philadelphia Evening Bulletin* put it this way: "He will take two blows to give one, for he has absolute confidence in his own power as a puncher, and his ability to stand punishment would certainly land him a winner in a longer contest with the Philadelphian."[4]

This was a very different contest than Lavigne's fight with McPartland where he spent the entire time chasing the fistic track star. At the beginning of the second round both fighters jumped to their feet and rushed to mid-ring. McKeever was game to slug it out with the Kid and that was preferable to the Michigan man. The fighting was fast and furious throughout the round with few clinches and many rights and lefts landed by both men. Lavigne did most of the rushing in the third, but McKeever was very quick with his hands when in close. The fight was fairly even at the end of the round.

In the fourth, Lavigne redoubled his efforts to get to the body of McKeever landing several hard blows to the ribs. "As the bout progressed," noted the *Philadelphia Evening Bulletin*, "it was seen that Lavigne's blows had more steam in them and he landed several blows to McKeever's head."[5] The bodywork was having its intended effect to open up his opponent for head-shots. The Kid finally got to McKeever in the fifth. Early in the round he threw a couple of light blows and then sent a right to McKeever's ribs. He stepped in and followed with a nasty right on the jaw and McKeever toppled. He got to his feet perceptibly groggy but was able to back-peddle and stay out of range until he regained his senses.

"No one could complain about the sixth round," reported the *Philadelphia Record*. "It was a whole show in itself. The two men went at it hammer and tongs."[6] McKeever desperately rushed the Kid and landed a couple straight lefts but they didn't faze him. After some good in-fighting, the round ended with both men throwing hard in the center of the ring. The *San Francisco Call*, from across the continent gave the newspaper decision to McKeever. Another newspaper from the day gave a more measured perspective on the outcome of the fight when it wrote: "Of course great things are always expected of the champion, and consequently there is always a disposition shown to magnify that which is done by the underdog, so to speak. While the crowd waxed enthusiastic by the points secured by McKeever, it did not always size up to the real execution done by the champion. In the first four rounds McKeever did undoubtedly land with the greater frequency but his blows did not have a tithe of the punishing power of those dealt out by Lavigne."[7]

And the final word from the *Boston Daily Globe*: "This one blow [the knockdown punch in the fifth round] and the body punches he landed on McKeever stamps Lavigne as a fighter of the first water."[8] It was generally agreed by those who witnessed the bout that Lavigne would have won in a longer contest particularly if McKeever was held to the lightweight limit.

The Passing of the Torch

On March 7, the night before the McKeever bout, a gathering was held in honor of undefeated lightweight champion Jack McAuliffe. "John L. Sullivan, Kid Lavigne, Sam Fitzpatrick, Lavigne's manager, and Jack McAuliffe formed a rather imposing group on the stage of the Star Theater in New York Sunday night," stated the *Syracuse Standard*. "It was the occasion of a benefit to McAuliffe incidental to his permanent retirement from the ring."[9] "Permanent" was an interesting and inaccurate word to describe yet another announcement from McAuliffe that he was once and for all hanging up his gloves. Since being outpointed by the younger, stronger, Michigan lad in a six-round go the previous spring, there were rumblings that Jack was pining for a longer fracas with the Kid. But rumblings was all it ever amounted to as no serious effort was made by the McAuliffe camp to arrange a longer contest that surely would have ended badly and put an indelibly negative stamp on an otherwise stellar and unblemished career. It was time to pass the torch.

One source, the *Daily Evening Herald* of Oskaloosa, Iowa, believed that the benefit included some short exhibition bouts when it stated, "At the testimonial benefit to be given under the auspices of the Broadway Athletic Club tonight, Jack McAuliffe, for twelve years champion lightweight pugilist of the world, will retire from the fistic ring. He will box Jack Everhardt, Kid McPartland, Kid Lavigne and Charles McKeever for one round each, presenting to the one making the best showing his old championship belt."[10] This appears to be a dubious claim as no evidence of these bouts could be found and it would be a grave insult for McAuliffe to consider naming one of the other three as his successor when Lavigne was the titleholder. The Kid had also beaten each of the three within the last six months and outpointed McAuliffe the year before. The choice was clear in the matter.

Sullivan was the master of ceremonies for the gala event. He stepped to the center of the stage and the crowd, which packed every nook and cranny of the house, gave a loud shout and began to applaud. "The noise kept up for fully half a minute," the *Standard* continued, "and when it subsided the former champion said in his usual deep, guttural voice: 'Ladies and gentlemen: I am here tonight to present to you Kid Lavigne, who will succeed Jack McAuliffe as lightweight champion of the world. He is a young fellow and I hope he will defend it as well as McAuliffe has done.'"[11] The crowd burst into applause. John L. stepped to one side and presented the Saginaw Kid and the crowd cheered again with gusto. Speaking for McAuliffe, Sullivan said that Jack had all the faith in Lavigne to do justice to the title he now would relinquish. "McAuliffe then came upon the stage in a dress suit and was called upon to say something," finished the *Standard*. "He merely looked at the audience, bowed and retired."[12] As brilliant of a fighter as Jack had been, and as polished a Vaudeville star as he had become, it was apparent that he had no love for public speaking.

At this juncture of the ceremony it was time for Jack to part with the diamond-studded, gold championship belt that was awarded him in 1887 by Richard K. Fox, proprietor of the *Police Gazette*. Unfortunately, he was no longer in possession of it. It had been with him only a few hours when needing money to lay down a sizable bet on Blue Wing, a race horse at the Brooklyn Handicap, he pawned it for $250.

John L. Sullivan stood and gave a few remarks. "He then passed a square slip of cardboard to the Saginaw Kid," wrote Nat Fleischer in his biographic work on McAuliffe. "'Jack wants you to have his belt too,' said Sullivan. 'But it bein' in hock, the next best thing he can do is let you have the ticket. So here it is. All you have to do is pay the interest.' The accumulated interest amounted to over $1,000!"[13] After that banquet, one sports writer later penned, "Not a lightweight contested McAuliffe's action. Not a fighter challenged the Kid."[14]

Perhaps the *Saginaw News* writer meant, not a fighter challenged the Kid's claim to the title, as several were lined up to get their chance at wresting it from the current champion. Of course this passing of the torch was merely pomp and circumstance, as Lavigne was already the undisputed world lightweight champ, having won it in England and defended it on American soil. McAuliffe, while conceding the active crown to Lavigne, would continue to engage in exhibitions as late as 1920 when in his last bout, at the age of 54, he fought an exhibition match with the gifted French champion, George Carpentier. One year later, Carpentier would fight his most famous contest when he was knocked out in the fourth round by the great heavyweight, Jack Dempsey.

At this point in his boxing career Lavigne was a wealthy man and with all the clubs clamoring to sign him to a lucrative match in their venues, a seemingly endless string of bouts and paydays stretched out before him. Many wondered how Lavigne would handle the money, fame, and adoration shown him by the fistic faithful. Whispers of his love affair with the bottle persisted. Sportswriters began to speculate. The Kid was travelling to his home town of Saginaw, Michigan in late March to visit his mother Agnes and await his next bout. He would stop on the way to take mineral baths at Mt. Clemens, a site later famed for its clientele of movie stars, sports figures, and wealthy heads of industry. While passing through Detroit, a local sportswriter ran into the Kid and commented on his conditioning and rumors of his imminent decline: "The Michigan boxing wonder is in splendid shape physically and weighs stripped within eight pounds of his fighting weight. The story circulated by a New York paper that Lavigne was travelling the pace that makes bums of prizefighters is without foundation."[15] From time to time, the rumors would resurface.

A Contrast in Body and Style

Eddie Connolly
- Courtesy of Cyber Boxing Zone

The Kid's second defense of his title would come against a true lightweight, Eddie Connolly, on April 30, 1897. Several New York clubs positioned themselves to host the battle but the bid went to the prosperous Broadway Athletic Club of New York which offered a purse of $5,000 for a 25-round match for the lightweight title, with the loser taking $500 for training expenses. Connolly was a savvy boxer with fast hands. His style and physique were a contrast to Lavigne's. "He was a slashing, long range fighter with advantages over Lavigne in height and reach," stated the *Police Gazette*.[16] Eddie was five inches taller than Lavigne and slender of build while the Kid was short and broad. He was not the type to sprint around the ring in an effort to stay the distance as McPartland had done with Lavigne. He would stand up to the Kid and either win the fight or be decisively beaten.

Coming into his contest with Lavigne he had fought professionally for a little over three years but had 20 bouts to his credit, with only two losses. He had beaten quality opponents such as Jimmy Dime and Johnny T. Griffin, and fought a draw with Stanton Abbott. Connolly, who hailed from St. John, New Brunswick, held the title of featherweight champion of Canada. He would later hold the world welterweight title for a few months. But perhaps his calling card to Lavigne was his recent draw with Dick "Iron Man" Burge.

Just three months previously, Connolly fought Burge in Birmingham, England and by all accounts had Burge nearly put away when time was called at the end of the scheduled 10 rounds. He, like Lavigne, allowed Burge to come in at over 140 pounds. Pundits had it that if it took Lavigne 17 rounds to knock out Burge and Connolly was on the verge in 10, then a Connolly victory over the Kid was a probable conclusion. The *San Francisco Post* saw it differently: "Connolly, however, has failed to take into account that with him, Burge, feeling himself to be the stronger hitter, rushed in and mixed it from the start, while with Champion Lavigne the Englishman, getting a cue early in the proceedings that the Kid was too much for him, made a defensive fight of it. It thus took Lavigne seventeen rounds to hunt Burge up and whip him—about thirteen to find him and four to whale him."[17]

Nonetheless, many thought Lavigne would have his hands full trying to whip the lanky Canadian. A prescient opinion was given by the *Post* when it continued, "Connolly, however, is no sort of match for Lavigne and if the go is brought about they will likely find there is but one man in it at any stage of the proceedings. . . . [Connolly] is not experienced or strong enough for the Saginaw youngster, who would undermine him and dent holes in his abdominal region."[18]

Yet Connolly was confident. "I understand that Lavigne is a pretty good hitter," he said, "but I can handle my own mitts at a fair rate and am ready to take my chances at any time that it is agreeable."[19] That time had come and in front of 3,000 spectators the gong sounded at 9:40 p.m. with odds in favor of Lavigne 100-to-70. Those who bet on Connolly did so for his ability to win fights quickly by an aggressive attack. But he'd never been in a 24-foot square with a raging bull like Lavigne. Two other fighters known for their overpowering rushes, Joe Walcott and Dick Burge, were shocked by the sheer will of the Kid forcing them to yield their usual dominance to a higher power in the ring. Connolly was about to meet the same fate.

The first round, like most in the fight was fast and furious. Lavigne, somewhat uncharacteristically, went more for the head and neck landing some solid rights that puffed up Connolly's left eye. Eddie repeatedly worked his left on Lavigne's nose until near the end of the round Connolly was staggered by a right on the neck. In the second round the Kid began to bore in with body blows but took several lefts to the face in doing so. There was "fierce work at close quarters," noted the *New York World*, "in which Connolly held his own and made himself solid with his friends. Once again, neither had a pronounced advantage and Lavigne looked amazed as he sat down and talked to his seconds."[20]

Round three was clearly for Lavigne as he smashed Eddie with a hard right that staggered him and backed him into the ropes. Connolly recovered only to be hit by another jack-hammer right that knocked him down. He was up in a flash and stayed the round with fast footwork. Lavigne bore in on the body in the fourth and Connolly clinched with both fighters using a free hand to hack away at the other. The fifth was much of the same with honors going slightly to Connolly as he finally staggered the Kid with a cascade of blows. "Lavigne's left eye was swelling and blood was coming from Connolly's nose at the end," wrote the *World*.[21]

The sixth was a fairly even round with Eddie doing effective counterpunching to the delight of his fans who gave him a round of applause as he walked to his corner at round's end. The fight began to turn in the seventh. "Finally, at close quarters Lavigne got a cross-counter to the jaw and staggered Connolly," the *World* continued. "In rushed the champion with body blows and Connolly for the first time showed no strength in his returns."[22] Lavigne worked his left for the jaw and his right for the body in the eighth. Connolly's counters had less and less steam as he seemed to have shot his bolt. Eddie caught his second wind in the ninth round and began to mix things up successfully. "Connolly did some stiff jolting, but the blows were not to be compared to the powerful smashes that the Saginaw boy sent into the head and ribs," reported the *World*. "It was now only a question of time when Connolly would be vanquished, for he was weakening rapidly."[23]

The beginning of the end came in the 10th round. The Kid worked hard for the body and after landing several on the ribs, "Lavigne again jabbed left on the ribs, with a crack which sounded like a bone breaking," noted the *Boston Daily Globe*. "The champion kept working like a beaver until the gong sounded. Connolly was very weak going to his corner."[24] The 11th round was all Lavigne smashing Connolly at will and forcing him to clinch to survive. Near the end of the round the Kid caught Eddie with a solid right to the jaw and he went down. He got back up immediately. "Five times in succession Lavigne sent Connolly down with rights on the head, and Connolly gamely got to his feet every time in a couple of seconds," continued the *Globe*. "The bell clanged when he came up for the last time and he staggered to his corner in a very weak condition."[25]

"'It's all over', was the cry all through the house," noted the *New York World*, "for the veterans knew that Connolly could not win."[26] Bravely, Eddie did not stay on the canvas and milk the count to regain his senses which may have allowed him to recuperate enough to make it a few more rounds. It is doubtful whether that would have helped and his corner knew it. Joe Choynski, who was Eddie's principal handler, jumped in front of him as he wobbled to scratch in the 12th. He saved Connolly from further punishment and a probable knockout by throwing up the sponge. Referee Billy Roche awarded the fight to Lavigne. "Poor Connolly was heartbroken over his downfall," continued the *World*, "and when his seconds had pulled off his gloves he burst into tears."[27] The Kid had proven simply too strong for yet another in a long string of great lightweight contenders.

Ziegler Tests the Kid

Since Lavigne's last contest with Owen Ziegler in January, the fighters had faced two common opponents in Kid McPartland and Charles McKeever. The Kid had fought a no-decision bout with McKeever and outpointed McPartland. Ziegler had drawn once with McKeever and defeated him in the second fight, both newspaper decisions, and lost a six-round contest to McPartland. Ziegler fought five times in the five-month span and gained valuable experience each time. It would show when he and the Kid mixed it up in their second six-round, no-decision bout at the Quaker City Athletic Club in Philadelphia on May 17, 1897. The fighters agreed to a 138 pound limit for the contest.

"Ziegler had all the physical advantages over his opponent," wrote the *Boston Daily Globe*, "being heavier, taller and with a longer reach."[28] The first three rounds were back and forth with both men trading rushes. Ziegler gave ground when the Kid was attacking but only long enough to mount his own rush in return. At one point Lavigne threw left and right and the only thing Owen could do to escape it was to squat very low, causing Lavigne to stumble over him, his momentum nearly propelling him through the ropes. The Kid recovered and sprung upon Ziegler as Owen was getting up. To keep from getting nailed by a shot from the Kid, Ziegler went to the floor and referee Crowhurst stepped between the men as the bell sounded to end the round. Lavigne worked a bit more for the head in these early rounds, knowing that his normal routine of pounding the body paid greater dividends in a longer fight.

The fight was even at this point and in the beginning of the fourth, "Ziegler caught Lavigne flush in the face with all the force of his good right," noted the *Philadelphia Record*. "The force of the blow knocked Lavigne's head back but the champion kept coming right along for more, and got it too."[29] The hometown house roared their approval. Near the end of the round Ziegler again squatted to avoid a rush and ended up on the canvas rolling away while inadvertently tripping Lavigne. The Kid had seen a lot of ways to avoid his onslaught in the past but this "crouch and roll" technique was a creative one.

In the fifth there was more back and forth with both fighters connecting on the exchanges. "Again Owen swung his right on Lavigne's ear," wrote the *Record*, "and the house was in an uproar."[30] Ziegler got the best of the exchanges in a hotly contested sixth round. Lavigne scored with a smash to the stomach that doubled his man over and the bout ended with a clinch. "But the champion was all there at the finish," concluded the *Record*. "In fact, both men could easily have continued."[31] The "unofficial" newspaper decision was given to Ziegler and was reflected in headlines such as, "Ziegler Bests Lavigne," "Ziegler Outpoints Lavigne," and "Ziegler Holds His Own." Referee Crowhurst did not render a decision. Newspaper decision aside, the boxing world did not consider it a defeat for the champion. The *Boston Daily Globe* a few days later reported that the Greater New York Club was offering a purse of $3,500 for a 25-round bout to settle the matter once and for all. The fight never came together as most probably Fitzpatrick demanded that Ziegler come in at the lightweight limit for a contest of 20 rounds. It would have been a cracker to watch.

Mr. Hyde Comes Calling

Fitzpatrick was evaluating all possibilities for the Kid's next fight and casting a wide net. An effort was made for a match with English lightweight champion George Causer at the Olympic Club of Birmingham, England. Causer had won the title from countryman Dick Burge on a TKO in the seventh round of a bout in late May. Causer was a "heavy" lightweight who fought at the English lightweight limit of 138 pounds. Although Causer agreed to that weight in early negotiations the fight never came to pass, perhaps Lavigne and Fitzpatrick feeling they could make good money in the states without a long trip and without giving weight. But plenty of beefy lightweights continued to nip at the Kid's heels here at home as well. Referring to a list of possible fighters itching to get a crack at the title Lavigne said, "Plenty of them challenge me to battle for the title I hold as lightweight champion of the world, but they want to weigh in up in the forties."[32]

One such challenger was Kid McPartland. His manager, Jack Dougherty, "is out with a bellicose challenge to fight Kid Lavigne for the lightweight championship of the world," reported the *Waterloo Daily Courier*.[33] Dougherty cited McPartland staying 25 rounds with Lavigne as his entitlement to the next shot at the champion and even agreed to fight winner-take-all. But again, Lavigne reminded Fitz that he didn't want to fight a man who ran to escape him the entire bout as McPartland had. The negotiations broke down when Dougherty refused to let his man take on Lavigne at the 133 pound lightweight limit.

"Slugger in Trouble—George Lavigne Tries to Wrestle with an Officer and Gets Put to Sleep," was the headline in the *Syracuse Daily Sentinel*. Having returned to New York after his match with Ziegler, and awaiting word on who his next challenger would be, Lavigne was out painting the town one night . . . which he probably did most nights. "George Lavigne, the lightweight champion, varied his training at Coney Island June 8 by making a tour of the Bowery resorts and indulging in potent stimulants," wrote the *Police News*.[34] It's odd that alcohol was so often referred to as a stimulant back in the day. While more accurately qualifying as a central nervous system depressant, about the only thing it stimulates is the tiny, ancient part of the brain that connects to the flight or fight syndrome. Therefore the mixture of alcohol and pugilist does not a good outcome make. And it didn't on this occasion either.

The Bowery was originally a little alleyway between larger streets running down to the sea. It was later surfaced with planks and became the heart of Coney Island amusement lined with dance halls, saloons, and cheap stands. At 1:00 a.m. the Kid and a couple friends stopped into an all-night restaurant where Lavigne, in full-on Mr. Hyde mode, engaged in combat with three waiters. "He proceeded to sprinkle them with catsup," stated the *Syracuse Daily Sentinel*. "He finally became so boisterous that detectives Vachis and Eckoldt decided to lock him up. Lavigne fought the officers and Vachis decided to punch the prizefighter. The knockout blow, or something much like it, settled Lavigne and he was taken to the station house with a very black eye. Today he was fined $10 and held on $500 bail for abusing the officer."[35] He spent the night in jail, not his first and definitely not his last. Echoes were in the air of "travelling the pace that makes bums of prizefighters," and "he will go the John L. Sullivan route." It would certainly fit the profile of many a great champion if he was on his way to such an ignominious fate.

Another fistic marvel who also liked his alcohol had recently resurfaced and was looking to Lavigne for a match to help him get back on his feet. Albert Griffiths, better known as Young Griffo, was a veteran of two draws with the Kid. He had recently been released in mid-June from the King's County penitentiary. Nat Fleischer, in his 1928 biography of Griffo wrote: "The year 1896 found Griffo in only a few fights for he was sentenced to serve a year in jail for a disorderly conduct."[36] Griffo did spend a year in jail but Fleischer's account that it was for "a disorderly conduct" was a less than accurate description and perhaps was Nat's way of glossing over the far more heinous truth of his crime. Albert Griffiths was put away for sexually assaulting a young boy. It would irreparably harm his career, as his manager soon learned when he tried to book a match with Lavigne. "It is not very likely that Young Griffo will ever get a chance to fight in San Francisco," wrote the *Centralia Enterprise and Tribune*. "Recently the manager of the erratic Australian wrote to the match-maker of a certain club in San Francisco asking how much money the organization would give for Griffo and Lavigne. The reply which came back stated that Griffo was not wanted on the Pacific Coast."[37]

Putting aside any concerns he and Fitzpatrick might have about Griffo's unconscionable transgression, a match was made to fight him on June 28, 1897 at the Quaker City Athletic Club in Philadelphia. This was not a fight Lavigne needed as it was to be a six-round, non-title fight. He had plenty of other suitors with less baggage than Griffo. It appeared that the Kid was doing it out of empathy for a legendary fighter who had fallen on hard times although "fallen" would not be the correct characterization as Griffo clearly chose his fate, this time through his own actions.

Since his release from prison Griffo had fought once and it wasn't a pretty go. On June 21 he stepped into the ring in terrible shape against Philadelphia Tommy Ryan, not to be confused with one of the great middleweights of all time with the same name. Ryan was a few years into his career at the time and was a middle-tier light-weight/middleweight. Ryan had the better of Griffo in the first two rounds. "It was very apparent that Griffo was not in good shape and his well-known style of defense was not in evidence," reported the *Boston Daily Globe*.[38] Ryan was landing at will in the third and Griffo's

Young Griffo (left) and Sam Fitzpatrick – Courtesy of Don Scott

retorts lacked steam. In the middle of the round Griffo quit. While pulling off his gloves he said, "I'll give you the decision. I cannot box tonight." Cat-calls and hisses erupted across the arena. The *Globe* continued: "Griffo walked to the ringside and said: 'I am in no condition tonight. You all know I have been on a long vacation and not in shape. A week from tonight I will meet this man and box him ten rounds.' That did not satisfy the sports and they denounced Griffo in very strong terms."

In the work-up to his fight with Lavigne a week later, the *Globe* added this: "The Lavigne and Griffo contest will not be a lively one, as neither man, especially Griffo, is in condition to make an interesting bout."[39] Griffo's lack of condition was no mystery as he rarely, if ever, conditioned properly for a fight. Penitentiary's of the day were not conducive to spending hours working out, as many are today, to emerge in better shape than when one went in. But the *Globe's* comment on Lavigne's lack of conditioning was telling. The Kid's own brief incarceration for drunken behavior earlier in the month in Coney Island was a sign that he was not training as an athlete determined to keep his crown for long and reporters in the sporting world were taking notice. And then the other shoe dropped.

On fight night, June 28, the Kid was a no-show. "His manager, Sam Fitzpatrick, was in the building," wrote the *Philadelphia Record*, "and after the show had started, notified the management that Lavigne would not be able to keep his engagement, and was in bed in the Hotel Walton in a beastly state of intoxication."[40] This was an incredibly cavalier move on the part of Lavigne and signaled to all that dissipation was taking its toll on the champion.

Griffo had been training hard over the course of the week leading up to the fight abstaining from drink as well. He claimed that this would be the first time he ever entered the ring against Lavigne in "proper condition." Proper condition? Just seven days prior he quit in the third round because he was in terrible condition. Such was Griffo's concept of training that he felt he could whip himself into proper condition with just seven days of workouts and abstinence. The *Record* quoted Griffo's comments to the disgruntled crowd, doing its best to mimic his heavy, working-class Australian accent: "Ladies and Gentlemen: I am 'ere to box Kid Lavigne, but 'e ain't 'ere, an' it's nobuddy's fault but 'is. I am keepin' good faith wid dis club, and I kem 'ere last Thursday in condition myself. I'm willin' ta box Lavigne nex' Monday, er any time er place 'e says. I ain't agoin' ta trow de public down, an' I'm 'ere ta fill me contrack."[41] The fight was not rescheduled but the Kid would need to be sober and trained to the hour for his next mill, a rematch with the Barbados Demon.

CHAPTER 21

He Seeketh the Demon Again

The *Mirror of Life* of London was first to describe a growing rift between Lavigne and Fitzpatrick when it wrote, "The best of feeling has not existed between Lavigne and his manager for some time back. Those who are in the 'know' say that Sam and the Kid used to have a battle royal after each fight."[1] Speculation centered on the Philadelphia no-show incident as the final straw. Fitzpatrick contended the Kid was in no condition to fight that evening but Lavigne denied it, saying he did not keep the engagement because he thought Griffo may quit on him as he had done to Tommy Ryan. It's also possible that Fitz had enough of Lavigne's continued boozing ways and saw the end of his champion's reign looming in the near future. So the man who had taken the Kid to the American title and then the world championship threw in the towel. The business relationship ended that August although the two remained friends over the coming years.

The Kid's brother Billy, would reassert himself as manager in the absence of Fitzpatrick. Billy had managed George in his early career until Sam had taken the Kid under his wing in 1894. Lavigne had bested a good crop of contenders and it was time to up the ante a bit. On August 28, 1897, Billy and the Kid agreed to a rematch with the Barbados Demon, Joe Walcott. The next day bidding began between the Occidental Club and the National Club of San Francisco. The Occidental was managed by Young Mitchell, born John L. Herget, a fixture of the San Francisco fight scene and one of only nine men to retire unbeaten over his entire 10-year career. He was also personal friends with both Tom O'Rourke, Walcott's manager, and Billy Lavigne giving him a leg up in the bidding. Both clubs proposed to hold the fight at the Mechanics Pavilion.

Mechanics Pavilion, San Francisco

The Occidental won the bid. The men would fight for 75% of the gate receipts with the winner taking 80% of it. With a packed house and some of the select tickets selling for ten bucks apiece, the winner stood to make in excess of the going rate of a $5,000 purse for a top- flight lightweight bout of the day. It was to be a 20-round affair "but will be carried on to a decision if not decided within that limit," reported the *Saginaw Evening News*.[2]

While it didn't take long, there was a liberal amount of haggling over the weight at ringside. O'Rourke was guarding against a repeat of what happened to Walcott in the first bout where he weakened considerably over the final rounds due, it was conjectured, to making the 133-pound limit for the contest. He wanted his man as close to 140 as a result of the negotiation. Billy gave O'Rourke three choices: 133 at 3 o'clock, 135 at 6 o'clock or 137 pounds at ringside. O'Rourke settled on 135 at 6 o'clock knowing Walcott would end up close to 140 when the gong rang for round one at about 10 o'clock that evening.

A well-known and well-informed sport of the time, Macon McCormick, gave his opinion on weighty matters when he wrote: "Not long since after he failed to put Charley McKeever out in Philadelphia, Lavigne, at Fitzpatrick's urging, resolved that 'hereafter I will not give away weight. I will fight any man living at 133 pounds, but will not go any higher.' I think that was a good resolution. Now he practically agrees to fight Walcott at 138 or 140 pounds, and I think he will find the 'Barbados Demon' a far better man than he was when he met him in New York. Lavigne has not been taking the best care of himself of late, I am sorry to say. I wish him luck with Walcott, but I know that he is going up against hard game."[3]

So much for the previous constraint vowed by Lavigne; it appeared that under the guidance of his brother such discipline in negotiations had gone by the wayside. However, agreeing to the heavier weight for Walcott brought with it two positives: Were Walcott to lose, he could not effectively argue that his stamina suffered as a result of having to reduce to the lightweight limit of 133 pounds, and, as noted by the *Saginaw Evening News*, "Should Lavigne be licked, Walcott cannot lay claim to the lightweight championship."[4] Modern fight records however, still show the bout as being for the lightweight championship of the world. Jumping weight classes to wrest a title from a champ in another division was not a two-way street. Only the lighter man could claim a title by defeating a man in the higher of two weight classes. The *News* had it right, Walcott could not claim the lightweight title if he was fighting above the lightweight limit.

Training at Pop Blanken's

Pop Blanken's Six-Mile House, just outside San Francisco - Courtesy of San Francisco City Guides

The fight, now scheduled for October 29, was to attract sports from all over the country. "It was felt that the greatest match since the Jim-Bob one [Corbett versus Fitzsimmons for the heavyweight title in March 1897] had been effected," noted the *San Francisco Bulletin*. "Walcott, beyond a shadow of doubt the greatest welterweight, and Lavigne, the undisputed lightweight champion were poised to scrap."[5] Another of the Bay area papers reported on Lavigne's presence: "He is splendidly built and has the reputation of being one of the most aggressive fighters that ever entered a ring. He will take up training at Blanken's Six-Mile House."[6] "Pop Blanken's" Six-Mile House was a stately old hotel down a dirt road a few miles out of town that was a regular training venue for area fighters.

Lavigne was confident that he would win and said so in a letter written to Detroit businessman, boxing manager, and personal friend, George Considine. "I am fit to fight the battle of my life. I was never in better trim. . . . I know my friends think I have given away too much weight, but if I didn't give away weight I would never secure any matches. . . . I expect to give a good report of myself next Monday. My training quarters are first class and I feel certain that I can again take Walcott's measure. I know that he is a hard and wicked hitter, but I am willing to take several of his blows to get in one of mine."[7] The Kid had such faith in his hitting power that he built his entire strategy in every fight around that certainty. Take two, or four, to return one. Add to that his super-human stamina and he was satisfied with his odds from there.

Lavigne was not a fan of rigorous training. One of his trainers for the Walcott bout was Biddy Bishop who in 1928 looked back at the challenges Lavigne presented. "It was a difficult job to train the Saginaw Kid viewed from any angle," he wrote in *Ring Magazine*. "But the hardest part of it was to keep Lavigne sober between matches. The record achievement along this line covered a period of eleven days, and I still point with pride to this feat."[8] However, when a fight of this magnitude presented itself, particularly against a foe who had given him the most savage beating of his career, the Kid would rise to the occasion. Of his training ethic his now former manager, Sam Fitzpatrick, wrote to the *San Francisco Call:* "In training he is a faithful worker. The only trouble a trainer will find with him is to prevent his doing too much work . . . and when he meets Walcott, if he has been properly trained, the lucky sports who witness the bout will see the greatest fighting machine of the present time at 133 pounds, his proper weight."[9]

Two days before the fight Lavigne's camp broke with their tradition of training outside the eye of the public when they invited all comers to watch the Kid go through the gymnasium portion of his preparation. He had finished his road work in the morning when fans and newsmen began to arrive on foot and by buggy for the afternoon session at Blanken's Six-Mile House. A hundred people watched Lavigne hammer away on the punching bag for two, 10-minute sessions with a jog around the gym in between, followed by a 20-minute, non-stop session on the bag. The Kid then worked with one of his trainers, Billy Armstrong, for a bit of clinching work. The Kid finished up with 1,000 revolutions of rope skipping and later remarked, "I cannot recall a single battle during my career as a boxer for which I prepared myself so thoroughly as I have done for this one."[10] He knew he'd need it against the Demon.

Lavigne rarely sparred as part of his preparation for a fight. Tommy Ryan, the great middleweight and sometimes corner man for

The "Kid", Billy Lavigne (seated) and Tommy Ryan - Courtesy of John Cuthbertson

Lavigne, once said of Lavigne's training routine: "Do you know, Kid Lavigne never spars when he is in training. The theory for this I don't understand, but it is a practice with Lavigne just the same."[11] The *Chicago Daily Tribune* shed light on Lavigne's theory when it wrote, "In training Lavigne does not do any boxing. He cannot deliver a light blow, and he would quickly do up a sparring partner. He believes that boxing is not necessary and does more harm than good. 'I used to box while training, but I've given it up,' explained George. 'Down at Long Island I had two fellows boxing with me every time I trained, and as a result I often went into the ring with a sore face. That's why I quit.' Then he added: 'I guess I will get enough punches in the face after I get in the ring without going into it with my nose raw or my eye bunged up.'"[12]

Lavigne's reticence to spar went back many years. In a 1909 article by Bill Blunt about the role of sparring partners, he wrote that when it came to holding back a bit, Lavigne was the worst of them all. "It was a case of fight from the start, and woe be unto the sparring partner. The first time Lavigne ever boxed on the stage the writer happened to be present. The Kid's brother Bill was carded to work with him. The Kid was very fond of his brother, but as soon as he saw the lights, the sea of faces and felt the gloves on his hands he forgot for the instant just where he was. He thought it was a real battle and as soon as the bell rang he tore after Billy like a hurricane. The first punch, a left swing, ripped Billy's eye open and almost sent him sprawling into the orchestra. He had a difficult time getting through the three, one-minute rounds. Down in the dressing room the Kid cried and said he didn't mean to hit so hard."[13]

Walcott was also working hard in preparation at his training grounds in Croll's Gardens, Alameda. Droves of spectators made their way to the camp but were turned away as Joe and his handlers preferred their man not lose focus with outside distractions. Walcott used some creative training techniques including shadow boxing while holding light dumbbells in each hand and doing some unusual road work as well. "Sometimes he 'hitches on' to a delivery wagon or other passing vehicle, as small boys are wont to do, and is hurried along until the pace begins to tell on him," noted the *San Francisco Examiner*.[14] He finishes up with a long ride on a bicycle. "As the day of my meeting with George Lavigne draws near, I find my bodily condition is gradually approaching perfection and I am confident that on Friday night I will be fit to fight for my life," Walcott told the *Examiner*.

As the fight date approached the *Police News* reminisced on the first clash between the warriors two years past when it waxed in a uniquely descriptive prose of the time: "The stamina encased in the makeup of Lavigne has been shown by actions too many times to need any extended notice on the present. Walcott with one smash nearly tore off the Kid's ear, yet, though bathed in the bright, gory dress of his own blood, the lad stood there with that smiling visage that is his habitually, forcing his way into the black, troubled lad who had never met such an unflinching white man in the ring before. It was a sight which can never be forgotten, one that would arouse life into the inanimate, and a crowning glory to the already great record achieved by the man from Saginaw."[15]

Crooked Concerns

A few days before the fight, Billy Lavigne received a letter from Sam Fitzpatrick in New York. He told Billy that betting there had Walcott the favorite, but he personally believed Lavigne would win. Local odds were 10-to-8 in favor of Walcott yet as the fight grew near the odds gradually settled into even then moved slightly in favor of Lavigne. And there was the question of the referee. Both managers opted to keep the name of the referee under wraps until the day before the fight. This was based on concerns that crooked interests may try to ply the referee with generous sums of money to influence his decision. One local bettor gave this opinion: "We all know that San Francisco has had some crooked referees in the past, and the thing has got to a pitch where very little money will be bet on a big fight until it is known who is to officiate. Let us know who is to be referee. If he is a man who has the confidence of the sporting community there will be a big play on this fight."[16] The man chosen was Ed Graney and sports in the know were confident that he would officiate the bout fairly.

The fighters were very well matched and the boxing world anxiously awaited the moment the two would step into the ring to do battle. "Good judges of boxing who have seen both men in action seem to consider Walcott the cleverer boxer of the two," wrote the *San Francisco Examiner*. "At the same time it is generally conceded that both men are remarkable more for the pace they set than the precision of their blows. They are of the order of hurricane fighters and as is the case with all of their kind, they sacrifice good marksmanship to a desire to strike early and often."[17] Given their styles, no one expected the fight to go the distance. Surely Walcott was itching to avenge his unexpected loss to the Kid two years prior.

At the appointed time of 6 o'clock the men weighed in at the Hammam baths. Lavigne moved the scale to 132 pounds. Having no concern about the weigh-in, he had rested all day. Walcott was just under the required weight of 135 although he again had to spend the

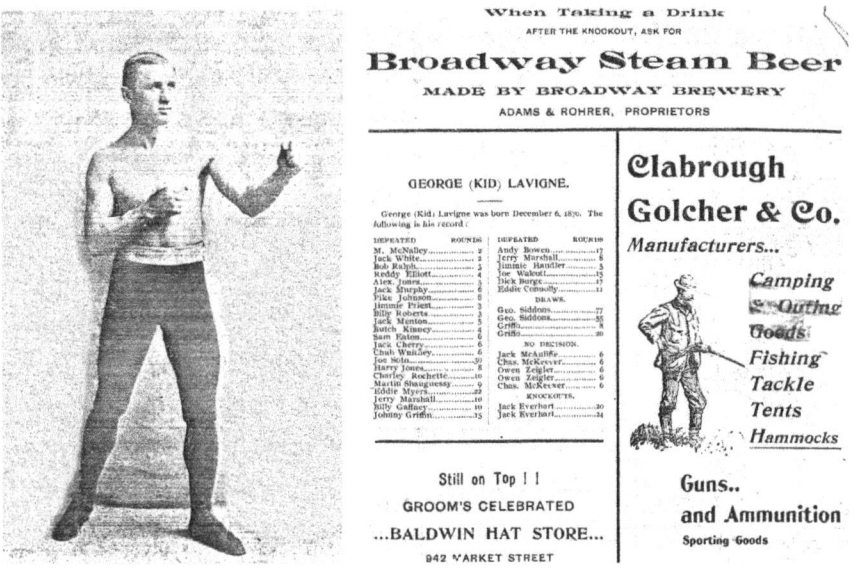

Part of the fight program showing Kid Lavigne and his record
- Courtesy of John Cuthbertson

day working hard, going for a long run, and finally taking a steam bath to sweat off the last pound. "Fifty sporting men witnessed the weighing in," reported the *San Francisco Chronicle*, "and as soon as they saw Walcott's condition, went back to the poolrooms and hedged on Lavigne."[18]

At this point the betting went from nearly even to 10-to-7 in favor of Lavigne. Two days prior a story was published in a San Francisco newspaper insinuating that a fix was in for Walcott to win the bout. "Up to 7 o'clock last night the betting was strongly in favor of Walcott," noted the *Boston Post*, unaware of the story of a fix circulating in San Francisco. "About that hour a flood of telegrams reached this city from San Francisco and immediately the odds were swung until the white boy was the reigning favorite. Just what caused this remarkable change was not clear."[19]

The telegrams to the east coast were no doubt the result of the witnesses to the weigh-in. This sudden shift in the betting just three hours before the fight strengthened the rumors of a fix. Most sporting men paid little attention to the rumors citing the fact that Walcott was trained fine after losing 19 pounds for the fight and why would he go to that effort if the fight's outcome was predetermined. The Occidental Club ascribed the rumor to its rival, the National Club, who failed to secure the fight bid and threatened to get revenge. And finally, of the newspaper insinuation the *Chronicle* opined, "The general tenor of the yarn shows that the writer is not familiar with well-known facts, but that he swallowed a lot of wild talk from some of the many 'knockers' here in San Francisco."[20]

JOE WALCOTT.

Joe Walcott was born April 7, 1872. The following is his record:

Defeated			Defeated (Knockout)	Rounds	Yr.
4 Men in Final's Boxing, New England States.			Dan Murphy	1	'95
			Paddy McGinon	10	'93
3 Men in Wrestling, New England States.			Mike Harris (lost)	4	'93
		Rounds	Yr.	Mike Harris (decision)	6	'93
Tom Powers	2	'91	Tom Tracy	16	'94
Fred Morris	4	'94	Dick O'Brien	12	
Joe Larg (knockout)	3	'93	Austin Gibbons	2	
Andy Watson	3	'93	During season '94 and '95 Joe Walcott as a member of Geo. Dixon Co. knocked out 100 men.		
Wolf Cohen	1	'93			
Jim McNamara	4	'93			
Buck Hamilton	1	'93	Mysterious Billy Smith (Draw), 15 rounds.		
Jim Lawson	1	'93			
Max Pierce	2	'93	Defeated Mike Dunn, of Australia, Knockout in 8 rounds, '95.		
Jack Cox	4	'93			
Prof. Green	2	'93	Defeated Dick O'Brien, 1 round, '95, (Knockout).		
Bob Reardon	4	'93			
Jim Mitchell	3	'93	Decision (lost) Geo. (Kid) Lavigne, 15 rounds, Dec. 20, '95.		
Lee Damro	3	'93			
Defeated (Knockout)			Defeated "Bright Eyes," Dan Stuart's Prodigy, 7 rounds, '96.		
Tommy West	3	'93			
George Gibbons	1	'93	Defeated "Seldy Bill" Quinn, 20 rounds, '06.		
Jack Dobson	4	'93			
Jack Homons	2	'93	Knockout, "Seldy Bill" Quinn, 17 rounds, '06.		
Bill Dougherty	4	'93			
Jack Rehan	4	'93	Tommy West (draw) 19 rounds, '96.		
Don Mason	2	'93	Decision (lost) Tommy West, 20 rounds, '96.		
Black Pearl, Phil.	3	'93			
Talbot Daley	3	'93	Draw, Jim Watts, 4 rounds, '97.		
Prof. Leon	2	'93	No Decision, Tom Tracy, 6 rounds, '97.		
Bill Morse	3	'93	Complete Knockout, Geo. Green, 18 rounds, Aug. 4, '97.		
Joe Johnson	4	'93			

Part of the fight program showing Wolcott and his record
- Courtesy of John Cuthbertson

At 9:45 p.m. the combatants entered the ring. Six thousand spectators crammed the Mechanics Pavilion arena. Walcott slipped through the ropes first in a long gray bathrobe with his seconds being, Tom O'Rourke, George Dixon, who had lost his world featherweight crown to Solly Smith earlier the same month in San Francisco, and welterweight Joe Cotton. Lavigne came next with his entourage of his brother Billy, Ted Alexander, and lightweight Billy Armstrong. The ring announcer, Billy Jordan, addressed the crowd, saying he had been requested by referee Graney to announce that if Graney saw anything crooked he would "declare the contest a fake and walk out of the ring."[21]

The Demon Kid

Both men sprang to their feet at the sound of the gong and sparred at a distance for a few seconds, then Lavigne landed a tremendous right on Walcott's jaw and the two clinched. Graney separated them and Lavigne rushed again landing a left and a right on Walcott's body. Joe countered with a stiff right on the jaw which didn't faze the Kid and the Saginaw lad was back at him like a terror landing a hard left on Walcott's neck. The round was all Lavigne. The next three rounds were more even. "The pace was terrific," reported the *Chronicle*. "Both men were doing hard, clean work, but clinched frequently. The referee was kept busy separating the men, who were vicious and powerful. At no time was there a sign of fouling."[22] The Kid chased Walcott around the ring with Joe stopping suddenly to launch rights to the body.

In the fourth, Lavigne rushed Walcott to the ropes landing a hot one to the ribs and Joe went down, partly slip, partly punch related, but was up instantly and back at it. The Kid began to target the heart landing consistently over the next few rounds with Walcott seemingly unable to block the punch. "Newspaper accounts gave me the best of the first five rounds," recalled Lavigne years later. "I was on top of the Barbados Demon every second, driving him to the ropes, staggering him with heavy smashes. I did not escape punishment. I took plenty. The black dwarf woke up in the sixth. Goaded by his manager, Tom O'Rourke, he cut loose with a terrible bombardment. The howl of the mob could be heard for blocks."[23] The *Police Gazette* saw the round similarly when it reported, "The men went at each other like butchers in the sixth. Lavigne hammered Walcott wickedly in the stomach and on the jaw with his right. Joe chopped the Kid on the neck with overhand blows, but Lavigne showed no distress."[24]

The Kid continued his rushing tactics in the seventh and the fighting was the fastest of the bout. "Lavigne rushed Walcott to the ropes and uppercut him with his left in the face," wrote the *San Francisco Examiner*. "Lavigne hooked his right on Joe's jaw, and he staggered and clinched. Lavigne went after his man and hammered him right and left on the jaw and head. The colored fellow was greatly distressed, giving ground and clinching to avoid the rushes. Lavigne sent Joe to his haunches against the ropes."[25] The eighth marked the turning point of the bout for Walcott. He began to complain of cramps and before the gong sounded for the beginning of the round his corner men began to vigorously massage and knead his legs.

The Kid sprang upon him trying to finish it. "The black fellow holds his guard high and escapes the knockout blow," noted the *Saginaw News*. "Walcott is clinching after every lead."[26] It was within the clinches that Lavigne took the measure of his opponent. "Once more I felt the strength of a foe waning," the Kid remembered.[27] "Toward the end of the eighth, the two men came together like steam engines and their heads bumped," described the *San Francisco Chronicle*.

"Lavigne's forehead was cut and the blood soon covered his face. In every round afterward Walcott made for this wound with his left and kept the blood flowing, much to Lavigne's discomfiture."[28] The head butt infuriated Lavigne and he pounded Walcott relentlessly as the round ended sending Joe limping and groggy to his corner.

The ninth and tenth rounds were slightly in favor of Walcott who sensed the fight was slipping away from him and redoubled his efforts to meet the Kid's fearsome rushes. Lavigne kept coming, scoring heavily on the body and over the heart. "In the eleventh I turned loose everything I had," the Kid recalled. "I slugged Walcott from rope-to-rope. I drove him back on his heels with punches that made me marvel at his gameness and stamina. When that round ended, Walcott was barely able to creep to his corner. O'Rourke wanted his fighter to quit then, but Walcott asked for another round."[29]

The 12th started with Joe resurgent, fighting at a terrific pace hoping to land the lucky one and end it. He caught the Kid with a strong right hook to the ear and followed it with a left to the body that doubled him over. Lavigne clinched to clear his head as the crowd went wild. The Kid came roaring back battering Joe against the ropes with a ceaseless number of rights and lefts leaving his man in a nearly helpless condition at round's end. "Walcott looks to the referee to assist him to his corner when time is called," reported the *Saginaw News*.[30] Instead, Tom O'Rourke met him and half carried him to his corner. Seconds before the gong was to be sounded for the beginning of the 13th O'Rourke called Referee Graney over and told him his man could go no further. A sponge "floated through the air from Walcott's corner, flung by O'Rourke as a signal of defeat," said Lavigne. "Walcott couldn't get out of his chair. He was carried from the ring."[31] Young Griffo, who had watched the bout from ringside, jumped into the ring and threw his arms around Lavigne. "You're the greatest fighter in the world," he bawled; "the greatest of 'em all – damn your tiger heart!"[32] And the crowd roared their acclaim.

Of Fixes and Cramps

Several questions lingered after the fight. Was the fight rigged? Did Walcott's training to make weight cost him yet another contest with Lavigne? Did he really have cramps in his legs? Should O'Rourke have let his man try to go the distance and was it a sign of a fix that he threw up the sponge?

Young Mitchell, the highly respected manager of the Occidental Club was first to weigh in on the rumors of a fixed contest: "It was the best fight I ever witnessed in my life. The people of this city know my reputation and they know that I would not countenance anything that was not straight. Lavigne went right at his quarry from the jump, and he never quit until O'Rourke threw up the sponge. After looking at the fight, and knowing intimately the men who participated in it, principles and managers, as well, it riles me to hear these rumors of fake. That fight was 'on the square,' and any intelligent, unprejudiced man who witnessed it will bear me out."[33]

Lavigne addressed the issue as well when he said, "I am not that kind of a fighter. I have fought all over America and England, and I have never had any one cast the finger of suspicion on any battle in which I was interested. It's the first time in my life that any one cried fake before or after any of my fights. My reputation as a square and upright pugilist has never been assailed."[34] The rumor was focused on Walcott and his manager and when reminded of this by one of his seconds Lavigne continued, "I know that, but it robs me of the credit of the victory. Walcott fought like a tiger. He couldn't fight any harder if he tried. I started a hot pace and he couldn't go over the route. That is all there was to it . . . Tom O'Rourke knew I would knock Walcott out, else he would never have thrown up the sponge."

The Kid also spoke of the issue of Joe's cramps: "I have no doubt the cramps he complained of were genuine. I think the punishment I gave him in the stomach was what gave him the cramps, for there is no doubt I did land into him awfully. For all that, though, I never saw anyone fight so fast with cramps in his legs as he did."[35] Walcott also spoke of his cramps and alluded to the weight as the cause when he concluded, "If it hadn't been for my legs—well, there's no use talking; but if anybody ever asks me to get to this weight again, there will be a fight right there."[36] Walcott was highly complementary of the Kid saying, "There is no use in my trying to disparage Lavigne. I think he is the greatest fighter at that weight in the world. I have never failed to knock a man down when I landed my right on his jaw. I landed repeatedly on Lavigne's jaw with my right last night and in our contest at Maspeth but I could not 'tip' him."[37] No greater accolade could Lavigne have gotten from the likes of Joe Walcott.

The *Saginaw News* ran a thought provoking story countering accusations of a fix when it wrote, "That part of the sporting world which contends that the Walcott-Lavigne fight at San Francisco last Friday night was a 'fake' will be interested to find out that Walcott is under the care of a doctor in his hotel and has been confined in bed since the night of the fight and that Lavigne is continually spitting blood. Two men who fake a contest would not batter each other into such condition. Lavigne has now gained a pedestal never before attained by any lightweight in ring history."[38] The Kid also suffered two badly broken ribs in the battle that would plague him for the rest of his career. For all their suffering the Kid's take of the gate receipts was $9,000, or about $225,000 in today's dollar, and Joe got $2,100 for the loss.

On the issue of throwing up the sponge O'Rourke was fairly livid: "Is my personal honor to be assailed, because I acted in a humane manner? When I threw up the sponge Joe Walcott was punished as much, if not more, than any fighter who ever received a bad beating within the ropes. He didn't stand a single chance of winning out. His legs were gone and he simply stood there for Lavigne to punch as he might a punching bag. Because Walcott was game, was that any reason why I should allow him to stand up and probably be beaten to death?"[39] And directly to the claim of a fake, O'Rourke continued, "I am known all over the United States as a square sportsman, and this is the first time I have ever received a deal like this." Fifteen years later O'Rourke was still defending his honor when he sued the British periodical, *Boxing Magazine,* for libel after it published a story alleging fight fixes by O'Rourke over the years including the Walcott-Lavigne match of 1897.

Peter Jackson, the eminent black heavyweight of the time, at ringside for the fight, gave his opinion as well supporting O'Rourke's decision. "Walcott met a better man; that's all there was to it. I don't know about the cramps, but Walcott was being punished so hard and in so dangerous a portion of the body that O'Rourke did right in ending it up just as he did. I would have done the very same thing myself."[40]

The second of their fights was now one for the history books. The fighters remained friends over the coming years. Walcott would continue his stellar welterweight career fighting five epic battles with the incomparably tough and crafty, Mysterious Billy Smith, winning three, with one loss and one draw. He would knock out heavyweight Joe Choynski in 1900 then finally claim the world welterweight title in 1901 holding it, on and off, until 1906. He retired from the ring in 1911. Nat Fleischer in 1950 listed Joe Walcott as the greatest welterweight of all time. In retirement he worked as a fireman, a porter on a freighter, and as a handyman at Madison Square Garden, a job arranged for a down-and-out fighter by the Mayor of New York, Jimmy Walker. He worked there for a month or two then vanished. Joe died in 1935 when he was hit by a car in Massillon, Ohio.[41] He was buried in an unmarked grave and it wasn't until the late 1950's that an Ohio boxing fan, Bill Cereghin, went searching, found the burial site, and put a modest headstone on the grave.[42]

After his retirement from the ring Lavigne recalled the effects of the second go with Joe in a letter to the editor of the *Police Gazette*: "That was the fight which finished me as I was never again the same. He broke two of my ribs and I neglected to have them attended to for two years, thinking there was nothing seriously wrong. Then I went to a doctor and learned that my ribs had been broken."[43] In a 1928 recollection to the *Los Angeles Times* Lavigne summarized the toll of the Walcott battles: "I am credited with two victories over Walcott, but I feel I lost the championship through those fearful struggles. I never had the same legs, wind, or vitality after that last Walcott fight."[44] The Barbados Demon wasn't the only thing that cut short his dominance in the ring. As Lavigne himself would also admit in a moment of reflection, "Liquor, as well as the punishment of the Walcott battle, had much to do with cutting short my fighting career. Many a row I had with my brother Billy over my love for drink."[45]

Walcott too had a profound perspective on the enormity of the second bout. Lavigne recalled a humorous encounter with the Barbados Demon years later in Boston: "While we were talking in front of his house, several youngsters came up. 'Children,' said Walcott, 'here's Kid Lavigne, de man who mighty near made orphans out o' you.'" Tom O'Rourke would have agreed. The two bore no ill-will towards each other over the years. In the fall of 1904 Wolcott accidentally shot himself in the hand and was out of action for some time temporarily vacating his word welterweight title. He signed to meet Willie Lewis on November 1, 1905 in Detroit and after a chance meeting with Lavigne asked him if he would assist him in his training for the fight, which he readily agreed to do. The fight, however, was cancelled by Governor Warner.[46]

CHAPTER 22

26 Rounds with Wilmington Jack

It was several months before the Kid was able to get back in the ring again after the damaging encounter with Walcott. In the meantime he went home to Saginaw to visit with his mother who lived in a brick house at 2034 Michigan Avenue from the early 1890s until her death in 1911. He would often stay with her while he was in town. He was then off to the Mt. Clemens baths for rest and recuperation. The city of Mt. Clemens, about 30 miles northeast of Detroit, was named for its founder, Christian Clemens, and was a mecca for those seeking the local mineral baths' restorative waters. It was recommended that one spend three weeks at the spa to obtain the maximum curative powers of the soothing liquid.

Lavigne had been an undefeated professional pugilist for over 11 years now. He had taken on the best of the best and strayed from the lightweight division to defeat some of the best welterweights of the day as well. He had captured the American and world championship titles. What was left? He was drinking more and training less. Dissipation began to take its toll. With few exceptions, it didn't show in the ring . . . yet. But as the calendar turned to the beginning of 1898 it was all about to catch up to the champ. Jack Kofoed, in his two part life story of the Kid published in a 1931 edition of *Fight Stories* magazine, wrote of Lavigne's decline: "In 1898 . . . the champion had begun to slip a little. It was inevitable that he should. People had been looking for him to break under the strain of a continued flow of punishment, but he still remained unbeaten. A little of the speed had gone from his legs, a little of the explosive power from his fists. This was not apparent to the casual observer, but it was unquestionably true."[1] And Lavigne knew it as well.

FINALE.

The "Lavignes"

In Three Hot Rounds of

SCIENTIFIC * SPARRING.

"KID" LAVIGNE,

The World's Champion Lightweight.

"BILLY" LAVIGNE,

The well known Scientific Sparrer.

Announcement of Lavigne brothers exhibition in Saginaw fight program. When in town the two sometimes sparred as the highlight of a fight card to the delight of local fans. - *The Saginaw News.* Copyright 1899. All rights reserved. Reprinted with permission.

The Kid resurfaced in Detroit where he was the main event of a five-bout program on February 3, 1898 fighting a four-round exhibition against a young middleweight named Jack Hammond. The night before the fight, Lavigne found his way to the theatre where he met Bob Fitzsimmons, the current heavyweight champion. The two champs exchanged courtesies before Bob dazzled the crowd with a bag punching exhibition. Bag punching exhibitions and contests were quite popular in the 1890s and the preeminent bag-man, William St. Mary, a Saginaw fellow, was on tap for the Lavigne program the next night. St. Mary had been touring the U.S. and Europe with a vaudeville act demonstrating his bag punching mastery. He later became a successful fight promoter in Saginaw after boxing became legal in Michigan in 1919. To add a bit of carnival to the event, George Considine, Detroit businessman and fight manager, had his bag-punching dog on the ticket that night.

This would be Hammond's second professional bout and at the time he was audaciously billing himself as the welterweight champion of Michigan. Referee Jim Burns introduced the Kid as the "lightest lightweight who ever held world's championship honors."[2] Lavigne was becoming more opinionated on the topic of weight. "There are not so many genuine lightweights in the business," he told the *Detroit Free Press* at the time. "They can all talk about matches in the lightweight class, and then when the subject of weight is brought up they want a special class for themselves and want to make it 135 or 137 or some other weight."[3] The *Free Press* reporter then asked him who he thought was the best lightweight aside from him. "Leaving aside the question of who is the best of the other lightweights, though, I can say mighty easily who is the hardest man I ever went up against. It is Joe Walcott, and I was in earnest when I said that, after having whipped him twice, I don't want to go against him again."

Hammond and Lavigne ended the evening with their bout. It was truly an exhibition, with two-minute rounds and neither fighter lighting up the other to any degree. It was understood, with the police commissioner and several of his officers in attendance, that the contests were to be strictly within the limits. The Kid did some excellent infighting to the delight of the crowd. "Some had said that Lavigne is a fighter only and not a clever boxer at all," noted the *Free Press*, "but the way he handled himself in this set-to would indicate it would take a pretty clever man to outpoint him in a boxing match."[4]

After the match the Lavigne brothers headed for Hot Springs, Arkansas by way of Louisville, Kentucky with a vaudeville troupe. It was quite common for famous athletes to tour with vaudeville shows of the time. Vaudeville was a sanitized outgrowth of the bawdy saloon hall and burlesque acts of earlier days. It became immensely popular in the 1880s playing to the middle class a variety program of mostly unrelated acts from musicians to trained animals, and acrobats to celebrities. It lasted until the early 1930s when the fledgling motion picture industry began to flex its muscle as the coming dominant form of entertainment. John L. Sullivan, Kid Lavigne, Jack McAuliffe, and many other larger-than-life sports figures participated during and after their careers in the ring. It was an effective way to increase a fighter's popularity, cashing in at the box office, come fight time. It also gave an "ex-fighter" a venue to continue to relive his heyday.

On February 3, 1898 the *Syracuse Daily Herald* noted in the fine print that a fight between lightweight Wilmington Jack Daly and Kid Lavigne was "in prospect" as the two sides were talking about a match. Three days later, Daly penned a letter to the *Herald* editor which was published by the paper on February 8, challenging Lavigne to fight for the lightweight championship. Perhaps the Daly camp knew such a brash public challenge might motivate Lavigne to wrap up negotiations for the fight. And perhaps the reason they knew it was that an old master was behind this bit of psychology being played on the Kid. Aside from his brother Billy, only one person knew the Kid that well and that man was his former manager, Sam Fitzpatrick. Sam was now the manager and coach of a fine lightweight in Daly, his latest in a long line of great fighters that would later include socially-controversial heavyweight, Jack Johnson. If anyone knew how to defeat the Saginaw Kid it was Fitzpatrick. The agreement was consummated a few days later.

"Wilmington Jack" Daly - Courtesy of BoxRec

Lavigne was also looking for matches with middleweight Jim Franey of Cincinnati and lightweight Frank Garrard of Chicago. But neither bout ever came together. Perhaps it was a blessing that he never fought Franey. Franey was knocked unconscious in the 14th round of a fight with Frank McConnell the following year. He regained consciousness a few hours later but died the next day; eerily reminiscent of the Kid's bout with Andy Bowen in 1894.

Once arriving in Hot Springs, Lavigne would settle into a training routine for his upcoming title match with Wilmington Jack Daly on March 17, 1898 in Cleveland. As a warm-up for Daly, Lavigne had arranged a six-rounder with Hot Springs native Billy Layton for

February 21st. Layton was a better-than-average lightweight of the time having been in the ring for nine years. He'd faced some serious customers with wins over brawler George LaBlanche—of pivot punch infamy—and an undersized Johnny Van Heest. Layton was knocked out by Tommy Ryan. He was coming off his last fight in early February, a respectable six-round draw with Jack Everhardt. Unfortunately there is no evidence of the outcome of the Kid's fight with Layton as no newspaper account of the contest was found.

Daly, who hailed from Wilmington, Delaware, was born Cornelius T. Moriarity. He had taken on all the best of the lightweight division and done well. He fought draws with Everhardt, Gans, McPartland, McKeever, Abbot, and Connolly. He lost to Griffo and Ziegler. He had experience with 28 wins, 14 draws and 4 losses, and was a muscular, fast, and rugged boxer. Daly was four inches taller than the Kid, had a decided advantage in reach, and outweighed Lavigne as well. Fitzpatrick was insisting that his man be allowed to weigh 138 but Billy and the Kid refused to go higher than 137. Odd that after all those years working to force welterweights to come down to the lightweight limit to fight Lavigne, Sam was now in the other corner trying to ensure that his man remained a "Philadelphia lightweight" for the contest. Daly would weigh 137 on fight night and Lavigne 133.

The Daly bout was to be 20 rounds held at the Cleveland Central Armory for a purse of $1,500 with the winner getting $1,000. It was not a very large purse at this point in the Kid's career as the world champ with 32 wins, eight draws, and no defeats. It might be that out of respect for his former mentor, Lavigne decided to give a shot to Daly knowing it was a meager payday. Kid McCoy, rated the top light-heavyweight of all time by Nat Fleischer, was the referee for the bout. McCoy was an interesting choice for a referee as he was known for his brutality in the ring using his infamous "corkscrew" punch to rip opponents' flesh. However, he was also one of the craftiest boxers of all time and surely understood better than most the science between the ropes.

Round one was typical of the entire bout with both fighters mixing it up with jabs and landing lefts and rights. Lavigne had the better of the fighting. In the second, "After Lavigne had landed heavily on the face several times," reported the *Chicago Daily Tribune*, "Daly caught him unawares, and sent in a straight left drive, bringing blood and bruising Lavigne's eye. The round was decidedly warm."[5] The third round was marked by sharp infighting. Daly nailed the Kid on the nose but Lavigne laughed at Daly's punches and at the end of the

Cleveland Central Armory circa 1898 - Courtesy of Library of Congress, Prints and Photographs Division, Detroit Publishing Company Collection.

round connected on a fierce blow to the stomach. "In a swift exchange both men landed right and left in the face," noted the *Saginaw Evening News* of the beginning of the fourth round. "Lavigne laughed outright, but scowled when Daly banged a hard right-hander on the jaw."[6] The Kid returned fire with a hard left on Daly's jaw. Daly landed a left "full on the jaw" and Lavigne went down with one paper calling it a knockdown and a second a slip. He was up in a flash. "A hot round with Daly in high feather," noted the *News*.

Rounds five through seven saw more brisk exchanges and effective infighting with honors even. In the eighth, "The Kid landed viciously with his left on the face—the hardest blow yet," stated the *Oregonian*.[7] The fast pace continued and in the ninth both fighters began to show signs of weariness. Lavigne feinted a punch and slipped in the tenth putting his head through the ropes. Over the next three rounds the Kid made a concerted effort to get to Daly's body landing several solid blows to the chest and stomach while taking some headshots in return. At this stage of the fight Daly's strategy was evident and had Fitzpatrick's cleverness written all over it. He was meeting Lavigne's incessant rushes with his left, then clinching and looking for the uppercut when in close. When not clinching he was trying his best to get away and as the *Saginaw Evening News* described, "Daly's sidestepping is a feature . . . and is fighting shy of Lavigne's lunges"[8]

In the 17th round Lavigne began to pick up the pace even more, forcing the fighting. It looked as if he saw the end of the fight looming and wanted to give one more push to end it now. It was to no avail as the round ended in Daly's favor with the cut over Lavigne's eye reopened and bleeding freely. Both fighters appeared confident but cautious at the beginning of the 18th and, "Daly led his blows for Lavigne's wounded optic."[9] Two rounds left.

Both men began fighting to avoid a knockout in the 19th. They sparred for an opening and then clinched for some close infighting, hammering away with their free right hands. "They exchanged vicious blows in the center of the ring," noted the *Washington Post* of the beginning of the final round, "with fierce slapping and jabbing." At one point Daly landed two successive lefts on the jaw forcing Lavigne to the ropes. Lavigne countered with a left and two rights on the body. The round ended with both men sparring.

"Referee Kid McCoy was unable to decide between them," reported the *Chicago Daily Tribune*. "Indeed, it would have been hard for anyone else to decide justly in favor of either man."[10] His announcement of a draw was met with a mixture of cheering and hissing. It was the general opinion that had the battle continued to a finish Lavigne would have succeeded in beating down Daly's defenses and won the bout. But one famous sport—and it should be noted, personal friend of the Kid—felt certain Lavigne should have gotten the victory. "The decision was an outrage," said George Considine. "Daly went into the ring with instructions from Sam Fitzpatrick to stay twenty rounds at any cost. I sat next to Fitzpatrick and heard him coach his man. The Kid did all of the leading and Daly never made an effort to fight until the twentieth round, when Sam urged him to do his best. Sam saw that the crowd was with Daly who came out of the ring with his left side looking like hamburger steak."[11]

From Considine's description it was apparent that Fitzpatrick copied the strategy employed by Kid McPartland in his 25-round bout with Lavigne the prior year. McPartland's goal was to make it through without being knocked out and did so by a combination of jabbing, clinching and using his legs to escape Lavigne's rushes. Sam employed the same fight plan here with his man Daly. When musing about a return match between Lavigne and Daly, the *Detroit Free Press* agreed with this assessment when it wrote: "Some are saying that it is not Fitzpatrick's wish or intention to make another fight with Lavigne, at least not right away. These people think that he carefully held Daly back at Cleveland for the purpose of having him sure to stay the twenty rounds and then make a rally that would make a showing for him in the last round. They say that he will now take Daly back east where he can get all sorts of chances for him on the strength of his new reputation."[12] Lavigne was eager for a rematch and the sports who subscribed to Fitzpatrick's alleged intentions were waiting for him and Daly to get finicky about the terms for a second bout. That would be their proof.

Should the Kid have had an easier time in this bout? Opinions of the day strongly suggest so. "Jack Daly held him to a twenty-round draw in Cleveland, and although Daly is a very able ringman, he would have been ruined by the Saginaw Kid of several years back," wrote Jack Kofoed. "But it wasn't the same Lavigne, you see, only a rather tired edition of that merciless puncher."[13] And again the specter of his social pursuits would prompt the media when one sportswriter noted, "It is said that the Kid has been travelling very fast since he defeated Walcott. If true, the result at Cleveland may bring the Michigan lightweight to his senses."[14]

Many years later Lavigne recalled the fight: "I fought a listless sort of scrap. I simply was not there with the old-time bounce and iron vigor. There was no spring in my legs and my timing was off. The minute's rest between rounds seemed far too short, for the first time in my life. Several times I tried to get going but it was no use. The decision was rightly a draw at the end of twenty rounds."[15] But at the time, Lavigne was ready and eager for another scrap. He announced immediately that he wanted a 20-round go at the same weight. "I want to see if he will stand the same medicine for another twenty rounds," was Lavigne's remark.[16]

Nothing Settled

Neither man was satisfied with the outcome of the Cleveland fight and a verbal battle ensued between Lavigne and Daly over when and under what circumstances the two would meet to settle things. "Lavigne's manager [Billy Lavigne] announced last night that he is willing to put any sum from $5,000 to $10,000 in Cleveland or New York for a fight to the finish between the two," wrote the *Republican News*.[17] This would be a side bet in addition to the purse. It's odd that they were proposing a "finish-fight," as this late in the 1890s these often lengthy affairs were becoming rarer as states accelerated their legal crack down on prizefighting. Finish-fights by their very definition were designed to incapacitate one of the fighters, something the laws strictly forbade.

Odder yet was the result of the haggling between the two parties. Daly admitted he couldn't secure backing in that amount. The parties finally agreed to hold the bout in Philadelphia, where of all places, they allowed no decisions over bouts and permitted only six- round contests. Lavigne's friends in the east, a bit perplexed by this move, pondered the bout's merits: "Considering the amount of gush that is being accorded to Daly in the east now, it is plain that this bout with Lavigne, set for April 11, will likely help his boom along in his own home and in the east generally. Perhaps that is what Lavigne and his brother are figuring on, as they want the best possible offer for the finish-fight that is bound to come sooner or later between these two lightweights."[18] So the Lavigne camp was cultivating Daly for a bigger payday down the road with a no-risk, short publicity builder.

"Six rounds for such men is not a long enough mill to warrant a decision, and to say the least, such contests look suspicious," opined the *Sandusky Morning Star*. The people who pay anywhere from $1 to $10 for a seat at a boxing match want to see a 'real thing' fight, which usually brings a decision. The six-round draw act at one night stands is getting to be a style card and top-notchers like Daly and Lavigne put hard earned reputations in jeopardy when they play such engagements."[19]

Returning from Hot Springs on his way to New York, Lavigne stopped in Louisville for a couple of exhibition bouts as tune-ups for his next mill with Daly. He fought two, three-round bouts on March 31st with Ed Rucker and Jim Watts. Both men were Louisville natives. Rucker, a lightweight, was fighting his first professional bout. Watts was a more experienced fighter whose first professional bout, halted in the fourth round by police, was against Joe Walcott. Watts was billed as the "colored middleweight champion of the south."

Meanwhile, the war of words between the Lavigne and Daly camps was not abating and perhaps it too was a calculated show. It was now elevated to the appearance of acrimony between the Kid and his former manager. "Lavigne has threatened to 'punch' Sam Fitzpatrick, his ex-manager who is now handling Daly," reported the *Sioux City Journal*. "Sam is not scared, but as a precaution he always has Daly and a stout club with him while out. Daly and Lavigne are both in New York, and as the Kid is very aggressive, may get together without the formality of a ring and referee."[20] A sober Lavigne would not tempt such fate but the inebriated Mr. Hyde was surfacing with greater frequency and would not hesitate to remove his bowler hat and engage his adversary on a street corner. Fortunately for all, no public altercations came to pass.

Thirty-five hundred spectators were on hand at the Philadelphia Arena on fight night. It would turn out to be as fast a six-round bout as had ever been seen in that city. The fighting was furious all the way through with the Kid doing most of the leading in the early stages. It was a smaller mirror of their previous 20-round battle. "At the end of the fourth Lavigne had the better of the set-to," wrote the *Chicago Daily Tribune*, "but Daly assumed the aggressive at the start of the fifth and clearly outpointed his opponent in the last two rounds, landing many hard blows on the head and jaw. Lavigne tried nearly all the time for the body and Daly's objective point was the face."[21]

No decision was rendered at the end of the fight as mandated by Pennsylvania law. And again the sports in attendance were split on who had the better of it. The *Milwaukee Evening Wisconsin* concluded that those who favored a decision for Daly did so on the merits of his focus on Lavigne's head. Body punching as an art form was no more appreciated in that era than it would be through the years. Looking back from the 1920s Lavigne chimed in on his second go with Daly and on the careening direction his fistic career was heading: "A few weeks later I met Daly in Philadelphia, for six rounds. There was no decision. Again the result was about even. I had to admit I was no longer the Saginaw terror, a tireless man of steel. I began drinking harder than ever."[22]

The much talked about final showdown between the two was in the works, to be held in New York in May, 1898 for a purse of $2,500 and for not less than 25 rounds. For unknown reasons the bout never happened. New offers surfaced weekly. A matchmaker in Trenton, New Jersey offered $1,500 for a bout between Lavigne and either Bobby Dobbs or Jim Judge. While Judge was a mediocre welterweight Dobbs was one of the greatest lightweights of all time.

Of all the matches that might have happened that didn't, this would have been perhaps one of the greatest of the era. Dobbs had a phenomenal ring career with 198 bouts over 26 years. It was estimated that he actually fought as many as 1,000 fights in that time span including many carnival bouts where he would take on several all-comers in a single day. He had defeated the master, Joe Gans, for the "colored lightweight championship" in September of 1897. He had also knocked out Billy Lavigne in five rounds in 1894. According to Tracy Callis' description of Dobbs he was "quick, agile, and clever and possessed a good left and a stiff right." Dobbs had plenty of science but he was also a rough fighter having been a wrestler as well in his early ring career.[23] He was skilled enough, tough enough and fit enough to make a great challenger for the Saginaw Kid. It would have been one heck of a match but it never came to pass.

In early May, a bauble from the past would make news. "A belt of silver, garnished with gold, diamonds, sapphires and rubies, that lightweight pugilists have fought for in England, California, New Orleans and New York, was recently auctioned off in a sale of a pawnbroker's unredeemed pledges on the Bowery in New York," noted the *Logansport Pharos Tribune*. "The former owner was Jack McAuliffe, who had pledged it with a Brooklyn pawnbroker. It is said to have cost $1,000 . . . 'I bought the belt partly because I am one of McAuliffe's old time followers and partly on speculation,' said the purchaser, John B. Hurley, at the South Street shop. 'Kid McPartland is a friend of mine and should he whip Lavigne I will give the belt to him.'"

Featherweight "Torpedo Billy Murphy" with Fox's Championship Belt, 1890. This belt was similar to the one given to Jack McAuliffe. - Courtesy of BoxRec

This was the famed belt given to then lightweight champion McAuliffe by Richard K. Fox, proprietor of the *Police Gazette*, in 1887 and promptly hocked for betting money by Jack. At a benefit in honor of McAuliffe in March 1897, the title had been ceremoniously conferred upon Kid Lavigne by McAuliffe. The pawn ticket for the belt was passed to Lavigne, partly in gest, by John L. Sullivan at the gala event. Lavigne never sought to reclaim the belt from the pawnbroker's establishment. McPartland never got another shot at the title and so most probably John B. Hurley kept the famous piece of boxing memorabilia. The story of the belt would resurface again in 1922.

Drunken Defeat

With no fights on the immediate horizon, Lavigne did what he did most often between bouts; he drank and looked for excitement outside the roped square. He was staying in New York in between fights, his home away from home, when he got into trouble at a hotel. The tale as told by the *World* of New York is worth recounting here in its entirety as it is colorfully described in the vernacular of the day:

"Kid Lavigne champion lightweight boxer of the world, was knocked out last night in one round. Unfortunately for the rest of the sporting world, the mill had not been advertised, and in consequence the audience was a small one. Kid Lavigne, dressed in his Sunday clothes and looking every inch a swell, was walking down Broadway last night. Jack McVey, Jim Corbett's sparring partner, who is well versed in the art of self-defense, accompanied the lightweight. They both felt warlike. 'Nobody can do me', said the Kid, who, it is said, had been looking upon the wine. 'You are all right,' responded McVey, and the two shook hands.

A moment later, Lavigne and McVey strolled into the lobby of the Metropolitan Hotel at 27th Street and Broadway. There were but few people in the place at the time. Among them was George P. Herdling, proprietor of the hotel. He is short and fat and knows nothing about the rules of the prize ring. He never wore a boxing glove and never saw a fight between professional boxers. Nobody ever saw Mr. Herdling angry. He tips the scale at 170 pounds and is about 50 years old. Clerk Peters, another quiet young man was behind the hotel counter. He was busily engaged in making out a bill for a guest who was about to leave the hotel.

'Hello there!' shouted the Kid as he stepped up to the hotel counter. 'What in thunder are you doing there anyhow?' Mr. Peters looked up in astonishment. 'Say, who do you think we are?' insisted Lavigne. 'I have knocked them all out, and I can knock out any man in this house, see?' 'You gentlemen will have to behave yourselves, if you want to remain here,' said Mr. Peters very quietly. 'This is not a barroom. You must observe the rules of the house.'

'We must, eh?' shouted Lavigne. 'Did you hear that Mac? He said must, eh?' The Kid stepped over to the hotel counter and picked up a heavy iron bell. He aimed it at the clerk's head and let fly. Had not Mr. Peters dodged, he might have been badly injured. Mr. Herdling, who had heard the language used by the fighters, but who did not know who the men were, stepped over to the hotel counter. He was about to interfere on behalf of the clerk when the Kid swung around and delivered a blow on Mr. Herdling's neck which awoke his wrath.

Before Lavigne knew just what had happened, he felt a stinging blow over his left eye. This was followed up quickly by another tap on the other eye. The fight was on. McVey was astonished when he saw Mr. Herdling sail into his friend. He saw that the Kid was getting the worst of it and McVey rushed forward to help him. 'Here, here! fair play,' shouted Prof. J. M. Laflin, who fought Sullivan some years ago and who is an expert with the gloves. Laflin had just entered the hotel in time to see the beginning of the fight. He threw his arms around McVey and held him until the heavyweight promised he would not interfere. In the meantime Mr. Herdling was making short work of the lightweight champion. The Kid fought back as well as he could but he was outclassed for once in his life. First Mr. Herdling closed one eye, then he closed the other, and finally he cut the Kid's nose. Then he managed to reach the boxer's jaw with a left hand swing, and finally, as a wind-up, he delivered a genuine solar plexus blow, which made the Kid sick.

'Now,' shouted Mr. Herdling, who was thoroughly aroused. 'I will teach you to come around here and act the part of loafers.' Then he picked Lavigne up by the back of the neck, shook him as a terrier does a rat, and a moment later the Kid was on the sidewalk. McVey followed and the crowd that had gathered jeered the fighters. The Kid did not come back to look for more. When last seen he was nursing two black eyes, a cut nose, a split lip and a much bruised forehead. He had spoiled a suit of clothes to say nothing of his reputation.

'So that was a real prizefighter?' said Mr. Herdling when seen last night at the hotel. 'There is nothing to say about the matter. They came in here and acted like rowdies, and I simply gave that man a good licking. I bet he will remember me as long as he lives. I am a very quiet man but if that fellow wants more he can get it quick.'"[24]

This was the third time in a little over two years that Lavigne's caustic, and no doubt, drunken behavior resulted in a knock-down outside the ring: at the hands of a reporter in Martin Dowling's saloon in February 1896, at the mercy of two policemen at a Coney Island restaurant in June 1897, and now again in June, 1898 by the fists of a hotel owner. All three incidents took place in New York. The fact that three different times the Kid was beaten by those with much less fistic skill, speaks volumes of just how inebriated he must have been. Drunk to the extent that he would pick these fights, and too drunk to defend himself when the melee began.

This latest incident sounded plausible enough given the detail with which it was described. A quick fact check confirmed that Prof. J. M. Laflin, the heavyweight who kept the contest even, did indeed fight John L. Sullivan in 1884, and was "considerably" larger than Sullivan. In the fourth round of the contest Sullivan shoved Laflin into a corner whereupon he hit his head on the ring post and was rendered unconscious. Sullivan won by a knock out.[25] In the bareknuckle days of the London Prize Ring rules, apparently a knock-out was a knock-out, regardless of the means used to achieve it.

By mid-June, a match with Frank Erne was in the works. The two agreed to fight a 20-round bout for a purse of $2,500 at the Olympic Athletic Club in Buffalo on July 11. Lavigne later got fussy about the purse and the fight fell through although the match would be rescheduled as Erne was to play a significant role in the Saginaw Kid's future. Days later the Montreal Athletic Club offered a "big inducement" for the Kid to fight Jack Bennett. Bennett was an accomplished welter with wins over Horace Leeds and Stanton Abbott. He also held his own in draws with Charles McKeever and Owen Ziegler. He had racked up 20 wins against three losses and a handful of draws. Lavigne wasn't interested.

Over the month of July two additional matches were rumored to have been made. The *Police Gazette* had brokered a rematch with Dick Burge to be fought in the U.S. at 144 pounds for a purse of $3,500.[26] The weight reportedly allowed was a clue that perhaps this bout was not as sure a thing as the *Gazette* was making it out to be. Lavigne gave that much weight away to the Iron Man when he won the world title but he would not be so brazen as to risk it a second time against a fighter of Burge's caliber. The bout was never fought.

The second bout that was purported to be a done deal was with Spike Sullivan, aka William Clothiers. Spike was an undefeated welterweight and a veteran of 27 bouts with 23 wins and four draws. It would be a risky proposition for him to put his unblemished record on the line in a bout with the Michigan mauler as the competition in those 27 fights was not on a par with opponents Lavigne had dispatched. The two were matched, according the *Milwaukee Evening,* for a 25-round go for a side bet of $5,000 and each went so far as to put down $1,000 to bind the contract. Sullivan wanted to put the bout off until later in the fall and when Lavigne suspected Sullivan was evading him the bout was cancelled.

At the same time that Dick Burge was making a pitch for a rematch, another Englishman, John Hughes, was offering to fight Lavigne for $1,500 in England. Hughes was an accomplished "booth fighter" taking on all comers on the fairground circuit. He only had two professional fights to his credit at the time from which he claimed the 134 and 138 pound English titles. He was not ready for Lavigne and the purse was far too small for a trip across the pond. Billy was still working on resurrecting a fight with Frank Erne and his efforts would soon pay off.

CHAPTER 23

Two More Go the Distance

It was now August of 1898 and the Kid had been idle since April with the exception of the beat-down he took in the Metropolitan Hotel in early June. There was a newspaper account that claimed Lavigne was to box against an "unknown" at Riverside, Rhode Island on July 16 but no record of that fight was found. On August 3 the match with Frank Erne was inked for 25 rounds at Buffalo on September 12. This was the same night and venue as a scheduled heavyweight bout between Jim Corbett and Kid McCoy.

Corbett, who had lost the heavyweight championship to Bob Fitzsimmons the year before, and had not fought a real bout since, was engaged in a series of exhibition bouts during July and August against a variety of fighters. These were his tune-up for the McCoy match, fighting as many as five bouts a day. Billy Lavigne, now managing his brother's affairs, had gone to New York in early August to begin preparations for the Kid's fight with Erne. Billy's last professional match in 1894 ended when his corner threw up the sponge in the fifth round when he was getting bludgeoned by the fast and furious Bobby Dobbs. With Corbett in need of sparring partners Billy decided to kill some time bobbing and weaving with the ex-heavyweight champ. He fought two exhibitions with Corbett of an unknown number of rounds on August 9 and August 15 at Corbett's training headquarters at Asbury Park, New Jersey.

The Kid was training at Corbett's facility and would routinely spar with the champion, do road work, and swim as part of their daily regimen. "I am very fond of road work," wrote Corbett in a special to the *St. Louis Republic*, "and start out with Kid Lavigne for a short run. We jog to Long Branch at a fair clip and on our return hit it up to almost a sprint. On these jaunts we cover 14 miles, and the work does not seem to exhaust me in the least. Kid Lavigne, the lightweight champion, is quite a swimmer, and together we take many a dip in the surf."[1]

Corbett was probably looking for lighter, quicker fighters to simulate what he could expect from Kid McCoy, who at this point in his career fought at a weight between 156 and 167. McCoy was described as "quick, agile, and slippery."[2] Billy was a clever, scientific boxer who fit the bill well and probably gave Corbett a good workout. The day after his second go with Billy Lavigne, Corbett learned of the tragic deaths of both his parents on August 16th. His father, who had been in declining mental health, murdered Corbett's mother with a revolver then killed himself in their home in San Francisco. Corbett cancelled his bout with McCoy to attend to his parents' estate.

The Kid was given permission by Jim Corbett to use his training camp and all its equipment while Corbett was laying his parents to rest. But before leaving New York, Lavigne had another close encounter with imminent bodily harm. It was a warm Friday night when he boarded a trolley car for Coney Island. Also on board was the private secretary of the owner of a local casino. "About three miles from Coney Island, when the car was running at a terrific speed, the secretary saw a car standing on the track a little ahead," reported the *Landmark*. "Being a theatrical man, of course he was on the alert. So he yelled at the top of his voice: 'Collision! Hold fast!' There were ten passengers in the car, but none of them took his advice. On the contrary, they allowed themselves to be hurled in all directions. One gentleman, said to be Kid Lavigne, the boxer, was thrown out of the car altogether, but was not hurt beyond a few scratches and bruises."[3] It could have been a career ending accident but luck was with the Kid that night.

Frank Erne, born Erwin Erne, was yet another of the great lightweights of the period from 1890 to 1910. Swiss born, he emigrated to the U.S. in 1882 at the age of seven. The family settled in Buffalo, New York. Erne was employed as a pin boy at a bowling alley when he began fighting professionally in 1891. He faced several fighters that Lavigne had also met including George Siddons, Solly Smith, and Young Griffo, although the Griffo bout turned out to be a four-round farce with Griffo dominating the short contest. By the fall of 1898 Erne had notched 41 fights against only two losses. One of the losses came at the hands of the wonderful featherweight, George "Little

Chocolate" Dixon. He fought Dixon, then world featherweight champion, in late 1895 to a 10-round draw, though all those present clearly saw Dixon the winner. Suspicion was rampant when it became known that the referee was a close friend of Erne's manager.

The two battled again in late 1897 with Erne winning on points in a 20-round bout. The majority of the sports in attendance saw the result clearly as a draw. "The referee explained that he had given the fight to Erne because the latter had outpointed Dixon," noted the *Boston Daily Globe*, "but he also said that the title of champion featherweight still belonged to the little colored pugilist, who would have to be beaten in a finish-fight to lose his laurels."[4]

Frank Erne - Courtesy of BoxRec

It is perplexing how one referee could sway public opinion with this standard to the degree that none of the record books show Erne as wresting from Dixon the featherweight title. Across the spectrum of boxing matches of the time it was understood that when a winning verdict was rendered titles exchanged hands whether it was a finish-fight or not. The fight should have been ruled a draw and in essence, the referee's declaration that the title should not change hands was an admission of such. Given that both fighters weighed in at 121 pounds, the featherweight title should have gone to Erne. Even though the record books don't reflect that outcome, a 1945 article by Arthur Daley in the *New York Times* clearly has it that Erne held the world featherweight title for three months between his defeat of Dixon and his loss to Martin Flaherty in early 1897.[5]

Police Intervention

The match, set for September 12, was to be held in the newly opened Hawthorne Athletic Club in Cheektowaga, New York, a town just east of Buffalo. Rumors were circulating that the authorities may intervene and stop the proceedings. With the cancellation of the Corbett-McCoy bout it became public knowledge that the club was using the Lavigne-Erne fight to test its legal right to hold such a match given the restrictions of New York State's Horton Law. And as if on cue, two days before the fight District Attorney Keneficke stated his intention to stop the fight.

Along with the legal questions there were also questions on the matching of the fighters. "Just what Frank Erne has done to give his backers any hope that he can successfully compare to the greatest lightweight in the world is hard to figure out," wrote the *Syracuse Sunday Herald*. "He received a disputed decision over George Dixon, a featherweight, and that at a time when it was acknowledged that Dixon was to be on the backward path." The same article cast doubt on Lavigne's fitness for battle. "If Erne wins on Monday night in the event of the fight being allowed to go on, it will be because some of the ugly rumors regarding Lavigne's methods of training that have been floating around the country are true. It is said that Lavigne is not keeping away from the flowing bowl as a man who expects a hard battle should, and this fact may influence some people to pin their faith on the Buffalonian."[6]

Lavigne was only 28 years old and for the first time he began to hint at retirement. He knew by now how his drinking was affecting his fighting and perhaps concluded that the end of his reign was but a short distance in the future. Jack McAuliffe had retired, at least for the time being, undefeated. Few boxers in history, nine to be exact, managed to do so and maybe Lavigne thought it a noble way to end his stellar career. The *Milwaukee Evening Wisconsin* broke the news. "Kid Lavigne, the present lightweight champion, says if he wins from Frank Erne of Buffalo, whom he meets before the Hawthorne Athletic Club on the night of September 12, he will again meet Kid McPartland and Jack Daly, and after whipping these two men he will retire from the ring."[7]

Four thousand people packed the new arena the night of the fight. The preliminary bout was set to start between Lon Breckwith and Jack O'Donnell when Sheriff Kilgallon and 20 deputies entered the ring. The sheriff declared that he would not allow any contest to take place. John Fisher, county attorney who was both legal advisor

George "Kid" Lavigne - *The Saginaw News.* Copyright 1898. All rights reserved. Reprinted with permission.

for the sheriff and counsel for the Cheektowaga town board, demanded that the club be given the use of its property and the fighters were ordered to shake hands. The sheriff disagreed. "Before a blow could be struck the deputies seized the boxers and forced them to their corners then released them," reported the *Titusville Herald*.[8] A second attempt was made to start the fight with the same result. "Erne and Lavigne were then introduced 'to box under the provisions of the Horton Law,'" continued the *Herald*. The sheriff was resolute and the matches were called off. Club officials, who had intended all along to force the showdown, declared they would bring an action against the sheriff for damages.

While the protest was making its way through the courts, the fight was rescheduled for September 28 at the Greater New York Athletic Club in Coney Island for a purse of $5,000. Lavigne was favored in the betting at 3-to-1 odds. Jim Corbett, whose training camp Lavigne had been using was to be in the Kid's corner for the fight. Kid McCoy would second Frank Erne. At least that is what fight fans were told as many of them had come to see the famous pugs in the fighters' corners. But something unpredictable happened the afternoon of the fight.

Corbett and McCoy, in New York for the Lavigne/Erne bout, had been trying to find a date for a contest after the postponement of their bout in early September. They were to meet at the Gilsey house to come to an agreement. Things didn't go as planned. As the two men and their managers met in the hotel lobby, William Gray, the manager of the Hawthorne Athletic Club, remarked to Corbett: "I don't think you want to fight." "What's that?" inquired Corbett. Gray repeated the remark and Corbett loudly said that he was ready to fight McCoy anywhere and at any time. "I'll fight him now and right here on the street," said Corbett.[9] McCoy stepped up to Corbett and knocked his hat off, whereupon several of Corbett's friends seized Jim by the arms to keep him from tearing into McCoy. Just as they grabbed Jim, McCoy kicked him in the groin doubling him over in extreme pain. McCoy then ran out of the hotel and disappeared on Broadway. Corbett was not in Lavigne's corner in the evening as he was back at the hotel in bed with an ice-pack on his private parts.

A Close Call With Erne

On fight night there were 7,000 souls in attendance with Sam G. Austin as the referee. Austin was the sports editor for the *Police Gazette* and was one of the more knowledgeable individuals on fistic concerns of the time. Lavigne was seconded by his brother Billy, and Owen Ziegler stood in for the injured Corbett. Erne's principal second was Kid McCoy. Both men weighed in at 133 pounds. They touched gloves at 10:30 p.m.

Lavigne rushed at Erne in the beginning of the first round unloading a long right which missed its mark causing the Kid to lose his balance and fall to the canvas. Up quickly, he rushed Erne again but Frank countered with a hard left on the neck. The fighting was fast and fierce with Erne holding his own. The second began with the

Kid getting a solid left on Erne's eye. Frank ducked another right swing from the Kid and was chased around the ring by a pressing Lavigne. "Lavigne reached the jaw with a corking right at close quarters," reported the *Syracuse Evening Herald* of the third round action.[10] After delivering the blow he had a hard time connecting while Erne did some effective work from long distance landing several on Lavigne's eye. By the fourth round Lavigne's left eye was showing signs of punishment. Erne blocked a vicious left hook but then caught another left that "drew the claret from Frank's nose and from this stage the Kid seemed to take on a new life."[11]

The next three rounds were tamer by comparison with Erne's left continuing to land on Lavigne's face and the Kid beginning to work more for the body. The fifth and sixth were honors even. In the seventh round the Kid began to press the infighting. Lavigne was unable to reach Erne on three consecutive rushes in the eighth but landed hard with a right on the kidneys that was the best blow of the fight so far. Rounds nine and ten saw Lavigne chasing Erne, rushing him into corners and unloading with body shots and a hard chopping left but also taking some lefts to the face in return.

Erne changed his tactics in the 11th and began to lead. The Kid blocked the lead blows and countered with hard rights and lefts to kidney and ribs but took two jabs to the right eye which caused more swelling. In the 12th, "Lavigne put a vicious right on the kidney that turned Erne around," noted the *World*. "Lavigne swung his right and caught Erne's jaw, Erne staggering, but clinched." The Kid pounded Erne's kidneys in the 13th causing Frank to grimace from the blows. "In quick succession Erne delivered a couple of facers, which made Lavigne wince," wrote the *Herald* on round 14. "Erne staggered Lavigne with a left flush on the face and cleverly blocked a right hand swing for the body as the gong sounded."

Speed of foot marked the 15th round for Erne as he danced away from the onrushing Kid. Frank reached the Kid's eye repeatedly and when the Kid forced the action his swings often caught nothing more than air. Midway through the 16th the Kid became even more aggressive and after a mix-up Erne began to spit blood from a jab on the mouth. Lavigne jarred Erne with a left hook on the chin in the 17th, and in the 18th they came together in the center of the ring, both fighters intent on rushing the other. Time after time, Erne successfully countered Lavigne's rushes with his left jab.

Erne seemed to be fresh in the 19th while the Kid looked the more tired of the two although he continued his rushes and swung wildly for a knockout blow. "As far as science goes Erne had showed more proficiency than the lightweight champion," wrote the *Mirror of Life*, but the latter was the heavier puncher and the more relentless fighter."[12] The 20th and final round was all honors to Erne who jabbed Lavigne repeatedly in the face and at one point staggered the Kid who now appeared weak and tired. "When the men went to their corners there were wild yells of 'Erne, Erne,'" reported the *Herald*, "but the referee declared the bout a draw. The announcer stated that it was understood between the men that if both were on their feet good and strong at the end of the twentieth round the bout should be declared a draw. This decision did not satisfy the sports, the majority of whom said that Erne had won. Erne from his showing last night has the championship almost at his mercy."[13]

Post-Fight Reflections

Aftershocks reverberated through the opinions of the sports writers. "Kid Lavigne, lightweight championship pugilist of the world, came very near losing his title tonight at the Greater New York Athletic Club in a twenty-round bout with Frank Erne of Buffalo," scribed the *Detroit Free Press*.[14] "Erne proved a Tartar for the Saginaw boxer, who is not the Kid Lavigne of three years ago by any means." The effects of the Kid's over-indulgence in alcohol since winning the championship were in evidence for all to see in those twenty rounds in New York. The *Milwaukee Evening Wisconsin* agreed when it wrote, "It is the same old story over again. Fast living proved too much for the fighter. Three years ago Lavigne would have made a chopping block of Erne, but not so last night. The Kid has been living a life of dissipation since his big victory in England and the result is that he has gone back 50 percent in his fighting. He lacked the old-time power of recuperation and seemed unable to put the force to his blows that he formerly possessed. This will probably teach Lavigne a lesson and he may get down to work now and prepare properly for the next battle."[15]

In Lavigne's own words, "Erne was a graceful boxer, a crafty ringster, and he could sock. Against him I found myself, once more, unable to strike my natural pace. The best I could do was to make it a draw after twenty rounds."[16] This was an admission that his skills were suffering yet there was no acknowledgement that had the fight been awarded on points he may have lost, suffering the first defeat of his career. Others would contend that Lavigne was not in peak shape for the fight. "At the end of the fight the champion was perfectly satisfied that the referee called it a draw," wrote Jack Kofoed.[17] "He was tired and puffing. That wasn't like him. Something was wrong."

Actually a few things were wrong that didn't surface until years later. In 1899, the Kid admitted "he had a bad ankle at the time but did not let anyone know about the sprain for fear it would give Erne too much confidence."[18] It's possible that the injury occurred the previous month when he was thrown from the trolley car in New York. And there was something else that when it came to light five years later, made sense of Lavigne's wild crash to the canvas in the first round of the fight. Remembering such a detail five years hence may not have been possible for the Kid had it not been attached to a precipitating event with a plausible story behind it.

The story emerged in 1902 when the Kid recalled his struggle to make the 133 limit for the Erne fight. "The night of the fight I was ill," Lavigne remembered. "I had not eaten a mouthful of food all day for fear that I would not weigh in and thereby forfeit. On the way to the clubhouse I felt so weak that my trainer, Paddy Gorman, told me to take a brandy in order to brace up. But it did me no good, and as I stripped I was as weak as a rat in a trap. When we began to fight I decided that if I did not knock Erne out quickly I would be beaten. So I let go a hard punch at him and fell sprawling on my face. I was drunk and the brandy on an empty stomach had done me completely up. I was accused the next day of having been intoxicated, but it was not in the sense that it was usually meant. It was a lesson to me, for I made up my mind that I would never take chances with my weight again."[19]

Excuses aside, Kofoed continued, "George didn't train as hard as he might have done. He was having a grand time running around with Mysterious Billy Smith, that queer wildcat who was in the way of being recognized as welterweight champion." Smith was convinced that the Kid would demolish Erne in five rounds. Lavigne bought it and had simply underestimated Erne. The two would meet again in July of the following year.

An Unimpressive Win

Lavigne had some soul searching to do. He couldn't continue on this path and hope to retain his title. Billy worked to secure the Kid's next match continuing to entertain offers from welterweights. And yet there was one marvelous non-welter out there that if matched with Lavigne may have been the last great bout of the century with all of fistiana clamoring to attend. That was Joe Gans.

For the reason why this bout never came to pass we look to Kid Lavigne who recalled the circumstances in a 1928 article in the *Los*

Angeles Times: "By this time some of my readers may have found themselves wondering why I never met Joe Gans, the great Baltimore colored lightweight. The fact is that Gans refused to meet me. This has never been printed before and I want to say that I was glad he didn't care to fight me. After the Erne fight I went home to Saginaw and left Billy in the East. He got back a week later and told me of stopping over in Pittsburgh, where he met Al Herford, manager of Gans. He said they discussed a match between Gans and me. 'Let Gans alone,' I shouted. 'There are plenty of white boys around for me to fight.' Billy suddenly cut in on my protests. 'Quit your raving,' he growled. 'Gans refused to meet you.' Gans would have taken the championship from me at that time had he known my condition, but apparently my victories over Walcott and Burge had awed him."[20]

By any boxing historian's measure, Gans is in the all-time elite of boxing's greats. He was named the top lightweight of all time by Nat Fleischer. His nickname was the "Old Master." At the time that he and Lavigne were looking for a match, Gans was the veteran of 77 fights with only four losses, one to Bobby Dobbs for the colored light-weight championship. His boxing resume reads like a who's-who of featherweight, lightweight and welterweight fighters of the era from 1893 to 1909. He became world lightweight champion in 1902 by defeating Frank Erne. Again, a contest with the Saginaw Kid would have been a dream match of a front-door pressure pugilist versus a ring-savvy, cat-quick, scientific boxer.

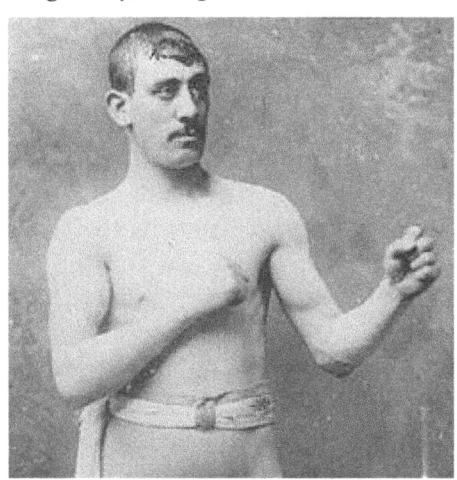

"Smiling Tom" Tracey – Courtesy of Cyber Boxing Zone

Instead, Billy secured a 20-round match for the Kid against Australian born welterweight, "Smiling Tom" Tracey, for November 25 at Woodward's Pavilion in San Francisco. The agreed upon weight for the bout was not to exceed 142 pounds. Why the Kid kept giving away this much weight was anyone's guess. Surely had Sam Fitzpatrick still been managing Lavigne he wouldn't continue to put his fighter in harm's way with the welters, particularly knowing the Kid was slowing down and losing some of his hitting power and legendary stamina.

Tracey had come to the U. S. in 1892, having just won the Australian lightweight championship. At the time of his bout with Lavigne, he had 37 fights to his credit with seven losses. Tracey was not a top-tier welterweight but had some respectable battles including three contests with Walcott, one lasting to the 16th round before being knocked out, and getting draws in the other two. He also fought the very tough, Tommy Ryan, losing both by technical knockouts.

"The men contrast at every point," wrote the *San Francisco Chronicle*. "Lavigne is short, sturdy, and a stand-up-and-hammer-away fighter. Tracey is tall, slender in limb, but very strong, shifty on his feet and a man who plays long for an opening, rather than enter into a give-and-take battle."[21] Tracey would enter the fight at 142 pounds and Lavigne just north of 134. The Kid was seconded by his brother Billy, John Herget, Tim McGrath, and Ted Alexander, and Tracey by Al Smith, De Witt Van Court and Arthur Walker. The betting line was 10-to-8 in favor of Lavigne and the referee for the bout was Jim McDonald who also happened to be a popular baseball umpire. The purse, to be split 75% for the winner and 25% for the loser, was for 60% of the gate receipts. A large crowd was expected as both fighters were known to the Bay area sports and "are expected to put up one of the finest fistic arguments ever seen here."[22]

By all outward appearances the Kid was as fit as could be. He had taken up training at Blanken's Six-Mile House where he prepared for his second fight with Joe Walcott. Noted the *Chronicle*, "Lavigne, the human battering ram, has got himself in great condition and is heavier than he has ever been. . . ."[23] Tracey, a terrific puncher, had been used to fighting heavier opponents depending on his footwork to keep out of harm's way, then drawing his man in until he could land his overhand right. Of this devastating punch the *Chronicle* continued, "This is generally a sufficient soporific, if he lands it, to give him the long end of the purse. His admirers claim that, as Lavigne is willing to take a blow or two to get one in, Tracey can land one of these effective blows of his, and the Saginaw Kid's career will be checked." Those who followed Tracey wondered whether he would change tactics and stand up to Lavigne now that the tables were turned and he had a weight, height, and reach advantage on the Kid.

According to the *Oakland Tribune*, Lavigne expected to meet an "artful dodger." "'Although I will be handicapped in weight probably seven or eight pounds,' Lavigne said. 'I nevertheless expect by persistent effort to corner my man at some stage of the game, and once I get him in a tight place I think there will be something doing.' Lavigne does not look for a short fight. In fact he expects the contest to run on pretty well to the finish of the twenty rounds, as Tracey is said to be a natural born racer, 'who never grows weary of carpet dancing.'"[24]

The Kid had, in the words of Jack Kofoed, "a rather quiet contempt for cream-puff hitters, these stabbers and dancers." Lavigne felt they weren't fighters because they wouldn't stand and fight. In the lexicon of the day they were known as "parlor style" pugilists. Continued Kofoed, "If it wasn't for their jumping-jack tactics they wouldn't last a round with a real fighter."[25] Billy Lavigne concurred with Kofoed as he was fond of saying, "The Kid fights best when his opponent walks right up to him and slams him a couple hot ones in the mush. I never like to see the Kid's opponent try to get fancy and box with him. Then he fights like a bum."[26]

The battle began at 9:24 p.m. and in typical fashion Lavigne stalked his man throughout. "One round was like all the others," reported the *San Francisco Chronicle*.[27] "Lavigne led time and again with his left only to have Tracey block it or let it land as he was going away so that it would have no effect. Lavigne, however, succeeded in getting in some good ones on Tracey's wind, and raised red marks all over his body." In the third round Tracey got in a couple of left jabs to the face but the Kid just laughed and came back in hot pursuit. Near the end of the fifth Lavigne landed a hard left to the body which made Tracy wince. Tracey was beginning to tire from his continued avoidance of the Kid's rushes.

For 13 rounds Lavigne kept boring in on his man with Tracey avoiding his straight lefts and vicious right hooks by side stepping and blocking. "The crowd was forced to admire Tracey's footwork and general shiftiness, but it did not like the kind of fight he put up," continued the *Chronicle*. "Frequent cries of, 'Take a chance, Tom,' were heard from the gallery when the work became tame."[28] Perhaps emboldened by the energy and urging of the crowd, Tracey started the 14th by fighting in close, landing several jabs on Lavigne's face. The crowd began to sense a turning point in the fight and cheered Tracey to renew his efforts. Then the Kid disabused all in attendance of their momentary excitement when he mounted a terrific rush crashing rights and lefts on Tracey's stomach, kidneys, mouth and nose which caused Tom's ever-present smile to disappear. At round's end there was no question who held the upper hand.

In the 15th, Tracey made a few stands but always came out with the worst of the mix while trying and failing to connect with his vaunted overhand right. "Lavigne held his lead with a little more added during the sixteenth, seventeenth and eighteenth," reported the *Washington Post*, "landing his right on Tracey's body with perceptible distress to the latter. Tracey seemed the weaker of the two and resorted to purely defensive tactics."[29] The 19th saw Tracey come alive one more time and try to force the fighting. He was successful for a bit then Lavigne came back banging to the body on Tracey's swollen right side. Tracey buckled under the assault and got back on his bicycle dancing away.

Both men fought carefully in the 20th and final round with neither taking chances although there were still plenty of hot exchanges. The round ended as the fight had started with the Kid chasing Tracey across the ring. Referee McDonald promptly gave the decision to Lavigne which was met with satisfaction from the crowd. "He tried his best to make Tracey fight," summarized the *Chronicle*, "but the latter would only box a little occasionally and spent most of his time avoiding Lavigne's blows by clever footwork. It was a case of an aggressive give-and-take fighter trying to mix things and of a shifty boxer declining the invitation that meant to defeat him. Tracey sensibly kept away from a dangerous man."[30] The *Chronicle* shared Lavigne's contempt for "stabbers and dancers" when it continued, "The decision was a good one and it will be a precedent from which defensive fighters may take warning, for it means that a pugilist must get in and fight or take the short end of the purse."

It was a vote of confidence and approval—from the crowd who chanted "take a chance Tom," from the referee who awarded the decision to Lavigne, and from the *Chronicle* which served notice—that "real boxing" was still the bastion of those who waded in to do battle laying all on the line. Yes, another victory for the Saginaw Kid but not without mounting doubters. "I don't think Kid Lavigne is anywhere near as good as he used to be," said Jack Everhardt to the *Police Gazette*.[31] "He's not there with the steam behind his punches as he used to be. You notice that he didn't do Tracey much damage." Everhardt would know better than anyone having gone 44 bruising rounds with Lavigne in two epic bouts when the Kid was at his fighting peak. Just how much Lavigne had gone back would be seen in this same building in San Francisco in a few months' time, when the Kid's 54-fight streak without a loss would be put to its greatest test.

CHAPTER 24

The Gathering Dark

Before heading east in December Lavigne had yet another run-in with local police. He was out for an evening with local featherweight, Dennis "Kid" McFadden. As part of their festivities they attempted to enter a theater holding a fight show. It's quite possible that alcohol played a role in what happened next. "The champion had a ticket but his partner was unprovided," reported the *Sandusky Star*. "Lavigne was admitted and when McFadden was not, the trouble began. 'Let him in; he is one of the profesh,' insisted the champion. 'What is the profesh?' quizzed the policeman, holding the brick-top fighter closely in his clutches. 'He is a scrapper,' explained Lavigne, advancing to the side of his chum. 'We don't recognize the profesh, as you call them,' said the officer tightening his grip upon the struggling McFadden. 'Oh, is that so? Well, I like your style. You are a peach,' was the roast which fell from Lavigne's lips. The remark landed him in the cooler and he remained there until the sport was over."[1] After securing his freedom, the Kid returned to Saginaw to ring in the New Year.

On New Year's Day 1899, welterweight champion, Tommy Ryan, wrote a piece for the *New York Herald* titled, "Pugilism Should Boom."[2] It delivered his prognostications of fistic events for the coming year. In it he predicted that the heavyweight champ, Bob Fitzsimmons, would not fight anymore, content to sit on his well-earned laurels. He was wrong, as Fitzsimmons lost the championship to Jim Jeffries by an 11th round knockout in June. He believed with Fitzsimmons idle, the title would then pass to the winner of the Kid McCoy-Tom Sharkey match in early January, noting that if Sharkey didn't get McCoy early he wouldn't win. Ryan was right about this bout. Sharkey knocked out McCoy in the 10th round of their 20-round fight. Settling any question as to who ruled the heavyweights, Jeffries defeated Sharkey in 25 rounds in November to close the year as the champion.

Ryan continued, "In the lightweight division there is likely to be a most interesting struggle. Kid Lavigne and Jack Daly are both bound to go by the board, in my opinion, and the contest for supremacy lies between Dal Hawkins, the Californian, and Joe Gans, the Baltimore Negro." Ryan's lightweight crystal ball proved to be quite hazy. He was correct on Daly who was savagely knocked out by middle-of-the-road lightweight, Tim Hearns, in 1899. He was wrong on Gans who would be knocked out by "Elbows" McFadden, and on Hawkins who would be knocked out by Frank Erne. Three of the four went "by the board" in '99. Would Lavigne join them? Given this jumble it was beginning to look like Erne was the one to beat.

Through the early days of January several fights with Lavigne were the talk of the newspapers. "Spike" Sullivan turned down an offer from a San Francisco club for a $4,500 purse to fight the Kid. It was clear that although he boasted of being ready and eager to battle the champion, his actions said otherwise when he countered the offer, demanding $10,000 plus $1,000 for training expenses and an eastern referee. He used a well-worn ploy of countering with outrageous demands to scuttle the potential match. Late in January he challenged Lavigne to a finish-fight in Carson, Nevada. Sullivan's reputation as one who talked big but avoided the big matches was well intact. On another front, a deal was struck for Lavigne to fight a third bout with Owen Ziegler for six rounds on January 21 in Chicago. That fight never came to fruition either.

Somehow emboldened by his lackluster victory over another welterweight in Tracey, the Kid took a careless step. In late January he issued a challenge to meet any boxer in the world at the welterweight limit of the time, 142 pounds. On February 1, one of the Kid's close friends, welterweight champion Mysterious Billy Smith, decided it was time, once and for all to see who the better of the two was. Smith abandoned his attempts to make a match with middleweight champion, Tommy Ryan, and accepted the Kid's challenge. By mid-month, an agreement had been made to fight 20 rounds at Woodward's Pavilion in San Francisco on March 10, 1899. They would fight for 60% of the gate receipts with the winner taking home 65% and the loser 35%.

The "Dixie Kid" versus Joe Wolcott in 1904 at Woodward's Pavilion, San Francisco
- Courtesy of BoxRec

The Mysterious One

Mysterious Billy Smith was one of the more enigmatic and colorful pugilists from the beginning of his fistic career in 1890 to his last bout in 1915. Born Amos Smith in 1871, in Nova Scotia, Canada, there are several accounts of how Smith got the moniker, "Mysterious," with one story that seems to be the most plausible. As told by Murray Greig in *Goin' the Distance*, Smith dropped in on Captain Cooke, editor and noted sports writer for the *Boston Police News*, asking Cooke if he could assist him in getting some bouts. Cooke agreed but only on the condition that Smith change his name to Billy as he felt Amos was too delicate. Instead, in his very early career Smith used the name "Jack Nickle" as he didn't want his family to know he was fighting.[3] He had a few bouts on the "smoker" circuit of Boston that impressed no one. Then he disappeared.

Several months later Cook began to get dispatches from the West Coast about a fighter by the name of Billy Smith who was getting the better of some well-known fighters from feathers to welters. As Greig tells it, "Reading one of the dispatches one day, Cooke casually remarked to an assistant: 'Here's another story about that mysterious Billy Smith. Put his picture with it and run it on page one.' Sure enough, the picture appeared above a caption that read, 'Mysterious Billy Smith Wins Again!'—and the handle stuck."[4] Other versions have Smith disliking his given name and changing it on his own, as well as never disclosing his age or where he learned how to fight, adding to his mysterious aura.

Perhaps his most infamous characteristic was his style of fighting. By all accounts and descriptions he was one of the dirtiest fighters of all time. Before his career was through he would lose 22 fights of which 12 would be lost due to disqualification for any of a number of offenses. "He came to fight and he used every possible tactic to win. Grabbing, holding, pushing, pulling, shoving, biting, butting, kneeing, hitting low, hitting after the bell, rabbit punching, and stepping on his opponent's feet were all part of Smith's arsenal," noted Tracy Callis.[5]

"Mysterious" Billy Smith – Courtesy of BoxRec

As a teenager he worked the docks in the Bay of Fundy and tussled regularly with larger men, honing the street fighting skills that would mark his brawling ring style throughout his career. One writer noted that if he fought in an earlier era when there were far fewer rules he would have been unbeatable. He was the last man you'd want to meet in a dark alley.

Early in his career Smith managed his own affairs and booked his own matches. In Spring Valley, Illinois, in 1894 he was scheduled to fight a coalminer by the name of Eddie Butler, built up by the locals as the "Terror of the Midwest." Stewart H. Holbrook, author of *Holy Old Mackinaw*, was a personal friend of Smith's and recounted the story of the fight as told to him by Billy in the 1940s. "When Billy arrived at the Spring Valley fight arena, he noted that although there was a man at the door to take tickets, a majority of the fans were entering by way of four open windows. Billy complained to the lone policeman. 'They're only kids,' said the officer, wholly uninterested. Billy remarked that he had never before seen kids with walrus mustaches and full beards. He threw off his coat and got busy plugging these woeful leaks, moving swiftly from window to window, punching in the nose every face as it came up over the sill. 'I just couldn't afford to lose all that money,' he told me, still righteously indignant."[6]

After calm was finally restored and the fight had started Smith noted that he did all his fighting in the center of the ring as getting near the ropes was sure to tempt payback from one of the mugs he slugged earlier. His plan was to let Butler go eight rounds or so to give the natives their money's worth but in the first round chunks of coal began whistling into the ring. Instead, he made short work of the 200 pound Butler, knocking him out in the second round. Mayhem broke loose as he left the ring, his escape aided by a handy water bottle he used to cold-cock three spectators. He needed a police escort out of town after collecting his pitiful purse of $117. Smith simply loved a good donnybrook inside the ring or out.

One of his more infamous scraps was when he fought fellow brawler, Billy Gallagher in July of 1896. A minute into the first round the men clinched and Smith used a hip throw to toss his man to the boards then stepped on his head. An enraged Gallagher got to his feet rushing Smith who repeated the same sequence with a boot-to-the-head encore. The police captain on duty objected to the brutal display. The referee immediately stopped the fight and ruled it a draw perhaps fearful what might have happened had he disqualified Smith. Smith and Gallagher met two days later at a saloon and after Smith knocked his man down he proceeded to kick and bite him until others broke it up with a bucket of hot water.[7]

Smith's next bout was with "Australian" Jimmy Ryan. In the seventh round Ryan slipped to the canvas. Before he could regain his feet Smith hammered him. The police intervened and the referee awarded the fight to Ryan on a disqualification. Smith was not happy and promptly knocked out the referee.[8] The referee was apparently not wise to Smith's recent ring history. A ruling of a draw may have spared the official from his own ten-count.

The Mysterious One had plenty of bravado to go with his extensive bag of rough-cut fighting skills. As legend has it, at the very beginning of his professional career he was in New Orleans 10 days prior to a middleweight title fight between "Nonpareil" Jack Dempsey and Bob Fitzsimmons scheduled for January 14, 1891. Smith, hearing that Dempsey was short on sparring partners sought out Dempsey's manager and volunteered to lend a hand, literally. He was told to show up the next day at the gym.

Smith, although knowing he was about to spar with the storied middleweight champion still declined the offer of protective head gear. Referring to Dempsey he flippantly said, "Give it to the dandy over there." Those who looked on were amazed as the two fighters went at it hammer and tongs with neither giving an inch. When they were through, Jack told young Smith he would be the next welterweight champion of the world.[9] And indeed he was, when in September of 1892 he knocked out Billy "Shadow" Maber in the 26th round of a finish-fight.

He was the first of five "Mysterious Billy Smiths," the second one being his son, a lightweight who fought from 1923-1925 out of Portland, Oregon like his father. He would eventually lose the welterweight title to Tommy Ryan in 1894 and regain it in 1898 when Ryan vacated it to seek the middleweight title. Smith lost the title in 1900 on a disqualification in the 21st round of a fight with Rube Ferns. Ferns had been down 15 times over the course of the fight. The fact that Smith dominated the fight and lost on a foul allowed him to keep his title in the court of public opinion. He "officially" lost it three months later when he was knocked out in the 19th round by Matty Matthews.

"Kid Lavigne has a contract upon his hands that is worrying some of his friends and ardent admirers," noted the *Detroit Free Press* of the upcoming bout with Smith. "Smith was ever a tough proposition, no matter whom he faced, and as he has been fighting fairly as well as fiercely lately, he is looked upon as one of the most dangerous men in the ring. Lavigne is a wonder, and no mistake, but he has made a bad match this time and is more in danger of defeat than he has been at any time in his long and creditable ring career."[10] Smith had plenty of professional experience as well, having fought 58 bouts before signing to meet the Kid, losing eight times, with five the result of fouls.

Not only were the Kid's friends concerned about the match-up, they were also a bit perplexed by it. Those close to Lavigne knew that the Kid and the Mysterious One were good chums. They also knew that the Kid's brother Billy had a strong dislike for Smith, most probably because he saw the ruinous effect the hard-partying Smith had on George. Billy and Smith had a "row" several weeks before the Kid and Smith were matched to fight. As the story goes, Billy was so angry with Smith that he pushed the Kid into fighting his good friend. George begged Billy to back off but he was insistent. Billy wanted his brother to punish Smith in the ring to settle his own grievance with him. The Kid finally relented and agreed to the bout.

Lavigne-Smith Fight Program – Courtesy of Don Scott

Lavigne knew this would be an impossible task. He described Smith as "a savage, ruthless, welterweight of enormous strength."[11] Smith would enter the ring at the peak of his fistic career while Lavigne was seen by all as having lost a step and a bit of the fire that marked him. The two fighters had one thing in common: both had fought the "Barbados Demon" Joe Wolcott multiple times. The Kid defeated Wolcott twice, once by knockout. Smith fought Joe three times; 15- and 25-round draws, and a 20-round win on points.

Most of the newspapers of the day reported that Lavigne was in top shape for the fight, training once again at Blanken's Six-Mile House. His training routine consisted of 10 to 12 miles of road work in the morning followed by bag punching and rope skipping in the afternoon. Not all sources agreed. He had been idle for nearly four months and one writer asserted that he was in no shape to fight "after weeks of trying the gin mills."[12]

A Foul Filled Affair

Five thousand sports were on hand the evening of the fight with odds in favor of Lavigne at 10-to-8. Smith weighed in at 142 pounds. He had a five inch height advantage and three inches in reach. Lavigne tipped the scales at just under 138. Once again baseball umpire Jim McDonald was the referee for the bout. At 9:15 p.m. the principals entered the ring. While the combatants' gloves were being inspected by Captain Gillen of the San Francisco police, Billy Lavigne lodged a protest with Smith's corner regarding his hand wraps which he contended far exceeded the standard of one band. After several minutes delay and shivering in his corner while he waited, the Kid went to Smith's corner and told his brother to drop the objection. That settled, the ring announcer informed the crowd that the contestants had agreed to break away clean without hitting. At 9:30 p.m. the gong rang for the start of the first round.

Round one was marked by hot exchanges with Lavigne the aggressor. He flailed away with rights and lefts forcing Smith to clinch frequently to save himself from further punishment. Each time the two clinched, Smith worked his free hand on the Kid's ribs. The crowd howled their displeasure at what they saw as a blatant disregard of the agreement to break cleanly. Each time it happened the referee admonished Smith. At the end of the round Smith spoke with the referee claiming he was not in violation of the agreement. He made the argument that it was within the rules to hit with a free hand while in the clinch. He believed the agreement meant that the men could not hit while breaking from the clinch.

The second round was all Lavigne again rushing Smith from corners to ropes. Smith opened the round with a stiff right to the Kid's head. "In the succeeding clinch Smith resumed his old tactics of hitting and was roundly hissed," reported the *San Francisco Call*.[13] Smith continued to hit in the clinches throughout the second and third rounds, disregarding the referee's cautions each time it occurred. The *Call* noted by the third, "Cries from the gallery and pit of 'Foul,' and 'What is the referee there for?'" were numerous. The crowd was decidedly in favor of Lavigne.

By the end of the fifth round the *Call* estimated that Smith had thrown at least twenty foul blows. Finally, Referee McDonald warned Smith that if he continued he would award the fight to Lavigne. By this time, Lavigne had begun to hit a few times in the clinches as well but only after he was convinced that the referee would not uphold the original agreement. The *Boston Daily Globe* noted that by the end of the fifth round, "The Kid's side was red from the effects of Smith's punching in the clinches."[14]

Lavigne would later recall, "He committed every foul possible. Twice the referee awarded me the decision but I refused to take it that way."[15] This quote, uttered nearly 30 years later, is evidence that the passage of time often distorts events of the past. There is no record in any of the newspaper accounts of the day that corroborates the Kid's version of McDonald awarding the fight to him and him refusing it.

The Kid drew first blood in the fifth. In the sixth frame Lavigne began to work for the body and landed several powerful rights to the stomach and ribs of Smith. Near the end of the round while in a clinch, Smith hit the Kid with a right to the ribs and then on the jaw. "The latter blow jarred Lavigne, who, while holding on, looked around as if appealing to the referee," wrote the *San Francisco Chronicle*.[16] Referee McDonald did nothing.

The seventh was marked by both men throwing wild but rarely connecting flush followed by repeated clinches. Again Smith struck Lavigne on the jaw in a clinch. "Lavigne quietly dealt Smith a blow in return," continued the *Chronicle*, "and while pushing him away Smith said, 'That's right George. You do the same.'" Lavigne was the aggressor in the eighth with Smith throwing left leads but moving away as he did it to keep clear of the Kid's hard body smashes. Then in a furious rush Lavigne went past Smith as he sidestepped. The Kid ended up with his head through the ropes and Smith wasting no time in getting in a hard right hand in the small of the back. Unfazed by just about any tactic from this converted street fighter, "Lavigne pulled himself away from the edge of the ring and grinned."[17]

The ninth round was tame by comparison with few telling blows landed while Lavigne chased Smith back and forth. The round saw lots of feinting, ducking, clinching and smothering of blows. To this point the fight was honors Lavigne. In the 10th, the tide began to change. Both fighters exchanged rushes with Smith getting the better of it. Late in the round Smith got in two rights in succession to Lavigne's jaw. The Kid spread his legs as his head popped back and forth from the blows. He clinched quickly to clear his head. He returned to his corner with a look of concern on his face at round's end.

Rounds 11, 12, and 13 were unremarkable as the men both seemed to tire a bit. An occasional stiff body blow punctuated the fray. Lavigne tried hard to land his right but Smith was shifty and got inside the blow. For his part the Kid was doing a good job of crouching, ducking, and evading Smith's repeated attempts to land on his head. The three rounds were slightly in favor of Smith.

"The end came in a curious way in the fourteenth round," wrote the *San Francisco Call*. "After several counters and blocks Lavigne landed hard on the head without a return. The blow warmed up Smith, who came back at his antagonist swinging his left and right for the head. He landed twice on the face and a hard right on the jaw. The Kid reeled as if nearly out, but essayed a weak rush back covering his jaw with his left hand. Then his brother Billy jumped through the ropes and threw his arm over the Kid's shoulder, saying something to the referee about Smith having fouled him long enough and led the Kid to his corner."[18]

The referee had no choice but to award the fight to Smith on a technical knockout on Billy's breach of the rules by entering the ring. Based on this one description of the final round it remains plausible that the Kid could have recovered and made it to the bell as the round was almost over. But listen to another version of the end as told by the *San Francisco Chronicle*. "Lavigne was in a bad way, he came in with his legs wide apart, and Smith stood in close and put in snapping blows on the jaw with his right. The Kid tottered along with his back touching the ropes. His arms were dangling and his body swaying. Smith watched him as a hawk watches its prey, and was on the point of stepping forward and delivering a knockout blow when Lavigne's brother jumped into the ring. He ran toward the reeling champion and clasped him around the neck with his left arm waving Smith away."[19]

On The Retrograde

To an unbiased eye it was clear that Billy had stepped in to save his brother from unnecessary punishment. "He has been with George at many a ringside," continued the *Chronicle*, "and he saw last night what he never saw before—his brother bending beneath a rain of furious blows and almost ready to sink to the floor. He saw that a knockout was inevitable and the prospect of witnessing it was too much for him."[20]

The Kid had gone 12 years and six months without a loss. Over the course of 54 fights he had never been knocked down for a count. It's possible that as much as any other motivating factor, Billy stopped the fight in the way that he did to spare his brother a physical knockout, knowing that by doing so he would take the blame for a technical knockout through his rule violation. It may have had yet another angle. He despised the Mysterious One so much that by stopping the fight he robbed Smith of bragging rights as the first person to ever "legitimately" knockout the Saginaw Kid.

But there is yet another point to chew on. The "dirtiest" boxer ever, if he wasn't a personal friend of his foe in the ring, would not have stopped when he saw Billy enter the ring. With his man in dire straits, he would have let fly that last blaster and dropped his foe before his corner could have rescued him. He did not. Instead he backed off, and then went to the Kid's corner to shake his hand. Two things we will never know: Did the friendship of the two predetermine a merciful outcome of the fight? And, just how close to the end of the round was it when Billy caused the referee to stop the bout?

On the first point, it is possible that the two close friends agreed behind the scenes to box a hard 20 rounds to a draw. The fouling that Smith was accused of was quite tame by his standards. A Smith fight would lack credibility if he didn't do some amount of roughhousing adding an air of authenticity to the match. Smith would gain little by a victory over a man in a lower weight division and would not be able to claim the lightweight title as he was nine pounds over the limit. Lavigne would have gained greatly with a win over a welter of Smith's caliber and would have captured his title as well. Neither result would have been acceptable to both fighters.

The *San Francisco Call* made a statement that supported the theory of a pre-arranged draw when it wrote: "The old saying that a good little man cannot cope with a good big man was fully exemplified all through the mill. But although Lavigne has proven to be a wonder in several battles, it must be said that according to the display he gave last evening in hitting and staying qualities he is fast on the retrograde. Smith made no apparent endeavor to deliver to his customer any of the hard goods which he is in possession of until the thirteenth round arrived. In fact, he toyed with Lavigne for several rounds and let opportunities pass . . . But for some reason best known to the mysterious gentleman he allowed the interest in the affair to go on until the fourteenth round, near the end of which he smashed Lavigne a brace of left-handers on the jaw in a mix-up which apparently dazed the receiver."[21]

Adding a bit of fuel to this fire, the Kid, who was relatively unmarked but for some redness on his ribs, would say, "I admit I was a little bit on queer street, but was not a bit distressed and could have gone on and finished if my brother had not come into the ring." And after some of Lavigne's epic battles, the first Walcott bout of note at which John L. Sullivan was calling for the Kid's corner to throw in the sponge, who could doubt that he may have yet again risen from the ashes to stay the 20 rounds and at least gotten a draw with Smith. And the question persists, would Smith have held back a knockout blow and allowed Lavigne to recover, had Billy not intervened?

"Lavigne is the best lightweight that ever breathed," Smith said after the bout, "but he was a little out of his class when he tried to tackle a welterweight. He is the fastest fellow I have ever seen for his size. I had him going a dozen times, but he would not go down. I walloped him on the jaw time and again but he stood it like a little man. . . . I am glad Billy Lavigne jumped into the ring when he did as I did not want to knock the Kid out and another punch might have settled him."[22]

Billy Lavigne chimed in after the fight as to his reasons for entering the ring. "The referee should have awarded the fight to my brother earlier in the contest. Smith repeatedly fouled him and kept up these tactics right along. He had a great advantage in fouling. I got tired of seeing him continuing it and jumped into the ring. I did not do so to save my brother from a knockout, but simply because I would not stand for Smith's rough work. Had George followed Smith's game I would not have interfered, but as he didn't and was getting the worst of the deal, I jumped in."[23] Billy's credibility on this point is suspect. The *San Francisco Chronicle* would go so far as to say that "it wasn't the best excuse that could have been offered at that particular moment, for Smith was doing no fouling just then."[24]

Referee McDonald gave his own assessment of his decision to halt the match and award it to Smith as a result of Billy entering the ring. "Had that not occurred, and the fight had gone the limit, I would have declared it a draw, because in my opinion Lavigne had the best of the fight up to the tenth round. From the tenth to the fourteenth Smith showed to advantage. I could not decide differently as the rules expressly prohibit any of the seconds entering the ring during the fighting."[25]

So by the referee's own admission they were headed for a draw after all. Again, it's possible that the two agreed to have Lavigne take the first 10 rounds and Smith the next 10. When the Kid landed hard to Smith's head in the beginning of the 14th and "the blow warmed up Smith," the Mysterious One may have gone off script because he was pissed and overreacted by catching the Kid with some hard returns. The Kid staggered, his brother panicked, jumping into the ring to stop the fight, and the best laid plan was scuttled. Plausible? Definitely. Provable? Not 113 years later.

The 58-year-old Lavigne would remember the aftermath of the fight differently than did the 29-year-old Kid. In late March of 1899 reports surfaced that Lavigne was "laid up" with a broken rib as a result of the Smith contest. He scoffed at the suggestion and maintained that he never felt better in his life. The Kid was accepting of his loss to Smith, brushing it off with, "those things are bound to happen once in a while."[26] It appeared he was ready to move on both physically and mentally. He'd only lost the bout, not his championship title.

The older Lavigne was unrestrained by the ego of his early days when he looked back over nearly three decades to tell possibly a more accurate version of events. After the fight he recalled, "I felt a severe pain in my side. Later, back in Saginaw, my physician found this was due to a new injury to the ribs which Joe Wolcott had cracked for me. . . . Although beaten by Smith, I still retained the lightweight title because we fought over the lightweight limit. But I saw that my days as champion were numbered."[27]

The *Police News* in poetic tone summarized the fistic career of Lavigne before his loss to Mysterious Billy Smith: "Upon the scroll of fame where rests Lavigne's name the vellum is as yet unspoiled—not a black mark or defeat hovers near his record."[28] All that had now changed. The Kid's record was tainted and the gathering dark was upon him.

CHAPTER 25

Reign's End

By several accounts, the Kid was furious with Billy for stopping the fight with Smith. One source from the 1940s claimed that he didn't talk to his brother again for two years. Newspaper accounts of the turn of the century contradict this assertion reporting that Billy was in the Kid's corner for his very next fight four months later. It may have been a short-lived riff in the relationship. "Judging from the telegraphic reports from San Francisco, Lavigne has had a falling out with his brother and manager and hereafter will do his own matchmaking," wrote the *Milwaukee Evening Wisconsin*. "It was a mistake for Lavigne to go out of his class to fight a champion welterweight, and as mistakes of this kind have been common with him since separating from his old manager, Sam Fitzpatrick, he may be expected to make them in the future."[1] On the contrary, the record clearly shows that Billy remained the Kid's manager.

For months now the Lavigne camp had been trying to reach an accord to fight a return battle with the "Iron Man" of England, Dick Burge. Finally a deal was put together to fight at 144 pounds for a purse of $2,500 and a side bet of $2,500 at the Bolingbroke Club on the evening of Derby Day, which happened to be three years to the date of Lavigne's defeat of Burge for the world championship. Lavigne had put off all other suitors and was making plans to sail for England in mid-April. Then word from England delayed the Kid's travel plans and on April 24, 1899 a cablegram from London scuttled the deal altogether. "Burge's backers decline to back Burge except to fight at the National Sporting Club. Consequently match off," read the terse communication.[2]

George Lavigne and Billy Lavigne Poster - Courtesy of John Cuthbertson

Burge had gotten into an altercation with the gifted black pugilist, Bobby Dobbs, at the National Sporting Club. In the vernacular of the day, "Burge is reported to have considerably damaged the darkey's visage," reported the *Police News*. As a result of their brawl, both boxers had been barred from the Club. In refusing to back Burge at an alternate venue, it appeared to the London press that Burge's people "practically acknowledged that Lavigne's game is tougher than they want for their money."[3]

With the cancellation of the Burge bout several suitors began making offers to fight the champ. Some came from top-flight lightweights and some from boxing neophytes. Bobby Dobbs, returning from England after a very successful tour in which he defeated Dick Burge, wanted a match at 133 pounds. And as an example of the other end of the spectrum there was Jig Stone for whom it would have been his fourth professional bout, having lost his first three.

Spike Sullivan had played a cat and mouse routine, harassing Lavigne for a match for several months. Lavigne finally capitulated and booked a match at 133 pounds for May 15 at the Lenox Athletic Club in New York. In an ironic twist of fate it would be Lavigne who would cancel the match claiming he was sick saying, "When I get in the ring with that fellow I want to give the people their money's worth. I couldn't do it now. I also want to hold my title and when I get ready to meet this Boston man I will be ready to beat him."[4] It may have been that the effects of the Kid's broken rib persisted and he wisely wanted to give himself more time to recover before stepping back in the ring. A more jaded explanation

253

held that he had been drinking hard and wasn't ready or willing to do the necessary training.

A Second Go With Erne

Even before the Burge cancellation Lavigne said that he felt he could still get the better of Mysterious Billy Smith and intended to make a rematch with him upon his return from London. Instead, Frank Erne got the nod and in late May a match was set for July 3, 1899. It would be 20 rounds at the cavernous, 15,000 seat Hawthorne Athletic Club in Cheektowaga, New York for a purse of $7,500. This was the site of their first scheduled match that was cancelled as a result of interference by the sheriff. That match had been rescheduled and fought in New York City, a 20-round draw.

Since the draw in September, 1898, Erne had impressive victories in a seventh-round knockout of hard punching and crafty Dal Hawkins, and a 25-round win over a top-tier lightweight in George "Elbows" McFadden. Erne had steadily improved while Lavigne had lost a step and some of his relentless fire. The Kid knew from their last battle that there wasn't much separating the two in their ability to scratch out a win. Lavigne thought highly of Erne. "This boy Erne is a good one," the Kid commented. "He has shown up well in all of his fights and there is no reason why any man should expect to find anything but a tough proposition. He is clever—that is a cinch—and he can hit some as his knockout of Dal Hawkins and others showed. A mighty decent fellow too is Frank."[5]

At the end of May, the Kid left for Oceanic, New Jersey where he would begin his preparation for the bout. "Lavigne intends to train as he never did before," noted the *Detroit Free Press*, "and says he would not dare return to Michigan if he loses this fight."[6] While training he sent a letter to Billy who was already in Cheektowaga, saying he never felt better or stronger and figuring on the form shown by Erne in their former battle, he thought he should win in 10 or 12 rounds. But in order to do so, he would have to get to Erne first. "From reliable sources the information has come that Erne intends to make a long range fight of it if possible," continued the *Press*, "and may be able to keep out of harm's way for twenty rounds." And yet rumors would persist that the Kid was "out on the town" often and not training as conscienciously as he should have for a fight of this magnitude.

Even though Lavigne was quite popular in New York, the easterners believed Erne would wear the lightweight laurels on the evening of July 3. The Michigan folk, along with the old time fight fans, were skeptical and like the man from Missouri would say, "Show me the fighter who can whip Lavigne. I will believe it after I see the act performed and not until them."[7] They argued about what chance Erne would have against the tough welterweights the Kid had fought in Joe Wolcott, Dick Burge, Jack Everhardt and Mysterious Billy Smith. "All of these fellows, with the exception of Smith, went down before the powerful blows of the lightweight champion, Kid Lavigne, the greatest fighter of his inches the world had ever known . . . he has more than an even chance with men of his weight, no matter how clever or strong they may be."[8] Even so, the odds were 100-to-90 in favor of the Kid.

A chiseled Lavigne in 1899 - Courtesy of Antiquities of the Prize Ring

Over 7,500 fight fans were in attendance the evening of the bout. Both fighters looked finely trained with Erne at 133 pounds and Lavigne at 135. Lavigne's seconds were his brother Billy, Jimmy Robinson, Jack Hanley and Billy St. Mary. Erne's seconds were Frank Zimpfer, George Salie, and Billy Huber. Leading up to the contest there had been some controversy as to who would be acceptable to both camps as a referee for the bout. It was finally settled with satisfaction. The crowd cheered its approval when referee "Honest John" Kelly stepped into the ring. "You're all right," one of the ringside sports said. "We know we will get an honest run for our money."[9] With the moniker of "Honest John" one would expect no less.

At last time was called to begin round one. After both fighters fiddled a bit for an opening Lavigne made the first lead but his left to the head was blocked. The men traded head and body blows with Erne blocking and dodging several. Near the end of the round Erne's nose began to bleed. In the second, Lavigne again opened with a rush and was blocked but then got in a hard left on Erne's stomach. The

Kid got in a left smash to the face but was countered with a tremendous left on the stomach. Erne continued to show his cleverness by blocking Lavigne's blows and countering effectively to body and head.

The Kid led in the third and "then Erne electrified the crowd with a beautiful left on the Kid's face."[10] Lavigne attempted several feints to try and draw Erne in but Frank didn't bite. The Kid landed a right and left on the jaw and got two hard body shots from Erne in the exchanges. "Lefts and rights were exchanged on the breast and neck and Lavigne, boring in, sent an awful left over the heart," reported the *Detroit Free Press* on the fourth-round action. Erne fought back but Lavigne landed another smashing heart blow. Erne straightened the Kid up from his crouch with a right uppercut. The men were sparring as the round ended.

Erne led first in the fifth and got the best of the infighting throughout the round. At one point Lavigne appeared to get angry and swung wildly which Erne ducked. The first minute of the sixth round saw both fighters trying to draw the other in with little success. The men each landed some good shots to body and head in the round with Lavigne forcing the pace toward round's end. At this point in the contest it was honors even.

The seventh round would prove to be the turning point in the fight. After some heavy exchanges, Erne caught Lavigne with a terrific left on the face drawing blood from his nose. A moment later he landed a hard left on the jaw staggering the Kid. He pounded Lavigne with a series of rights and lefts to his head and face. "A fusillade sends the Kid staggering away and groggy," wrote the *New York World*. "Bloody and weak with blood flowing, the Buffaloan punched the champion at will."[11] The Kid fought back wildly and it looked as if the Saginaw Kid would go down. "His seconds cried to him, 'Block George.'"[12] As the bell rang the groggy, staggering champion fell into his seconds arms.

The eighth round was tame by comparison. Lavigne recovered well but it was evident he had lost much of his speed. Erne, instead of pressing the fight inexplicably hung back, waiting for the Kid to come to him. Even without leading, Erne's clever punching gave him the honors for the eighth and ninth rounds. "Frank has Lavigne's face covered with blood and is fighting a cool, clever battle," wrote the *World* of the 10th round, "jabbing Lavigne's face to a jelly and taking no chances of catching one of Lavigne's bad swings. The champion's left eye is closed and the Buffalo boy is unmarked."[13]

The 11th was an even round and in the 12th Erne seemed to tire and lacked the aggressiveness of his opponent. Lavigne was still throwing with both hands but was having a hard time blocking Erne's straight left which was pummeling his face. The 13th and 14th were marked by Lavigne getting stronger and forcing the pace but still taking a lot of punishment for his efforts.

"Erne was as cool as the proverbial cucumber while Lavigne was in evident trouble when they came together," reported the *San Francisco Call* on the 15th round. Erne continued to play for the Kid's body to create openings on his head and neck. Near the end of the round Erne blocked two left leads then landed three hard lefts on the Kid's wind. "George returned to his corner much the weaker of the two."[14] Between rounds one of Lavigne's seconds told him to take a chance. As the fighters came together at the beginning of the 16th, the Kid tried one of his monster right hooks but missed by a hair. From that point on, the round was all Erne's and any counters the Kid threw lacked steam.

Of the 17th the *New York World* wrote, "Not a clean blow landed, though a couple of assays were blocked. The fight is Erne's by a round margin and he is content to block the leads and hold his advantage." The 18th was Erne's round as he punished Lavigne with body punches and continued to work on his badly swollen eyes with his left jab. In the 19th the Kid was wary but continued to try desperately for an opening. Erne got in a hard jab that once again brought blood from the Kid's nose. The fighters were sparring at the bell.

After shaking hands for the final round Erne slipped a Lavigne left to his head and came back with a right and left on the face. The intensity and finality of the round was best described by a special dispatch to the *San Francisco Call:* "Lavigne's countenance at this moment was anything but prepossessing, both eyes being closed. Right and left blows to the body brought Lavigne's guard down, and then Erne smashed his right to the neck and hooked his right to the face without a return. Game to the core Lavigne withstood this punishment and went to his opponent as if he were only beginning the bout. Erne was relentless, however, and forced the pace, fighting his man as if his life depended on the result. Lavigne never weakened but took his punishment like a stoic, but it was all day with him, and though beaten almost to a standstill, he returned to his corner having lost the championship, but none of his many friends and admirers."[15]

Champion No More

As expected by all, Referee Kelly awarded the fight to the new lightweight world champion, Frank Erne. "Lavigne's staunchest admirers could not but recognize the justice of this ruling, and many of them congratulated Erne before he left the ring and wished him the best of luck in defending his newly acquired title," reported the *Police Gazette*.[16] The *Chicago Tribune* was succinct in its summary of the bout when it wrote, "The Buffalo boy simply battered the title out of his opponent . . . he administered a terrific drubbing to Lavigne. Toward the end of the bout Lavigne's guard was useless and nothing but sheer gameness kept the Saginaw Kid from going under."[17]

Injuries to both men played a prominent role in how the fight unfolded. Early in the fight, Lavigne realized that the rib he broke in his fight less than four months earlier with Mysterious Billy Smith had not healed properly. The rib problem actually had its origin in the Kid's second bout with Walcott in late 1897. After the Erne fight he admitted the rib hampered him and changed his fight strategy. The *Detroit Free Press* reported, ". . . a blow on the ribs caused him to wince early in the fight, with the result that he devoted his time and attention to protecting his 'slats' and made little effort to prevent Erne from landing on his face. That being the case it is little wonder the battle was so one-sided."[18]

Erne's backers were puzzled when he didn't redouble his efforts to knock Lavigne out after the dominating seventh round. "It was a matter of great surprise to the spectators that Erne did not put the Kid out at once, but the mystery was made plain after the fight when it was learned that Erne broke his hand in the seventh round and was afraid of consequences," noted the *Fort Wayne News*."[19] Erne finally cut loose with everything he could muster in the twentieth round, throwing caution to the wind knowing he would need the damaged mitt no longer. Had he not broken his hand early, many at ring side believed Lavigne's undoing might have happened in half the time that it took Erne to win it.

Speculation aside on the impact of injuries to the outcome of the fight, Lavigne made it known that Erne had won fairly and cleanly and predicted that he would be champion for some time. "But it would be rather peculiar if I should come back and take it away from him, wouldn't it," said Lavigne.[20] Those close to the Kid learned that he intended to "cut out the habits that have been a handicap with the expectation of cutting a figure in the lightweight ranks for some years to come".[21]

However, the grip the alcohol habit had on the Kid would prove to be his most powerful opponent of all. Looking back from 1928 he reflected on the fight and the role that dissipation continued to play in the disintegration of his boxing skills and stamina when he wrote:

"The Buffalo lad was fast and he could hit, but he couldn't take it. Had I been able to speed up as in the old days, and give punishment, I would have stopped him. Considering that I had been drinking heavily for eighteen months, I think it is marvelous I was able to fight twenty rounds."[22] The beginning of this drinking binge coincided with his second defeat of Wolcott.

Two famous fistic sports were at ring side for the fight and each offered their thoughts on the end of the Kid's reign atop the lightweights. The first was former heavyweight champion, Jim Corbett. Late in the fight with the Kid taking a tremendous beating, bloodied and staggering with both eyes nearly closed but gamely fighting on, Corbett uttered, "Kid Lavigne and [Nonpareil] Jack Dempsey, the two gamest men the ring has ever known."[23]

And from Sam Austin, editor of the *Police Gazette*: "I am sorry, indeed, to see Lavigne lose his title, but he lost it as I always believed he would, fighting gloriously in defense of it. It was no disgrace to be beaten by a man of Erne's acknowledged ability. To have gone down in a conflict to some second or third-rate 'dub' would have been a disgrace indeed, but in resigning his title he leaves it in the care of a man who has proven his fitness to defend it with honor and credit. Lavigne's greatness as a fighter will never be disputed: he was a valorous champion."[24]

Austin believed that Erne's win over Lavigne signified a further stamp of legitimacy on the prevailing school of pugilism at the time. "Frank Erne, of Buffalo," he wrote, "fought one of the greatest championship battles in the annals of pugilistic history and only defeated him [Lavigne] by reason of his ability to demonstrate the superiority of the methods of the new school over the old. His work in the ring is an object lesson in the beauties of scientific pugilism and the acquired art of fighting."[25] Many a sport still preferred to watch a slugger stand the gaff and bang his opponent into ultimate submission. Even so, it was becoming harder to argue with Austin's assertion that the dominant style was that of the ring scientist. There just weren't many of the old-time pugs left to bear the standard of muscle and mayhem.

The *London Daily Mail*, perhaps still smarting from the Kid's knockout of their champion in '96, embellished their account of the final round of Lavigne's loss when they reported, "Erne had his man beaten, but Kid took his punishment wonderfully gamely, and it was near the end of the round when Erne knocked him out with a left uppercut."[26] Badly beaten, yes, but not knocked out, or down for that matter.

It's possible that writers at the *Detroit Free Press* read the *Mail's* inaccurate account. Being partial to their Michigan lad, they may have felt a pang of fistic patriotic duty to right the record when they expounded on Lavigne's vertical resilience putting to rest any association of the Kid with the canvas. The *Free Press* wrote, "Much consolation is found by the followers of the famous lightweight when they make the statement that in his long and wonderful career, not once has Lavigne been knocked down. More than that, he has not even been knocked to his knees and the distinction is his of being the only man to lose a championship without going to the floor."[27]

Erne had a tough go as a champion. A year after his defeat of Lavigne he would take on a featherweight, Terry McGovern. He agreed to fight at 128 pounds and knock McGovern out in 10 rounds or less. It was a disaster for Erne. After being knocked down twice in the third, his corner would throw up the sponge with nearly a minute remaining in the round. McGovern was a Lavigne-style fighter who held both the world bantamweight and featherweight titles when he fought Erne. In fairness to Erne, McGovern was as tough and powerful of a fighter, albeit in a slightly smaller package, as Lavigne was when in his prime. He was well deserving of his nickname, "Terrible" Terry. McGovern has been rated by various boxing authorities as the number one bantamweight and featherweight of all time.

"Terrible" Terry McGovern
- Courtesy of BoxRec

Against the prevailing wisdom of Sam Austin, this time a slugger beat the man with more science. Since Erne had agreed to train down to 128 pounds he was not willing to put his lightweight title on the line, even though 128 was still within the lightweight class. Had it not been for the fighters' agreement, McGovern would have been the first man to hold three division titles at the same time. Some in Erne's camp said that because their man made the lighter weight it robbed him of his power. A sound argument for a fighter who begins to fade in the 10th or 12th round but not for one who gets knocked sideways midway through the third. Erne was totally outclassed.

The Michigan sports and the old timers who had said that Erne would never hold up against the tough welters that Lavigne fought were proven to be prophets when Frank was knocked down by welterweight champion, Rube Ferns, in the first round, and knocked out in the ninth of a bout in September 1901. For comparison sake, while Ferns was a very good welter, when he fought Mysterious Billy Smith in early 1900, Smith had him down fifteen times before Smith lost on a foul in the 21st round.

Erne would defend his lightweight title four times, losing it to the "Old Master" Joe Gans in a first-round knockout in May 1902. He had beaten Joe in March, 1900 on a 12th round technical knockout. Gans asked the referee to stop the bout after getting a nasty cut from an accidental head-butt. Erne would not be so lucky the next time the two met. "I'd hardly warmed up," chuckled Erne. "I made one or two feints and, bang!—that was all—Gans had knocked me out with his first punch."[28] Erne's recounting of the short-lived battle might have put it in the record books as one of the fastest knockouts in a championship bout. However, this was the memory of a 70-year-old Erne recalling the fight for the *New York Times,* and that's not exactly how it happened. Erne lasted one minute and forty seconds and after being dazed by a Gans combination to the head he was knocked cold by a wicked right hand from Joe. The sands of time had erased the prelude for Erne, leaving only the searing memory of the moment the lights went out.

Lavigne would move on with no ill will toward Erne. "I am going to rest for a while," he said to the *Police Gazette.* "I am having my injured rib attended to. I should have done so long ago—before my fight with Smith. I haven't decided yet on any plans for the future, but you can gamble that I will do some more glove work."[29] The Kid was planning on getting one more shot at Erne down the road. "Lavigne should have no trouble in getting on matches in the future, as some of the other genuine lightweights may now screw up courage enough to fight him although they could not be dragged into the ring with him prior to his battle with Erne unless a derrick had been called into us. . . . A battle with Lavigne would not only show whether they are entitled to a chance at the champion, but would at the same time determine Lavigne's right to ask for another meeting with his conqueror."[30]

CHAPTER 26

Three Strikes and You're Out

While publically the Kid was nonchalant about what was shaping up to be the worst year of his fistic journey, privately he had to be gravely concerned when taking stock. His love for drink was a ball and chain he couldn't shake. Years of wading into the pummeling blows of skillful opponents, betting on wearing them out before they inflicted too much damage, had taken its toll, not just physically, but emotionally as well. A few months shy of 30 years old, he was a step slower and his indefatigable tenacity was waning. Most of his power was still there but he could no longer sustain the maniacal pace that made him the most formidable of opponents.

The Kid was very clear as to the primary reason for his fall from grace as reported by the *Sandusky Star*. "Kid Lavigne does not attempt to deny the decisive nature of his defeat at the hands of Frank Erne. Nor does the Saginaw wonder hesitate to give the reason for his downfall. He admits that his long dalliance with the stuff that has put better men than himself in their coffins has transformed him from a champion of champions into a has-been. 'A fighter holding the title of lightweight champion and able to defend it can easily make $15,000 a year,' says Lavigne. 'The only thing that can destroy his money making power is booze.'"[1]

In late July the Kid returned to New York and in an introspective mood pledged to lick his problem. "The former lightweight champion says that he has made up his mind that there is nothing in dissipation, and in the future will take care of himself," wrote the *Milwaukee Evening Wisconsin*.[2] But could he shake his demon and would it be enough to revive his speed and stamina at this late stage of the game?

It appeared that the Kid's vow to quit the "stuff" was short lived when on August 1, 1899 word came of his latest drunken escapade. "Kid Lavigne's friends sustained a severe mental shock the other day," wrote the *Police Gazette*, "when they read that he had enlisted in Uncle Sam's army and on his way to the Philippines had stopped off at Battle Creek, Michigan long enough to get gloriously drunk."[3] The dispatch is quoted in its entirety:

> "George, better known as Kid Lavigne, disappeared from public sight shortly after his defeat by Erne for the lightweight championship and remained quiescent until Tuesday, when he broke out in this city and attempted to clean out the police department. He was one of 12 recruits bound from Saginaw or Detroit for Fort Sheridan to join Colonel Gardner's Thirtieth volunteer regiment for Manila. When the station was reached a number of the recruits got off, among them Lavigne. He found a policeman standing on the platform and said he longed to lick the whole police force of Battle Creek. He and Policeman Gore mixed it up lively for a while, but Gore finally floored him with a smash in the eye. He chased Gore with a revolver until Policeman Bancroft came to Gore's assistance. Bancroft knocked him down with a club and the two officers hammered him good and plenty. They could not arrest him, as he was in the United States service and bound for the front. The Kid was badly battered up when the sergeant in charge of the party finally got him and his load of whisky aboard the train."[4]

It certainly sounded like the Kid, at least that person who was prone to drunken forays that landed him in trouble with the law on several occasions past. And maybe after losing two in a row, in a fit of depression he decided to do something as extreme as joining the army in hopes of fighting in an altogether different arena. Who would blame him or doubt he would do such a thing? However, this time it was an imposter using the Kid's name and fame to get a few headlines. "It was the grossest kind of a counterfeit in all particulars except that he could, according to reports, fight like a house afire," wrote Sam Austin.[5] The real George Lavigne was reportedly back in New York working hard to remain sober.

Back With Fitz

Confirmation of his abstemious ways was reported in the *Sandusky Star* in late August along with news of a reunion of sorts. "Kid Lavigne is once more under Sam Fitzpatrick's management. The Saginaw wonder is said to be fighting shy of the red stuff and to be anxious to regain his lost laurels."[6] Lavigne was offering to meet Bobby Dobbs or any of the lightweights who challenged him as a champion. Sam's influence was already evident as Lavigne's challenge no longer included the welterweights that had exacted their toll on him.

The "red stuff" was the likely cause of the dissolution of the relationship with Fitzpatrick two years past after the Kid was too drunk to fight Griffo. And yet Sam must have seen something in the Kid's new resolve to put himself back in the director's seat of what was surely looking like the downward trajectory of Lavigne's career. Then on August 25 word came that Fitz had signed his ex-champ to fight George "Elbows" McFadden at the Broadway Athletic Club of New York on October 6 at a weight not to exceed 135 pounds.

Broadway Athletic Club circa 1899 – Courtesy of Museum of the City of New York

The Kid's abandonment of his brother as his manager and his subsequent reunion with Fitzpatrick had everything to do with his health. In Billy's words, "George has been suffering from a fractured rib for a whole year, in fact, ever since his bout with Mysterious Billy Smith, and he is in no shape to fight. When he met Erne, George was in bad shape, physically, and Dr. Diehl told him not to enter the ring again for another year."[7] The Kid began pressing Billy to find his next opponent. Billy refused, saying, "At Saginaw he told me that if I did not match him with Erne at once he would go to New York and get matched there. Rest is what George needs now and not matches, and I hope he'll take good advice and act on it. The Kid's my brother and I speak this way because I take an interest in his welfare. I am not going to see him race to destruction if I can help it."[8]

The bullheaded Kid was off to New York in defiance of his brother's sage advice. When word reached Billy that George had taken up with Fitzpatrick and signed to meet McFadden, he was not surprised. A reporter asked Billy's opinion of the report. "Now what do you think of that?" Billy replied sarcastically. "I have been expecting some such thing for some time. The Kid is really no more fit to fight than an invalid, and any man who meets him will beat him. That is, they will put him away, for he will stand and take a terrible punching, but what will be the use?"[9] Would Billy's ominous prediction hold true? Was Fitzpatrick fully aware of the Kid's current limitations having not been close to Lavigne for nearly two years? All would become clear on October 6th. The Kid returned to the familiar haunts of Oceanic, New Jersey to begin preparations for his final bout of 1899.

An Engagement with "Elbows"

George McFadden was a solid lightweight who by the time of his bout with Lavigne had fought 38 times losing only four. His forte as a boxer was his defensive stance in which he held his guard high and used his elbows to deflect blows, thus the "Elbows" moniker. This would prove to be a significant advantage over a hard hitter like the Kid. For most of McFadden's early career his competition was unimpressive with the exception of a knockout of Joe Gans in the 23rd round. Coming in to the fight with the Kid, he had a string of five KO wins including the Gans fight. He then lost on points to Frank Erne in 25 rounds, and managed a draw with Gans in their second go. The two Gans bouts with the Erne fight in between were wonderful preparation for his bout with Lavigne. No one knew Gans better or fought him more times. Between 1899 and 1902 McFadden would fight Gans seven times, losing two, winning one, and notching two draws and two no-decisions over the course of 73 total rounds.

Intrigue was building as the fight date neared. "Lavigne's reputation will suffer materially if he fails to whip his opponent, and some of the smart followers of the pugilistic sport are inclined to favor McFadden's chance.... The latter has youth, ability and gameness in his favor," reported the *World*. "McFadden never really trained for a fight before, but realizing the importance of this battle, has been preparing himself industriously and will be in better condition tomorrow night than he was ever in before for a fight."[10] Under the guidance of Sam Fitzpatrick, Lavigne proclaimed he was never in better shape to fight as well.

George "Elbows" McFadden
- Courtesy of BoxRec

The men entered the ring at 9:50 p.m., each weighing 133 pounds. Lavigne was favored 100-to-90 in front of a record-breaking crowd of more than 6,000 "sporting men" that packed the building to the eaves. The first round was a hot one with Lavigne leading repeatedly but often failing to get by McFadden's puzzling defense. The Kid forced the fighting for three rounds. "He punched McFadden furiously," wrote the *World*. "His swings were wild and most of them were cleverly stopped, but now and then one landed that hurt."[11] Toward the close of the fourth round McFadden staggered the Kid with a left and right combination to the head.

"In the fifth McFadden took the aggressive, getting in on the Kid's wind and stopping the latter's rushes in a way that set the spectators cheering," recorded the *Saginaw Evening News*.[12] The Kid swung a hard right to the body that dropped McFadden to his knees, but he was up without hesitation. The next three rounds were more of the same with the Kid forcing the fighting to the point that many of his swings were wild. Near the end of the eighth round McFadden's straight left jabs began to close Lavigne's right eye. In the ninth, "Lavigne kept on leading ineffectually and getting smashed in the face," the *Evening News* continued. Lavigne's right eye was now completely closed yet he kept up his relentless onslaught of swings and jabs.

Twice in the 11th McFadden went to his hands and knees after taking some wicked shots to the stomach. The referee cautioned McFadden warning him to stay on his feet. It looked like a strategy McFadden employed much like a clinch . . . when he was in trouble he would drop to his knees, and given the rules Lavigne could not hit him in that position. The referee had seen him use it in the fifth and wanted to put a stop to it now. The Kid had seen this tactic used against him as well, way back in 1891 when the San Franciscan, Joe Soto, used it often in their 31-round bout.

Lavigne had the better of the fight through the first 12 rounds although he was taking severe punishment for his work. In the 14th round the fight began to turn decisively in McFadden's favor, when he got in half a dozen hard lefts on the Kid's face. The *World* noted, "Both of Lavigne's eyes were now in trouble, but smiling wearily at McFadden's puzzling defense, he kept on swinging as fast as his arms could move."[13] In the 15th McFadden sent the Kid down and staggered him a short time later. Things were beginning to slip away for Lavigne who was tiring from the pace he was keeping and the blows he was absorbing.

In the 17th McFadden connected with a hard right on the jaw sending Lavigne to the canvas but he was up instantly and boring in on his man. Toward the end of the 18th the Kid went down from a left jab and a push but was up in two seconds. He was then hammered to his knees from a hard uppercut as the bell rang and he wobbled unsteadily to his corner. If the Kid couldn't recover with the minute's rest, he wouldn't last through the 19th.

"The nineteenth round was one of fearful punishment for Lavigne," described the *New York Times*.[14] McFadden sensed the end at hand and went after Lavigne from the outset. The detail of this round bears repeating in its entirety from the wire service report out of New York to the *San Francisco Call* as it was a spectacle never before seen in the Kid's 13 years in the ring:

> "In the final round McFadden went right to his man and had him reeling with right and left swings on the head.

A right swing to the jaw put Lavigne to the floor, where he lay for six seconds. He got up reeling and tried to clinch, but was sent down twice more with similar blows. Each time he took almost the limit to get up, but it was beyond doubt that he was unable to cope with McFadden, who stood waiting to give him a final blow. The Kid clinched as he got up and the referee separated them. Then Mac nailed Lavigne with a left back of the ear and the Kid went down for nearly nine seconds. A left to the body floored Lavigne for the fifth time. He got up only to go down again, this time from a clinch with McFadden on top.

McFadden jumped up at once but Lavigne rose slowly. He staggered across the ring with McFadden hot after him. He rushed to a clinch. When the referee broke them Mac swung right to the head and uppercut his left to the chin. Lavigne went down again, but got up within the limit. He stood in a dazed condition. Mac measured him carefully and with a left swing this time sent him down and out. Time of the round: 2 minutes and 3 seconds."[15]

The Gamest of Mortals

The Saginaw Kid had finally been knocked out. The sportswriters exploded with praise for the fallen ex-champion. "Down to defeat went the gamest man of the pugilistic profession, when little George fell before a fusillade of blows," scribed the *Sandusky Star*.[16] Perhaps he was mortal after all. The *New York Times* honored Lavigne when it wrote, "He succumbed only after he had been punched into a state of complete exhaustion and was unable to keep his hands up to protect his jaw. An ordinary fighter would have had to quit sooner, but Lavigne is not an ordinary fighter. He took a grueling such as even a pugilist is seldom called upon to endure, but he was game to the last, and although he was knocked down seven times in the nineteenth round before the knockout came, he got to his feet seven times, dazed and helpless, but still ready to fight."[17]

One reporter noted that Lavigne's display of gameness was as remarkable as McFadden's blocking. Those crafty elbows may have proved the difference. Lavigne was so battered that several minutes elapsed before he realized what had happened. He would recall the fight in 1928: "McFadden gave me a terrific pounding, not any worse, perhaps, than I had taken in earlier years from greater fighters, but I lacked the staying power that once was mine. After the sixteenth round I remember nothing until I found myself in my dressing room."[18] Lavigne remembered one important detail incorrectly when he told the *Los Angeles Times* in the same article that his seconds later told him they had thrown up the sponge after he went down eight times. As all the news reports of the day concurred, Lavigne was knocked cold—no sponge or towel was involved.

Back in his home town of Saginaw Lavigne's defeat was no surprise to some of his friends, "for the Kid has not trained as he should have done and gone the pace that kills," wrote the *Saginaw Evening News*[19] The "pace that kills" being another veiled reference to his uncontrolled drinking habits. Detractors of Fitzpatrick emerged as well. The *Police Gazette* stated that "not a few criticized Sam Fitzpatrick severely for not 'throwing up the sponge' before the knockout blow was administered when it was apparent that nothing could save him from defeat."[20] One of the most vocal critics was Billy Lavigne who vented, "It was a mean shame to allow George to fight after a point when there was no chance for him to win, and I don't admire Fitzpatrick's way of handling a boxer. I guess George's fighting days are over."[21]

In the days after the fight, Lavigne's boxing demise was the talk of the sports world with comments like this from the *Racine Daily Journal*: "Kid Lavigne has decided to quit the ring and will probably join the ranks of retired pugilists who have gone into the saloon business in New York."[22] The saloon business was in the Kid's distant future but for now, the spunky former title holder remained undaunted in his desire to claw his way back up the championship ladder.

Fitzpatrick was convinced that Lavigne had it in him as well and kept working to make matches for his fallen lightweight. Just five days after the Kid's shellacking by McFadden, Fitz had nearly completed the arrangements for him to fight the hard punching Dal Hawkins at 133 pounds at the Broadway Club in New York on November 14. Hawkins, like Lavigne, had endured a humbling 1899 losing two of three fights. The match with Lavigne was not to happen. As the fight date neared Lavigne had to cancel. He had sustained a spine injury in the McFadden bout that had not yet healed.

Undeterred, Fitz pressed on and booked a six-round return match with McFadden for the 28th of November. Still not well, Lavigne had to cancel this one also. He said he intended to take a long rest. And the career's-end comments kept piling up. "A New York paper of recent date said the Saginaw lad has gone back to a battle with his old enemy, the booze," continued the *Daily Journal* a few weeks later. "Whatever the cause of his present lack of condition, it looks like a cinch that the once great Michigan boy has ended his career as a boxer."[23]

The Saginaw Kid entered the last year of the century as the undefeated lightweight champion on top of the world. Twelve months, three fights, and three defeats later he had, as Tommy Ryan had prophesied on New Year's Day, "gone by the boards." The Kid was in a deep hole. He never contemplated losing, let alone three in a row, or for that matter ever getting knocked off his pins. His rib, and now his spine kept him from getting back in the ring. He was slower and had lost a great deal of his stamina. And most importantly, there was no end in sight for his affair with John Barleycorn. The turn of the century may have been a joyous time for many revelers but for the ailing Lavigne it brought depression and uncertainty. He was out of the game for now.

CHAPTER 27

The Long Drought

Things were changing and people were moving on. On the first day of the new century the *Mansfield News* reported, "Billy Lavigne, brother of George (Kid) Lavigne, the former lightweight champion, will shortly take hold of the new athletic club at Cleveland."[1] This wasn't Billy's first business venture. He worked in a bathhouse in Saginaw in the early 1890s and by 1896 owned his own place on the corner of Washington and Tuscola streets, Hammam Bathhouse, which featured Turkish, Russian, and an oddity of the time, electric baths. The electric bath was a precursor to the modern tanning bed where a customer was "showered" with light rays, although not the type that burn the skin, while seated in a mostly enclosed cabinet.

He left the bathhouse business behind when the opportunity at the Business Men's Gymnasium, Cleveland's top sporting club, presented itself. The 1890s saw a dramatic increase in the number of athletic clubs in many states as laws grew more tolerant of "sparring exhibitions" in the more controlled environments of the clubs. The Cleveland club was tailor-made for Billy's experience in the fight game and he got busy promoting fights and fighters in his new position.

Given the last year the Kid had what better way for a famous wealthy fellow to shake the blues than to go on an excursion. Without explanation, he sailed for Paris on the steamship Champagne on January 11, 1900. How fitting, given his weakness for drink, that he would board a ship with the same name as an effervescent alcoholic beverage. He was mum as to his plans when reaching France but rumors were afloat that he was there to fight, but whom? The *Boston Daily Globe* had a source. "George Lavigne, that pugilist, better known as 'Kid' Lavigne, sailed for Paris, France yesterday. According to a friend, Lavigne has an offer to fight in Paris with the winner of the O'Brien-Erne fight. From the same source it was learned that the 'Kid' probably will fight in England with Dick Burge."[2]

The Kid and the Kicker

Erne and Jack O'Brien had fought to a 25-round draw in December and were working to make a rematch. Lavigne was still in no shape for another fight so the next piece of news was even more unbelievable. "The unexpected departure of Kid Lavigne for France last week is due to wealthy businessman M. Gahbell who is taking Lavigne there with the intention of matching him against Charlemont, the French champion kicker," claimed the *Mansfield News*.[3] "Champion kicker" was reference to a French form of martial art known as "Savate." It derived its name from the French word for "old boot," a heavy type of footwear that used to be worn during fights. Its origins go back to street fighting techniques of the early 19th century where combatants used their feet to strike each other.

In the early days of savate it lived up to its street fighting roots where almost anything was permissible. Just as boxing had gone through changes to make it less brutal and more acceptable to the masses, so too did this French form of foot fighting. Michel Casseux was the first to open a savate school in 1825 practicing a more respectable form of the art which disallowed eye gouging, head butting, biting, grappling and other, less savory forms of contact. Casseux's pupil Charles Lecour witnessed an English boxing match in 1838 and began training in boxing. He later put this newly acquired skill together with his foot techniques to create the modern form of savate or "boxe francaise," as it is known today.[4]

Lecour's pupil Joseph Charlemont and his son Charles Charlemont were responsible for the professional development of the sport. Charles was the French champion that Lavigne would face. As old English pugilism was going into decline, French savate was reaching its peak at the end of the 1890s. The French issued a challenge to determine which system was superior once and for all. Their best, Charles Charlemont, fought Jerry Driscoll, a good English middleweight with only three losses, one of which was a 14 round knockout at the hands of the very skilled welterweight, Bobby Dobbs. On October 28, 1899 Driscoll was counted out in the eighth round from a savate knee to the groin.[5]

Charles Charlemont (on left),
French Savate Champion

It made sense that an ex-world champion like Lavigne would hear of this contest and, looking for a new challenge, decide he would train in savate and test Charlemont. "The Kid has had considerable practice at the game," wrote the *New York World*, "and a good judge thinks well enough of his ability to take Lavigne to Paris to beat Charlemont at his own style of fighting."6 Unfortunately, no record of the Kid and Charlemont kicking and punching was found.

Charlemont and savate were fascinations of the sporting world at the turn of the century. Even the "Barbados Demon," Joe Wolcott was working on getting a match with him in July 1900. "It was to be a battle of fists, feet and skulls, with a special clause in the articles of agreement barring the use of the teeth," noted the *Boston Daily Globe*.7 Wolcott was well aware of the details of Charlemont's victory over Driscoll. Driscoll claimed that he was bitten by Charlemont in round one of their bout and Joe wanted to ensure that he would not be another victim of the Frenchman's teeth. No record of that bout, if it happened, was found.

When not fighting, Lavigne did what he did best outside the ring—imbibe. It's possible that one of the reasons he sailed for France in the first place was not only to leave the ring behind for a bit and convalesce but also to take in the sights of the Paris Exhibition, the world's fair that opened its gates in April 1900. With people converging from all over the world to attend the fair, the night life in Paris at the time was second to none. Having been raised in a French speaking household, his language skills would make him feel right at home. The popular pugilist would be in his element here.

In early May a report surfaced in New York that the Kid had tied the knot causing disbelief by one of his family members. "Kid Lavigne has found a wife and is now living in his own home in Paris, enjoying matrimonial bliss," noted the *Mansfield News*. "It is said that he first met Mrs. Lavigne in California when he fought Wolcott and has been in correspondence with her since. She heard of his recent bad luck and sent for him. After a few weeks' courtship they were married. She is said to have plenty of the 'long green.' Frank Lavigne doubts the story and says he recently received a letter from the Kid, who is now in London."[8] Frank, one of the Kid's younger brothers, was right to be skeptical. The Kid would get married eventually but, according to available records, it would happen in New York in 1905 not in Paris in 1900.

However, the marriage rumor would continue to gain some traction when the *Saginaw News* wrote in February 1900 that a Saginaw businessman had just received a letter from Lavigne wherein the Kid states that he is having a good time in Paris, and tells of other activities. "Since leaving here Lavigne married a young lady of French parentage and he and his wife are spending some time with her parents a short distance from Paris. George writes that Paris is not so fast as it had been painted, in fact he thinks it is considerably behind the times in a good many respects."[9]

Further proof that Lavigne was not enjoying matrimonial bliss in Paris and that he hadn't returned to the ring came from the *Milwaukee Evening Wisconsin*. "A Paris cable to the *New York Journal* says: 'Kid Lavigne, the prizefighter from Saginaw, Michigan, has been painting Paris lurid lately. Not finding any men to fight he set upon a poor little French woman. With her eyes black she entered the United States consulate and said Lavigne had beaten her but all she wanted was that he be sent back to Saginaw, where he might be out of temptation and do better. Consul-General Gowdy persuaded her to have the Kid arrested, and he is now in the hands of the police."[10] Mr. Hyde had struck again, this time quite literally. Still, it may have been that the "poor little French woman" he allegedly abused was his new wife, and seeing what a boor he was under the influence of drink, she sent him packing back to the U.S.

Lavigne may have been forcibly deported as the outcome to his arrest and by early July he was back in the U.S. He returned to Cleveland where his brother Billy was making a go of it as a fight promoter. A somewhat cryptic quote from the *Milwaukee Evening Wisconsin* hinted at the Kid possibly seeking professional help with his alcohol problem when it wrote, "The Kid has been at Green Springs for the last four weeks and is feeling like a 2-year-old colt."[11] It may be that he got more than rest and hot mineral baths while there.

On the one hand, the Kid was fond of visiting Mt. Clemens, just north of Detroit when he was staying in the Saginaw or Detroit areas between fights. He enjoyed the famed mineral spring's recuperative powers. So it wouldn't have been unusual for him to seek out a mineral springs close to Cleveland. Green Springs, Ohio, about 75 miles from Cleveland boasted the world's largest natural sulfur spring. It also was the home of Green Springs Sanitarium and Water Cure, a world class facility for the treatment of "liquor, tobacco and drug habits" since 1885.[12] It's quite possible that after boozing it up in Paris, getting arrested and then being asked to leave, Lavigne was ready to get some help and spent four weeks "at Green Springs" working on curing his addiction.

Off the Booze and Ready to Rumble

Reports began to circulate that Lavigne had finally kicked his habit. "Kid Lavigne says he has not taken to the booze again," confirmed the *Police Gazette*. "The Kid says he is through with the stuff for all time and that he intends to get back to the place he occupied in pugilism a year ago."[13] It was easy to read an amount of skepticism in the press reports of the time relating to Lavigne's alleged sobriety. They had a certain "Chicken Little" quality about them as they'd heard it so often. Only time would tell. Lavigne was looking for a match with a "top-notcher," and several bouts were contemplated. Dal Hawkins indicated he was willing to give the Kid a shot. In mid-September the Kid began training for a proposed bout with George "Young" Gibbs, a black Cleveland boxer on the rise who was being called the Joe Gans of Ohio. For unknown reasons neither of these matches came to fruition.

However, the boxer Lavigne preferred to fight over all others was Terry McGovern. The Kid saw "Terrible" Terry as his style of fighter; one who would meet him in the center of the ring and sock until only one man was standing. Lavigne's last two losses to Erne and "Elbows" McFadden were against fighters who were defensively crafty and who used the full ring to escape Lavigne's pressure rushes. McGovern would not go there. He would wade in and slug until the best man won. That appealed greatly to the Kid who had a well-known disdain for dancers. He also saw it as his best chance to regain the title. Erne was dominated by McGovern in a non-title, third-round loss. Beat McGovern and it would be hard for Erne to deny Lavigne his title shot.

The *Racine Daily Journal* announced Lavigne's intentions in a piece covering his trip to the windy city: "Kid Lavigne, the ex-lightweight champion, looking in splendid condition, arrived in Chicago last night from Cleveland, where he has been getting himself in fine condition for a battle with some of the crack lightweights in the west. Lavigne was unsuccessful, however, and now states he is ready to tackle either Terry McGovern at 130 pounds, or Frank Erne or Joe Gans at 133 pounds, before any club that will offer a good purse for the battle."[14] Yet the matches were not made. These men were not fools. Even though the Kid was nowhere near the fighter he had been just a few years past, he was still a very dangerous go in the ring for anyone. Rumors of his sobriety and his conditioning would elicit further pause in those who would dare to make a match with him.

In the meantime, Billy Lavigne's foray into the boxing promotion business at a Cleveland athletic club was meeting with significant legal resistance. Cleveland and Cincinnati authorities were working to shut down prizefighting in their cities causing matches to be cancelled and moved to other states more lenient and agreeable to fistic contests. Billy would leave as well and took a job as the manager of the Nonpareil Athletic Club in Louisville, Kentucky. The Kid followed Billy there to train with him and await news of a date with McGovern or other challenger.

It is difficult to determine when, but Lavigne and Sam Fitzpatrick went their separate ways again, most likely when the Kid sailed for Paris and didn't return for six months. Since arriving back in the U.S. the Kid and Billy were never far apart including taking time in October of 1900 for a visit with their mother in Saginaw and a hunting trip across northern Michigan.[15] While none of the news clippings researched show evidence of Billy representing the Kid in his quest for bouts, it's a safe bet that Billy was managing his brother's boxing affairs again that fall. A report in the *San Francisco Call* does make reference to Billy Lavigne as the Kid's manager in the spring of 1901.

Injured and Waiting

The lengthening string of bad luck would continue to hinder Lavigne's comeback efforts when he took a fall in mid-November 1900. "Kid Lavigne has been singularly unfortunate of late," wrote the *Police Gazette*. "He had been taking care of himself and was about to begin training with a view to fighting Terry McGovern when he met with an unfortunate accident at Saginaw, Michigan, which came within an ace of compelling him to retire from the ring forever. As he was leaving his mother's home in company with his brother Billy, he slipped upon some ice on the porch, falling headlong down nine steps upon a stone sidewalk. He was unconscious for some time. A physician made an examination of the ex-champion's injuries, and at first it was thought that his right arm had been broken, just above the wrist but later it was announced that no bones were broken, although the injured member is frightfully swollen. It is believed that Lavigne has sustained internal injuries."[16] And again Lavigne was off the market for a while.

The Kid had been an active fighter for 15 years and 1900 marked the first year in that span without a bout. As 1901 dawned, Lavigne continued to train and refuse the booze, determined to rise again. "Kid Lavigne again announces that he is in fine condition and anxious to fight somebody," reported the *Oshkosh Daily Northwestern*. "Other people also announce that the once great lightweight is giving John Barleycorn a grand tussle, and the listeners can take their choice of the stories."[17]

"Once great" was a label that had to be hard to swallow, yet even the one who vanquished him made similar reference to the Kid. Frank Erne, still the current lightweight champion, was lamenting that he could not get a rematch with McGovern when he uttered this slight of Lavigne picked up by the *Racine Daily Journal*: "The latest talk is a match between McGovern and 'Kid' Lavigne, a has-been, and I am out of it."[18] The *Trenton Times* added to this bit of cruelty when it wrote, "There is some talk of a battle between Terry McGovern and Kid Lavigne. It would be a shame for Terry to take the money for beating the poor old Kid."[19] And of course what would this pile-on be without a subtle capper from the often hyperbolic *Police Gazette*: "Kid Lavigne seems to have a picture of himself boxing Terry McGovern. A picture of him after Terry got through with him would be something of a curiosity."[20]

And so the months went by. A proposed fight between Lavigne and McGovern was to have taken place in Chicago on February 12, 1901, however the bout had to be moved when Chicago authorities shut down professional boxing in early 1901 . . . a ban that lasted for a quarter of a century.[21] And the ban had everything to do with a fight between "The Old Master" Joe Gans and "Terrible" Terry McGovern. It was a fight on December 13, 1900 in Lou Houseman's Tattersall Athletic Club at 16th and Dearborn. McGovern, giving away several pounds to Gans, nonetheless dominated the Old Master and knocked him out in the second round. Gans hardly put up a fight and while there was no indication that McGovern was in on it, the fight was seen by all who witnessed it as a fake. Six years later Gans would admit to such with much remorse. It was suspected that he was helping his manager, Al Herford, get out from under substantial gambling debt.[22]

The doctor that attended to Lavigne after his fall down the steps said that he should be able to return to training in 10 days or so. Two months had passed since the accident and surely he was ready to fight yet the bout was not moved to a new locale for reasons unknown. Even the press was starting to tire of this phantom match that defied culmination when the *Oshkosh Daily Northwestern* opined, "Lavigne is on the wrong trail. If he waits till he gets a bout with McGovern he will be gray headed. What Lavigne should do is to take on lesser lights and prove he can still fight."[23]

Several months later the *Northwestern* continued to drive home its point slamming both fighters when it wrote, "If McGovern has consented to meet George Lavigne next fall it goes to show that the featherweight champion is still in quest of easy game. Lavigne is out of the champion running and it would prove a slaughter. There are half a dozen 130-pounders who can now defeat the once invincible Saginaw boy. It is questionable if the public will regard with favor the proposed McGovern-Lavigne match."[24]

In May he was offered $400 for a ten round go with Kid Ashe, born Albert Laurey, a black lightweight out of Cincinnati whose ring name was the "Pork Chops King." The money offered was a paltry sum compared to what Lavigne was used to earning yet the competition, while still green, was not a pushover. Sure, Ashe had only begun his professional career in 1899, but in his eighth fight that year he managed to stay 15 rounds with Joe Gans for a draw. In his 17th and last bout before he would step into the ring with Lavigne he stayed 20 rounds with Bobby Dobbs for a draw. Maybe it was the money or lack thereof. Maybe it was Lavigne's unrealistic expectation that he deserved a bout with a top-notcher. The fight never came together.

Waiting for someone to fight, Lavigne tried his hand as a referee when he agreed to officiate a bout in Sault Saint Marie, Michigan in May. The Kid was frustrated that in spite of both his and Billy's concerted efforts to secure matches he had now gone nearly 22 months without a fight. Getting desperate, the Kid again left his brother's oversight and signed with a new manager to guide his sputtering career.

Under New Management

The *Trenton Times* made the announcement in early August 1901: "Billy Roche, manager of George McFadden and Tim Callahan has taken hold of Kid Lavigne and will manage the ex-light-weight champion in the future. Roche declares that Lavigne is now in better trim than ever. He says the Kid has been taking good care of himself. Roche says that he will not go after Terry McGovern right away, but will content himself by pitting Lavigne first against some of the lesser

135-pounders."[25] Roche had managed some of the best which also included Mysterious Billy Smith, Eddie Connolly and Jack Everhardt. Lavigne was hopeful and agreed to Roche's initial focus on some of the "lesser" men of the ring.

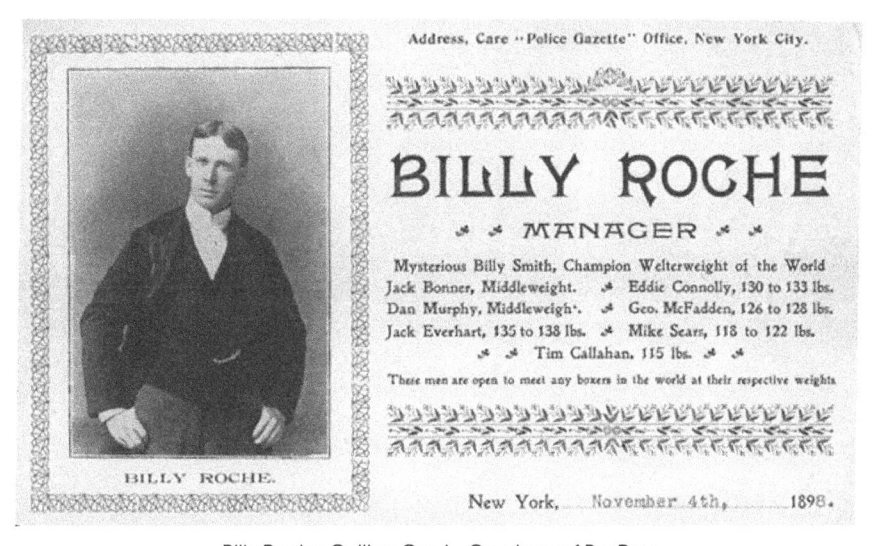

Address, Care "Police Gazette" Office, New York City.

BILLY ROCHE

⁂ ⁂ MANAGER ⁂ ⁂

Mysterious Billy Smith, Champion Welterweight of the World
Jack Bonner, Middleweight. ⁂ Eddie Connolly, 130 to 133 lbs.
Dan Murphy, Middleweigh*. ⁂ Geo. McFadden, 126 to 128 lbs.
Jack Everhart, 135 to 138 lbs. ⁂ Mike Sears, 118 to 122 lbs.
⁂ ⁂ Tim Callahan, 115 lbs. ⁂ ⁂

These men are open to meet any boxers in the world at their respective weights

New York, November 4th, 1898.

BILLY ROCHE.

Billy Roche Calling Card - Courtesy of BoxRec

While waiting for a fighting payday, Lavigne used his considerable cachet to help with a worthy cause. He fought a three round exhibition in Saginaw at the police department's 10th annual outing in Union Park on August 23, 1901. His opponent was Ed Sholtreau (also Sheltraw), a rangy middleweight from Bay City. Ed had lost twice earlier in the year to one of the more underrated heavyweights of the early 20th century, Tommy Burns, who would go on to become world champion from 1906 to 1908. The picture captured from that event is the only known photograph of Kid Lavigne inside the squared circle.

Several possibilities emerged including bouts with Young Corbett and Dave Sullivan. Both were top-level journeymen featherweights. Corbett was coming off a defeat of long-in-the-tooth George Dixon in August and would wrest the world featherweight title from Terry McGovern in November. These two were hardly lesser pugilists but at least they were smaller than the Kid. After a lot of challenging with few takers, Roche got the Kid a 20 round match at 133 pounds with Artie Simms of Akron, Ohio on Oct. 14. Two days after the

"Kid" Lavigne in a boxing ring with exhibition opponent Ed Sholtreau
- Courtesy of *Boxing Illustrated*

announcement of the match it was called off by the Fort Erie Club that was to host the bout.[26]

Simms was a true up-and-comer. He was an undefeated veteran of 28 fights. It might have been an interesting, and possibly disastrous, bout for Simms. Roche took a big step down and inked a bout for Lavigne with Barney Furey in Cincinnati later in the month. Furey was inexperienced with only seven fights to his credit, one being a ninth round KO at the hands of Joe Gans. Mysteriously, this fight was also cancelled. Looking at the dynamics and timing of events, a conclusion can be drawn, with a modest level of probability, that Simms and Furey decided they were a better match for each other and both wisely bypassed Lavigne.

Simms's decision may also have been influenced by ominous news from Lavigne's training quarters. Tim Callahan, another of Roche's fighters was training with Lavigne and Roche wanted to measure the Kid's progress against a top-notch featherweight of Tim's caliber. "In a tryout bout a few days ago Kid Lavigne knocked out Tim Callahan in less than three rounds and there was only seven pounds difference in the weights," reported the *Brooklyn Daily Eagle*. "This would mean a big difference under certain conditions, but it must be remembered that Callahan has been fighting regularly for a long time and is in grand shape . . . while the old champion has not had a fight in many months. Unless Artie Simms is the wonder those who have seen him say he is it looks as if the Kid would win the fight which takes place in Fort Erie in a few days."[27]

Simms had already beaten Kid Lavigne in November of 1899. It was decisive. He knocked the Kid out with one second remaining in the first round. However, this was not the Saginaw Kid. It was Dave "Boston Kid" Lavigne, champion lightweight of New England. Pondering a possible fight in late October 1901 with ex-world lightweight champ Kid Lavigne, didn't look like an easy go from any angle, particularly from a fighter who would risk his unblemished record against the hungry, swarming man from Michigan. Instead Simms met Furey on October 25 in Cincinnati and fought a ten-round draw. Fortunate for both of them perhaps. Simms' undefeated career went over the cliff at that point, losing four of his next seven bouts. Furey lost three of his next six bouts and quit boxing. Given the trajectory of both of their careers, at least they would have gone out with a bang getting mauled by the original Kid Lavigne.

While the Kid was still in the hunt for a fight, his brother Billy had moved on from the Nonpareil Athletic Club in Louisville to take the position of general manager and physical director at the Acme Athletic Club in Oakland, California in September. The Acme A. C. would be the site of the Kid's first fight in 26 months since getting pounded into submission by "Elbows' McFadden. Most likely with a little assistance from Billy Lavigne, Roche finally landed a big fish for the Kid. His opponent would be an Aussie champion just off the boat from Down Under.

CHAPTER 28

Into the Ring at Last

The *Oakland Tribune* broke the news. "Tim Hegarty, the Australian boxer who came to this country especially to meet Terry McGovern, has agreed to meet the redoubtable "Kid" Lavigne."[1] Hegarty was "a clever, shifty fellow with a good punch in either hand" according to a paper across the bay.[2] Clever enough that he was undefeated in 47 fights. At various times he held the Australian bantamweight, featherweight, and lightweight titles. So much for going after lesser 135-pounders. The only thing lesser about this opponent would be his weight as he would come in at 128, two pounds lighter than the Kid. The fight would be 15 rounds on the evening of December 12, 1901 for a purse of $1,200 to be split between the contestants.

Three separate sources reported that this would be Hegarty's first fight in America. This was not true as he had fought two bruising battles with Californian, Aurelio Herrera in Bakersfield in July and September, winning in 20 rounds in the first and getting a draw in 20 in the second. The Cyber Boxing Zone page says "Herrera was a murderous puncher. . . . He was a rough, tough customer who came to brawl."[3] His record corroborates the hard hitting claim. At the time of his first go with Hegarty he had fought 26 times with 20 knockouts and one loss, to world featherweight champion Terry McGovern, in San Francisco earlier in 1901.

Herrera was well known on the boxing scene and with his last fight being for the featherweight championship he should have been fresh on the sportswriters' minds. So why then would the *San Francisco Call, the Los Angeles Times,* and the *Police Gazette* all make the same mistake, saying this was Hegarty's first bout since stepping off the boat? The most plausible explanation may be race, which often played a role in who fought who at the turn of the century and possibly on what was deemed noteworthy on a white fighter's record.

Lavigne began his finish-training at Blanken's Six-Mile House, outside of San Francisco. This would be the fourth time he had used this popular venue for his pre-fight preparation. "There is fire in the eye of 'Kid' Lavigne when he plows along the highways adjacent to Blanken's Six-Mile House through fog and rain, mud and slush," wrote the *Oakland Tribune*.[4] The Kid was training hard for a month prior to the fight putting in five to six hours each day. All eyes were on him in hopes of making an assessment of his readiness after the layoff. "Lavigne's long rest from the fighting game and his temperate habits have made a new man of him, and those who have seen him work at his training quarters down at Blanken's say he will show his old-time form," was the positive report from the *San Francisco Call*.[5]

The Kid responded to some of the speculation on his fitness when he said, "There may be something in that talk about me being a has-been. How do they all know it so well without seeing me go some? I know I fought when I was in no condition and put up some bad fights although they were the best I had in me at the time. . . . I feel as strong now as ever in my life and I know I am just as clever with my hands as ever. All I ask is fair treatment from the public and if I should fail in my present condition to show on the night of the 12th that I am no longer the Kid Lavigne of other days I will not take to strong drink again for there is nothing in that game, but mix with the fighters of my class. If the old fire is in me and I triumph over Hegarty I want another try at the biggest fish in the pond."[6]

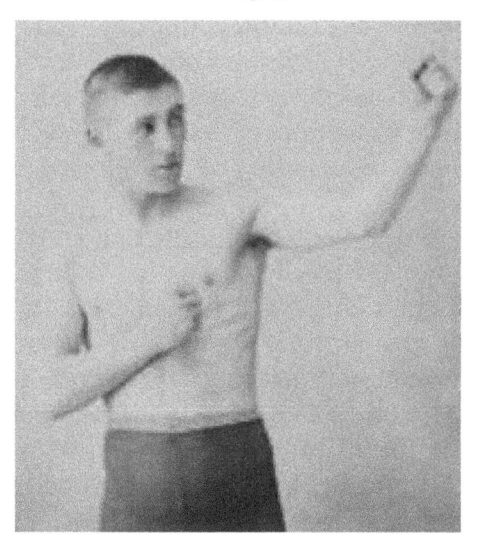

Tim Hegarty - Courtesy of BoxRec

Hegarty was also rounding into peak shape for the bout. His trainers knew that Lavigne was one of the most formidable challenges in the lightweight division and had worked hard to prepare him. Hegarty admitted that it was the most important contest of his career in the ring. While his pedigree was well known to knowledgeable sports, few had seen him fight since coming to the states and it had a bearing on the betting which remained light days before the match. The other side of the betting coin was that the general public really didn't have a read on Lavigne's present condition compared with his championship form. The odds were slightly in favor of the Australian but were expected to swing to Lavigne as fight night approached.

A Doomed Game Plan

Hegarty's strategy going into the fight was sound and would have worked against most men. "Hegarty tells his friends that he intends to go after Lavigne from the sound of the gong and put him on the defensive if he can from the beginning," reported the *Oakland Tribune*.[7] "In this manner he hopes to test the strength of his opponent without allowing him time to get his bearings in the ring or the caliber of the man before him. . . . Lavigne has pretty much the same notion as Hegarty so far as forcing the fighting is concerned and he promises his friends that the Australian will not be allowed a moment's rest from the call of time."

This was shaping up to be a war in the center of the ring, much to the Kid's advantage. Several great fighters, including Joe Walcott, Dick Burge, and Eddie Connolly had employed the same strategy against Lavigne only to be beaten at their own game by an indomitable foe. Hegarty had learned nothing from reports of how Lavigne was bested in 1899 by Erne and McFadden. No one had ever beaten Lavigne by taking the fight directly to him. The prognosticators at the *San Francisco Chronicle* opined, "It will probably develop into a give-and-take battle . . . and the man who can digest the most punishment and hit back will win."[8]

The latest in reporting technology was installed for the fight. The management of the Acme Club arranged to have special wires at the ringside to accommodate eastern sports writers given the three hour time difference between coasts. This allowed the blow-by-blow to be transmitted within seconds all over the U. S. The first use of ringside voice transmission would not happen until the Dempsey-Carpentier heavyweight championship bout twenty years later in 1921.

Fight date had arrived and at last the old-time idol of fistiana stepped through the ropes into the ring. The *Oakland Tribune* described the reaction of the crowd best when it wrote, "Kid Lavigne is on earth again. When he stripped in his corner last night and his chest, arms and legs showed with muscles standing out and his skin clear and pinkish in color, this gave evidence that he had indeed trained well and faithfully and an exclamation that voices surprise and pleasure escaped from everybody in the house, and then applause, spontaneous and hearty, gave further evidence that the boy from Saginaw was still the public idol, and from that moment the house was with him."[9]

At 9:30 p.m. referee Jack Kitchen was in position and the fighters were ready to mix it. Lavigne's seconds were Tommy Gilfeather, Jim Lawler and Teddy Alexander. Hegarty was seconded by "Australian Billy" Smith and Jack Hill. At the sound of the gong Lavigne was now favored 10-to-6 in front of a crowd of about 2,400. Hegarty began his assault of the Kid and "set a pace in the first round and part of the second which seemed beyond endurance to maintain."[10] Lavigne sized his man up and began boring in, meeting Hegarty's rushes and forcing him back. In the first round the Australian had a slight advantage on points but the Kid was the aggressor the entire round.

In the second, the *Los Angeles Times* noted "Lavigne was cool and collected," while Hegarty went at his man fiercely.[11] Hegarty got in with a number of straight lefts cutting Lavigne's lip and one on the jaw that staggered the Michigan man. Undaunted, the Kid kept coming, smiling as he landed rib-bruising body blows. Hegarty, now confident he could land on the Kid stayed close and traded blows in the third round.

Those close to him believed he would use his cleverness, jabbing and moving while keeping the Kid from boring in. Instead they saw Hegarty either incapable of keeping the Kid off of him or deliberately exchanging punches with the idea of wearing him out. The Kid spent the round pounding rights and lefts to Hegarty's stomach which began to weaken him. "Time practically saved Hegarty from going out," the *Times* continued.[12]

As the fourth canto began, Lavigne sensed he had gained the upper hand and went at his man with renewed ferocity. The *Police News* called the end of the fight 49 seconds into the round: "He ripped in several rights and then sent a clean right to the jaw, which knocked Hegarty to the floor. He took seven seconds on the mat. When he stood up he seemed dazed, but instead of clinching to avoid punishment, he started to exchange blow-for-blow with Lavigne. The latter had all his fighting spirit stirred up and never allowed Hegarty a moment's respite. He went at him hammer and tongs, and the second right hand punch, this time on the neck, sent the Australian down and out."[13] Hegarty could not move until his seconds carried him to his corner and "was fully five minutes recovering from the knockout."[14]

Resurrection

The Kid was back! The crowd was in frenzy, shouting themselves hoarse with delight as nearly everyone wanted to see the Kid prevail. According to Billy Lavigne's recollection, "They pulled him around and hugged him until he was almost dizzy."[15] Though he won the fight in spectacular fashion the Kid was not without damage. When he got back to his quarters after the fight it was found that he had a hole in his upper lip one could put a finger through. Having lost his upper front teeth long ago, a small stub remained, and in the days before the use of mouth-guards it punched through the lip with the force of a Hegarty left hand; just another battle scar for the resurgent ex-champion.

Lavigne surprised even his most ardent backers. He fought with his old savagery. While he didn't show the same speed of his past, he had plenty of power and cunning. Hegarty's only chance would have been to stay away and count on the Kid losing steam as the fight went on. His supporters felt that his strategy was a huge mistake. "Hegarty fought the most aggressive fight of his life and was worsted because Lavigne was willing to take a punch to get one in, and his forte is mixing it," wrote the *San Francisco Chronicle*.[16] The blame was also placed on Hegarty's handlers who believed Lavigne would be easy pickings given his reputation as a boozer who was a long way from his old form. They may have had their fighter in top condition for the bout but failed to give him the best advice on how to stop the Kid.

Boxing pundits from across the land weighed in. "Everybody is enthusiastic about Kid Lavigne's return to form, and justly so, for no more popular fighter ever stepped into the ring," gushed Sam Austin, editor of the *Police Gazette*. "If he had taken a continuous passage on the water wagon there is no telling how far he could have gone without being beaten, but he writes me that he has declared his entry out of the booze stakes and intends to make up for lost time."[17]

Lou Houseman was a well-known Chicago sportswriter, boxing promoter and manager of the time. He created the light-heavyweight division in 1903 and one of his boxers, Jack Root, won the first light-heavyweight championship bout when he defeated Kid McCoy that year. Houseman knew boxing as well as anyone. He added his perspective on the impact of Lavigne's stunning victory when he wrote, "The resurrection of George (Kid) Lavigne from the ranks of the 'has-been' brigade and his knockout of Australian Tim Hegarty at Oakland, California, was beyond a doubt the most important event of recent pugilistic history. The much touted champion of the antipodes was pounded to a standstill and put to sleep in four rounds. His defeat was so thorough and decisive as to not allow any argument and the result of the match proves that Lavigne must once more be looked upon as an important factor among the premier lightweights of the day."[18]

Given that Hegarty was the current lightweight champion of Australia and was soundly defeated by the Kid, it could be argued that Lavigne, while no longer the world lightweight champion, had a legitimate claim to the Australian lightweight title with his victory although no mention of the claim was found in any publication of the time.

While Lavigne's stock was on the rise again, Hegarty's prospects turned sour. The loss to the Kid, particularly in the manner that it happened, ruined Hegarty's chances of getting quality opponents in the States. He fought five times in 1902, winning two, losing two by knockout and getting one draw. To add insult to injury, five days after his loss to Lavigne a San Francisco judge issued a warrant for his arrest for a $400 debt owed to his uncle for unpaid rent. It didn't help matters that he also socked his uncle in the jaw.[19]

If only he had been patient and played for Lavigne to fight himself out, all may have turned out differently. By the end of 1902 he had returned to Australia where he was knocked out defending his Australian lightweight title. He tried in vain to recapture it, later settling for the lightweight championships of Victoria and Tasmania. He ended his career getting knocked out three consecutive times in 1907. It was time he quit as Hegarty had joined the ranks of the "has-beens."

CHAPTER 29

Hard Times on the Comeback Trail

Following his disastrous 1899, the Kid fled to Paris where he got mixed up with the gendarmes and was sent packing. Back in the states he hit rock bottom, then climbed slowly back to the land of the fit and sober. After more than two years absence he had reentered the game with a resounding victory and his world was now righted again. His new manager, Billy Roche, posted $1,000 with east coast promoter and old friend of the Kid's, George Considine, to bind a match with any featherweight in the world at 126 pounds. "Roche says that his boy would like to hear from 'Dave' Sullivan, 'Kid' Broad and 'Terry' McGovern, and that Lavigne will take the latter on a winner-take-all basis," noted the *Trenton Times*.[1]

Some of the luster had gone from a Lavigne-McGovern match-up as McGovern lost his featherweight crown quite unexpectedly in late November to one of the original trash-talkers, Young Corbett II. Yet he was still the Kid's preferred match. He knew that "Terrible Terry" fought with the same strategy that the ill-fated Tim Hegarty had. No longer possessing the extraordinary stamina he was once noted for and painfully remembering how a couple of hard hitting dancers destroyed him a few short years ago, the Kid knew his best chances from now on would be against those who dared to stand toe-to-toe with him.

And he wasn't limiting his challenges to the featherweights. "Kid Lavigne, who has convinced his admirers that he has recovered his old-time form, is out with a challenge to any of the lightweights, all of the purse to go to the winner," continued the *Times*. "'I am ready to face George McFadden, Spike Sullivan or any man weighing 135 pounds,' says Lavigne, 'and am prepared to sign articles for a match to be decided within three weeks after affixing my signature. I never felt better than I do now, and I intend to keep my health In the future.'"[2]

The Kid was relevant again after his signature knockout of Tracy and suitors began stacking up. New York Jack O'Brien notified Billy Lavigne at the Acme Athletic Club that he wanted a match with the Kid. O'Brien had several notable bouts to his credit including a 25-round draw in a lightweight championship bout with Frank Erne in which he had Erne on the canvas three times. Roche also heard from Billy Gardner, Kid Broad, Young Corbett II and even the champion, Frank Erne.

While most fighters scaled up in weight at the far end of their careers, Lavigne appeared more comfortable moving back toward the feathers, a weight at which he had great success very early in his Saginaw days. The last time he had issued a challenge to all the featherweights was 1894. "With advancing years Lavigne has learned a wise lesson," wrote the *Milwaukee Evening Wisconsin*. "He will pass up men heavier than his true class in the future and will also cut out second-raters. The Kid views the situation wisely. 'What's the use of fighting these fellows that everybody had licked?' he said. 'They're pretty nearly as hard to beat as the top-notchers and then you have everything to lose with them and nothing to gain. Do you suppose Corbett will give me a chance? He's a mixer; and that's the kind I want. Let them come at me and I will take care of them all right enough.'"[3]

Meanwhile, Roche was working with Billy Lavigne at the Acme to put the finishing touches on a match between the Kid and Young Corbett, born William Rothwell, for late February 1902 and the deal was reported to be all but done on February 7. Unfortunately Corbett got finicky about the weight. Lavigne said he would come down to 128 but Corbett and his manager, John Corbett, held out for 126 and the match fell apart. Roche must have had a queue of bouts lined up because the very next day the Kid was signed to fight New York Jack O'Brien at 134 pounds before the Yosemite Athletic Club on February 28. Lavigne settled in at Blanken's to train for the bout.

An Injurious Setback

Midway through February disaster struck. "Lavigne had enjoyed his usual tromp over the hills about Ingleside, and after a rub down and rest put on the gloves with Mike Donovan," reported the *Oakland Tribune*. "The Kid has never given much attention to boxing while training for a fight and it was at his brother Billy's request that he agreed to change his tactics this time and use Donovan for a boxing partner. When Lavigne fought Hegarty before the Acme Club in this city he missed the Australian in a dozen leads. His wild leads showed plainly the lack of practice at boxing during his training and a change was made this time in his preparation for Jack O'Brien, and Donovan engaged. Yesterday Lavigne swung and Donovan stepped in and was struck on the head with Lavigne's arm instead of his glove. The wounded boxer did not discover the injury for some moment, and it was not until he reached the surgeon's office and the arm given a twist that he became convinced it was broken."[4]

A new technology, only available since its practical development by Thomas Edison in 1896, confirmed the initial diagnosis. It was an X-ray that showed a break in one of the bones in his left arm. His arm was splinted and the bout was cancelled as it would be at least three months before the limb was sufficiently repaired to get back in the ring again. It was the first time the Kid had ever suffered an accident of this type that caused him to cancel a match. It was ironic that it happened on one of the few occasions in his career that he used a sparring partner in his training. It was a serious setback on the comeback trail.

While Lavigne went back east to convalesce, the lighter weight divisions were busy with great contests. Two former featherweight champions, Terry McGovern and Dave Sullivan squared off in Louisville on February 22. Sullivan had been boasting of a new punch he invented that he was certain would make the difference in the fight. "He calls the punch the 'Mauser,' and says it is almost as deadly as the rifle from which he borrowed the name," wrote the *Fort Wayne Journal-Gazette*. "Sullivan starts the punch by feinting with the right, making a bluff swing but instead of letting it go shoots out the left . . . expecting it to reach Terry's jaw as he comes in."[5] McGovern got the best of Sullivan and knocked him out in a brutal fight. Sullivan spent too much time backing up and getting battered by the raging McGovern to use the Mauser. He was counted out in the 15th.

Erne, still atop the lightweight world, did a little boasting as well in a run-up to a bout with Joe Gans. "If I can beat Gans, and I surely will, I will fight any man of my weight in the world. I mean to fight every two weeks if I can possibly secure the matches, and I will continue along these lines until I am beat at the lightweight limit. After losing the title I'll never fight again. That's final. [Rube] Ferns will probably be the next after Gans. If the Rube won't give me a bout I will take on Lavigne or any other boxer in the world. I only wish Terry McGovern was heavy enough to fight me at my weight. I think I can beat that fellow and would bet some money that way if Harris

[McGovern's manager] would only give me the chance. Watch me when I meet Gans."[6] There was not much to watch as Erne lost the lightweight crown to Gans by a first round knockout on May 12, 1902. He continued to fight, albeit sparingly, getting knocked out by Jimmy Britt later in the year and closing his career as the welterweight champion of France in 1908.

Almost an Amateur

On April 21, 1902 Roche got the Kid a match with San Franciscan, Jimmy Britt, for May 29. It was six weeks away so it gave the Kid's broken wing more time to knit. Britt was an amateur sensation who had just begun his professional career earlier in the year with two victories, the second over the Australian, Tim Hegarty, scoring a technical knockout in the eighth round. Ironically, it was Lavigne who had encouraged Britt to join the professional ranks. He saw Britt fight when he was in San Francisco in 1897 for his second go with Walcott noting that he had won many medals in amateur competitions. He told the young pug, "You are good enough to get real money for fighting. Why don't you get into the game? You can't eat those medals."[7] A few years later he offered the same suggestion to Britt's brother and manager, Willus, who finally convinced Jimmy to turn pro.

The upcoming bout with Lavigne would only be Britt's third professional bout yet some odds makers had the fight 10-to-7 in favor of the 22 year old. He was wildly popular with the locals and it was his youth, speed and cleverness, as well as his ability as a power puncher with either hand that tipped the betting in his favor over the rode-hard, 32-year-old Kid.

Jimmy Britt – Courtesy of BoxRec

Britt would be more of a challenge than the Kid and his followers anticipated. He held the amateur lightweight championship of the Pacific Coast and used a peculiar crouching style that would make it very hard for Lavigne to land his sledge hammer right hand. It was reminiscent of the style of defense employed by Jim "Iron Bark" Burge in his 50-round bout with Lavigne, also in San Francisco, way back in 1892. In that bout, the Kid broke his right hand in the 5th round trying to punch his way through Burge's crouching defense. Fighting a crouching fighter was rarely a problem for Lavigne as the majority of the men he had faced were several inches taller than he was. But Britt was only 5 feet 5 and 1/2 inches, just two inches north of Lavigne's height. A croucher of Britt's size would be a very compact target. Advantage Britt.

The fight was held at Woodward's Pavilion in San Francisco and both fighters appeared to be "trained to the hour" as they stepped to the center of the ring for the beginning of the first round with Ed Smith officiating. Lavigne's left arm that had been broken only 14 weeks ago was heavily taped. The Kid's brother Billy was one of his seconds. "Contrary to expectations, Britt forced the fighting from the start," noted the *San Francisco Chronicle*.[8] He caught the Kid with a left and in the Kid's signature style, he grinned and kept coming, only to have his head snapped back by another left. It was clear from the outset that although Lavigne was game, Britt's speed was dominant. Several fast exchanges left Lavigne puzzled as to how to penetrate Britt's crouching defense and avoid the youngster's fast, powerful returns.

Lavigne forced the action in the second but again had trouble landing. The Kid tried two rights to the head missing both. "Britt followed this with a right and a left to the head, which dazed Lavigne for the moment," wrote the *San Francisco Call*. Lavigne came back and "missed a terrific right swing, the swish of his glove being heard throughout the pavilion."[9] Near the end of the round Lavigne appeared dazed but Britt couldn't capitalize on it. "After he had gone a couple of rounds he took on a careworn expression," continued the *Call*, "and when he missed his desperate swings, as he did repeatedly, he shook his head and smiled dubiously." The careworn expression may have been the result of something that would not be revealed until after the fight.

In the third, Britt let Lavigne come to him and the Kid got in his best blow of the match which for him were few and far between. Britt was boxing fast and cleverly. When Lavigne landed a right to the body Britt responded with a left to Lavigne's body and continued to use this return successfully throughout the bout. "Britt was clearly the best in this round, Lavigne already looked beaten," surmised the *Call*. The Kid opened the fourth with renewed vigor and while Britt got the best of the round little damage was done by either fighter.

It was apparent in the fifth round that Lavigne was having trouble finding Britt with his punches and was taking a pummeling in return. In mid-round he backed Britt into a corner and the two engaged in a slugging match. "There was a buzz around the ring that Lavigne was fighting in his old style," noted the *Call*. The Kid was using every bit of his considerable ring generalship but was clearly growing frustrated at the marvelous skill of his young adversary. At the close of the round Lavigne caught a wicked smack in the mouth which staggered him and started blood flowing from his lips. As they went to their corners Lavigne said to Britt, "You are a hard nut."[10] Quite a compliment from the Saginaw Kid.

In the sixth, Britt's speed was overwhelming the Kid. He hit Lavigne with a half dozen solid left jabs, jerking his head back and causing his right eye to swell. Near the end of the round the Kid landed two solid rights to body but Britt, taking a page from Lavigne's book, laughed at the effect of the punches. Britt retired to his corner showing no fatigue at round's end. Sensing he was in complete control of the fight Jimmy increased the tempo in the seventh. "Britt went after his man like a tiger," wrote the *San Francisco Chronicle*.[11] He nailed the Kid with a crushing right to the jaw which staggered him. "Britt again sent his right to the head," reported the *Call*, and the spectators marveled that Lavigne could take the blows which Britt was delivering."[12] Another clean right to the head knocked the Kid to the canvas but he was up in a few seconds and after Britt like a demon fighting desperately for a knockout blow. Britt went down to his knees, slipping on some water as Lavigne rushed in. He was up in a flash, bobbing and weaving his way out of danger.

Billy to the Rescue

The Kid was wild in the eighth, missing several hay-maker right hands. Britt rushed at Lavigne and in a collision both men toppled to the floor with the Kid on the bottom of the scrum. "Both men arose quickly and Lavigne showed the effects of the jar," noted the *Call*. "He reeled about like a drunken man and was at sea."[13] The *Chronicle* described what happened next: "The laugh which the Kid had worn in so many victories had faded away; his right eye was almost closed and a thin stream of blood was coming from between his lips. . . .

Lavigne tried to regain a standing position but it was evident that the fight was near an end for he staggered and fell back. By a great effort he came up for further punishment. Again he went down under a rain of blows and once more showed his gameness. This time as he arose, Jimmy rushed him into a corner. He was in a perfectly helpless condition and to save him unnecessary pain, his brother climbed through the ropes and mercifully led the beaten man to his corner."[14] Referee Smith did the only thing he could under the circumstances and awarded the fight to Britt.

The Kid was lucky that his brother Billy was in his corner this night and acted with compassion to remove him from harm's way. He had done the same thing in the very same ring in the Kid's loss to Mysterious Billy Smith three years ago. A comment from the Kid caught by a *Chronicle* reporter spoke volumes of his condition and the rightness of Billy's action to stop the carnage. "The Kid mumbled something about a man having a chance until he was knocked out. In the next breath he asked how it all happened."[15] Addled he was.

After the fight it was revealed that the Kid broke his arm early in the bout when he threw a left and his forearm collided violently with a right from Britt. "He went at once to the office of Dr. Leonard," wrote the *Call*. "When the tape bandage was removed from the arm the member fell limp by the boxer's side. Dr. Leonard found the large bone broken near the old fracture and the small bone broken in two places. It is apparently a bad fracture."[16] "It snapped," said Lavigne, "in that second round. Although I felt no sharp pain I did notice that the arm seemed to be numb. It was not until Dr. Leonard removed the tape that I realized I had been fighting a formidable man with only one good arm. I did the best I could and have no apologies to offer for the stand I made."[17]

It was the final death-knell for Lavigne's comeback. This was no longer the Lavigne of old who climbed through the ropes. His power to punish had vanished with the years. His speed diminished. The fire in his eyes had dulled. Even so, those who saw him fight on this night were witness to his heart. Britt would remark after the fight, "One thing, though, you can't get away from the fact that he is game to the core. The more I hit him, the harder he came back." Lavigne, forever humble, was equally complimentary of the young victor. "Britt is a great little fighter," he said, "and he beat me fair and square."[18]

Game, tough as nails, relentless; these were but a few of the descriptions that labeled Lavinge's indomitable character in the ring. How many modern fighters would fight 45 rounds with a broken hand as he did back in '92 against Jim "Iron Bark" Burge? How many would be beaten to a bloody pulp as he had been against the Barbados Demon in '95 and refuse to quit, prevailing in the end? How many would continue to do battle for six more rounds with a badly broken arm as he did against Britt, getting up off the canvas three times to suffer more punishment before his brother stopped the carnage? The Saginaw Kid was truly the quintessence of a waning era of pugilism marked by its grit, its savagery, and its brutality.

The Belladonna Scandal

Forty-six years after the fight an accusation was made that would have shocked the fistic world had it been known back in 1902. It came from an unnamed sportswriter with the *Saginaw News* on January 25, 1948. Near the end of the far ranging mini-biography of the Kid titled, "Lavigne Won City Prize Ring Fame," the author asserted that the Kid was doped before the Britt fight by crooked seconds. Fact checking the entirety of this mini-biography against multiple sources of the time periods it covered confirms it is highly accurate. This single event as reported, however, may be an outlier, and if true, is an outrageous accusation and worth repeating as written in its entirety here:

> "The Kid's last fight brought a dismal ending to a great career. His handlers, the Kid always believed in later years, had been bribed. They doped him with belladonna. Three years later, the Kid never remembered the fight only that his memory faded at the start. Britt knocked him out in the eighth round. The Kid wrote in one newspaper story, that the Britt crowd knew that Lavigne was to be doped. Just before the fight they delayed the opening bell so that the belladonna would have time to take effect. For weeks the Kid lay in a hospital bed, recovering. A bone in his arm had snapped during the fight and the dope muddled his thinking for weeks."[19]

Parts of the story are known to be true. Lavigne did break his arm and did spend an inordinate amount of time in the hospital convalescing after the fight. The events that led to his hospitalization are a story in itself and will be told shortly. It is possible that belladonna may have been one of the factors that sent him there as the story will illuminate. Ingestion or absorption through the skin of this powerful narcotic can cause staggering, hallucinations, and delirium. In addition, the central nervous system effects of the drug include memory disruption, which may lead to severe confusion. Flashback to the Kid asking Billy what happened at the end of the fight and the doping accusation gains some traction. The Kid missed a larger than usual number of his patented knockout blows in this bout. Could a drug have affected his timing and coordination? Again, it's possible.

Only two additional clues were found that would lend credence to the belladonna debacle. One was a cryptic comment in a piece written by the *Milwaukee Evening Wisconsin* in 1912. It wrote, "Lavigne will publish a book of his ring career in a couple of months, in which he promises to spring a sensation regarding his fight with Jimmy Britt."[20] Lavigne never wrote that book but in 1921 he did an interview with Jack Veiock, the *International News* sporting editor out of New York regarding the upcoming heavyweight title fight between George Carpentier and Jack Dempsey. In that interview he stated that Jim Jeffries was doped when he lost to heavyweight champion, Jack Johnson, in 1910.

Then he spilled the "sensation" referred to in 1912: "They doped me, too, when I fought Britt out there on May 29, 1902. They get a handler to rub belladonna in your hair. Then when you get in the ring your vision is affected. I saw two Britts. They hung it on me out there in California, where the native sons play the game safe."[21] In the same article he spoke of his broken arm. "I had broken my left arm three months before my Britt fight. I knew it wasn't strong enough in such a short time to do the work but rather than disappoint the matchmakers I went through with it. And then they had to dope me in the bargain. No western fights for me if I was able to take 'em on."

Jimmy Britt's career continued to ascend when he took on Frank Erne in November knocking him out in the seventh round. Britt had perhaps one of the best first-year records as a professional boxer of any era. Consider that in his second fight he knocked out the current Australian featherweight and lightweight champion, Tim Hegarty, in eight rounds. Next he dispatched the previous two world lightweight champions, Lavigne and Erne, by knockout. He was well on his way to the top of the lightweight ranks and reached the goal when he defeated Oscar "Battling" Nelson in 1904 for the world title. He lost the title the following year in a return match with Nelson.

After what was by comparison a short career in the ring, Britt retired from boxing in 1909 and began a successful second career in vaudeville. While doing a show in 1913 in Cleveland a reporter asked him, "You defeated Kid Lavigne once didn't you Jimmy?" "Yes, but that did not count," replied Britt. "I am entitled to no credit whatever for that incident. You see Lavigne was only a memory of the Lavigne who had conquered the world in the lightweight division when I boxed him. I never could have defeated George Lavigne when he was at his best, and there is no other lightweight alive today who could have beaten the little giant when he was good. Lavigne was the most wonderful fighter of his weight and inches ever known to the history of pugilism. Put that down as a fact and don't let anyone tout you away from it, for I know."[22]

The little giant was through by his own admission. "My defeat by Britt convinced me that there was no comeback for me and I quit the ring forever, except for some minor exhibition appearances," he recalled many years later.[23] The *Oakland Tribune* concurred when it wrote, "George Lavigne of Saginaw, Michigan, had fought his last fight when he fell dazed and defeated before the skill and youth of 'Jimmie' Britt in the ring at Woodward's Pavilion Thursday night. Once more it has been shown that no matter how able and strong and game a boxer may be, if he doesn't leave the arena for good with the laurel fresh on his brow he will quit the business finally a man demonstrated to be what the world of sports calls a 'dead one'"[24] The Kid, mourning the death of his 17-year fistic journey, sunk into a deep depression.

CHAPTER 30

From the Asylum to Paris

The aftermath of the bout was painful both physically and mentally for the Kid. His left arm, badly broken in three places, was causing so much pain that it was depriving him of sleep. What reserve he had left was rapidly wearing thin. Then a shocking headline made the morning news in papers across the country two weeks after the Britt loss. "Kid Lavigne Goes Insane at Stockton: The Great Boxer's Reason is Dethroned in the Slough City," was the headline above the fold in the *San Francisco Call*. "Kid Lavigne Insane," was another from the *Brooklyn Eagle* on the East Coast. "Kid Lavigne, the well-known pugilist, is at the detention hospital suffering from mental aberration. Physicians are doubtful of his recovery," reported the *Eagle*.[1]

His brother Billy committed him to the most prominent facility of its kind in the state at that time, Dr. F. P. Clark's Sanitarium at Stockton, for what he described as an "attack of dementia and melancholia." It was thought to be a combination of depression, pain, and lack of sleep that sent the Kid over the edge. But given this event it is worth reflecting on the drugging accusation by the *Saginaw News* reporter once more.

Assembling all the facts; first there is the possible absorption of belladonna which causes delirium, hallucinations, insomnia and restlessness. Add to the mix a severely depressed fighter who is in tremendous pain and has not slept for ten days. To treat the pain Lavigne was most likely given either laudanum, a mainstay of turn of the century painkillers which was a mixture of alcohol and opium, or another in the opiate family, morphine. The totality of these circumstances surely makes it more plausible that the Kid would end up in an asylum for the insane as a result of aberrant, and by one paper's quote, "violent" behavior. We'll never know if the Kid's seconds committed this heinous act but suffice to say, whatever the cause, Lavigne was in a very bad way.

Lavigne lay wasting away in Clark's Sanitarium by one account for several weeks. The *Oakland Tribune* reported that Lavigne "came near having a severe case of brain fever, but fortunately that was averted."[2] Brain fever was a Victorian era term used to describe what now days would be diagnosed as encephalitis or meningitis but it was also used to describe someone who was in a state of shock over a traumatic incident. The latter fit the Kid.

Nearly a month after Lavigne entered the hospital his manager, Billy Roche, recalled visiting him before leaving for the East Coast. "I saw the Kid before I left. His condition is pitiable. He is strapped in bed and I don't think he will ever get well. A little while ago he was out and the first thing he did was to punch at a tree until he broke his hand nearly to pieces."[3] The *Police Gazette* added, "Reports from San Francisco are to the effect that the condition of Kid Lavigne who went insane a few weeks ago is serious. The once-noted lightweight champion is now a shadow of his former self and is weak as a kitten."[4] The dire turned into the optimistic when an early August article in the *Gazette* noted the "fever" had left him and the doctors were hopeful for his complete recovery.

In mid-September he was well enough to travel and returned to Saginaw by way of Chicago. By now he must have been much better as a friend who saw him in Chicago noted, "He did not look like the broken down boxer reports from the Pacific Coast would lead one to believe he was. With a good rest, the Saginaw Kid will probably be all right again."[5] He didn't linger long in his hometown. After a few weeks visit with his mother Agnes, he was off to Europe for a long needed rest and a change of scenery. He would find an opportunity there that would keep his feet firmly planted on the canvas for a change.

Once the Kid sailed for Europe he dropped out of the news for a while. It is known that he settled in Paris with the intention of staying there for a time. Every so often a dispatch from the continent or a letter home illuminated his latest pursuits. It came as a bit of a surprise to folks stateside when his brothers Billy, Frank and James received a letter in December telling them of his plans to get back in the ring. He had been matched, presumably of his own doing as Roche was no longer his manager, with Ben Jordan, the featherweight champion of England at a London club on Derby day, June 1, 1903.

It was apparent that Lavigne had learned little from his drubbing by Britt. Why would he make a match with Jordan who had only one loss and had gotten the best of George Dixon twice? He was not a second-rate boxer. Surely fighting a quick featherweight would further expose the Kid's glaring loss of speed. For unknown reasons the fight never materialized and instead he opted for the stage where, "according to his letter, he is coining money in the vaudeville line."[6]

Professor of Pugilism

In the spring of 1903 on the advice of a friend, the Kid opened a boxing school at the Pelican Club of Paris. It is assumed that this club was a reincarnation of the Pelican Club of London which was a boxing mecca from its inception in 1853 until its demise in 1891 with the founding of the National Sporting Club of London that year.[7] "The French nobility and aristocracy have gone in for boxing with a vengeance," Lavigne declared. "Their own style of fighting—'La Savate'—has lost favor and the clean fighting of the American and British pugilists is now the popular thing of the schools and clubs."[8]

One of the fistic aristocracy Lavigne had the honor of training was Prime Minister, Emile Combe's son. There were also many Americans living in Paris who found their way to the Kid's school of boxing and physical culture. He made a good go of it for a while but all was not roses. "There were several drawbacks," explained Jack Kofoed many years later, "the principal one being the ex-champion's temperament. He was a good instructor. He knew the mechanics of the game, and had the knack of imparting his knowledge. But, in the first place, he was not a good mixer. He failed to develop a wide circle of friends. This was most important in a venture like this. In the second place, the Kid was impatient with stupidity. He didn't see why his students should not do exactly as they were told and the students resented his manner. In short, attendance fell off and finally the school closed down."[9]

Lavigne ran the school for a bit over two years after which he returned to the U.S. in the summer of 1905. During his time in Paris he stayed in excellent health, abstaining from drink and keeping himself in fine condition. Thoughts of another comeback were never far from his mind. Every so often he would write to Sam Austin of the *Police Gazette* with the latest goings-on, as he did in March 1904. "An interesting letter from him last week tells me that he has entirely recovered the use of his 'glass arm' and is satisfied that a permanent cure has been affected," noted Austin. "He says he is anxious to fight Jimmy Britt again and have the use of two arms."[10]

After a couple years the school was on the decline but the Kid had already made his mark on the Parisian boxing movement. "Lavigne has met with flattering success since he went to France and he is credited with the responsibility for the enthusiasm displayed in the boxing game in Paris at present," reported the *Boston Daily Globe*. "Regular boxing competitions are held weekly in the French capital and the Kid is arranging for an international tourney between the best English boxers and the foremost French exponents of the art."[11]

Many years later Lavigne would reminisce of his time in Paris and his impact on the French boxing world. "I claim that George Reynolds and I put the boxing game on its feet in Paris. We went on for a benefit. There were many women present. We didn't do any boxing but sailed in. The women at first cried, 'merchant,' (brutal), but they soon liked it and the cries turned to 'bravos.' From then on the French public couldn't get enough of professional boxing."[12]

One of the French up-and-comers was lightweight, Fernand Charbrier, of whom Lavigne thought highly. "This is a smart lightweight boxer I am working with," he wrote, "and I would like to get him a match in the United States, for I am confident he will give a good account of himself."[13] The Kid got some assistance from Frank Erne who visited the school and helped with the instruction of pupils for some time. Frank was born in Switzerland and although he came to the U.S. as a child was probably familiar enough with the French language to be of assistance to Lavigne. Erne would open his own boxing school in Paris just a few years later.

In addition to the Prime Minister's son, the Kid had another famous pupil under his tutelage in Paris, one George, "The Orchard Man," Carpentier.[14] Carpentier was the most famous of all French pugilists who went on to claim multiple titles in France and Europe from welterweight to heavyweight. He also achieved the title of light-heavyweight champion of the world in 1922. He was 10 or 11 at the time Lavigne contributed to his fistic education at the Pelican Club boxing school and had his first professional bout at the very young age of 14 in 1908. He ended his long career nearly 20 years later.

While training Charbrier, Carpentier, and others, the Kid was working himself back into ring condition. After a lay-off of over three years he signed to fight Jack Roberts of London at Chiarini's Nouveau Cirque in Paris on July 1, 1905 as a 10-round headliner to an international card between France and England. The other bout on the card was to match the English world bantamweight champion, Joe Bowker, and the French champion, Louis D'Or. As it turned out, Bowker did not fight D'Or that evening and no information was found on a French champion by that name. Bowker was still on the card and ended up fighting a novice by the name of Wally Pickard defeating him in six rounds.

Roberts was a middling ex-featherweight champion of England who was on the long end of his time in the ring. He had several things in common with the Kid. According to the *Boston Daily Globe*, he was stockily built, tough and capable of taking severe punishment.[15] He and Lavigne also shared the searing memories of a fight each would carry with them the rest of their lives. For Roberts it was a bout in 1901 against Billy Smith of Philadelphia. He was no relation to the great welterweight, Mysterious Billy Smith, who started the Kid's slide to boxing oblivion. But he took a page out of the Mysterious One's book in using the name "Billy Smith" as he was born Murray Livingston.

In Smith's second professional fight he found himself in London at the National Sporting Club facing Roberts. He dislocated his right arm in the fourth round of their 15-round bout. Fighting mostly one handed from then on, he was taking a severe beating. In the eighth, he was nearly defenseless when Roberts knocked him down and he was counted out. He, like Lavigne's specter, Andy Bowen back in 1894, never recovered consciousness and died the next day.

Little information of Robert's round-by-round with the Kid could be found but Lavigne got a technical knockout when Jack broke his hand in the fifth. His loss to Lavigne would send him on a seven-fight losing streak to close out his career. Fresh off a victory, Lavigne began making plans to return to the states, sailing for home in late August.

Jack Roberts - Courtesy of Tony Triem

The Kid Says "I Do"

Upon his arrival on August 29, 1905 he had some additional personal business to attend to. The Kid wed Julia Drujon in Manhattan the very day he stepped off the boat. Drujon was born in a small town outside Paris on May 22, 1865, making her four years older than George. On her headstone in Saginaw's Forest Lawn Cemetery the surname is spelled Drugon but the marriage record has it as Drujon. Census records indicate that she first came to the U.S. in 1899.

It's hard to say when and where they met as this was the Kid's third trip to Europe; the first when he won the world title in 1896, the second in 1900 after his meltdown, and the last, this recent stint from 1902 to 1905. Records show it was her second marriage as she wed Louis Ballet as a teenager in 1882. There was little if any mention of her in news articles of the day and she and the Kid never had any children. It is possible that Julia may have been the woman Lavigne was reported to have married in Paris in early 1900 just prior to being evicted by the Parisian authorities for physically abusing a woman. It would also fit a pattern that would develop near the end of his career in how he treated Julia when Mr. Hyde came calling. Without finding a record of his Parisian arrest this would be pure speculation.

On his return from France the *Milwaukee Free Press* wrote, "The erstwhile great fighter says that he has had all he wants of the other side, and that hereafter he will remain on his native heath."[16] One of the reasons for his return was his mother Agnes. She was 62 and her health was failing. Lavigne and his new bride settled in Detroit but he would make the 100-mile trek to visit Agnes two or three times a month to look after her.

The Kid was full of plans for the future. He continued to show a fascination with the French style foot-fighting. "It is my intention to show America two of the best of the French experts at La Savate," he declared, "and I have arranged to bring them over within a few months. These men can strike as heavy a blow with their feet as our fighters can with their hands. An exhibition of fighting along these lines will be nothing if not interesting."[17]

The Kid's stateside ambitions, however, were all over the map. While no record of the savate exhibition was found, one news report told of his desire to go into the hotel business in Detroit, another of his plans to open a boxing academy in Michigan City, and yet another that he would purchase an interest in one of the lumber mills in Saginaw in which he worked as a teenager. It has often been said that if you go into business do so in a field in which you are very familiar. For the Kid the choices were lumbering, boxing, and drinking. Having already spent his youth in the lumber mill and managed a boxing school, he decided to make a buck in a way so many retired boxers did; he opened the "Kid Lavigne Triangle Café", a little saloon at 185 Randolph Street in downtown Detroit in mid-October, 1905.

It's a bit odd that the very same month Lavigne was launching his saloon the *Milwaukee Evening Wisconsin* relayed a story out of Detroit declaring him threadbare. "Kid Lavigne, the lightweight champion and idol of the ring, the most prominent fighter ever turned out in the state of Michigan, is said to be 'all in' financially . . . 'I am coming close to the mark,' said a friend of the ex-champion, 'when I say that Lavigne has squandered a couple of fortunes. He was good-hearted and could never refuse a friend a favor, and like John L. Sullivan, Lavigne loved the sound of popping of corks.'"[18] This friend of the Kid's estimated that he had earned and spent over $100,000 in his career. That would be between 2.5 and 5 million dollars in today's money depending on which conversion calculator is used—an enormous sum in 1905. It's possible that the Kid spent the last of his nest egg to open the saloon.

Settled in Detroit, married, and running his own business again, what more could a retired pug ask for? He had now been sober for five years and outside of the time he was nursing injuries, he kept in remarkably good shape. His body was toned and hard and his weight was still within a few pounds of the lightweight limit. Then delusion crept in. He thought he had another run in him. He began talking about getting a match in Philadelphia where the bouts were limited to six rounds. Even if his stamina wasn't what it used to be, surely he could throw leather for eighteen minutes. He began training harder and looking in earnest for a fight.

CHAPTER 31

Kid Palooka

Though retired and running a suds joint, the Kid's head was still in the ring. In addition to running his "café," two newspaper sources claimed he was conducting a physical culture school in Detroit although no record of this assertion was found. He was a regular at the Detroit Athletic Club and was coaching some of the local boxers while there which is probably what gave rise to the claim. He was often seen ringside at Detroit's boxing venues and again tried his hand at refereeing, officiating a match between Saginaw lightweight Joe Cherry and Paddy Nee in late September 1905. His heart and soul were in the fight game and he couldn't shake the feeling that was willing him back to test what he had left.

Reports of matches made began to surface over the next few months. "Lavigne is back in the game," flashed the *Washington Post* in December, "and a match is being put together for him to fight Young O'Leary, the hard hitting lightweight of Chicago for 10 rounds at the Saginaw Athletic Club later this month."[1] The bout never came together. In late January, 1906 he was said to have inked a deal to fight Kid Sullivan at Baltimore but this too did not come to pass.

In April, after several failed attempts to get a match, the Kid signed on with his old boss, Sam Fitzpatrick, for the third time in his career. If anyone could get him a match, the master Fitzpatrick could. But why would he? Fitz knew better than anyone that the nearly 37 year old Lavigne no longer had it. Was it done out of friendship because he knew how badly the Kid wanted back inside the roped arena? Or was it simply business, knowing that memories of the Saginaw terror of a few years past were still vivid in the minds of sporting men and they would clamor to see a legend fight? Lavigne wanted Joe Gans, Jimmy Britt or "Battling" Nelson. It would be hard to envision any tougher competition of the time. Gans was the current lightweight champion, with Britt holding the title a few years before and Nelson a few years later.

Many thought the Kid's dream of recapturing the title was a failed sanity check. "George Lavigne, the former great boxer, should be restrained," wrote the *Fort Wayne Journal*. "He threatens to get into the ring again and talks of fighting Gans or any of the other good ones in that class. Lavigne is mentally sound, but he is possessed of the hallucination that afflicts so many back numbers. They never can be convinced that their fighting days are over. Gans would beat Lavigne in a punch, and the Saginaw Kid also would be easy meat for any of the other husky lightweights of the present. The trouble is that the deluded back numbers are deceived by designing managers, who hope to make a killing financially on the reputation of once great fighters. The boxer is easily persuaded that he is all that he once was, and goes into the ring for a humiliating beating. It is unfortunate, but it is human nature never to admit defeat."[2] Was Fitz guilty of the veiled charges of being a "designing manager?" Time would tell.

After avoiding the Kid all these years Gans finally toed the scratch with Lavigne but not with anything on the line. "In 1906, Gans and I met for a three round boxing exhibition in Detroit at the Gayety Theater," recalled Lavigne many years later. "Of his marvelous skill, plenty has been written. Gans was a crafty ringster and a gentlemanly fellow. I don't want to take any glory away from him but I can't help feeling there has been a tendency to overate him."[3] It's a shame these two didn't meet in their prime

Joe Gans, "The Old Master"
- Courtesy of BoxRec

for a 20- or 25-round contest. As good of a boxer as Gans was, Lavigne the fighter, though battered and a bit bloodied, would most probably have prevailed. In the words of Sam Austin of the *Police Gazette*, "Time was when this same Lavigne had it on every lightweight in the business, and the very mention of the Saginaw Kid's name used to make Joe Walcott and Joe Gans tear to the tall and uncut."[4] No newspaper summary of the exhibition match was found.

The next possibility was presented in early July by a local Saginaw promoter, James Bowen, who was working to get Lavigne a fight with another "back number" searching for relevance, Joe "Pride of the Bowery" Bernstein out of New York. Bernstein had battled many of the greats including Solly Smith, Terry McGovern, George Dixon, Young Corbett II, and Young Griffo. Although eight years younger than Lavigne he was two years from career's end and it would have been an entertaining match of two fighters whose skills were equally ravaged by the passing of time. This one never made it from contract to canvas either.

Judging from the prospects that were being considered it looked like Fitzpatrick was wisely steering clear of the top-notchers and looking to match the Kid with other fighters who had name recognition and were on their way up or, like Lavigne, were in the twilight of their careers. The next offer came from the camp of Mike Ward, a Canadian lightweight who, after five very successful years in the ring, had retired to run a pool hall. He had only two losses, one of which was a technical knockout at the skilled hands of Joe Gans.

It was to be a contest held at Lansing, Michigan but it too never came to pass. Unfortunately Ward did find a match that fall against Harry Lewis. It was held in Grand Rapids, Michigan and it was to be Ward's final match and final breath. Lewis knocked him down in the ninth round, Ward striking his head frightfully hard on the ring surface. He regained consciousness momentarily, and then lapsed into a coma from which he died.[5] No doubt Lavigne heard of the tragedy and perhaps he reached out to Harry Lewis, having lived through an identical nightmare with Andy Bowen, so eerily similar in its detail. If only Ward had resisted the temptation to crawl through the ropes one more time. That part didn't register with the Kid.

In one more false alarm, it was reported that Lavigne would meet Ed Granger at Jackson City, Michigan on September 12. Fitz was now bottom feeding as a search for Granger's ring record yielded nothing. Then in early November, the *Police Gazette* declared that Lavigne had signed to meet Kid Sullivan at Baltimore. When this bout also failed to culminate some sports began to wonder if Lavigne's come-back attempt was on the up-and-up. Detractors passed negative remarks about his age while those close to him saw that his level of preparation at the Detroit Athletic Club was ample evidence he was serious about giving it a go. "Lavigne is as hard as nails now, without an ounce of superfluous flesh, and although his wind is not as good as it might be, he expects soon to have his breathing apparatus in good order, ready to supply atmosphere in any quantity desired," reported the *Salt Lake Tribune*.[6]

Hearing some of the talk, Lavigne responded: "I'm only 36 and I'm in good physical shape. There ought to be a few more fights in me. Bob Fitzsimmons won the championship of the world by beating Jim Corbett when he was 35." He talked of a match "already half negotiated" with Young Corbett ll and then continued excitedly with his lucid dream spouting, "Say, wouldn't it be great—for me—if I showed them I wasn't all in? You see, I spent about three years over in Paris, and they kind of lost sight of me. When I did come back they looked upon me as an awfully old man. They've been writing my obituary before I am quite dead."[7]

Another Erne

The Kid was focused on Corbett because he was a rough, tough brawler, who would wade in and let the chips fall where they may. He was tailor-made for the long-in-the-tooth Lavigne who would need to stop his man early before losing steam to have any hope of a victory. Instead of Corbett he got perhaps the most experienced lightweight of the new century's first decade, Young Erne. It was clear now that the Kid was back to managing himself as there were no signs that Fitzpatrick was still steering the ship. His third go with Fitz had been a short one.

Erne, born Hugh Frank Clavin in Philadelphia, began his fistic marathon in a preliminary bout July 16, 1900, on the card that saw Terry McGovern knock out lightweight champion Frank Erne. Young Erne collected a whopping $2.50 purse for his six-round draw with another neophyte, Kid Egan. "Clavin was known as "Young Erne" elsewhere in the United States but as 'Yi-Yi' in Philadelphia," noted an obituary in *Box Rec*. "The name 'Yi-Yi' came from the battle cry of the gangs in the Gray's Ferry district, where Mr. Clavin was known as the champion rock thrower of his day."[8]

He fought six more times that year, only four times in 1901, and then the explosion, fighting 45 times in 1902. He was incredibly busy measured by any standard from the late 1800s to the present day. By the time he was to face Kid Lavigne he had notched 144 bouts losing 20 in a 6 and 1/2 year span. When he finished after 17 years it was reported that he had fought over 400 times. And he scrapped with some of the best including Packey McFarland, Tim Callahan, Aurelio Herrera, Kid Goodman, and champions Young Corbett II, Abe Attell, and Willie Ritchie.[9]

This fight, set for February 1, 1907 at the National Athletic Club in Philadelphia, was one of desperation. Maybe the Kid really needed the money and it was the best purse he could get. Maybe he figured it was his best shot given the six-round limit in Philly. But why a fighter of Erne's experience, speed, and youth? Was it all about the money at this point? Lavigne himself would shed light on the reasons and once again show that he was in fanciful denial of his age-diminished abilities.

Young Erne (Hugh Frank Clavin) - Courtesy of BoxRec

In a January 1907 letter to a sport in Louisville the Kid said that while he was making money in the saloon business he could make more money in the prize ring. "It really makes me blue," said George, "to see the lightweights of today getting all that easy money, and to be frank with you, I think that my chances of licking any one of the bunch are as good now as they ever were. At any rate, I want to get on with some of them and show the public that I can still go some."[10] Though the Kid was confident, sports in the know were not, and looking back on his "palmy days" one concluded, "If Lavigne is making a pretty fair living with his Detroit café, he had better stick to it and let the fighting game run . . ."[11] And so he should have.

Fight night. The preliminaries were over and the Kid climbed through the ropes wearing a little cap to cover his hairless pate. He was followed by his seconds, Willie Fitzgerald and Johnny Loftus, as the crowded house cheered appreciatively. Fitzgerald was a lightweight who went by the ring name, "The Fighting Harp," denoting his Irish heritage. He was a veteran of over 100 fights and would be good counsel in the Kid's corner. The referee was Burt Crowhurst. The long and rangy Erne while only 5 feet 7 seemed to tower over his older and squatter opponent.

The bell rang for the first round and Lavigne shook with a case of the nerves after having been out of the ring for so long. The Kid did what he did best . . . put his head down and rush his man but Erne was too quick and skillfully blocked his punches. "Toward the end of the round he clipped him on the ear and the Kid tottered toward the ropes, the bell coming to his rescue as he straightened for more," reported the *Los Angeles Herald*. "In the gallery, where the bloodthirsty sit, there were yells to Erne to 'knock his bald block off.' 'Put the old stuff out Erne,' and such."[12]

For three rounds Lavigne fought fairly well but it was clear that Erne could hit him whenever and wherever he pleased. He took it easy on the Kid, perhaps out of respect for the aged ex-champ. The Kid's timing was dreadful, his power was gone and all he could do was to keep coming forward, however feebly. "Erne was considerate," noted the *Herald*. "He stood in the center of the ring and let the poor shadow of the once great fighter fling his arms about and try to fight. Lavigne was determined but harmless."[13]

Erne was trying to let Lavigne go the limit of the six rounds when in the fifth round the Kid missed a roundhouse swing and fell on his face. When he got up he began to verbally abuse his man which was out of character for Lavigne. His young adversary had heard enough. "Erne sailed in," reported the *Saginaw Courier Herald*. "He sent Lavigne reeling to the ropes and then pounded his body while the Kid covered up his face with his gloves to prevent a knockout. Jack McGuigan, Erne's manager called to him to ease up and not to hit the old champion hard."[14] Erne backed off and instead of banging Lavigne he began tapping him softly until the bell rang.

Erne started the sixth and final round moving and lightly jabbing under explicit orders from McGuigan. The crowd began to jeer as they paid to see a fight and expected Erne to knock the old-timer out. About two minutes into the round Erne again reached his breaking point as Lavigne had resumed his trash-talk. He advanced quickly and showered a series of deadly fast punches on the Saginaw man. "Hammering Lavigne about the body with both hands, Erne then shot his right against Lavigne's jaw," continued the *Herald*. "The Kid was sent half-way across the ring and fell up against the ropes. To these he clung desperately with his back turned toward Erne while the referee sprang forward and pushed him toward his corner signifying that the unequal combat was at an end."[15] Had Erne wanted to he could have ended it in three or less.

"The old time fighter had run his race," wrote the *Los Angeles Herald*.[16] Hopefully, mercifully, it would be his last race. Lavigne had become a tomato can, a ham and egger, a palooka. He had shown he could still draw a crowd but at a terribly degrading price. Ten years ago a fighter of Erne's caliber would have been fresh meat for the hungry, unstoppable Kid. On this night he was but a shadow of his former self.

CHAPTER 32

El Último Título En México

Eleven years since winning the world title and eight since losing it, Kid Lavigne was on a slow slide into obscurity. By all accounts his saloon was doing well and those who frequented it said the Kid looked good and quite healthy. Some wondered how long he could continue to abstain from drink while making a living selling it to all who wandered through his door. Perhaps as long as he held on to the illusion that he had one more go left in him, the longer he would continue to stay in shape and off the bottle. Then personal tragedy came calling. The Kid's brother Billy died after contracting spinal meningitis in Seattle at the age of 42, on April 29, 1907.

"Lavigne, who died recently at Seattle, was a welterweight boxer a decade ago," reported the *Washington Post*, "though he never attained the prominence that did his brother "Kid" Lavigne. It was he who managed the Kid in his second fight against Joe Wolcott, out on the Coast. Billy was a long-headed young man and a true sportsman. He had high ideals and lived up to them. He was of a retiring nature and good-hearted, and the sport has lost one of its pillars by his death. Unlike his brother, Billy took the best care of himself and accumulated quite a little money as a promoter of a fight club in Seattle."[1]

In early 1903 the Oakland, California Police Chief put an end to boxing in that city. Billy then left the Acme Athletic Club of Oakland to become the Manager of the newly formed Athenian Athletic Club in Seattle on December 16, 1903. In March 1904 the new Phoenix Athletic Club opened its doors and Billy was tapped to be their head referee while still employed at the Athenian A.C. He finally left the boxing business behind when he took a job as the advertising manager for the *Seattle Post-Intelligencer* sometime in 1905 or 1906. He was in perfect health and preparing to go on a fishing excursion on Friday when he became ill, dying just three days later on Monday afternoon.[2] Billy's body was returned to Saginaw where his remains were laid to rest in the Lavigne family plot in Forest Lawn Cemetery.

Billy's sudden death surely rocked the Kid's foundation as the two had been close for so many years. It was Billy who came home with boxing gloves in the mid-1880s, teaching his younger brother the crude fistic skills he would refine, bringing him fame and fortune ten years later. It was Billy who stood by the Kid through thick and thin, through his rise and fall. It was Billy who would pick up the pieces when twice the Kid split with his on-again, off-again manager, Sam Fitzpatrick. And it was Billy who jumped into the ring twice to save George from senseless beatings at the hands of Mysterious Billy Smith in 1899 and Jimmy Britt in 1902.

In January of 1908 the *Milwaukee Evening Wisconsin* reported that the Kid would soon appear in a vaudeville sketch with his lightweight champion predecessor, Jack McAuliffe. He also began working with a few young fighters and in June he was trying to arrange a match for one of his protégés, Saginaw featherweight, Billy Johnson. He proposed a winner-take-all bout against fellow Michigander, Ad Wolgast, in a Milwaukee club. Pitting a raw young fighter, for whom no boxing record could be found, against the talented Wolgast was extreme.

Adolphus Wolgast, the "Michigan Wildcat," who would later become the lightweight champion of the world, had 44 fights under his belt with only two losses. The question has to be asked as to whether Lavigne was living vicariously through the green talent he was coaching. The end result of the proposed bout between his neophyte and the stiff punching brawler Wolgast would be little different than if he got into the ring himself—a disaster. Lucky for Billy, the fight never materialized.

One month later, the same paper that reported in January that Lavigne was doing vaudeville scribed the headline, "Kid Lavigne Another Example." The story that accompanied it read: "Last week, up in a little New England town, Kid Lavigne, a bum of the direct description, applied for admission to a poor house for the winter. He was worse than all-in, he was a hobo of the most out-and-out character." The article then spoke of Lavigne's successful past, his penchant for top hats and fur coats, and his engaging nature. It ended with, "He made all kinds of money and could have made tens of thousands more. But—that 'old openin' wine' habit got him, and from that the old red-eye claimed him for its own."[3]

Fortunately the article was only half true. The latter half of the description of Lavigne was spot-on but the Saginaw Kid never sought the poor house in New England. The real hobo was one of two Massachusetts fighters who also went by the nickname of "Kid" Lavigne. It was either "Boston" Kid Lavigne, the former lightweight champion of New England who had a short ring career from 1898-1899, or a middleweight who had one professional bout in 1907. Like the case of Lavigne allegedly joining Uncle Sam's army in 1899 and drunkenly taking on the entire Battle Creek, Michigan police force, this was another case of mistaken identity.

As the months rolled by periodic articles would pop up extolling the merits of one old-timer over another as the best lightweight ever. An article in the *Oakland Tribune* opined, "Whether Gans is the best lightweight that ever lived is very doubtful. Some of the very best judges give that honor to the great "Kid" Lavigne."[4] The Kid, staying close to the goings-on in the fight game, no doubt read such assessments by news pundits and it kept his fantasy alive. The draw was powerful, similar to his addiction to booze which for the moment was still under control. His head swimming with stories of his past, he decided it was time to tempt fate once more.

Socking South of the Border

A most unusual and head-scratching piece of news was published by the *San Antonio Daily Express* on August 27, 1908. It was a tiny article in the fine print of page eight, sandwiched next to the box scores of a Galveston versus San Antonio baseball game. The headline reads, "Lavigne Still In the Ring – Lightweight Champion of Mexico Given Decision on a Foul." Could this be the Saginaw Kid? The *Daily Express* continued, "Kid Lavigne was given the decision over Bert Davis on a foul in the seventh round last night."[5] Davis was a native of San Francisco but not a fighter of any renown as no fight record for him was found. A theory needed to be developed to make this fight, and another to come in 1909, plausible and perhaps probable.

The Kid's chances of getting a bout in in the U.S. were slim as even though he was game, no one wanted to humiliate an ex-champion of Lavigne's storied stature. He decided to look south of the border. But how does one become "lightweight champion of Mexico?" It wasn't until 1921 that the first boxing sanctioning organization was created to counterbalance the influence that the New York State Athletic Commission (NYSAC) had on U.S. boxing at the time. It was called the National Boxing Association, precursor to the World Boxing Association. The NYSAC was still in its infancy having been created by the Walker Law of the state of New York in 1920. One of the functions of both these organizations was to confer championship titles on fighters.

In the early days of boxing, before the advent of sanctioning organizations, fighters would often self-anoint. Lavigne, having already legitimately held the American and world titles would be most comfortable travelling to Mexico and calling himself the lightweight champ of that country. This would be *el último título*, his "last title." Any lightweight in disagreement could step in the ring and prove him wrong. Given his credentials and the aura that surrounded the ex-champ's famous deeds, few would tempt to do so. So far, so good.

In March of 1909 a story broke with the *San Antonio Light* that Lavigne was in Mexico. Might this be his second trip there or had he spent the winter there since his bout in August of 1908? The *Light* said he had challenged the Alabama Kid, and arrangements for a bout were in progress.[6] As bizarre as this all might seem, it wasn't out of character with Lavigne's past. Twice before he had sailed to France when emotionally out of sorts and needing a change. Facing another harsh winter in Detroit with his boxing juices still percolating, he may have decided to sample the warm winter hundreds of miles south. A Mexican adventure might be just what he needed.

In a follow-up story on April 6 the *Light* reported, "The Alabama Kid has been matched to fight Kid Lavigne, former lightweight champion, in Aguascalientes, [central] Mexico next month. . . . Alabama has secured an unlimited backer in the person of Dr. Orsini, a noted Mexican sport, who not only has posted a side bet of $1,000 on the [Alabama] Kid, but will take all money offered at the ringside that his protégé will win by the knockout route."[7] The last part of the article told of Lavigne "leaving in a few days for Aguas to get into shape."

It's very likely that this bout, scheduled for some date in May of 1909, for whatever reason, never happened. There was never a follow-up story by the *Light* and no record of such a bout could be found, although there was an Alabama Kid, from Mobile who fought between 1899 and 1918. But another bout did happen in central Mexico on May 16, 1909 in the town of Tlalnepantla, a suburb of Mexico City.

Lining up the evidence, it looks as if Kid Lavigne had been in Mexico City looking for a bout. He thought he had one set with The Alabama Kid and the report said he was leaving in a few days for

Aguas. Aguas was a few hundred miles north of Mexico City so he may have been leaving there to travel to Aguas to begin training. When this bout fell through, he returned to Mexico City and began looking for another match. He found one quickly.

The *Lowell Sun* and several other U.S. newspapers reported on a bout between Kid Lavigne and Bert Davis on May 16 for the lightweight championship of Mexico. This would appear to be a rematch of their bout in August of 1908. The *Sun* headline on the story out of Mexico City read: "Bert Davis Had Kid Lavigne in Helpless Condition."[8] Bert's ring skills had improved just enough to take out the worn and weathered, 40-year old Lavigne. "Bert Davis of San Francisco yesterday won the lightweight championship by stopping Kid Lavigne, holder of the title, in eight rounds," the *Sun* continued.[9] "Lavigne was helpless when the referee stopped the fight. The bout was fast throughout, Davis being the aggressor."

Twice before, someone else had been mistaken for the Saginaw Kid in news stories that stretched the imagination. Could the Mexican escapade be a third time? One way to rule it in or out was to do a thorough search of all the Kid Lavignes fighting at that time. A search was completed for the time period of 1907 to 1910 of all lightweight Kid Lavignes, as well as featherweights and welterweights, as fighters of that era often fought on one or both sides of their weight class.

Only two possible candidates were found. One was an Erie, Pennsylvania fighter named Young Kid Lavigne who had two, four-round professional bouts to his credit, one in 1907 and the second in 1910. He lost the 1907 bout. It was not the sort of pedigree to bolster a claim to the Mexican lightweight title in 1908. And a further complication, according to the *Williamsport Daily Gazette,* Young Kid Lavigne also fought another bout not in his official record against "Cyclone" Bill Larry on May 23, 1909. While not impossible, it's hard to believe a fighter of Young Kid Lavigne's means would fight for and lose the lightweight championship of Mexico, then turn around and rush back to Williamsport, Pennsylvania to fight a six-round undercard bout eight days later. Add to it that the *Daily Gazette* did not mention his loss of the Mexican championship just days ago.[10] It was easy to come to the conclusion that the possibility of this being the right "Kid" was beyond remote.

The second Kid Lavigne was a lightweight who had only one professional fight on his record, a six-round no-decision in 1908. That left only George, "The Saginaw Kid," Lavigne as the leading contender for the mystery man and now *ex campeón de peso ligero*—former lightweight champion—of Mexico.

Cracking the Case

But not so fast. Later research developed a lead exploding the premise that the Saginaw Kid was the Mexican champion. It is a good example of the need for exhaustive research when piecing together events of 104 years ago. In this case, an article from the *Los Angeles Herald* from May 29, 1908 was stumbled upon while searching for something else. The title of the article by Harrington Jones was, "Kid Lavigne Is Globe Trotter." The article was based on a compilation of Kid Lavigne's ring battles and global travels as told to the author by the Kid. But which "Kid" was this?

In the article Jones states that the Kid "was born at sea under the French flag in 1880."[11] If true, this was not the Saginaw Kid. It also mentioned that he had fought in England, New York, the Philippines, Australia, New South Wales, Acapulco, and Mexico City. Several opponents were identified in the article but most of them had no ring records, yet one did. It said he was knocked out in the second round by John Dorman in New York City. That lead cracked the case. Dorman had a ring record and in it was found a bout on May 13, 1907 with a "Lavigno II," in which Dorman prevailed by a second round knockout. Not quite Kid Lavigne but getting close.

A search for Lavigno II found a Box Rec record of a Mexican fighter with only one bout . . . the one with Jack Dorman. It's safe to say that Lavigno II and the Kid Lavigne of the article were one in the same. This "Mexican" Kid Lavigne told Jones that he was the veteran of 39 battles, having been knocked out three times. So who was this Harrington Jones? Perhaps knowing that might add more certainty to this Mexican mystery. More research identified Jones as a writer for the *Mexico Daily Record*. It was all fitting together now.

The final conclusion of the Mexican conundrum is that the fighter known as Lavigno II was also known as Kid Lavigne and he was the man who claimed the Mexican lightweight title. He was also the man who fought Bert Davis in 1908 and 1909, losing his championship to Davis in the second battle. Hopefully someday, someone with interest in early Latin American fighters will research and do justice to the Mexican Kid Lavigne's record. If he truly did have 39 globetrotting bouts, it should prove to be quite a good story.

CHAPTER 33

Not Yet Dead

At this point Lavigne's itch to get back in the roped square was probably more about the life-affirming feeling of being in the ring rather than chasing a dream of recapturing his old glory. Like so many people in so many professions who over-identify with the work in their life, they cannot quit. Having little else that makes them tick, they keep on doing it, year after year, far beyond when others have quit the game. This was a picture of Kid Lavigne, still not ready to hang up his gloves.

Confirmation came from the *Police Gazette* when in October of 1909 it wrote, "Kid Lavigne, ex-lightweight champion, feels like many of the other old-timers that he can still put up a good bout and wants a chance." He got another chance in December 1909 when he landed a bout with "Fighting" Dick Nelson in Detroit. As a tune up on December 17, Lavigne climbed in the ring at the Avenue Theater in

Oscar "Battling" Nelson – Courtesy BoxRec

Detroit with another Nelson, current lightweight champion, Oscar "Battling" Nelson, aka the "Durable Dane," for an exhibition of a few rounds.

The prime years of these two fighters were about 10 years apart, Lavigne having held the title from 1896 to 1899 and "Battling" Nelson on and off from 1905 to 1910. Had their peak years aligned, a go between these two would have been an epic match. Their aggressive fighting styles were very similar and their remarkable stamina and capacity to absorb punishment were legendary. They were known in the day as true "iron men," and it was fitting that they were joined at the hip by Nat Fleischer whose 1958 ranking had them as the 5th and 6th all-time lightweights. On the quality of the mill the Denver Post reported, "The terror of the lightweights ten years ago showed flashes of his speed but was a little short of wind at times."[1]

The Last Real Go

Dick Nelson was another Scandinavian, born Richard Christensen in Norway. It's hard to figure why he took this bout with Lavigne other than to say he had stepped in the ring with a legend. He would gain nothing else by beating the ex-champ who was 11 years his senior and had just turned 40 that month. At the time of the fight on Christmas Day, Nelson was the veteran of 116 fights with only eight losses. Admittedly, Nelson had not fought many of the top tier lightweights of his day with the exception of a 10-round draw with an aging George Dixon in his first professional bout four years past, and a 10-round newspaper decision win against Young Corbett II in May of 1909, when Corbett was past his prime as well. Nonetheless he was a journeyman of the ring and would be a formidable foe for the Kid.

The result was predictable and no doubt quite humbling for Lavigne. "Detroit fight fans saw the last of the once famous Kid Lavigne, former lightweight champion of the world, in a pitiful boxing bout the other night," reported the *Grand Forks Daily Herald*. "Lavigne, a mere shadow of his former self, attempted to stay six rounds with "Fighting" Dick Nelson. Before the last round was half over Nelson dropped his hands and said to the referee: 'Stop this farce. I can't hit that poor old man. It's a shame to let him box anybody.' So Lavigne was spared the ignominy of a dead sure knockout and was led away, convinced that the prize ring has seen him for the last time. In his prime Kid Lavigne, the once famous Saginaw Kid, never knew when he was whipped and though beaten to a standstill on numerous occasions, he always came back with the sleep wallop."[2]

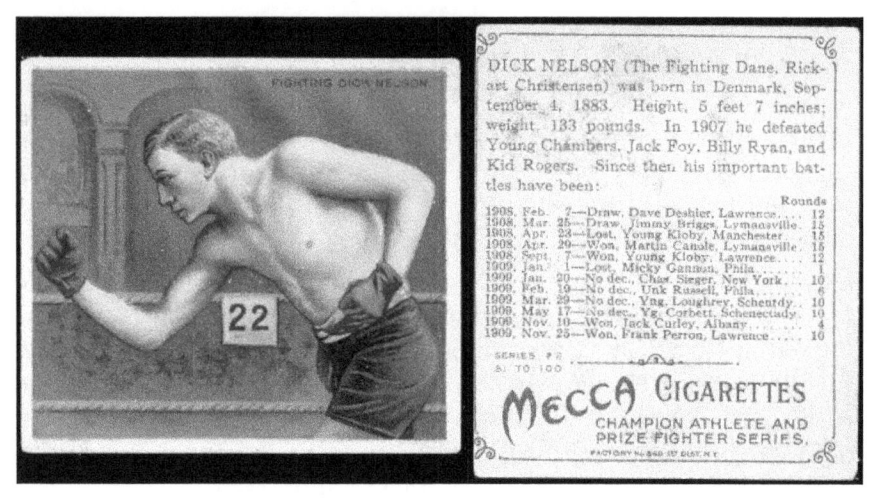

Tobacco card from 1910 of "Fighting" Dick Nelson

At this stage of the game, given his loss of speed and stamina and no longer possessing that sleep inducer, the Kid was whipped before he graced the canvas with his storied presence. Would this truly be his last go? He went back to running his watering hole but continued to dream about staying in the fight game. He fought Ad Wolgast, lightweight champion at the time, in a two-round exhibition sometime in 1910 although no newspaper confirmation of the bout was found.

In late December, 1910 the Kid and Battling Nelson teamed up again for a series of exhibitions in the theatrical circuit. On Monday night, December 19, they put on a sparring match at the Avenue Theater in Detroit.[3] Nelson had lost the championship to Ad Wolgast in 1910 and was knocked out in November by Owen Moran. Despite the decisive losses, he was still a very popular fighter and the show broke all of the theater's records for receipts.[4] Though Lavigne's glory days were long past, his popularity in his home state, and now his home town, helped to pack the house. But a packed house simply allowed more people to witness the Kid's state of decline. Of this exhibition the *Denver Post* wrote, ". . . the showing he made that night should convince him he hasn't a chance in the world to make good again."

Aside from their fighting styles and having both been lightweight champs, they had one more thing in common of the fateful variety. They both lost their mothers in 1911. Nelson's 52-year-old mother Ida died tragically in August when struck by a train in Burnham, a south suburb of Chicago. The Kid's 58-year-old mother

Mickey Sheridan - Courtesy of Library of Congress, Prints and Photographs Division, Bain Collection.

Agnes died a painful death in December from uterine cancer in Saginaw. With both parents and his brother Billy gone as well, the Kid was survived by his younger brothers Frank and James, and his sister Agnes, who had married a Detroit fellow named Clarence Smith in 1900. The Kid's parents had twelve children between 1864 and 1881. Only four were still living.

In what may have been the last action of his career in the ring, Lavigne fought two short exhibitions as part of a benefit for Bob Farrell in Windsor, Ontario on February 3, 1911. He traded gloves for three rounds with Mickey Sheridan, a promising lightweight of the time and he got his second short shot at a "first-rater," Ad Wolgast, for two rounds.

There would be more emotional trauma for the Kid in 1911. By all accounts Lavigne had been on the wagon since the fall of 1900. His temperate time started after he had been sent home by the Parisian authorities, followed by a lengthy stay at Green Springs, Ohio, quite probably the Green Springs Sanitarium and Water Cure, where he conquered his demons. He opened his saloon, the "Kid Lavigne Triangle Café" in Detroit in the fall of 1905. While it was reported that he was a lively patron of his own saloon, rumors of his succumbing to the booze circuit that marked his reputation of the past were non-existent. He may not have been entirely abstinent but it appeared that all was under control.

Rock Bottom and Insane Again

Then a different piece of news surfaced in August. One that showed he had fallen again. "Kid Lavigne, once champion lightweight of the world, was in police court at Detroit yesterday charged with another kind of fighting," noted the *Milwaukee Free Press*. "His wife made the complaint. Kid imbibed too much of his own wet goods, and when he went home, proceeded to start a rough house. The judge suspended sentence."[5] With the cold Detroit winter closing in his mother died on December 9 three days after his 42nd birthday. The Kid was once again struggling to make sense of it all and turned to the bottle for comfort.

From the depths of a boozy gloom, this fistic Phoenix rose once again from the ashes of imminent obscurity when he startled fans with an announcement that he was returning to the ring. "I am in better condition right now than I was when I left the ring," he proclaimed to the Detroit press. I am going into training for ten months. I will make the best of them sit up and take notice at the end of that period."[6] Just six months had passed between his arrest for drunken spousal abuse and his latest comeback proclamation. Was he truly "in better condition" or was Lavigne becoming delusional. A prescient statement from the *Denver Post* gave rationale for the Kid's affliction when it averred, "Strange when once they become inoculated with the 'comeback' germ all efforts to stay their desire fail."[7]

News of Lavigne's comeback announcement spread far and wide, and was met by a skeptical press. A Detroit news wire gave this opinion: "Sometimes a ball player, or an athlete in other lines, realizes that he is done. No fighter ever is convinced until he has spent a month or two in the hospital thinking it over, after a futile attempt to come back. Kid Lavigne, the greatest lightweight of his day is one of the latest of the pugilists to con himself into the belief that he is not yet dead."[8]

Lavigne's resurgence would have to be accompanied by yet another ride on the water wagon. And the talk was surfacing that that is exactly what he was committed to do. "The change from alcoholic drinks to the peaceful waters has wrought wonders with the ring hero of other days," noted the *Springfield Daily News*. "Some old friend of his went into his place several weeks ago, and advised him to cut out the intoxicants. The talk had such a thrilling effect on the former champion that he agreed to stop drinking then and there and prepare for exhibition bouts on the stage. He has kept his resolve most religiously ever since."[9]

Lavigne sounded steadfast when he recalled the friend's intervention. "I had been drinking when this friend commenced talking to me and I was sober when he quit talking to me, and I went out of the door with him a different man. I have quit the liquor for good and all time. Get that? It isn't religion I've gotten but common sense.

I am strong as ever and not much over the lightweight limit, and I believe I can lick the best of them at my weight. Wolgast is the toughest nut I will have to crack but watch me."[10] Ad Wolgast was indeed a tough nut, cut from the same fiber and fighting style as Lavigne. Two years prior he did what few thought was possible; outlast Battling Nelson to earn a 40th round technical knockout to win the lightweight championship. He would have taken the 42-year-old Lavigne apart in short order.

Mercifully, no shot with Wolgast materialized but according to a dispatch out of Cincinnati on April 5, 1912 the Kid had been matched with Boer Unholz. Unholz wasn't exactly a household name as only one bout could be found in the various boxing record sources for this German lightweight. The *Cleveland Plain Dealer* couldn't resist a sarcastic comment about the match when it wrote, "As long as the world rolls on men will try to cheat nature. Here's Kid Lavigne, who was pugilistically dead and buried many years ago, signing up to fight Boer Unholz. The contest is open for the club offering the largest purse. Come on, matchmakers, with your bids! Lavigne is only 42 and Unholz 31, but the latter can still fight."[11] The matchmakers didn't bite and no bout happened.

The next bit of news was testament to the Kid's see-saw battle with alcoholism and sanity. For a second time in his career the headline broke, "Kid Lavigne Is Insane."[12] The *Fort Worth Star-Telegram* was more colorful in its headline, "Kid Lavigne Off To The Bughouse."[13] First reports surfaced on June 29, 1912 when the *Milwaukee Free Press* noted, "George 'Kid' Lavigne, former prizefighter, appeared before Judge Stein today charged with creating a disturbance in his home. He was such a wreck from drink that he was sent to St. Joseph's retreat

Ad Wolgast, "The Michigan Wildcat"
- Courtesy BoxRec

in Dearborn. Lavigne's wife, with whom Lavigne fell in love in Paris while he was touring the world at the height of his glory, wept as she told Justice Stein of her husband's conduct toward her."[14]

Further news accounts painted a grim picture. "Wrecked physically and mentally, George 'Kid' Lavigne, one of the greatest lightweight pugilists the world has ever seen, is likely to spend the balance of his days in an insane asylum," reported the *Denver Post*. "He is at present confined in the Dearborn retreat until his wife can have him legally committed to an insane asylum. A blow on the head in one of his championship battles some years ago is believed to be responsible for his irrational actions. Recently, he has become so violent that his relatives have feared for their lives."[15]

When a fighter's mental capacities diminished as he aged, it was often attributed to repetitive blows to the head. In 1928 it was given the name, "dementia pugilistica," describing a neurodegenerative disease due to concussive or sub-concussive blows to the head. Dementia pugilistica (DP) would decades later be known as a variant of chronic traumatic encephalopathy (CTE). Symptoms include slurred speech, problems with memory, lack of coordination and tremors. Those suffering from DP are also prone to inappropriate or explosive behavior and may display pathological jealousy or paranoia.

It is entirely possible that Lavigne was suffering from DP as he certainly was displaying explosive behavior. His fighting style, which featured minimal defense, left him vulnerable to severe punishment which accumulated over the course of his career. However, the outbursts he experienced were the only symptom of DP that he exhibited. His memory was sharp and he was physically very capable late into his life. His Mr. Hyde behaviors most probably had their roots in the bottle.

The pattern was set as a teenager when drinking let loose a side of his personality that was highly inconsistent with his humble and genial nature while sober. Going back over his career, nearly every time he was arrested, roughed up his spouse, or ended up in an asylum, alcohol was in the mix. Countless news articles told of his decline at the hands of dissipation. It's more likely that he was coming to the realization that the absolute end of his fistic career was at hand. The finality of it all, fueled by his drug of choice, sent him into a rage. He took it out on Julia and she in turn, fearing for her safety, had no choice but to call the police. In court she vouched for his sober side when she told the judge, "When he is sober, he is one of the best of husbands, but he is rarely sober anymore."[16] This was further evidence that alcohol, not DP, was to blame for his aberrant behavior.

St. Joseph's Sanatorium, also called the Michigan Retreat for the Insane was opened in 1883 in Dearborn, Michigan, housing mainly Civil War veterans at first and later alcoholics, drug addicts and other "incurables." Sending someone here was usually a one way ticket with no return to society. Aside from his temporary hold at St. Joseph's there is no evidence to suggest that Julia had him committed for the long term. Several news items later in the year support this conclusion.

A writer for the *Detroit Free Press* on June 30 countered the report that Lavigne was again insane in an article which featured comments from Julia Lavigne. "Speaking English is a great effort for Mrs. Lavigne, but she managed to make herself understood. She repudiated the statement over and over again that she asked to have her husband taken to the county jail. It is true that George has been on a spree recently, but there was nothing violent in his nature nor was she in the least wise afraid he would do her an injury. . . . She believes the stories that sometimes appear in the papers are the concoctions of persons who do not like George and grasp those means to belittle him." The piece continued with Julia wishing her husband would seek out the writer of the negative article and even the score. "I jes lak for one tam for Schorge to tak wan poonch hen hees face and give heem black eye for six months."[17]

A story ran in the *Saginaw News* on August 7 about a charity baseball game between the well-heeled sports of Saginaw and Detroit. Kid Lavigne was named as the coach for the Saginaw team and Judge Stein, who had sent the Kid to the asylum just five weeks earlier, was playing catcher for the Detroit squad. Lavigne was no longer under lock and key.

One Last Match?

Then a headline in the *Milwaukee Free Press* in September trumpeted, "Ex-Champion Lavigne Has New White Hope."[18] Lavigne, as he had done on and off since the opening of his boxing school in Paris, continued to stay active in the gym, coaching and training new talent. The article talked of a heavyweight Wisconsin woodchopper named Art Nelson who the Kid felt was a "world beater." But it was not to be. Nelson failed to fill the role of the white hope losing six of thirteen in a short career. Working with fighters always seemed to keep the Kid thinking he had one more bout left in him and news was soon afoot that he was matched again.

A short announcement in the *San Francisco Call* in mid-December 1912 noted various bouts happening the coming week across the nation. The *Call* wrote, ". . . while they have old Kid Lavigne on the bill for a set-to with a lad known as Kattel in Cherry Valley, Illinois."[19] The fighter's full name was George Kattel and it was to be a 10-round go. A search of the Rockford, Illinois newspapers of the time yielded no mention of a fight between Lavigne and Kattel. No record was found for George Kattel either. It is assumed that this fight, for whatever reason, fell through. This was the last match that was ever made with the Saginaw Kid.

Further proof that Lavigne was not rotting away in an asylum came from two news items out of Ohio. "A friend of George (Kid) Lavigne, who is at Dayton, Ohio, says that the reports that Lavigne is confined in an insane asylum are untrue. He states that the Kid is breathing the good air and enjoying good health and will soon start writing a brief history of his wonderful fighting career."[20] Unfortunately, like so many matches that were made and postponed or made and never held, he would not make good on his promise to chronicle his fighting career for years to come.

CHAPTER 34

Decline and Revival in Detroit

Slowly, the memories of Lavigne's heyday were dissipating in the sporting world. Throughout the teens his name and deeds would be brought up in news stories, discussing the merits of the "modern" fight game versus those of boxing's first golden age of the 1890s. Comparisons were made between the new breed and the old-timers, often noting Lavigne's savage attack, gameness, and willingness to take on all comers regardless of their weight. Recollections of his greatness were also accompanied by stories of his darker side; how he succumbed to the "Great White Way," drinking himself out of the championship and into oblivion.

Items from his past made the news in 1913. A story broke in February about a libel suit brought by fight manager, Tom O'Rourke. O'Rourke, former manager of Joe Wolcott and one of the top promoters and managers of the 1890s, claimed he had been slandered by the English sporting paper *Boxing*. A dispatch from London to the *New York Times* identified the transgression. "Certain articles appeared in this publication [*Boxing*] alleging that O'Rourke had made fraudulent arrangements to contests in New York, San Francisco and other American cities in order to bring about pre-arranged results and to win considerable sums of money."[1] One of the bouts in question was Kid Lavigne's second fight with Joe Wolcott in San Francisco in 1897.

The *Boxing* editors printed comments by American journalist Robert Edgren claiming that O'Rourke made a secret arrangement with the referee whereby Wolcott was to lose and he placed his bets against Wolcott. O'Rourke vehemently denied the charges saying he lost $4,500 on that fight betting on his man to win. Called as the only witness on his day in London court, O'Rourke was on the stand for several hours and subjected to a "severe cross-examination" by counsel for the defense. He had obtained affidavits from Lavigne and Walcott as well as other fighters.[2]

Mr. Powell, the defendant's attorney, addressed the court likening O'Rourke's alleged libel charge to an ink spot on a sidewalk. "If the jury must give damages," continued the *Times*, "he suggested that the smallest coin of the realm was large enough for O'Rourke to carry away to America and wear on his watch-chain as a memento of the occasion." The Brits were peevish about an American making accusations against one of their beloved sporting rags. The jury was out for 25 minutes ruling in O'Rourke's favor and awarding him $250 in damages.[3]

Years later when asked by a reporter about the alleged "fix" Lavigne was shocked. "He first took it as a joke and then got serious," wrote Tad Dorgan in an *International News Service* column, "Tad's Tid Bits." "He was so serious that he started to cry. Then in order to cry better he took out his false teeth, put them in a tin box and cried his heart out."[4] It caused him great pain that anyone would associate his name with such a deception. An alcoholic-wife beater he may have been, but in the ring Lavigne saw himself as beyond reproach.

Another incident linked to the Kid's past hit the news wire in May of 1913. "Edward Congalton, 75 years old, who says he was at one time head athletic trainer for the New York Athletic Club, once trained John L. Sullivan, and for a time was manager of Kid Lavigne, is in New York today looking for someone who knew him in the old days to aid him, after having been taken starving from a locked freight car in the Lackawanna freight yards in Hoboken yesterday."[5] Hard times befell many a person associated with fistiana. No additional information was found on Congalton to support the claim that he managed the Kid.

A piece by the *Milwaukee Evening Wisconsin* stated that the Kid was soon to open another boxing school. "George Kid Lavigne, who in the opinion of many, was the greatest lightweight the game has ever known, not even accepting Joe Gans, has decided to open up a school of boxing at Dayton, Ohio. He has been keeping a buffet in Detroit for several years, but recently decided to get into some other line because he fears being around it all the time will keep him into the way of drinking more than is good for him."[6] No record of a boxing school venture in Dayton was found

In Need of a Benefit

Late in 1913 Lavigne closed the Kid Lavigne Triangle Café on Randolph street, however, his fear of being around the temptation of drink must have quickly subsided as he was next seen in June of 1914 tending bar at the Burns Hotel just a few blocks away. The Kid was now drifting with little in the bank to shield him from very hard times. Like many fighters that had climbed the ladder of fistic success he didn't prepare for his future, preferring instead to live in the pomp of his past.

Nearing the end of 1915 the Kid's economic plight was well known. "Only a year ago the once famous and admired fighter sent out an appeal for a job," wrote the *Trenton Evening News*, "any kind of a job—and announced that he would be tickled to death with a proposition that would enable him to pull down seventy-five bones—no, not a week—but a month! And this is the lad who used to consider such a sum as only a fair-sized outlay for a little dinner-for-two! Only the other day the Kid addressed a pathetic appeal to a New York sporting scribe, asking him to pull off a benefit for him in the Big Town. 'I would like to get hold of a piece of money now as I need it pretty bad,' wrote the Kid in a pencil scrawl. And doubtless he does need the money, with a long, hard winter coming on, and the memory of past glories but a poor substitute for food and shelter."[7]

Old friends of the ex-champ, led by the Kid's former manager, Sam Fitzpatrick, took up the cause and organized a benefit in his honor, hoping to collect enough money to get him squarely on his financial feet. "Lavigne is remembered as one of the honest fighters who never faked a contest," reported the *Milwaukee Free Press*. "He was not a money-grabber, although he won some big purses. He never saved his money, but like John L. Sullivan and other good 'sports,' he spread it all over the map and gave it away wherever it would do good for others. And so Lavigne has been scraping along and having a hard time of it."[8]

The benefit was set for December 22, 1915 at the Harlem Athletic Club. Five hundred sports came to see a "who's-who" from past and present pay homage to Lavigne. The list included John L. Sullivan, Jim Corbett, Bob Fitzsimmons, Jack McAuliffe, and Frank Erne from the bygone era, as well as a cadre of the best lightweights of the current ranks including Willie Ritchie, Freddy Welsh and Benny Leonard.[9]

It was late in the evening of bouts between old-timers and some boxers of the present when Lavigne made his entrance. "All but one of the exhibition bouts had been concluded when a little bald-headed man appeared in the ring to referee the bout of these two-minute rounds between Kid McPartland and Owen Ziegler," noted the *New York Times*. "He was greeted with a cheer and this seemed to unnerve him, for in the face of the tumult he was speechless. For a few minutes he stood looking helplessly at the sea of faces, and then Charley Harvey jumped into the ring and spoke of Lavigne's career in the boxing days long since passed. . . . It was but the shadow of the past flitting for a moment across the present."[10]

The benefit, although well attended, netted only $482 for the Kid. The gate receipts totaled $1,500, leading well known 'sport', boxing manager, and columnist for the *Denver Post*, Otto Floto, to cry foul at the hands of "the invisible mitt." Floto contended there was no explanation for why most, if not all, of the $1,500 didn't end up in Lavigne's pocket as those who contributed the funds did so with the expectation that the ex-champ would be receiving all of it. "Kid Lavigne expressed it correctly the other evening at his benefit," Floto continued. "'Now days the boys get a Standard Oil bankroll and don't have to do one-half as much fighting as we were compelled to do in our training quarters. I came just 20 years too soon and that's why I need this benefit I suppose.'"[11]

Descriptions of Lavigne, so often focused on his battle with the bottle, now noted his physical decline as well. A few days after the benefit another story out of New York, titled "Lavigne But Shadow Of His Former Self" depicted him in this manner: "The once robust little athlete appears a shadow of his former self. The sharp, clear eye that marked him in the ring a generation ago is gone. The George Lavigne of today is a 'squinter.' His sight is very bad and he wears glasses all the time. Whatever sign of the athlete he still bears is entirely removed when he puts on the 'cheaters.' He is just a plain little old man, and yet his years number but 46. And he talks of old times just like all little old men do."[12] The ravages of all the punishment absorbed and the booze consumed had aged him beyond his years.

Lavigne continued to keep his head in the fight game without risking life or limb in the ring. In early 1916 he was training Arthur Pelkey, Canadian heavyweight champion for a bout with Carl Morris in February. Both Pelkey and Morris had ten-round draws to their credit with then world heavyweight champion Jess Willard and it was widely assumed that the winner of the bout would get a crack at Willard next. Pelkey, born Pelletier, aside from being of French decent, had another thing in common with the Kid. He had killed a man in the ring. In 1913 he knocked out Luther McCarty

Drawing by Robert L. Ripley (of "Ripley's Believe It or Not" fame) from his "Talk with Lavigne" article, 1915

who collapsed and died from an apparent light blow in the first round. Up to that time Pelkey had lost only one bout but afterward, according to a description by Tracy Callis, Pelkey was never the same and won only a handful of bouts. Pelkey was knocked out by Morris in the fifth.[13]

A Dozen Arrests

Tending bar and training some up-and-comers kept the Kid busy and in a little coin. His drinking problem began to worsen. Bad news again was noted in a short piece by the *Portsmouth Daily Times* when it wrote, "George 'Kid' Lavigne, former lightweight champion pugilist has suffered a nervous collapse and is in a bad way at his home in Detroit."[14] Then the details from the *Saginaw News* on September 22, 1916: "George (Kid) Lavigne a former pugilist appeared in the bull pen of the court of Justice Sellers Friday morning charged with beating his wife. 'The woman,' said the officer, 'was taken to the Receiving hospital and discharged after her hurts were dressed.' 'How often have you been arrested?' asked the court. 'Several times,' said Lavigne, 'always because I got drunk.'"[15] Indeed, this was the Kid's twelfth arrest.

The Kid had accumulated quite a rap sheet for a pint-sized pugilist over a 29 year span. His first arrest was as a 17 year old for public drunken behavior. He was arrested six times for assault including once on a police officer, once on a woman in Paris, once on a man on a river boat, and three times on his wife. He was also thrown in the slammer twice for prizefighting, once for jumping bail, and once for disrespecting a police officer. His most famous arrest was for the murder of Andy Bowen for which he was exonerated.

After proving he beat her, Lavigne's wife, Julia, petitioned the court, asking that the Kid be committed to an asylum. Two physicians testified that he was the victim of alcoholism but that he could cure himself if he would. One of the doctors described the Kid as "easy going and extremely pleasing."[16] This was the conundrum of his condition. The doctors saw the sober and humble Dr. Jekyll. Julia lived with the drunken, hell-raising Mr. Hide and she'd had enough. This was the third time the Kid had roughed her up to the point where he was arrested and it would be anyone's guess as to how many times it happened when it didn't make headlines. He was given 30 days probation and released with instructions that Julia contact Judge Hulbert at the end of that time with a report on how he was behaving.

After 30 days another headline in the *Kalamazoo Gazette* read: "Kid Lavigne Escapes Asylum." The *Gazette* followed with, "The Kid hasn't beaten anybody lately—excepting his wife—but he has proved to the satisfaction of the probate court that he has downed the demon rum, for the time being, at least, and there is no reason to send him to an asylum."[17] Given the Kid's long and lurid track record there was also no reason to believe his latest ride on the water wagon would last.

Full Circle to Ford

Finally, the Kid caught a break when the research department of "a big automobile factory" became interested in his plight and offered him a job.[18] The auto maker was Ford and it's tempting to wonder if Henry Ford remembered his chance meeting with the Kid 22 years past, on that dusty road outside of Saginaw, if indeed it actually happened. Had Henry picked up the Detroit paper one morning, read that a local ex-champion was down on his luck, recalled that he had met the man and instructed his people to reach out to the Kid with an offer of a job? Plausible, yes. Provable, no. But a good story it makes. Lavigne started with Ford sometime in early 1917.

"Old friends of the once great Kid Lavigne will be interested in the news that he has been for several months a regular employ in the Ford factory, holding a responsible job as an inspector of automobile parts," reported the *Elkhart Truth* in late 1917. "This is much better than living from hand-to-mouth, as Lavigne did for many years, as proprietor of a roadhouse or a gymnasium. Lavigne never had any financial genius. His ring earnings as lightweight champion lasted only a short time, and he never saw much prosperity after losing the title to Frank Erne until he 'made good' in his present job."[19]

Lavigne would go on to hold several jobs at the Highland Park Ford Plant. In early 1918, a comment in a column by famed writer, cartoonist, and sport, Robert Edgren, regarding the occupations of some of the old-time pugs noted that Lavigne was "a moving picture film inspector" with Ford. Edgren noted that "there are many branches of work in the Ford shop," as if to shed light on why Ford would employ someone in a role seemingly unrelated to automobile production.[20] It's tempting to assume that Edgren got a bit mixed up and meant to write, "moving-parts inspector." It was only five years earlier that Henry Ford had perfected the first moving assembly line in the world at his Highland Park production facility. But indeed there was such a job as a moving picture film inspector in Ford's Art Department.

The Kid, after working at Ford for a few years took on two co-workers as borders. With George being the sole breadwinner on his $5 per day salary it helped to pay the bills. One border, 20-year-old Mr. Caslagne, was a recent French speaking émigré from Canada and the other was a 24-year-old recent émigré from Ireland named Mr. Spellman. No doubt, the Kid and his Parisian wife, Julia, welcomed the opportunity to keep their French language skills polished.

Perhaps the Kid's most interesting and little discussed job at Ford was as a member of Harry Bennett's "strong-arm squad." Bennett, an ex-sailor and boxer, was discovered by Arthur Brisbane, a Hearst newspaper editor who in 1916 was on his way to a meeting with Henry Ford. He witnessed Harry wading into a brawl between a friend and U.S. Customs officials. He was knocking them down right and left until the cops got the upper hand. Brisbane liked his pluck, got him released, and took him to his meeting with Henry. "Ford liked the idea of a young scrapper who could take care of himself. After asking Bennett, 24, if he could shoot, he offered him a job."[21] After a few years as night-watchman Henry had bigger plans for Harry making him the head of Ford's Service Department, a euphemism for internal security. He supervised over 3,000 crooks and retired police officers and became Henry Ford's right hand "muscle".

Bennett became very close to Henry doing all his dirty work including covering up Ford's infidelities, spying, firing employees, and administering beatings to others to keep them in line. Given Lavigne's drinking problem he probably wasn't the most reliable person to be inspecting moving pictures and a better use of his natural talents appealed to Bennett who liked the old ring-men, finding them useful implements for workforce intimidation. At some point in the early 1920s the Kid was drafted by Bennett into the Service Department. He had now come full circle from his job in 1890 wielding an ax handle on the steps of Saginaw's Michigan House, keeping rowdy loggers in line, to roughing up auto plant workers for Harry Bennett. Once a pug, forever a pug.

The Kid's employment status at Ford would be tested, when once again, on April 14, 1920, a troubling headline broke: "Kid Lavigne Adjudged Insane Man."[22] The accompanying article stated that the examining doctors Clark and Sterns recommended he be sent to an asylum. This was a repeat of the 1916 event when his wife Julia had started proceedings to have him committed only to have the doctors pronounce him sane. This time the same two doctors agreed with her, recommending he be sent to an asylum. "The report of physicians who examined him states that Lavigne suffers from hallucinations and hears noises that may soon deprive him of his self-control," noted the *Jackson Citizen Patriot*.[23]

Many feared Lavigne would be locked up for the rest of his days. One writer for the *Racine Journal-News* believed that it was his loss of the championship to Frank Erne in 1899 that caused him to become unhinged. "The Saginaw Kid never recovered from the beating administered by Erne, and since he became mentally unbalanced has been heard to mutter incoherent sentences that touched upon that one great battle in his career."[24]

Lavigne was not long in the asylum, most probably St. Joseph's Sanatorium in Dearborn, Michigan, where he was well known by now. Burt Coppelberger, a close friend of the Kid's living in Oakland, California received a letter from him just two months later on June 18th. "I received your letter some time ago but wasn't feeling well and was away for three weeks," wrote the Kid. "But you can tell all my California friends that I am feeling well again and am 'o.k.'"[25] It appears that Lavigne may have been a patient in the "short-stay unit" at St. Joe's, were there such a thing back then. This most probably marked the point when he gave up booze for good. Sane and sober again, the Kid was nearly 51.

Losses of Another Kind

On October 19, 1922, word began to circulate that Lavigne's long time, on again-off again manager, Sam Fitzpatrick was gravely ill in New York and was not expected to recover. Fitzpatrick first came to the U.S. in 1888 with Peter Jackson in tow. Jackson has been lauded by many boxing historians as possibly the greatest fighter of all time who never won the heavyweight championship. John L. Sullivan drew the color line, refusing to fight Jackson, ostensibly because he was black; however, it was clear at the time that Sullivan did it because he knew he wouldn't prevail.

Jackson, through Fitzpatrick, had a dramatic influence on Kid Lavigne's boxing style. Jackson was one of the first to make extensive use of body blows. It was a fight between Peter Jackson and the "colored" heavyweight champion, George Godfrey, in 1888 that convinced Fitzpatrick that a blow to the body was as deadly as one to the jaw. Jackson made for the body and punished Godfrey throughout until he admitted defeat in the 19th round after which he spent several days in bed healing the beating he took to his midsection and chest. Under Fitz's direction, Lavigne would become one of the greatest body punchers of all time.

Fitz was a bit of a boxer in his day. As an Australian middleweight he was nicknamed the "Australian Comet." He became Jackson's chief second. He became the Kids' manager in 1894 and was largely responsible for guiding him to the world championship. Sam later hooked up with Jack Johnson, becoming his manager in 1908 and taking him to the world heavyweight championship when he defeated Tommy Burns in Australia on December 26, 1908.[26] Fitzpatrick failed to recover and died six days later on October 28th. The fistic world mourned the loss of one the great managers of the time, "Honest Sam," as he was fondly called.

While this certainly rocked the Kid as he and Sam had been through so much together and remained close over the years, Lavigne had been dealing with his wife's illness at the time as well. Julia was suffering from breast cancer and after an eight-month battle she died on November 22, 1922 at their home in Detroit.[27] Her remains were taken to Forest Lawn Cemetery in Saginaw and buried in the Lavigne family plot, next to the Kid's mother and father, Agnes and Jean Baptiste, and his brothers Billy and John.

It was a rough year for Lavigne but he shouldered on and to the surprise of many he didn't drown his sorrows in the bottle. He was still stone cold sober and looked to stay that way.

Of Belts and Canes

When last we left the path of the lightweight championship belt first worn by Jack McAuliffe in 1887 it had been purchased from a pawn shop in Coney Island by John P. Hurley, a friend of McAuliffe's. McAuliffe had pawned it to bet on horse at the track that came in second "by a whisker." The belt next found its way back to the man who originally created it, *Police Gazette* proprietor, Richard K. Fox. Fox had the belt refurbished, replacing some of its missing baubles, notably diamonds, rubies, and sapphires. Fox then gave it to Terry McGovern, bantam and flyweight champion at the turn of the century.[28]

Why would a non-lightweight champion end up with the belt? The answer, quite possibly, is that Fox felt "Terrible" Terry deserved it after beating Frank Erne, then lightweight champion, in July 1900. An argument could be made that the title should have changed hands. They had agreed to fight at 128 pounds, still two pounds above the featherweight limit, making it legitimately a lightweight bout. Erne weighed in at 128 and McGovern at 123. Erne was slaughtered by Terry in three rounds, his corner throwing in the towel. It appears this was the *Police Gazette's* way of making a statement, conferring the title via the championship belt. Sam Harris, McGovern's manager, ended up with the belt. In the early 1920s the belt was a feature of an exhibition of one of Harris' shows, "The Champion."[29]

Another form of championship hardware was also on the move in the early 1920s. When Lavigne returned from England after winning the world lightweight championship in 1896 he was presented with a championship cane by fellow Frenchie, fan, and long-time Saginaw shoemaker, Edward Griguerre. This was no ordinary walking stick; not a popular wardrobe accessory, but a functional training aid. It was made of a thin, flexible, metal shaft, and strung under heavy pressure with round leather disks. It was topped with a gold handle and engraved with the words, "World Lightweight Champion."

This was a training stick, also called a road cane. A boxer would do miles of road work gripping the cane with both hands near the ends. This would compel the user to assume a fighting position with his hands and arms. While conditioning his lungs and legs he would also be training himself to keep his dukes up through the end of the fight. It no doubt came in handy as well if chased by an aggressive, teeth-bearing canine.

"Griguerre had intended it to be a championship trophy, and asked Lavigne to hand it to his successor," noted the *Nevada State Journal* in 1922. "However, the cane has remained in the Kid's hands until the present time."[30] Lavigne may have been waiting for the lightweight to come along that he believed worthy of the treasure. He found that man in Benny Leonard.

Leonard, born Benjamin Leiner, is the first person mentioned when debating who the greatest lightweight of all time is. His ring record is nothing short of phenomenal, losing only once in a 20 year span from May 1912 to October 1932. He was the world lightweight champion from 1917 until he retired in early 1925. He lost his fortune in the stock market crash of 1929 and was forced to make a comeback in 1931 and 1932 after which he retired again. His final go in the ring was an exhibition at the age of 45 in 1941 against 43-year old Lew Tendler whom he had battled twice and defeated in the early 1920s.

Lavigne, ever critical of the lightweights who jousted for the title after his decline, had nothing but the highest praises in a letter he penned to Leonard. "I have seen you box," he wrote, "and I am sure you are better than Gans or any of the old-timers. As for the present day fighters, you can handle all the lightweights and welterweights." The Kid had used the cane in his roadwork and when presented with the trophy, Leonard promised to do the same. The gift was made with the understanding that it was to be passed on by Leonard to his successor.

"Kid" Lavigne and Wife Flora on their front porch in 1927 - Courtesy of Antiquities of the Prize Ring

Cupid Strikes

Nine months after the death of Julia, the Kid was back in the news on the verge of a new marriage. His soon-to-be wife was 35-year-old, Margaret L. Dumont Morrisette.

Margaret was a "sales lady" and 18 years younger than the Kid. They received a marriage license at the courthouse on August 27, 1923 but for unknown reasons never followed through. The press had a bit of a field-day with the next announcement. "Saginaw Kid Gets His Second Marriage License Within Three Months" read the headline in the *Boston Globe*.[31]

"Kid Lavigne, once lightweight champion of the world, has just taken the count from a short right delivered by Battling Dan Cupid," wrote the *Chronicle Telegram*. "'The Saginaw Kid' has taken out a license in Detroit to marry Mrs. Flora M. Davey, a widow. Lavigne is fifty-three."[32] The Kid, on the verge of marrying a working woman 18 years his junior, tied the knot 99 days later with Flora, a 58-year-old housewife who was five years his senior. They lived at the house Lavigne had owned for several years at 111 LaBelle Avenue, just a few blocks from the Highland Park Ford Plant.

The Kid settled in to his new marriage and fortunately for his bride Flora, he was now a teetotaler. Gone were the days of drunken rages and insanity tinged violence. He was simply the sober, humble ex-champ and night watchman at the Ford plant. He had come a long way through a score of turbulent years, losing fortunes but perhaps not fame. He had battled many demons, those in the ring and out. The sun was beginning to set on this now modest old pug.

CHAPTER 35

The Long Count

Lavigne never wrote the book he had promised but he did pen a series of articles, installments on his life and times that were picked up by papers across the country in late 1927 and early 1928. These and letters he would periodically write to sports columnists and friends shed light on his character, his humility, his love of the sport, and his self-awareness of what proved to be his undoing.

It was now 1927. Gone were the accolades, the wealth, and the alluring bright lights. A story from just a few years prior in January, 1925 is testimony to just how cruelly time obliterates the past. The setting was a fight in Detroit between middleweight champ, Harry Greb, and the challenger; Detroit's own Bob the "Battling Barrister" Sage. Kid Lavigne was one of Sage's seconds. "Two boxers who have worn the title, 'Champion of the World,' faced each other in a Detroit ring last month," noted the *Ludington Daily News*. "One of them was a champion in fact, the other a champion only in memory."[1] Grebb, the "Pittsburgh Windmill" in the heyday of his career, was cheered wildly as he entered the ring. "The other man, one of the greatest of former champions mounted the stairs in the opposite corner unnoticed." Lavigne in his own state and in his own town, unnoticed.

The ring announcer began his script bellowing to the crowd the names of the fighters, their weights, and number of rounds to be fought. "A voice near ringside rose above the hubbub: 'Introduce the Kid! Introduce the Kid!' The announcer, taken aback, looked around the ring for a 'kid' to introduce. Finally his glance strayed to Sage's corner where a harmless appearing man in his shirt sleeves was watching the gloves being fastened on Sage's hands. The announcer's face brightened, and with a flourish of his hand toward the little bespectacled man in Sage's corner he shouted: 'And this, ladies and gentlemen, is George Kid Lavigne!'

"There was a momentary break in the excitement as 5,500 pairs of eyes turned inquisitively on the 55-year-old man who shuffled about nervously. There was scattered handclapping, over in a few seconds, and George (Kid) Lavigne bowed awkwardly." The Kid didn't wonder why the crowd failed to enthuse over him. He was an old-timer—a has-been. "Lavigne's glory days were 25 years behind him, when fights were fights, as the older men say, and the best man won."[2]

More signs of the passing of time were on the way. In a harbinger of what was to come for the Kid only a few months off, his two-time opponent of the old days, Albert Griffith, better known as Young Griffo, died suddenly in his basement apartment on New York's west side. He was 55. Griffo, penniless, was living nearly rent-free, compliments of the widow of a bar owner who had been best of chums with him. He had ballooned to 200 pounds from his fighting weight of 126. It was his lifelong pursuit of alcohol that finally killed him.

"The mold was broken after Griffo was made," commented Lavigne on hearing of Griffo's demise. "While it may have been an exaggeration to say that he could stand on a handkerchief and prevent a first-class opponent from hitting him there is no denying he was the cleverest boxer that ever pulled on a glove. I have boxed and witnessed boxing contests all over the world and I have never seen anyone comparable to Griffo for speed and deception."[3] Griffo was the latest in a long string of the great ones from the old-school of pugilism to meet their maker; Dixon went in 1909, Gans in 1910, Fitzsimmons in 1917, and Sullivan and McGovern in 1918.

News of Griffo surely caused the Kid to ponder his own mortality. Lavigne had begun feeling ill from heart disease in the fall of 1927. It is quite possible that he saw the end coming and it motivated him to write the story of his life in those 15 newspaper dispatches. His father, Jean Baptiste, had died suddenly in 1882 at the age of 54. No records were found to determine the cause of death but a heart attack would be a safe bet. In early February, 1928 Lavigne was able to work only irregularly and so took what he'd hoped to be a temporary lay-off from the Ford plant. Then at 7:00 p.m. on Friday evening March 9, Lavigne suffered a heart attack and died at his home on LaBelle Avenue at the age of 58.

On Saturday morning, March 10, newspapers across the country from Bismarck to Bridgeport and Kalamazoo to Kalispell broke the news that the old idol of fistiana past was down for the long count.

"Saginaw Kid Answers Final Bell; Fans Mourn," read a headline from the sports page of the *San Diego Evening Tribune*.[4] Funeral services were held at St. Benedicts Catholic Church in Detroit on March 12. Father Thomas Hally said a requiem High Mass for the Kid. He noted that while the Kid was victorious in the ring he also won the greatest of his fights, that of his faith. Father Hally said the Kid had attended his church regularly over the past six years, training to be ready for "the last bell in this last battle." He finished with, "The Kid brought the same fighting spirit for which he was famous in the ring; now and then he slipped, but always came back with renewed determination, content with nothing short of victory."[5]

Grave of Kid Lavigne in Forest Lawn Cemetery, Saginaw, Michigan – Author's photo

His body was then taken to Saginaw where he was buried the next day at Forest Lawn Cemetery in the Lavigne family plot. Several months later, a memorial benefit was to be held in Detroit on November 2 for Flora Lavigne. The proceeds were to be used to erect a monument over the Kid's grave in Saginaw. "The remainder will be turned over to the widow who is said to be financially stressed," noted the *Ludington Daily News*.[6] The benefit was cancelled the night of the event when creditors of the promoters had the authorities seize the gate receipts which totaled only $500. Worse than the benefit that yielded little for the Kid in 1915, this one produced nothing for his widow.

Mirror, Mirror on the Wall

Time moved on and the deeds of the Saginaw Kid were recounted with lessening frequency as the months and years rolled by. In the 30s and 40s, the fighters of the teens and 20s became the old-timers shuffling about the musty gyms and roped arenas. The men of Lavigne's time were relegated to a point further back, where most existed only in the annals of ring history and in the memories of fighters and sports old enough to have seen them in the now distant past. And that history was beginning to fade.

Where Kid Lavigne fits in the discussion of the greatest scrappers of all time is hard to determine looking back over all these years. Time distorts the debate with a bias found to be present in favor of the era of those doing the debating.[7] As a writer and kin of the Kid who spent nearly three years rummaging through the 1890s and the turn of the century boxing world, I found it critical to guard against my own bias in making an assessment.

It's somewhat impossible to rank fighters in their own weight class or across all weight classes when dealing with a period of nearly 120 years. In the case of an era where we cannot have witnessed the bouts, just before the advent of moving film footage, we must rely on stories and opinions of the time, understanding that there may be biases at work there too. Even boxing writers and historians such as the esteemed Nat Fleischer, now 40 years deceased, would have been but a young teen when Lavigne ruled the lightweights, casting doubt as to whether he ever witnessed the Kid in battle in his prime.

An examination of opinions of the day from sportswriters, "sporting men," referees, managers, and fighters who were witness to the rise and fall of Lavigne, who were knowledgeable about the fistic arts of the time, are the only sources on which to rely. Boxing historian, Mike Silver, in his book *The Arc of Boxing* defines the time period between 1925 and 1955 as the golden age of boxing. The time period chosen for this review roughly coincides with the beginning of the widespread use of the Queensberry rules, say, 1885 up to 1925. An argument could be made that this was the "first" golden age of boxing.

Four names immediately rise to the top when asked who was the greatest of the lightweights of this time: Benny Leonard, Joe Gans, Kid

Lavigne, and Jack McAuliffe. It is often written that the decade within this 40-year range that ranks the highest in terms of the number of top quality lightweights in the mix is the 1890s. Some conclude that the "Napoleon of the Prize Ring," Jack McAuliffe, who retired undefeated, should get the nod. A close examination of his record, however, reveals cracks in the veneer.

It is uncontested that McAuliffe was a wonderful ring general, a hard hitter with either hand, quick on his feet, and able to absorb a great deal of punishment. Beginning his career in 1884, by the time he reached the 1890s many of his fights were limited-round exhibition and no-decision bouts making it harder to determine just how good of a fighter he was. Two of his more prominent bouts, 74 rounds versus Jem Carney in 1887 and 10 rounds against Young Griffo in 1894, should have counted as losses on his record but didn't.

McAuliffe had been an inveterate gambler nearly his entire career. His passion was horse racing and by the early 1890s he was in deep debt much of the time to book-makers and gamblers. It was suspected that many of his fights were "arranged" to settle his arrears. He clearly dodged a challenge by England's Dick Burge in 1892, over a three pound weight difference, when both were in their primes. Jack, from my perspective, belongs in the top five but does not deserve the title of "greatest" lightweight of the era, nor should he be seated at the table as one of the top three. Fleischer, who never saw McAuliffe fight in his prime, did not include him in his 1958 top ten list of all-time lightweights.

Joe Gans was called the "Old Master" for good reason. He fought nearly every great of the time period from feathers to welters. He amassed an incredible record of 196 fights, losing only 10 and collecting 100 knockouts. The only fighter he opted to side step along the way was Kid Lavigne. Billy Lavigne tried to secure a match for his brother with Gans in late 1898 while the Kid was still lightweight champ but Gans refused, assuming anyone who could lick Dick Burge and Joe Wolcott was simply too formidable a foe. Billy later revealed that given the toll dissipation had taken on the Kid at the time, Gans would have beaten him.

Gans was fast and clever with hands and feet. He could hit hard with either hand, throwing perfect punches, and was very elusive on defense. Fleischer rated Gans as his number one lightweight of all time in his 1958 rankings. Others agreed. Sam Langford, one of the greatest fighters never to win a title, believed Gans was the greatest boxer of all time. Heavyweight champ, Bob Fitzsimmons, thought

Gans was the cleverest boxer he'd ever seen. Featherweight champ Abe Attell said, "Joe Gans was the greatest lightweight that ever entered a ring."[8] Joe definitely belongs in the top three of the time period.

Benny Leonard, the youngster in this group, whose ring name was the "Ghetto Wizard," also amassed an unbelievable record of 219 fights losing only six bouts. He was tremendously popular setting many gate records of the time. He held the title for nearly eight years, the longest of any lightweight champ in history. As Tracy Callis puts it, "Leonard was as good as they get; He was quick and shifty, clever and game, could box and punch—and was super smart."[9] With Leonard there is ample film footage for review to compare him to other fighters yet not to the early ones in this group of four. Nat Fleischer rated Leonard as his number two lightweight of all time.

Modern day boxing historian, Mike Casey, compared Leonard and Gans this way: "Benny Leonard was one of the great students of the game, possessed of a brilliantly analytical mind. He is comparable in so many ways to his illustrious predecessor, the Old Master himself, Joe Gans. Joe shared similar gifts of perception, anticipation and what so often appeared to be effortless execution. Benny and Joe were never too proud to study other boxers and root out little gems of information. Both men were master boxers, but, more importantly perhaps, master thinkers."[10] Leonard and Gans as pure boxers deserve to be in the top two spots.

And what of the Saginaw Kid? He was anomalous to the previous threesome. While the length of his ring record pales in comparison to those of Gans and Leonard, the epic battles he fought are firmly emblazoned in early ring history as some of the greatest ever contested. He wasn't the ring scientist that McAuliffe, Gans and Leonard were nor did he possess half of their defensive talents. There was little need for defense when he unleashed his savage, muscle and mayhem attack. But Lavigne had a combination of four attributes that no one else possessed in similar quantities that keep him in the discussion for the greatest lightweight of the pre 1925 era.

First, the trait that made the other three possible; he was virtually indefatigable in the ring. He got stronger as fights wore on. Had he fought in a more modern era he would not have been able to rely on long-distance fitness. About the time a 12-rounder would be over today, Lavigne would still be battling with the tenacity of the first three minutes of the fight and could do so at that pace for another 10 or 15 rounds. Siddons, Soto, Burge, Everhardt, and Griffo experienced it first-hand. Listen to the words of heavyweight champ, Jim

Corbett when asked who was the greatest between Lavigne and Gans: "Kid Lavigne and Joe Gans? Why Lavigne had the fighting class, Gans the brains. Lavigne would have won in a distance fight, Gans in a short fight."[11] Distance he did best.

Second, for a little guy, he hit harder than many middleweights. "He hit so hard he often broke bones," recalled his trainer Biddy Bishop.[12] He put his power to use as a consummate body puncher ... the best of the era. From 1911, here are the words of "Iron Man" Dick Burge, the Brit from whom Lavigne won the world title 15 years earlier: "I fought lightweights, welters and middleweights in my prime" said Burge, "but never did a man hit me as hard as Lavigne did. He was a wonderful fighter and could hit like a heavyweight."[13]

Third, his ability to keep coming forward no matter what level of punishment was being absorbed was simply superhuman. It was often said he would take two punches to return one. It wasn't scientific. It was a purely instinctual and overwhelming style of fighting. This style only worked because, as Joe Wolcott so aptly bawled to his manager at the end of the eighth round of their famous battle at Maspeth, "This boy ain't human. . . . I cain't hurt him."[14] Wolcott had shredded the Kid's face and nearly torn off his ear, yet he kept coming. Everhardt had the Kid beaten, with both eyes swollen almost shut and nearly blind, yet the Kid kept coming and dropped Jack in the 24th. Who would know better than the Kid's brother Billy who put it this way: "There is no man alive that can live under punishment, who can thrive under chastisement that would kill an ordinary man like George can. That's why I'll bet he can beat Gans."[15]

"Hard as nails" and similar phrases were used to describe the Kid's gameness. In comparing him to lightweight champ and fellow Michigander, Ad Wolgast, one writer put it this way, "When the kid was at his best he was the roughest and toughest little fighting machine the game had known up to that time and the writers of sport very promptly and correctly added the 'Pine Knot' to his many other pet names."[16]

And finally, the Kid ducked no one. Not for lack of a larger purse. Not for the color of the person's skin. Not for how they tipped the scales. And not to protect his record or his title. Noted columnist Tad Dorgan, who witnessed his first prizefight when Lavigne met Joe Soto in 1891, offered this: "There was no color-line with Lavigne. There was no passing up of hard ones with him; there was no faking. He entered the ring to win or lose on his merits, and his battles are down in the books as the greatest ever fought by a man of his weight."[17]

When he cleaned out the lightweight division he went after the welters and was greatly respected by many for his bravery in doing so. In the words of John L. Sullivan, "Of all the fighters of the present day Kid Lavigne is the one I most admire. He is a pugilist, not an orator. He is the grandest little man of our time. I believe he can whip welterweights and middleweights; he took a chance with Dick Burge in England, a man five inches taller, but the Kid knocked him out."[18]

Nat Fleischer rated Lavigne sixth all-time lightweight in 1958. Here is a further sampling of comments from several of those who witnessed Lavigne's matches:

Writers and Sports

"In his class there never has been a fighter equal to the man from Michigan. . . . If he had taken a continuous passage on the water wagon there is no telling how far he could have gone without being beaten"[19] Sam Austin, *Police Gazette*

"Had Lavigne taken proper care of himself between fights, it is agreed by [Biddy] Bishop and all who knew him, that he would have retired undefeated and lived longer than he did."[20] George K. Franklin, *Boxing Illustrated*

"The greatest little man, I suppose, that was ever born was your own Kid Lavigne. He was my ideal of a fighting machine—hard as steel nails, quick as a panther, game as a bulldog. . . . I saw him when he fought Joe Walcott, the Barbados Demon and what a fight that was!"[21] Nat C. Goodwin

Trainers and Managers

"In all my experiences it is my opinion that Kid Lavigne was the greatest of all fighters."[22] Biddy Bishop commenting on his perspective after 40 years in boxing.

"Lavigne was a wonderful fighter. I do not think I am doing him wrong when I say that only one better lightweight ever fought—Joe Gans."[23] Harry Tuthill

"Lavigne was made of rawhide and iron, a bulldog in attack and bronco in staying power. No gamer, tougher man ever drew on a glove than the Michigan lumberjack."[24] Tom O'Rourke, Joe Walcott's manager.

"The greatest fighter that lived for his size and the most modest that ever stepped in a ring . . . and the finest athlete I have ever seen in any sport."[25] Michael "Dad" Butler, Kid Lavigne's trainer

Referees

"The greatest lightweight who ever laced on a boxing glove."[26] George Siler

"His memorable bout with Joe Walcott, at Maspeth, about fourteen years ago, was one of the affairs that is alluded to as the greatest and most stubbornly contested boxing match ever decided. Tim Hurst says it was the best glove argument he ever refereed."[27]

Fighters

"I do not think we will ever see Kid Lavigne's equal as a lightweight. He was a fighter pure and simple and none of the present day lightweights has reached anywhere the standing set by the Saginaw Kid."[28] Jim Corbett, heavyweight champion, 1892-1897

"Jeff thinks that Kid Lavigne was the greatest of all lightweights and is of the belief that he could have trounced many of the middle division had he been given the opportunity."[29] Nat Fleischer article with comment from Jim Jeffries, heavyweight champion, 1899-1905.

"Among the lightweights I think Kid Lavigne was the greatest of them all. I picked him as my successor when I retired undefeated and I made a good selection."[30] Jack McAuliffe, lightweight champion, 1886-1893

"George Lavigne was a born fighter and no less a judge than Bob Fitzsimmons [heavyweight champion 1897-1899] still claims that he was the best ever."[31] Joe "Buck" Kelly, referee

"Lavigne was the most wonderful fighter of his weight and inches ever known to the history of pugilism. Put that down as a fact and don't let anyone tout you away from it, for I know."[32] Jimmy Britt, lightweight champion, 1904-1905

"There never was a more courageous fighter than George Kid Lavigne."[33] "Gentleman" Jack Skelly, featherweigtht, 1891-1897

"I think as a simon pure fighter Kid Lavigne was the toughest man ever in the ring."[34] "Cute Eddie" Hanlon, lightweight, 1900-1914

"Well, it's a toss-up between Lavigne and Gans . . . I think Lavigne and Gans stand so far out beyond all other lightweights that there is no comparison, but to save my life I couldn't pick who was the better of the two."[35] Patsy Haley, lightweight, 1894-1915

The Measure of a Man

Few of the comments collected mention Lavigne as a ring general or recall his "science" as a pugilist. More of them refer to his toughness and indomitable will as a fighter. A fighter—not a boxer. Several men stepped in the ring with him that were his superior when it came to boxing skill, but none could match his ability as a pure fighter. It was his ability to impose his will on opponents that propelled his climb to the top. He did it with the utmost confidence.

A *Washington Post* article recalls Lavigne's manager, Sam Fitzpatrick, speaking of the Kid's demeanor before a fight: "Kid Lavigne was a cool proposition on the eve of a mill. The ex-lightweight champion was as indifferent to the outcome as if he thought it was all over and he had won. Lavigne had unlimited confidence in his prowess. His mind was occupied thinking just how long it would take him to win."[36]

Though the will and confidence were still there, it was his loss of power, speed and stamina that sent him tumbling from the summit in just a few short years. Some said he was through—that his will was broken—when, with the Kid fast on the rise, Andy Bowen died in 1894. That hardly seems true as he continued to climb the championship ladder until he attained the title in 1896. After beating Dick Burge and the "Barbados Demon," Joe Walcott, twice, there was little left to prove. As his one-time trainer, Biddy Bishop, said, the Kid loved liquor and hated to train. The Kid himself admitted it was booze that slowly robbed him of his championship form. He was famous, rich, and had slayed all the dragons. Dissipation beat the Kid.

Perhaps his greatest fight of all was the real beginning of the end. It was the battle at Maspeth in 1895 when he whipped Walcott in what many an early fight authority concluded was the greatest fight of the early Queensberry era. Lavigne was beaten to a pulp yet there was simply no quit. Shockingly battered, with John L. Sullivan at ringside pleading with the referee to stop the fight, the Kid fought on and finally turned the tables, overwhelming a stunned Walcott. That fight took a physical and mental toll on the Kid.

Six months later he took a pounding from the mitts of Dick Burge, but again prevailed late with a 17th round knockout. Four months after that he fought what many claimed was his second most desperate battle. In a grueling match he was disfigured by Jack Everhardt, before putting Jack to sleep in the 24th round. Twelve months hence, he fought the second scrap with Joe Wolcott in

October 1897, suffered two badly broken ribs in the contest but prevailed in 12 rounds. It was the accumulation of punishment that he endured through these four fights that marked the pinnacle of his career and the beginning of the long slide to has-been.

"After the second Walcott fight, George Kid Lavigne came home to begin a slow death that took exactly thirty years to see him in his grave," wrote George Franklin.[37] "'I never seemed the same after that,' he told intimates after he retired. 'It was the beginning of my decline.'"[38] He fought three, 20-round bouts the following year along with a couple of shorter contests. The old Lavigne was clearly gone. No knockouts. Two, 20-round draws and one unimpressive win in the third one. This followed by a disastrous 1899 and the loss of the championship title to Frank Erne.

Few in the know thought he would continue to rule the division. His drinking escapades had become legendary. His intense training regimen had fallen off. And the punishment in the ring kept piling up. A fighter who possesses great science can slow the decline using his experience and cleverness to continue to outpoint opponents. A brute-force, pressure pugilist like Lavigne could not. With the loss of his speed and his timing, he became vulnerable. His unbending will simply led him into a slaughter. This shooting star had burned out and although he mounted several comebacks, they were fueled by dreams alone and dashed by dissipation.

His absolute rock bottom came after he broke his arm and lost the Jimmie Britt fight in 1902. Suffering mentally and physically he ended up in an asylum for the insane, his first of four trips to the "bughouse." Off and on went his flirtations with gloved affairs, finally calling it quits in 1912. His career behind him now, his life took a turn toward stability when he became employed by the Ford Motor Company in 1917. It was shortly after his last visit to an asylum in 1920 that he conquered his greatest foe and rode the water wagon to his final sunset.

The Kid stayed connected to the fight game, coaching some of the young ones, seconding a few fighters, and attending local matches in Detroit. By the time of his death, his epic past was but legend. The little bespectacled old man with the blue twinkle in his eye was content and modest to the end. Was he the greatest of the lightweights of this era or of all eras? I believe that if Gans, Leonard, and Lavigne were all in their primes and fought 25-round bouts. Lavigne's will, stamina, power, and gameness would prevail. We'll never know, but he is deserving of inclusion in the debate.

Final Tributes

Famed boxing manager, promoter, and writer, Benjamin H. Benton, better known as Rob Roy Benton, wrote a piece in 1920 titled, "He Stands the Shadow of a Mighty Name." It was in response to news that Lavigne had been committed to an institution for a fourth time. Benton laments the ex-champ's confinement and continues by extolling the Kid's greater virtues in this passage:

> "He attained his record and fame prior to, and after he became champion, through ring efficiency, and decided merit, shown in public and not in the newspapers. It was personal achievement, and before the best patrons, and accepted expert judges of professional fistics of this country and Europe, and not through capacious agency of publicity men, or the favor of generous sports writers. It was successful public effort that earned for Champion Lavigne his tablet on the rolls of honor, which are indelibly impressed in the history of famous fights and fighters; and George Lavigne figures second to none.
> "The patrons of pugilistica in this country have created monuments for many deserving heroes of the squared circle, but none of them ever excelled George Lavigne, the Saginaw Kid, a real champion for efficiency, courage, fairness, good fellowship and genuine manhood and one who never had a blemish on his professional record. This great little gladiator . . ."[39]

And a final tribute from Robert E. Howard. Howard was a writer in the 1920s and 1930s who is probably best known for the creation of the character, Conan the Barbarian. He wrote pulp fiction with most of his work being published in the magazine, *Weird Tales*. I remember as a young boy in the 1950s finding stacks of *Weird Tales* and *Amazing Stories* magazines in the basement that my father, a sci-fi buff, had squirreled away. Howard, an amateur boxer was a fan of the fistic arts and wrote many fictional fight stories as well. Three months after Lavigne's death he penned this poem, first published in *The Ring Magazine* in June 1928.

Kid Lavigne is Dead

Hang up the battered gloves; Lavigne is dead.
Bold and erect he went into the dark.
The crown is withered and the crowds are fled,
The empty ring stands bare and lone—yet hark:
The ghostly roar of many a phantom throng
Floats down the dusty years, forgotten long.

Hot blazed the lights above the crimson ring
Where there he reigned in his full prime, a king.
The throngs' acclaim roared up beneath their sheen
And whispered down the night: "Lavigne! Lavigne!
Red splashed the blood and fierce the crashing blows.
Men staggered to the mat and reeling rose.
Crowns glittered there in splendor, won or lost,
And bones were shattered as the sledges crossed.

Swift as a leopard, strong and fiercely lean,
Champions knew the prowess of Lavigne.
The giant dwarf Joe Walcott saw him loom
And broken, bloody, reeled before his doom.
Handler and Everhardt and rugged Burge
Saw at the last his snarling face emerge
From bloody mists that veiled their dimming sight
Ere they sank down into unlighted night.

Strong men and bold, lay vanquished at his feet.
Mighty was he in triumph and defeat.
Far fade the echoes of the ringside's cheers
And all is lost in mists of dust-dead years.
Cold breaks the dawn; the East is ghastly red.
Hand up the broken gloves; Lavigne is dead.

-Robert Ervin Howard. *The Ring.* June 1928

George Henry "Kid" Lavigne was inducted into the Ring Hall of Fame in 1959, the Michigan Boxing Hall of Fame in 1965, the International Boxing Hall of Fame in 1998, and the Saginaw County Sports Hall of Fame in 2002.

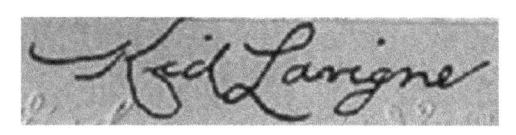

POSTSCRIPT

The First Lightweight Champion of the World

Being the first at anything carries a certain distinction with it. Based on my research for *Muscle and Mayhem* I found that many authorities and sources claim Jack McAuliffe as the first lightweight champion of the world under Queensberry rules while a few claim that honor goes to Kid Lavigne. What follows is an analysis of much of the information and data available with the goal of putting the question to rest once and for all. Of course, being a cousin of Kid Lavigne means I definitely have a dog, or should I say fighter, in this fight so I must declare a bias of bloodline in this matter.

As presented in Chapter 5, "The Early Lightweights," there were others who preceded McAuliffe in the record books. But a cut-off point needs to be established between the fighters of the London Prize Ring rules era and those of the Queensberry rules era. While the Queensberry rules were developed in 1867, they did not become widely used in America until the late 1880s. The last of the London rules lightweights, Arthur Chambers, came to America in 1871 after a successful seven years of fighting in England. He beat Billy Edwards for the American lightweight championship in 1872, defended his title once in 1879 and then retired.

The American title was vacant until "Nonpareil" Jack Dempsey at 138 pounds claimed it after defeating Tom Ferguson in a four round bout in 1884. He quickly outgrew the weight limit and vacated the title. Jack McAuliffe beat Jack Hopper for the vacant American lightweight title in 1886. Later that year McAuliffe defeated Billy Frazier and claimed the world lightweight championship, however, beating another untitled American hardly qualifies one to claim the world title. McAuliffe was the first of the lightweight champions to fight consistently under the Queensberry rules. But was he the first Queensberry world champion?

The first premise of this analysis is that one cannot win the world championship unless he defeats another person who, by virtue of an extensive and successful ring career, is considered to be the undisputed world champion by the boxing authorities and experts of the time. Failing that distinction, one must defeat the current champion of one of the four major centers of boxing in the world in the last decades of the 19th century, those being America, England, Australia, and South Africa. In these early days, fighters would claim to be a champion after winning a few fights, hardly meeting any prerequisite of championship stock.

Take the case in point of the rise of McAuliffe. After an amateur career of a few years he fought a couple of professional bouts. He then challenged Jimmy Mitchell for the "professional" lightweight championship. When Mitchell refused the challenge McAuliffe claimed the title. Mitchell, according to available fight records, had one professional bout to his credit at the time. This illustrates the second premise of this analysis; that one cannot claim a title without getting in the ring and earning it.

Next McAuliffe, very early in his professional career, defeated Jack Hopper in February of 1886 and claimed the American lightweight title. It was Hopper's third fight of his career. He had never fought for and won the American title or even a regional title so it was dubious that McAuliffe could now claim he wore the crown. In October of 1886 McAuliffe defeated Billy Frazier and claimed both the American and world lightweight titles. Frazier called himself the lightweight champion of the east and of New England but was born in the U.S. and held no claim to the American or world title. And to boot, the weight for the fight was to be at the American lightweight limit of 133 pounds. Frazier weighed in at 130 but McAuliffe exceeded the limit, weighing in at 138.

McAuliffe's only legitimate claim to the world title, and it falls apart under examination, is his victory over Canadian, Harry Gilmore in January of 1887. While McAuliffe was adding specious titles to his name, Gilmore was working at gaining the Canadian lightweight title. In September of 1885 he claimed both the Canadian title and the world title after a two round, no contest fight that was broken up by police. In 1886 he fought Sam Bittle three times in a span of 64 days, losing the first and third bouts, but claimed the Canadian lightweight title after winning the middle contest of the three. Bittle was over the lightweight limit when he notched his second victory. A review of the

Fights Rec, Box Rec, and Cyber Boxing Zone records for Bittle showed that he had only a handful of professional bouts . . . all against Gilmore. Defeating a man of Bittle's pedigree is hardly the quality of competition upon which to stake a championship claim.

Taking nothing away from Harry Gilmore's fighting abilities, which were impressive; his claim to the Canadian title given the men he had beaten or not beaten to get it was thin at best. This set up the battle for what McAuliffe considered the world title. McAuliffe prevailed over Gilmore after 28 hard fought rounds. McAuliffe at this point may have had an uncontestable claim to the title of lightweight champion of North America but that was all.

McAuliffe had his best shot at the world title in November of 1887 when he met Jem Carney, the recognized lightweight champion of England. In an epic, nearly five-hour battle, McAuliffe failed to get the victory that would have given him undisputed claim to the world lightweight title. "He was tottering on the verge of a knockout in the seventy-fourth round of his battle with British Jem Carney," wrote Nat Fleischer, "when the ring was broken into by the American's followers and the bout was called a draw."[1]

Serveral sources have McAuliffe winning the world title in a bout with Jimmy Carroll in March of 1890. Upon closer examination it appears that Carroll claimed the world title by defeating Sam Blakelock one year prior. Blakelock "claimed" the English 128 pound title in his second professional match, the first was a loss, in June of 1887. And the fellow he beat had a 1 win, two loss record. Again, lots of "self-annointing" by all the above with no ring record substance to justify their title claims.

By this analysis and through his efforts of defeating all comers on the continent, McAuliffe could certainly claim the American and North American lightweight titles, but not the world lightweight title. "McAuliffe's claim to fame," wrote Frank Butler in *A History of Boxing in Britain*, "was that he was the last American bare-knuckle lightweight champion and the first under the Queensberry rules."[2]

How does Kid Lavigne stack up in a similar analysis? In many early newspapers, sporting magazines, and record books, the Kid is credited with the American lightweight title as early as 1893. While he was undefeated at the time and widely recognized as the top lightweight of the day he had no legitimate claim to the American title yet. It seems that these early pundits conferred the American title on him with the announced retirement of Jack McAuliffe in late 1892. This was the first of three McAuliffe retirements between 1892 and 1897.

Lavigne met Andy Bowen in December 1894. Bowen was anointed by the *Police Gazette* as the lightweight champion of the South, and widely recognized at the time as the toughest competition for the Kid in America. The fight was billed as being for the American lightweight title. Given Bowen's death, it was a tragic way to earn the title; nonetheless, the Kid prevailed and was declared the American champion. But McAuliffe didn't see it that way as his first retirement had been short lived. He became very selective with whom he would risk his laurels, fighting mainly second-raters until he toed the scratch with Young Griffo in August of 1894. McAuliffe weighed 145 to Griffo's 133. Griffo embarrassed him over ten rounds and had referee Maxwell Moore been an honest bloke, he would have awarded the win to Griffo. The fight was a bellwether for Jack and after breaking his arm three months later in a bout with Owen Ziegler, he retired a second time.

Lavigne, ever modest and reverent toward those who went before him, still gave the nod to McAuliffe. "Although looked upon as the champion since McAuliffe's retirement, Lavigne has refused to style himself so, holding that he could only secure it in one way—by a battle with the man who held and defended it for ten years," wrote the *Detroit Free Press*.[3] But McAuliffe had no interest in trying the Michigan mauler until he came out of retirement a third time and a six-round bout was arranged for March 1896. Even then, McAuliffe claimed that his titles were not on the line. He was using it as a gage to determine if he had one more go in him for the money stakes. He and Lavigne met and according to most sources, McAuliffe was on "queer street" near the end of sixth when the police stopped the bout.

McAuliffe was now too heavy to even make the 133 pound lightweight limit, and in a move designed to preserve his undefeated status, was no longer willing to get in the ring with any of the first-raters. In the meantime Lavigne had taken on the best of the best in the division including Young Griffo, Jack Everhardt, Jerry Marshall and Joe Walcott. The Saginaw Kid now stood at the pinnacle of the American lightweight division. Finding it harder to get matches he looked overseas to the reigning lightweight champion of England, Dick "Iron Man" Burge. Though outweighed by as many as 15 pounds, he thrashed the Brit, knocking him out in the 17th round on June 1, 1896. Lavigne was now the undisputed, and first, world lightweight champion of the early Queensberry era.

Others agree with this assertion. Noted boxing authority, Nat Fleischer, in his book, *Jack McAuliffe: The Napoleon of the Prize Ring* came to the same conclusion when he wrote in reference to Lavigne's defeat of Burge, "That victory made Lavigne the undisputed lightweight champion, a feat his predecessor failed to accomplish when held to a seventy-four round draw in 1887 by Jem Carney."[4] Gerald Suster, in his book, *Lightning Strikes—The Lives and Times of Boxing's Lightweight Heroes*, recounted a debate between Fleischer and historian Herbert G. Goldman and concluded: "Fortunately both agree that the Lavigne-Burge bout was the first universally recognized as being for the lightweight boxing championship of the world."[5]

John Grombach concurred with Fleischer when he wrote in *The Saga of Sock*, "From 1885 to 1896, McAuliffe was considered champion, although, his claim to the world's championship was never fully justified, for his battle for the world crown with Jem Carney of England resulted in a seventy-four round draw. When the fight was stopped, Carney actually had much the better of it. . . . Kid Lavigne of Saginaw, Michigan, who succeeded the great McAuliffe, was able to do what his predecessor had failed to do—bring the world's title to America. In 1896, Lavigne went to London and knocked out Dick Burge, the British and European champion, in seventeen rounds."[6]

Several references, including the Box Rec website, identify the first fighter to win a world title under the Marquess of Queensberry rules as James J. Corbett, who defeated John L. Sullivan on September 7, 1892 at the Pelican Athletic Club in New Orleans, not Jack McAuliffe years earlier. I'm sure that Bob Fitzsimmons might have a bone to pick with this claim as he defeated "Nonpareil" Jack Dempsey in January 1891 under Queensberry rules for what was billed at the time as the world middleweight title. But if there remains a question as to who was the first Queensberry world champion of any weight division it must be left for a future debate among boxing historians.

The final nail in the coffin is provided by Jack McAuliffe himself. After he was nearly defeated by Lavigne but for the intervention of police in March 1896, he talked of his desire to fight Lavigne in a battle to the finish. He then said, "If I win I shall be ready to fight the much vaunted Dick Burge of England, and determine whether an Englishman or an American is to be lightweight champion of the world."[7] This can be interpreted as Jack acknowledging that, even though he considered himself to be the world lightweight champion, until an American fighter were to take on the European champion there could be no legitimate claim to the world title.

Appendix A

1890s WORDS AND PHRASES

A hard rub – A tough fight

All at sea – A fighter who is in a state of confusion and is groggy and out on his feet

Back numbers – A person or thing considered old-fashioned—in this case it refers to a boxer well past his prime

Bellows to mend – Out of wind, fatigued

Booze stakes – Alcohol consumption

Bowler hat – A round topped felt hat popular in the second half of the 19th century

Brace – A set of two similar things—in this case, a pair of like punches

Brain fever – An illness brought on by a state of shock

Brick top – A person with red or reddish-brown hair

Brown study – A state of thinking deeply about something

Bughouse – A mental hospital or asylum

Cotton – Be friendly with or take a liking to

Corker – A hard punch

Cracker – In British slang, a thing or person of notable qualities or abilities

Dead-head – A person attending a match who did not pay for admission

Dissipation – Unrestrained indulgence in alcohol, women, or gambling

Dub – A clumsy or awkward person

Fanning bee – A gathering for a specific purpose—in this case to discuss the merits of fights

Fettle – State of proper physical health

First water – Of the highest quality

Flowing bowl – The title of an 1892 book by William Schmidt which was a collection of classic cocktail recipes, used as a clever way to describe someone with a drinking habit as in, "drinking from the flowing bowl."

Four-in-hand coach – A carriage drawn by four horses

Gaff – Harsh treatment

Gage - Something, as a glove, thrown down by a medieval knight in token of a challenge to combat

Geezer – A queer, odd or eccentric person, used especially of elderly men

Go – A fight (see also: set-to and mill)

Go by the board – Finished with or defeated

Grampuses – Dolphins and whales that have a blow hole—in this case it is used to describe two tired fighters "blowing like grampuses"

Great White Way – Refers to the bright lights of Broadway and in this context it has to do with Lavigne's dissipation as a result of drink and the high life.

Ham and egger – A washed-up or unskilled fighter—from the old days when miners held boxing matches; the winner got money, the loser got a ham and egg meal.

Honors – Leading or getting the best of an opponent in a round or fight

In chancery – Holding one in a head-lock

In high feather – To be in high spirits

Kitchen – The stomach, as in taking a blow in the kitchen

Knockers – Those who spread real or alleged scandal about another

Lamped – Looked over with a critical eye

Long-headed – Astute or wise

Long in pickle – Nearing the end of a fighter's career

Looking upon the wine – Had been drinking heavily

Mill – Slang meaning to fight with the fists (see also: go and set-to)

Nettle – Irritate or annoy someone

Octoroon – A person who is one-eighth black

On the jump – An aggressive style of fighter who takes the fight to his opponent

Palmy days – Prosperous, flourishing or successful times

Parlor style boxer – Fighting at long range rather than slugging it out toe-to-toe; and a fancy, tricky fighter who prefers short bouts

Peaceful waters – Non-alcoholic beverages

Pins – Legs

Pippin – A person or thing that is admired

Pluck – Resourceful courage and daring in the face of difficulties

Profesh – Short for professional fighter

Queer street – Groggy and close to being knocked out

Road cane – A flexible cane carried in both hands while doing distance running for training

Roughs – Crude, unmannered men; rowdies

Sack suit – A style of suit which became popular in the 1880s that was the precursor to the modern business suit. It supplanted the frock suit which reached to the knees in length.

Scrapper – Slang for fighter or boxer

Set-to – A bout or fight (see also: go and mill)

Shot his bolt – To exhaust one's effort

Simon pure – Genuinely and thoroughly pure

Slats - Ribs

Sockdolager – A knockout or finishing blow

Soporific – Causing or tending to cause sleep—in this context a knockout punch

Tartar – A fearsome or formidable person

Trying the gin mills – Frequenting taverns

Water wagon – Abstinent from drinking alcohol

Wind – Used to describe a boxer's stamina as in "being winded" or to describe the stomach and chest as in "taking a punch on the wind."

Appendix B

George "Kid" Lavigne's Professional Fight Record
Wins – 34   21 by KO   No Decisions – 10
Losses – 6   4 by KO   No Contests – 1
Draws – 11   Exhibitions - 21
Total of all bouts - 83

1886

September 7	Morris McNally	Saginaw, MI	W KO 1
September 11	Billy White	Saginaw, MI	W KO 1
September 21	Billy Roberts	Saginaw, MI	W KO 3
October 19	Bob Ralph	Saginaw, MI	W KO 3
October 28	Jimmy Priest	Saginaw, MI	W KO 3
November 18	Red Elliot	Saginaw, MI	W PTS 4
December 28	Jack Cherry	Saginaw, MI	W PTS 8

1887

| February 12 | Red Elliot | Saginaw, MI | ND 3 |

This bout is marked as ND because no information was found as to the outcome. In the newspaper article it identifies Kid Lavigne as Charles Lavine "of this city." Also on the card was George's brother, Billy, who fought a three-round bout. In these early days Lavigne was spelled several ways and it is most assuredly a mistake by the paper identifying George as "Charles." Billy's and George's mentor, C. A. C. Smith, was the headliner on the card. Source: *Saginaw News*, February 12, 1887, p. 3

1888

| February 10 | Dan Connors | Saginaw, MI | W KO 5 |

"Lavigne had the best of it, Connors being knocked out in the middle of the fifth round." Source: *Saginaw Evening News*, February 11, 1888 page 3

March 2	Pike Johnson	Saginaw, MI	D 8

Source: *Saginaw Evening News*, March 3, 1888

June 10	Unknown	Manistee, MI	W KO 3
September 21	Jack Menton	Manistee, MI	W PTS 12

1889

February 28	George Siddons	Saginaw, MI	D 77

The bout lasted 5 hours and 8 minutes, the longest bout to date under Marquess of Queensberry rules.

March 10	Butch Kinney	Manistee, MI	W PTS 4
April 16	Billy Bushy	Saginaw, MI	EX 4

This was an exhibition bout as part of a benefit for local featherweight, Sam Purdy. Billy Lavigne fought a six-round bout with Purdy on the same card. Source: *Saginaw Evening News*, April 17, 1889, page 3

April 25	George Siddons	Grand Rapids, MI	D 55
May 12	Billy O'Brien	Detroit, MI	W PTS 4
December 23	Billy Bushy	Saginaw, MI	EX 4

Source: *Saginaw Evening News*, December 24, 1889 page 3 – No number of rounds given but assumed to be three or four.

1890

March 13	Morris McNally	Saginaw, MI	W PTS 3

Lavigne "had things his own way." Source: *Saginaw Evening News*, March 14, 1890

April 14	Billy Boucher	Saginaw, MI	D PTS 3

"It was lively and decided a draw." Source: *Saginaw Evening News*, April 15, 1890 page 3

May 19	Jack O'Brien	Saginaw, MI	EX 3

"The 'Kid' got the best of Jack O'Brien in three, two-minute rounds." Source: *Saginaw Evening News*, May 20, 1890 page 3

November 12	Sam Eaton	West Bay City, MI	W TKO 6

1891

October 15	Jimmy Lewis	San Francisco, CA	W PTS 4

No record exists of this fight in any of the San Francisco papers of the time or of a fighter named Jimmy Lewis. The *Saginaw News*, November 4, 1891, page 6, reported that Lavigne was given a tryout upon his arrival in San Francisco against a Jimmie Lucie, champion amateur lightweight of "the slope." Lavigne nearly knocked him out and the club's officers asked Lavigne to stop the carnage. Lucie might have been misidentified as Lewis. The *San Francisco Call*, November 17, 1891 mentioned a "tryout" but didn't report who Lavigne fought.

November 20   Joe Soto   San Francisco, CA   W TKO 30

1892

Date Unknown Danny Needham   San Francisco, CA   EX 4
March 17   Charles Rochette   San Francisco, CA   W PTS 10
May 25   Harry Jones   Portland, OR   W KO 8
August 10   Jim Burge   San Francisco, CA   D 50

Lavigne fought from the 5th round on with a broken right hand. Source: "Both Were Iron Men," *San Francisco Chronicle,* August 12, 1892

November 21   Martin Shaughnessy Bay City, MI   W KO 9

Lavigne weighed 122 and Shaughnessy 145. Source: *Saginaw News,* November 22, 1892, p. 9

1893

January 31   John Hayes   Saginaw, MI   EX 3

This was an exhibition bout as part of a benefit for Lavigne prior to his fight with Eddie Myer, most likely three or four rounds. Source: *Saginaw News,* January 31, 1893

February 12   Eddie Myer   Dana, IL   W KO 22
March 29   Billy Gaffney   Detroit, MI   ND 10

Police declared that arrests would be made if anything more than scientific sparring occurred and no decision was permitted. Source: "Tame Contest in Detroit," *Chicago Tribune,* May 30, 1893

April   Charley Mitchell   Ludington, MI   ND 4

This bout was listed as a No-Decision in "Lavigne's Complete Ring Record," published in the *Detroit Times,* March 11, 1928. No newspaper account of the bout was found.

August 21   "Mysterious" Billy Saginaw, MI   EX 3
              Smith

This was one of several exhibition bouts at a benefit for Kid Lavigne at the Park Rink in Saginaw. Billy Lavigne also fought two, three-round exhibitions during the event which drew 600 spectators. Source: *Saginaw News,* August 22, 1893, p. 7

1894

February 10   Young Griffo   Chicago, IL   D PTS 8
March 7   Solly Smith   Saginaw, MI   D 8
May 25   Dick O'Brien   Boston, MA   ND 6

This bout was listed as a No-Decision in "Lavigne's Complete Ring Record," published in the *Detroit Times,* March 11, 1928. Lavigne also mentioned winning this bout in "When Fights Were Fights," *Los Angeles Times,* December 18, 1927. No newspaper account of the bout was found and it's possible it never happened.

June 4	Billy Hennessey	Boston, MA	ND 4
September 17	Jerry Marshall	New York, NY	W PTS 10
October 29	Johnny T. Griffin	New York, NY	W TKO 15
December 14	Andy Bowen	New Orleans, LA	W KO 18

1895

February 4	Eddie Myer	Saginaw, MI	EX 3
April 11	Jerry Marshall	Chicago, IL	D PTS 8
May 30	Jack Everhardt	New York, NY	W PTS 20
August 26	Jimmy Handler	New York, NY	W KO 5
October 12	Young Griffo	New York, NY	D 20
December 2	Joe Walcott	New York, NY	W PTS 15

1896

January 9	Billy Woods	New York, NY	EX 4
January 9	Tommy Ryan	New York, NY	EX 4
March 11	Jack McAuliffe	New York, NY	NC 6

Police would not allow a referee and stopped the bout in the sixth round with McAuliffe in trouble. Lavigne would have won had a decision been allowed. Bout listed as a No-Decision in 1897 Lavigne/Walcott fight program. Sources: *Chicago Tribune* and *Milwaukee Evening Wisconsin,* March 12,

June 1	Dick Burge	London, England	W KO 17

World championship bout - Lavigne weighed 133 and Burge weighed between 145 and 150. Source: *Sporting Life,* June 2, 1896

July 20	Charles McKeever	New York, NY	ND 6
October 27	Jack Everhardt	New York, NY	W KO 24

Lavigne weighed 133 and Everhardt weighed 138 raising doubt as to whether this was a legitimate lightweight championship bout at the American 133 pound standard. It was considered a world lightweight title match at the 138 pound limit which was the limit in England at that time.

1897

January 11,	Owen Ziegler	Philadelphia, PA	ND 6
February 8	Kid McPartland	New York, NY	W PTS 25

This bout was for the world lightweight title. Lavigne weighed 131½ and McPartland 133. Source: *BoxRec*

March 8	Charles McKeever	New York, NY	ND 6
April 30	Eddie Connolly	New York, NY	W TKO 11

This bout was for the world lightweight title. Both fighters weighed 132. Source: *BoxRec*

May 17   Owen Ziegler   Philadelphia, PA   ND 6
October 29   Joe Walcott   San Francisco, CA   W TKO 12
This bout was for the world lightweight title although Walcott was two pounds over the recognized 133 pound limit. Lavigne weighed 132 and Walcott 135. Source: "Lavigne Wins Strictly on His Merits," *San Francisco Chronicle*, October 30, 1897

1898

February 3   Jack Hammond   Detroit, MI   EX 4
Hammond was a middleweight.

March 17   Wilmington Jack Daly Cleveland, OH   D PTS 20
This bout was billed as being for the world lightweight title even though the agreement between the fighters was not to exceed 137 pounds. Technically, it was not for the lightweight title. Lavigne weighed 132 and Daly weighed 137 according to the *Detroit Free Press* but the *Chicago Tribune* had Daly at 135. Sources: Both newspapers on March 18, 1897.

March 31   Ed Rucker   Louisville, KY   EX 3
March 31   Jim Watts   Louisville, KY   EX 3
April 11   Wilmington Jack Daly Philadelphia, PA   ND 6
September 28   Frank Erne   New York, NY   D PTS 20
This bout was for the world lightweight title and both men weighed in at 133 pounds.

November 25   Tom Tracey   San Francisco, CA   W PTS 20
Lavigne weighed 134 and Tracey weighed 142. BoxRec has this bout as being for the world 142 pound title and Cyber Boxing Zone has it for the lightweight championship of the world. It was neither, as both fighters were over the 133 pound lightweight limit and Mysterious Billy Smith was the current welterweight world champion.

1899

March 10   "Mysterious"   San Francisco   L TKO 14
               Billy Smith
This bout was for the world and American welterweight titles. Lavigne weighed just under 138 and Smith weighed 142. Lavigne's lightweight title was not on the line.

July 3   Frank Erne   New York, NY   L PTS 20
This bout was for the world lightweight title. Lavigne weighed 135 and Erne weighed 133. Erne wrested the title from Lavigne even though Lavigne was two pounds over the lightweight limit.

October 6   George "Elbows"   New York, NY   L KO 19
               McFadden

1901

| August 23 | Ed Sholtreau (Sheltraw) Saginaw, MI | EX 3 |
| December 12 | Tim Hegarty | Oakland, CA | W KO 4 |

1902

May 29 Jimmy Britt San Francisco, CA L TKO 8
Lavigne broke his right hand in the second round.

1905

June 1 Jack Roberts Paris, France W TKO 5
Roberts broke his hand in the fifth round and could not continue.

Date Unknown Oscar "Battling" Nelson Detroit, MI EX 3
Source: Nat Fleischer, *The Ring Record Book and Boxing Encyclopedia*, 1962 page 299. No newspaper account of this bout was found.

1906

Date Unknown Joe Gans Detroit, MI EX 3
Source: Nat Fleischer, *The Ring Record Book and Boxing Encyclopedia*, 1962 page 299 and 300. This bout is mentioned in Lavigne's column "When Fights Were Fights," in the *Los Angeles Times*, March 5, 1928, although no date is given aside from the year 1906. No newspaper account of the bout was found.

1907

January 19 Young Erne Philadelphia, PA L TKO 6

1908

Date Unknown Oscar "Battling" Nelson Detroit, MI EX 3
Source: Nat Fleischer, *The Ring Record Book and Boxing Encyclopedia*, 1962 page 299. No newspaper account of this bout was found.

1909

December 17 Oscar "Battling Nelson Detroit, MI EX
The bout took place at the Avenue Theater. No number of rounds given. Source: *Denver Post*, December 18, 1909.

December 25 Dick Nelson Detroit, MI L PTS 6
"Lavigne, a mere shadow of his former self, attempted to stay six rounds with Fighting Dick Nelson." Source: *Grand Forks Daily Herald*, December 29, 1909.

1910

Date Unknown Ad Wolgast Detroit, MI EX 2
Source: Nat Fleischer, *The Ring Record Book and Boxing Encyclopedia*, 1962 page 299. No newspaper account of this bout was found. This exhibition was mentioned in Lavigne's Cyber Boxing Zone record as happening on May 30, 1910, the same day as

another six-round exhibition in Cadillac Michigan but Cadillac is 200 miles from Detroit.

December 19   Battling Nelson   Detroit, MI   EX 4
This was an exhibition in the theatrical circuit at the Avenue Theater. The *Denver Post*, February 26, 1912 indicated it went four rounds, "and the showing he made that night should convince him he hasn't a chance in the world to make good again." Source: *Milwaukee Evening Wisconsin*, December 17, 1910.

1911

February 3   Mickie Sheridan   Windsor, Ontario   EX 3
This bout was held as part of a benefit for Bob Farrell at Windsor, Ontario. Source: *Chicago Examiner*, February 4, 1911.

February 3   Ad Wolgast   Windsor, Ontario   EX 2
The bout "was to go just as many rounds, not to exceed eight, as Lavigne can stand." The benefit consisted of a dozen, three-round bouts, and this was most likely one of them, as no other newspaper account of a Lavigne-Wolgast exhibition was found. Source: *Milwaukee Free Press*, January 21, 1911.

Additional Fights Reported But Unconfirmed:

Chub Whitney – W PTS 6 – Most likely early in his career in 1890 or 1891. (Source: 1897 Lavigne/Walcott fight program) It is also possible that Chub Whitney is the unknown from June 10, 1888 that is listed as a three-round bout in Manistee, Michigan.

Paddy Kelly – Kelly said he knocked out Lavigne near Detroit "many years ago" and was knocked out in a return bout. (Source: *Racine Daily Journal*, January 3, 1911) There was a Boston fighter, Patsy (Patrick) Kelly who fought George Dixon in 1888 and 1889 getting a draw in the first and losing the second. It's possible he fought Lavigne around that time and it never was recorded. It's also possible he mixed up Dixon with Lavigne and embellished the story although that is hard to believe as Dixon was black and Dixon won on points not a knockout.

Jimmy Popp – An article out of San Francisco of unknown origin talks about Lavigne and Popp in a 25 round match in Toronto sometime after Lavigne returned from England as the world champion. Toronto newspapers were searched and no record of the bout was found. The writer may have gotten this fight mixed up with the McPartland bout which was the Kid's only match that went exactly 25 rounds.

George Reynolds – This was an exhibition fought during Lavigne's time in Paris sometime between 1903 and 1905. (Source: *Republic*, April 19, 1921, page 10)

Billy Layton – According to the *Chicago Tribune* the bout was scheduled for six rounds at Hot Springs, Arkansas on February 21, 1898. No Hot Springs newspaper for that time was available to confirm that the fight actually took place. (Source: *Chicago Tribune*, February 6, 1898 page 7).

Freddie Green – According to a *Canton Ohio Repository* article from 1910 reminiscing about great bouts in their city, Kid Lavigne and Green fought a 20-round draw at the Grand Opera House. Green was a middle-tier Cleveland featherweight who's fighting career spanned 1895-1904. No newspaper record of this fight was found. (Source: *Canton Ohio Repository*, June 26, 1910)

Harry Gilmore – According to the *Daily Kennebec Journal* (Maine) article on May 1, 1912, Kid Lavigne and Harry Gilmore were to fight a bout in Windsor, Ontario that evening. No other corroboration of that fight could be found. If this bout occurred there is no doubt it was a couple-round, friendly exhibition between these two early boxing greats as Gilmore would have been 58 years old and Lavigne 42.

George Kattel – According to the San Francisco Call the 43 year old Lavigne was to fight a 10 round bout with Kattel at Cherry Valley, Illinois (near Rockford) on December 17, 1912. All Rockford area newspapers were searched and no record of the bout was found. (Source: "Bouts in Many Cities Hold the Fans," San Francisco Call, December 16, 1912).

Appendix C

George "Kid" Lavigne
Physical Measurements

Height:	5 feet 3 and 1/2 inches
Weight:	135 pounds
Reach:	67 and 1/2 inches
Neck:	15 inches
Chest:	37 and 3/4 inches
Biceps:	13 and 1/2 inches
Wrist:	7 and 1/8 inches
Forearm	11 and 3/4 inches
Waist	34 and 1/2 inches
Thigh	21 inches
Calf	14 and 1/2 inches
Ankle	9 and 1/2 inches

Source: *San Francisco Examiner,* September 11, 1897, seven weeks prior to the Kid's second fight with Joe Wolcott

Appendix D

LAVIGNE FAMILY HISTORY

Ancestry

Pierre Poudtre Lavigne and Philipotte Ouaroque (Rocquet) married in 1645 at St. Gery Valenciennes, Flanders, France

Andre Poutre Lavigne and Jeanne Burel married on November 3, 1667 at Quebec City

Jacques Poudrette Lavigne and Marie Ann Simon married on April 16, 1714 at Pointe Au Trembles

Andre Poudrette Lavigne and Marie Josephte Daoust married on February 6, 1746 or 1747 at Point Claire (possibly St. Joachim church)

Joseph Poudrette Lavigne and Marie Angelique Ranger dit Laviolette married on January 17, 1774 at St. Genevieve de Pierrefonds

Jacques Poudret Lavigne and Marie Louise Cousineau married February 21, 1814 at St. Genevieve de Pierrefonds

Jean Baptiste Poudret Lavigne and Marie Agnes Dufort married on February 20, 1860 at St. Polycarpe, Soulanges, Quebec

Jean Baptiste Lavigne and Agnes Dufort Family

Jean Baptiste Lavigne born October 26, 1828 – Died October 16, 1882 at Zilwaukee (cause unknown). Jean Baptiste was one of 12 children.

Marie Agnes Dufort born October 28, 1843 – Died December 9, 1911 at Saginaw of uterine cancer.

Jean Baptiste born November 20, 1860 at St. Polycarpe, Quebec – Died as an infant

Joseph Procul born August 24, 1862 at St. Polycarpe – Died July 22, 1863

William (Joseph Guillaume) born August 1, 1864 at St. Polycarpe – Died of spinal meningitis on April 29, 1907 in Seattle. Married Bertha Dewey April 30, 1894 at Saginaw.

Marie Louise born August 1, 1866 at St. Polycarpe – Died as an infant

George Henry born December 6, 1869 at Bay City Michigan – Died March 9, 1928 of a heart attack

John B. born June 7, 1871 at Bay City – Died May 18, 1892 at Saginaw of peritonitis

Frank J. born 1874 at Bay City – Died February 18, 1918 at Saginaw

Dennis born December 26, 1876 at Bay City – Died as a child

Ida born January 3, 1878 at West Bay City – Died July 15, 1878 at Bay City

Agnes M. born 1879 at West Bay City – Married Clarence R. Smith of Detroit on May 15, 1900 - Died ?

Jochin born February 8, 1880 at West Bay City or Zilwaukee (?) – Died as a child

James J (or H) born February 8, 1881 at Saginaw – Died July 23, 1959 at Saginaw

George Henry Lavigne Spouses

Married Julia (also Julie) Drujon (or Drugon – headstone spelling) on August 29, 1905 in Manhattan, New York – Julia was born on May, 22, 1865 in Paris and came to the U.S. in 1899. Died on November 27, 1922 at Saginaw of breast cancer. Father, Claude Adrian Drujon – Mother, Genevieve Conversat. Julia was previously married in 1882 to Louis Ballet.

Nearly married Margaret L. Dumont Morisett on August 27, 1923 – applied for a marriage license but never got married. Margaret was born in 1888 and was a 35 year old "sales lady" at the time.

Married Flora (also Florence) M. Morrison Davey on December 1, 1923 – Flora was born in 1865 and was 58 years old at the time. She was a house wife.

CHAPTER NOTES

Chapter 2

1. http://en.wikipedia.org/wiki/Cousin

Chapter 3

1. Lucile LeBlanc Constentino, *http://www.acadian-home.org/carignan-regiment.html*
2. Lucile LeBlanc Constentino, *http://www.acadian-home.org/carignan-regiment.html*
3. http://freepages.genealogy.rootsweb.ancestry.com/~havens5/fille_du_ roi.htm
4. Stewart Holbrook, *Holy Old Mackinaw* (New York: Ballantine Books, 1971) Back cover
5. Stewart Holbrook, *Holy Old Mackinaw* (New York: Ballantine Books, 1971) page 84
6. Jean Lamarre, *The French Canadians of Michigan* (Great Lakes Books, 2003) page 95
7. Name of Saginaw Derived From Sauk Indians, *Bay City Times*, February 27, 1937
8. Jeremy W. Kilar and Ronald Bloomfield, *Bay City Logbook* (G. Bradley, 1996) page 17
9. Stewart Holbrook, *Holy Old Mackinaw* (New York: Ballantine Books, 1971) page 80
10. Ibid, page 81
11. *The Lumber Region of Michigan*, (Making of America, Library of Congress Collection) July 1868, Vol. CVIIi. — No. 220. 6

12. Jeremy W. Kilar, *Michigan's Lumbertowns, Lumberman and Laborers in Saginaw, Bay City, and Muskegon, 1870-1905*, (Wayne State University Press, 1990) page 25

Chapter 4

1. *American Lumberman; the Personal History and Public and Business Achievements of Eminent Lumberman of the United States*, (Chicago: American Lumberman, 1905) page 148
2. *The Michigan Manufacturer and Financial Record*, August 31, 1912, page 9
3. Jeremy W. Kilar, *Michigan's Lumbertowns, Lumberman and Laborers in Saginaw, Bay City, and Muskegon, 1870-1905*, (Wayne State University Press, 1990) pp. 70-71
4. John Philip Schuch, *Michigan's Old Inn*, (1946)
5. "Directory of Bay City Hotels, 1868-69, http://www.bay-journal.com/bay/1he/dir/bcity-hotel-dir-1868-9.html
6. Jeremy W. Kilar, Ronald Bloomfield, *Bay City Logbook*, (G Bradley Pub edition, 1996)
7. Larry Gustin, "New Facts About Kid Lavigne," *Boxing Illustrated*, March 1964, page 46
8. Tracy Callis, *Charles A. C. Smith Ring Record*, International Boxing Research Organization, 2011
9. International Boxing Hall of Fame - http://www.ibhof.com/pages/about/inductees/nonparticipant/muldoon.html
10. *National Police Gazette*, August 4, 1883. p.14
11. Ibid, p.14
12. Jeremy W. Kilar, *Michigan's Lumbertowns*, (Wayne State University Press, 1990) p. 69
13. Tracy Callis, *Charles A. C. Smith Ring Record*, International Boxing Research Organization, 2011
14. "Lavine's [Lavigne's] Antagonist," *Saginaw News*, March 9, 1891
15. George Lavigne, "Real Lightweights Are Missing Since Leonard Retired, Claims Lavigne," *Los Angeles Times*, December 4, 1927
16. "Lavigne Won City Prize Ring Fame," *Saginaw News*, January 25, 1948
17. Larry Gustin, "New Facts About Kid Lavigne," *Boxing Illustrated*, March 1964, page 46
18. George Lavigne, "Real Lightweights Are Missing Since Leonard Retired, Claims Lavigne," *Los Angeles Times, December 4, 1927*

19. Tom Marter, "Kid Was A Man In The Ring," *Bay City Times*, August 30, 1998
20. Jeremy W. Kilar, Ronald Bloomfield, *Bay City Logbook*, (G Bradley Pub edition 1996)
21. Kilar, "Michigan's Lumbertowns," page 72
22. John Philip Schuch, *Michigan's Old Inn*, (1946)
23. Stewart Holbrook, *Holy Old Mackinaw*, (The MacMillan Company, 1971) page 84
24. George Lavigne, "Real Lightweights Are Missing Since Leonard Retired, Claims Lavigne," *Los Angeles Times, December 4, 1927*
25. "Death Defeats Kid Lavigne," *Detroit Free Press*, March 10, 1928
26. George Lavigne, "When Fights Were Fights," *Los Angeles Times*, December 11, 1927
27. "Lavigne Won City Prize Ring Fame," *Saginaw News*, January 25, 1948
28. "Bringing Back Boxing History: Kid Lavigne – Former Champion," 1929 article from Antiquities of the Prize Ring Archive (author and publication unknown)
29. "Among the Greatest Fighters: The Saginaw Kid Never Quit," *Saginaw News*, April 23, 1963
30. *Saginaw Evening News*, February 12, 1887, p. 3
31. *Saginaw Evening News*, June 27, 1887, p. 6
32. "Referee Knew His Business Second Time," *Mansfield News*, January 14, 1911
33. Jean R. Beach and Ed Miller, "George H. (Kid) Lavigne," *Saginaw Hall of Fame, 2000*
34. "Lavigne Won City Prize Ring Fame," *Saginaw News*, January 25, 1948
35. Tom Marter, "Kid Was a Man in the Ring," *Bay City Times*, August 30, 1998
36. George Lavigne, "When Fights Were Fights," *Los Angeles Times*, December 11, 1927

Chapter 5

1. John V. Gromach, *The Saga of Sock*, (New York: A. S. Barnes and Company) 1949, page 96
2. *Baltimore Sun*, October 19, 1858, page 1
3. *Baltimore Sun*, June 14, 1867, page 4
4. *Baltimore Sun*, August 25, 1868, page 1
5. Alexander Johnston, *Ten and Out!*, (New York: Ives Washburn) 1947, page 314

6. Johnston, page 316
7. "The Great Prize Fight," *Watertown Daily Times,* March 28, 1879, page 1
8. *New York Sun,* November 21, 1884
9. Johnston, page 318
10. *Newark Daily Advocate,* November 17, 1887

Chapter 6

1. "Kid Lavigne Was Greatest of Great Crop of Saginaw Fighters," *Saginaw Sunday News,* June, 17, 1934
2. Ibid
3. Larry Gustin, "New Facts About Kid Lavigne," *Boxing Illustrated,* March 1964, page 47
4. "Kid Lavigne Was Greatest of Great Crop of Saginaw Fighters," *Saginaw Sunday News,* June, 17, 1934
5. George Lavigne, "When Fights Were Fights," *Los Angeles Times,* December 11, 1927
6. John Philip Schuch, *Michigan's Old Inn,* (1946)
7. Ibid
8. "Declared Draw," *Boston Herald,* April 28, 1889
9. *Saginaw Evening News,* April 27, 1889, p. 7
10. George Lavigne, "When Fights Were Fights," *Los Angeles Times,* December 11, 1927
11. Stephen K. *Schroeder,* "The Saginaw Kid May Be Toughest Ever," *Saginaw News,* September 21, 1969
12. *Saginaw Evening News,* August 21, 1890, p. 6
13. "Lasted Six Rounds," *Saginaw Evening News,* November 13, 1890
14. George Lavigne, "When Fights Were Fights," *Los Angeles Times,* December 11, 1927
15. Ibid
16. "Soto Gave Up," *San Francisco Chronicle,* November 21, 1891
17. George Lavigne, "When Fights Were Fights," *Los Angeles Times,* December 18, 1927
18. *Soldier Beats Sailor,* (San Francisco Morning Call, November 21, 1891)
19. "Soto Gave Up," *San Francisco Chronicle,* November 21, 1891
20. Ibid
21. George Lavigne, "When Fights Were Fights," *Los Angeles Times,* December 18, 1927
22. "Soto Gave Up," *San Francisco Chronicle,* November 21, 1891

23. Tad Dorgan, "Tad's Tid Bits," *New Castle News*, January 4, 1923, page 16
24. George Lavigne, "When Fights Were Fights," *Los Angeles Times*, December 18, 1927
25. "An All-Night Fight," *San Francisco Chronicle*, March 18, 1892
26. George Lavigne, "When Fights Were Fights," *Los Angeles Times*, December 18, 1927
27. "The Lavigne-Jones Contest Attracting a Great Deal of Attention," *Portland Oregonian*, May 25, 1892
28. Ibid
29. "Both Were Iron Men," *San Francisco Chronicle*, August 11, 1892
30. Robert Edgren, Untitled Article, *Fort Wayne News and Sentinel*, May 10, 1919
31. "Both Were Iron Men," *San Francisco Chronicle*, August 11, 1892
32. Ibid
33. Ibid
34. Ibid

Chapter 7

1. Tommy Ryan, "Nineteen Years in the Ring," *Syracuse Herald*, 1911
2. Ibid
3. Ibid
4. *Bay City Times Press*, November 22, 1892
5. *Saginaw News*, November 22, 1892, p. 9
6. *Saginaw News*, January 31, 1893
7. *Milwaukee Evening Wisconsin*, February 3, 1893
8. "Hardships of the Ring," *Seattle Daily Times*, November 2, 1903 p. 9
9. "Billy Myer's Brother Beaten," *National Police Gazette*, February 12, 1893
10. *Milwaukee Evening Wisconsin*, July 2, 1893
11. "Tame Contest in Detroit," *Chicago Tribune*, May 30, 1893
12. "Lavigne Is Clever," *Detroit Free Press*, March 30, 1893
13. *Saginaw News*, August 22, 1893, p. 7

Chapter 8

1. *Milwaukee Evening Wisconsin*, September 2, 1893
2. Tommy Sullivan, *Tacoma Daily News*, March 6, 1916
3. *Illustrated Police News*, September 16, 1893

4. George Lavigne, "When Fights Were Fights," *Los Angeles Times*, December 18, 1927
5. Ibid
6. Tracy Callis, Solly Smith's Ring Record, Cyber Boxing Zone Website, *www.cyberboxingzone.com*
7. *Milwaukee Evening Wisconsin*, February 9, 1894
8. Tommy Sullivan, *Tacoma Daily News*, March 6, 1916
9. *Chicago Tribune*, February 11, 1894
10. George Lavigne, "When Fights Were Fights," *Los Angeles Times*, December 18, 1927
11. Ibid
12. *Police Gazette*, March 8, 1894

Chapter 9

1. "Lavigne's Complete Ring Record," *Detroit Times*, March 11, 1928
2. "Boxer Lavigne Cut," *Boston Daily Globe*, May 19, 1894
3. *National Police Gazette*, May 1894
4. "In the Pugilistic World," *National Police Gazette*, June 23, 1894
5. *Boston Herald*, June 18, 1894, p. 8
6. Dan Streible, *Fight Pictures: A History of Boxing and Early Cinema*, (Berkeley: University of California Press, 2008) p. 23
7. *Boston Herald*, June 16, 1894, p. 1
8. *National Police Gazette*, September 1894
9. *Boston Daily Globe*, September 18, 1894
10. Ibid
11. *Ibid*
12. *Philadelphia Item*, September 18, 1894
13. *Boston Daily Globe*, September 18, 1894
14. "Lavigne Wants a Fight," *Boston Daily Globe*, September, 21, 1894
15. Tracy Callis, Johnny T. Griffin's record, Cyber Boxing Zone website, *cyberboxingzone.com*
16. Unknown source from Antiquities of the Prize Ring archive, October 29, 1894
17. *Saginaw Courier Herald*, February 1913
18. *Milwaukee Evening Wisconsin*, October 29, 1894
19. Tom McDonald, "The King of the Light Weights" *Saginaw News*, September 1998

Chapter 10

1. Frank Butler, *A History of Boxing in Britain*, (London: Arthur Barker Limited, 1972), p. 13
2. Butler, p. 7
3. Broughton's Rules of 1743, *Cyber Boxing Zone Website*, www.cyberboxingzone.com
4. John V. Grombach, *The Saga of Sock*, (New York: A. S. Barnes and Company, 1949), p. 36
5. London Prize Ring Rules of 1853, Cyber Boxing Zone Website, *www.cyberboxingzone.com*
6. Tommy Ryan, "Nineteen Years in the Ring," *Syracuse Herald*, September 3, 1911, p. 8
7. Robert G. Rodriquez, *The Regulation of Boxing*, (North Carolina and London: McFarland and Company, 2009), p. 29
8. Elliot J. Gorn, *The Manly Art: Bare-Knuckle Prize Fighting in America*, (Ithaca and London: Cornell University Press, 1986) p. 204
9. George Lavigne, "When Fights Were Fights," *Los Angeles Times*, December 4, 1927
10. Ibid
11. John V. Grombach, *The Saga of Sock*, (New York: A. S. Barnes and Company, 1949), p. 28
12. London Prize Ring Rules of 1838, Cyber Boxing Zone Website, *www.cyberboxingzone.com*
13. Nat Fleischer, *Jack McAuliffe: The Napoleon of the Prize Ring*, (Ring Magazine Press, 1944) p. 66
14. *Milwaukee Evening Wisconsin*, February 9, 1894

Chapter 11

1. *National Police Gazette*, November 17, 1894
2. *Milwaukee Evening Wisconsin*, December 8, 1894
3. Alexander Johnston, *Ten-And Out! The Complete Story of the Prize Ring in America* (Ives Washburn, 1947)
4. Nat Fleischer, "Jack McAuliffe: The Napoleon of the Prize Ring," *Ring Magazine*, 1944
5. George Lavigne, "When Fights Were Fights," *Los Angeles Times*, December 25, 1927
6. Melissa Haley, "Storm of Blows," *www.common-place.org*, January, 2003
7. Jeffrey T. Salmons, *Beyond the Ring* (University of Illinois Press, 1988) pp. 13 and 262
8. *New Orleans Picayune*, December 15, 1894

9. George Lavigne, "When Fights Were Fights," *Los Angeles Times*, December 25, 1927
10. *New Orleans Picayune*, December 15, 1894
11. *Chicago Tribune*, December 15, 1894
12. "Lavigne Won City Prize Ring Fame," *Saginaw News*, January 25, 1948
13. George Lavigne, "When Fights Were Fights," *Los Angeles Times*, December 25, 1927
14. *New Orleans Picayune*, December 15, 1894
15. Tom McDonald, "King of the Light Weights," *Saginaw News*, September 1998
16. *Washington Post*, December 16, 1894
17. George Lavigne, "When Fights Were Fights," *Los Angeles Times*, December 25, 1927
18. *Chicago Tribune*, December 15, 1894
19. *New York Times*, December 16, 1894
20. Melissa Haley, "Storm of Blows," *www.common-place.org*, January, 2003
21. *Washington Post*, December 16, 1894
22. *Brooklyn Daily Eagle*, December 16, 1894
23. *New York Times*, December 16, 1894
24. "Andy Bowen's Body Borne To Its Rest," *Times-Picayune*, December 18, 1894, p. 3
25. *New Orleans Daily Item*, December 17, 1894, page 8
26. *New Orleans Picayune*, December 15, 1894
27. Ibid
28. *Milwaukee Evening Wisconsin*, December 28, 1894
29. *Washington Post*, December 16, 1894
30. *Chicago Tribune*, December 15, 1894
31. Tom McDonald, "King of the Light Weights" *Saginaw News*, September 1998
32. George Lavigne, "When Fights Were Fights," *Los Angeles Times*, December 25, 1927
33. Larry Gustin, "New Facts About Kid Lavigne," *Boxing Illustrated*, March 1964, page 47
34. "Fistic Contests," *Saginaw Evening News*, February 5, 1895

Chapter 12

1. Alexander Johnston, *Ten and Out! The Complete Story of the Prize Ring in America (Ives Washburn 1947)*

2. *National Police Gazette*, June 15, 1895
3. *Milwaukee Evening Wisconsin*, April 12, 1895
4. Tracy Callis, Jack Everhardt's Ring Record, Cyber Boxing Zone Website, *www.cyberboxingzone.com*
5. *Dallas Morning News*, April 29, 1894
6. "Lavigne Licks Jack Everhardt," *New Jersey Journal*, June 1, 1895
7. Ibid
8. *Sporting Review*, June 15, 1895
9. "Lavigne Licks Jack Everhardt," *New Jersey Journal*, June 1, 1895
10. George F. Franklin, "George 'Kid' Lavigne," *Boxing Illustrated*, September 1959, p. 25
11. www.fundinguniverse.com/company-histories/Ford-Motor-Company-Company-History.html
12. *Illustrated Police News*, September 1895
13. *New Jersey Journal*, August 27, 1895
14. Ibid
15. Ibid
16. *Illustrated Police News*, September 1895
17. *New York Illustrated News*, September 16, 1895
18. *Detroit Free Press*, October 8, 1895
19. George Lavigne, "When Fights Were Fights," *Los Angeles Times*, January 1, 1928
20. Stan Weston, "The Fighter Who Couldn't Be Hit," *Boxing and Wrestling*, March 1955
21. Ibid
22. George Lavigne, "When Fights Were Fights," *Los Angeles Times*, January 1, 1928
23. *Chicago Tribune*, October 13, 1895
24. George Lavigne, "When Fights Were Fights," *Los Angeles Times*, January 1, 1928
25. *Washington Post*, October 13, 1895
26. *National Police Gazette*, October 26, 1895
27. Jack Kofoed, "The Saginaw Kid," *Fight Stories*, February, 1931, p. 15
28. *Milwaukee Evening Wisconsin*, October 13, 1895

Chapter 13

1. Kelly Nicholson, *Hitters, Dancers and Ring Magicians* (Jefferson, North Carolina and London: McFarland and Co., 2011) page 83
2. Nat Fleischer, *Jack McAuliffe Napoleon of the Prize Ring* (The Ring Magazine, 1944)

3. Ibid
4. Nat Fleischer, *The Three Colored Aces: Story of George Dixon, Joe Gans, Joe Walcott and Several Contemporaries volume 3 of Black Dynamite: The Story of the Negro in the Prize Ring from 1782-1938* (New York: Ring Athletic Library, 1938) page 196
5. B. H. Benton, "Lightweight Champions of Today Lack Ability of the Old Timers," *(Unknown source from archive)*
6. Fleischer, *The Three Colored Aces*, pages 198-199
7. *Police News*, August 28, 1895
8. George Lavigne, "When Fights Were Fights," *Los Angeles Times*, January 8, 1928
9. Ibid
10. Ibid
11. "Lavigne the Champion," *National Police Gazette*, December 14, 1895
12. "What Critics Say Was the Greatest Prize Ring Battle," *Detroit Free Press*, March 17, 1912
13. Ibid
14. George Underwood, "'Greatest Fight I Ever Saw' When Lavigne Met Walcott" (Unknown newspaper of 1920)
15. "Kid Lavigne's Battle," *Washington Post*, December 3, 1895
16. Robert Edgren, "Two Ring Feats of Lavigne Made Him 'Stand Out' as Greatest of Lightweights," *New York Evening World*, 1913
17. George Lavigne, "When Fights Were Fights," *Los Angeles Times*, January 8, 1928
18. Ibid
19. B. H. Benton, "Lightweight Champions of Today Lack Ability of the Old Timers," (Unknown source from archive)
20. Ibid
21. George Underwood, "'Greatest Fight I Ever Saw' When Lavigne Met Walcott" (Unknown newspaper of 1920)
22. "What Critics Say Was the Greatest Prize Ring Battle," *Detroit Free Press*, March 17, 1912
23. "Lavigne Won City Prize Ring Fame," *Saginaw News*, January 25, 1948
24. B. H. Benton, "Lightweight Champions of Today Lack Ability of the Old Timers," (Unknown source from archive)
25. Alexander Johnston, *Ten and Out! The Complete Story of the Prize Ring in America*, (Ives Washburn,1947) p. 325
26. George Underwood, "'Greatest Fight I Ever Saw' When Lavigne Met Walcott" (Unknown newspaper of 1920)

27. George Lavigne, "When Fights Were Fights," *Los Angeles Times*, January 8, 1928
28. Robert Edgren, "Two Ring Feats of Lavigne Made Him 'Stand Out' as Greatest of Lightweights," *New York Evening World*, 1913
29. George Underwood, "'Greatest Fight I Ever Saw' When Lavigne Met Walcott," (Unknown newspaper of 1920)
30. Ibid
31. "Lavigne Won City Prize Ring Fame," *Saginaw News*, January 25, 1948
32. Johnston, *Ten and Out!* pages 325 and 326
33. George Lavigne, "When Fights Were Fights," *Los Angeles Times*, January 8, 1928
34. "Lavigne the Champion," *National Police Gazette*, December 14, 1895
35. 2 "Bringing Back Boxing History Kid Lavigne – Former Champion," (Early 1930s article "by an old-timer who saw them all in action," unknown source from archive)
36. George Underwood, "'Greatest Fight I Ever Saw' When Lavigne Met Walcott," (Unknown newspaper of 1920)
37. Robert Edgren, "Two Ring Feats of Lavigne Made Him 'Stand Out' as Greatest of Lightweights," *New York Evening World*, 1913
38. Johnston, *Ten and Out!* pages 325 and 326
39. B. H. Benton, "He Stands the Shadow of a Mighty Name," (Typed, unpublished letter, 1902)
40. George Underwood, "'Greatest Fight I Ever Saw' When Lavigne Met Walcott," (Unknown newspaper of 1920)
41. Ibid

Chapter 14

1. *National Police Gazette,* January 18, 1896
2. *National Police Gazette,* January 11, 1896
3. George Lavigne, "When Fights Were Fights, *Los Angeles Times*, January 29, 1928
4. *Detroit Free Press,* March 1, 1896
5. "Kid Seems the Better," *Chicago Tribune,* March 12, 1896, page 8
6. Type written note from the archive file. Most probably a transcription from the *Police Gazette* of February, 1896
7. "Lavigne Whipped by a Reporter," *Detroit Free Press,* February 8, 1896
8. *National Police Gazette,* October 3, 1908

9. *Milwaukee Evening Wisconsin*, March 7, 1896
10. *Detroit Free Press*, February 23, 1896
11. Ibid
12. "Jack McAuliffe's Challenge," *Brooklyn Eagle*, March 9, 1896
13. "Kid Seems the Better," *Chicago Tribune*, March 12, 1896, page 8
14. Ibid
15. Ibid
16. *Milwaukee Evening Wisconsin*, March 12, 1896
17. George Lavigne, "When Fights Were Fights, *Los Angeles Times*, January 29, 1928

Chapter 15

1. Robert Edgren, *Fort Wayne News and Sentinel*, May 10, 1919
2. Ibid
3. *Boxing's Book of Records to June 30, 1914*, Published by *Boxing*
4. B. H. Benton, "He Stands the Shadow of a Mighty Name," (1902 typed manuscript in archive)
5. B. H. Benton, "Kid Lavigne Surprised English Sportsmen in Go With Burge," (unknown publication, 1913 – From Antique Prize Ring archive)
6. "The Kid Is Confident," *Detroit Free Press*, March 25, 1896
7. Ibid
8. B. H. Benton, "He Stands the Shadow of a Mighty Name," (1902 typed manuscript in archive)
9. B. H. Benton, "Kid Lavigne Surprised English Sportsmen in Go With Burge," (unknown publication, 1913 – From Antique Prize Ring archive)
10. *Mirror of Life*, June 1, 1896
11. George Lavigne, "When Fights Were Fights," *Los Angeles Times*, January 29, 1928
12. Robert L. Ripley, "Sam Fitzpatrick Tells of the First International Battle for Lightweight Championship, *Washington Post*, July 8, 1914, p. 2
13. B. H. Benton, "Kid Lavigne Surprised English Sportsmen in Go With Burge," (unknown publication, 1913 – From Antique Prize Ring archive)
14. "A Coaching Party Visits Lavigne," *Mirror of Life*, May 1896
15. Ibid
16. Robert Edgren, "Two Ring Feats of Lavigne Made Him Stand Out as Greatest of Lightweights," *New York World*, July 20, 1913

17. A. J. Liebling, *The Sweet Science*, (New York: North Point Press, 1951) p. 62
18. Robert Edgren, "Two Ring Feats of Lavigne Made Him Stand Out as Greatest of Lightweights," *New York World*, July 20, 1913
19. "National Sporting Club Lightweight Championship of the World," *The Sporting Life*, June 2, 1896
20. "Burge and Lavigne at the National Sporting Club," *The Sportsman*, June 2, 1896
21. George Lavigne, "When Fights Were Fights," *Los Angeles Times*, February 5, 1928
22. Robert Edgren, *Fort Wayne News and Sentinel*, May 10, 1919
23. Lavigne's banter with a betting man are a composite taken from Robert Edgren's "Two Ring Feats of Lavigne Made Him Stand Out as Greatest of Lightweights," *New York World*, July 20, 1913 and an unknown English sports periodical from the Antiquities of the Prize Ring archive.

Chapter 16

1. "The Ring: London Sporting Life on the Lavigne/Burge Fight," *Detroit Free Press*, June 15, 1896, page 8
2. "No Match for Lavigne," *Washington Post*, June 2, 1896
3. George Lavigne, "When Fights Were Fights," *Los Angeles Times*, February 12, 1928
4. Ibid
5. "English Referees Severe in Interpreting the Rules," *Denver Post*, July 18, 1912 page 10
6. B. H. Benton, "Kid Lavigne Surprised English Sportsmen in Go With Burge," (unknown publication, 1913 – From Antique Prize Ring archive)
7. George Lavigne, "When Fights Were Fights," *Los Angeles Times*, February 12, 1928
8. B. H. Benton, "Kid Lavigne Surprised English Sportsmen in Go With Burge," (unknown publication, 1913 – From Antique Prize Ring archive)
9. "Two Much for Burge," *New York World*, June 1, 1896
10. "Kid Lavigne Greatest, Most Modest Fighter, Says Dad Butler, Trainer," *Detroit Times*, March 11, 1928
11. B. H. Benton, "Kid Lavigne Surprised English Sportsmen in Go With Burge," (unknown publication, 1913 – From Antique Prize Ring archive)

12. George Lavigne, "When Fights Were Fights," *Los Angeles Times*, February 12, 1928
13. "Two Much for Burge," *New York World*, June 1, 1896
14. Ibid
15. "Burge and Lavigne at the National Sporting Club," *The Sportsman*, June 2, 1896
16. "When Lavigne Fought Burge," *Los Angeles Times*, July 19, 1914
17. "Burge and Lavigne at the National Sporting Club," *The Sportsman*, June 2, 1896
18. George Lavigne, "When Fights Were Fights," *Los Angeles Times*, February 12, 1928
19. "When Lavigne Fought Burge," *Los Angeles Times*, July 19, 1914
20. Robert Edgren, *Fort Wayne News and Sentinel*, May 10, 1919
21. "Kid Lavigne" (unknown publication from Antique Prize Ring archive)
22. Robert Edgren, *Fort Wayne News and Sentinel*, May 10, 1919
23. "Lavigne's Appearance is Rather Deceptive," *Beloit Daily News*, February 13, 1917

Chapter 17

1. Michael T. Isenberg, *John L. Sullivan And His America*, (Urbana and Chicago: University of Illinois Press, 1988), p. 57
2. Guy Deghy, *Noble and Manly: The History of the National Sporting Club*, (London: Hutchinson, 1956), pp. 40-41
3. "Better and Safer Boxing: Ringside and Boardroom Medical Control of Boxing Careers in the Twentieth Century," published by De Monfort University, Leicester, England
4. Isenberg, p. 76
5. Jeffrey T. Sammons, "Boxing's Legal Status," *www.britannica.com*
6. Isenberg, p. 71
7. Adam J. Pollack, *John L. Sullivan: The Career of the First Gloved Heavyweight Champion*, (North Carolina and London: McFarland and Company, 2004) p. 10
8. Jeffrey T. Sammons, "Boxing's Legal Status," *www.britannica.com*
9. Melissa Haley, "Storm of Blows," *www.common-place.org*, January 2003
10. Jeffrey T. Sammons, *Beyond The Ring*, (Urbana and Chicago: University of Illinois Press, 1988) pp. 12-13
11. Pollack, p. 11
12. Sammons, *Beyond the Ring*, p. 19

13. *New York Times,* January 24, 1900
14. Sammons, *Beyond the Ring,* pp. 32-33
15. Randy Roberts, *Jack Dempsey: The Manassas Mauler* (Baton Rouge: Louisiana State University Press, 1984) p. 24
16. Robert G. Rodriguez, *The Regulation of Boxing* (North Carolina and London: McFarland and Company, 2008) p. 34
17. "Killed in First bout," *Baltimore Sun,* January 31, 1917, page 8
18. James B. Roberts and Alexander G. Skutt, *The Boxing Register: International Boxing Hall of Fame Official Record Book* (Ithaca, NY: McBook Press, 2002) p. 51
19. Rodriguez, p. 35

Chapter 18

1. "Lively Boxing Tonight," *New York World,* July 20, 1896
2. "Couldn't Hit," *Boston Daily Globe,* April 14, 1896
3. "Lavigne vs. McKeever," *Boston Daily Globe,* July 21, 1896
4. "Lavigne's Cool Reception," *New York World,* July 21, 1896
5. "Lavigne vs. McKeever," *Boston Daily Globe,* July 21, 1896
6. Ibid
7. "Lavigne's Cool Reception," *New York World,* July 21, 1896
8. "The Light Weights," *New York Herald,* September 5, 1872, page 4
9. Ibid
10. George Lavigne, "When Fights Were Fights," *Los Angeles Times,* February 19, 1928
11. "Lavigne and Everhardt," *Logansport Pharos,* October 12, 1896
12. *Boston Daily Globe,* October 16, 1896
13. *Milwaukee Evening Wisconsin,* September 29, 1896
14. "Lavigne and Everhardt," *Daily Iowa Capital,* October 28, 1896
15. George Lavigne, "When Fights Were Fights," *Los Angeles Times,* February 19, 1928
16. Ibid
17. "Lavigne the Champion," *New York World,* October 28, 1896
18. "Lavigne Wins A Stubborn Battle From Everhardt," *National Police Gazette,* October, 1896
19. Ibid
20. "Lavigne's Good Work," *Detroit Free Press,* November 3, 1896
21. "Lavigne the Champion," *New York World,* October 28, 1896
22. "Lavigne's Fight," *Boston Daily Globe,* October 28, 1896
23. "Lavigne Wins A Stubborn Battle From Everhardt," *National Police Gazette,* October, 1896

24. George Lavigne, "When Fights Were Fights," *Los Angeles Times*, February 19, 1928
25. Ibid
26. "Lavigne the Champion," *New York World*, October 28, 1896
27. George Underwood, "Kid Lavigne's Bout With Everhardt is Recounted," *Detroit Free Press*, August 21, 1921
28. Jack Kofoed, "The Saginaw Kid," *Fight Stories*, February, 1931
29. George Underwood, "Kid Lavigne's Bout With Everhardt is Recounted," *Detroit Free Press*, August 21, 1921
30. "Lavigne Wins A Stubborn Battle From Everhardt," *National Police Gazette*, October, 1896
31. Jack Kofoed, "The Saginaw Kid," *Fight Stories*, February, 1931
32. *Milwaukee Evening Wisconsin*, November 26, 1896
33. George Lavigne, "When Fights Were Fights," *Los Angeles Times*, February 19, 1928
34. *Boston Daily Globe*, January 8, 1897
35. "Bested By Kid Lavigne," *Washington Post*, January 12, 1897
36. "Lavigne Bests Ziegler," *Philadelphia Evening Bulletin*, January 11, 1897
37. *Sioux City Journal*, January 10, 1897

Chapter 19

1. Jim Wilson, "The Truth About Billy the Kid," www.shootingtimes.com , January 3, 2011
2. www.aboutbillythekid.com
3. *Tacoma Evening News*, February 10, 1900
4. As revealed by a search for all boxers with the nickname "Kid" at www.fightsrec.com
5. Jack Kofoed, "The Saginaw Kid," *Fight Stories*, March, 1931
6. "Fighter's Fancies," *Illustrated Police News*, February 20, 1897
7. "Stood Up Against Lavigne," *Washington Post*, February 9, 1897
8. "Fighter's Fancies," *Illustrated Police News*, February 20, 1897
9. Ibid
10. "Lavigne-McPartland," *Decatur Morning Herald Dispatch*, February 9, 1897
11. "Lavigne the Winner," *New York World*, February 9, 1897
12. Ibid
13. "Fighter's Fancies," *Illustrated Police News*, February 20, 1897
14. *Philadelphia Record*, February 9, 1897
15. "Stood Up Against Lavigne," *Washington Post*, February 9, 1897

16. George Lavigne, "When Fights Were Fights," *Los Angeles Times*, February 19, 1928
17. *Decatur Daily Review (Illinois)*, November 22, 1899

Chapter 20

1. "Lavigne – McKeever Match," *Philadelphia Record*, March 8, 1897
2. "Six Rounds," *Boston Daily Globe*, March 9, 1897
3. *Philadelphia Record*, March 9, 1897
4. "Lavigne And McKeever," *Philadelphia Evening Bulletin*, March 9, 1897
5. Ibid
6. *Philadelphia Record*, March 9, 1897
7. Article of unknown origin from Antiquities of the Prize Ring archive. Most likely a Philadelphia newspaper.
8. "Six Rounds," *Boston Daily Globe*, March 9, 1897
9. "Kid Lavigne Champion," *Syracuse Standard*, March 9, 1897
10. "His Last Round," *The Daily Evening Herald* (Oskaloosa, Iowa), March 5, 1897
11. Ibid
12. Ibid
13. Nat Fleischer, *Jack McAuliffe: The Napoleon of the Prize Ring* (The Ring Magazine, 1944)
14. "Lavigne Won City Prize Ring Fame," *Saginaw News*, January 25, 1948
15. *San Francisco Bulletin*, March 31, 1897
16. *National Police Gazette*, March 1897
17. "Connolly and Lavigne," *San Francisco Post*, February 24, 1897
18. Ibid
19. *San Francisco Report*, March 8, 1897
20. *New York World*, May 1, 1897
21. Ibid
22. Ibid
23. Ibid
24. "Still Champion," *Boston Daily Globe*, May 1, 1897
25. Ibid
26. *New York World*, May 1, 1897
27. Ibid
28. "Ziegler Holds His Own," *Boston Daily Globe*, May 18, 1897
29. "Ziegler Bests Lavigne," *Philadelphia Daily Record*, May 18, 1897
30. Ibid
31. Ibid

32. "Kid Lavigne Predicts Success for Yankee Pugilists in England," *Lowell Sun*, July, 31, 1897
33. "McPartland and Lavigne," *Waterloo Daily Courier*, June, 25, 1897
34. *Police News*, June 19, 1897
35. "Slugger in Trouble," *Syracuse Daily Sentinel*, June 10, 1897
36. Nat Fleischer, *Young Griffo : The Will-O'-The-Wisp Of The Roped Square*, (The Ring Publisher, 1928)
37. *Centralia Enterprise and Tribune*, July 31, 1897
38. "Young Griffo Quits," *Boston Daily Globe*, June 22, 1897
39. *Boston Daily Globe*, June 28, 1897
40. "Kid Lavigne Was Not There," *Philadelphia Record*, June 28, 1897
41. Ibid

Chapter 21

1. "Kid Lavigne Leaves Sam Fitzpatrick," *Mirror of Life*, September 22, 1897
2. "The Coming Battle," *Saginaw Evening News*, October 13, 1897
3. *San Francisco Bulletin*, September 16, 1897
4. "The Coming Battle," *Saginaw Evening News*, October 13, 1897
5. *San Francisco Bulletin*, September 10, 1897
6. *San Francisco Examiner*, September 5, 1897
7. "The Coming Battle," *Saginaw Evening News*, October 13, 1897
8. Biddy Bishop, "Kid Lavigne Greatest Lightweight of All Time," *Ring Magazine*, May 1928, page 4
9. Sam Fitzpatrick, Letter to the Sporting Editor of the *San Francisco Call*, October 4, 1897
10. *San Francisco Examiner*, October 24, 1897
11. "Ryan Will Take It Easy," *Syracuse Standard*, September 5, 1897
12. "Will Fight It Over," *Chicago Daily Tribune*, October 29, 1897, page 4
13. Bill Blunt, "Responsibility of Sparring Partner," *Anaconda Standard*, December 20, 1909, page 9
14. *San Francisco Examiner*, October 27, 1897
15. "Lavigne vs. Walcott," *Police News*, October 16, 1897
16. Ibid
17. *San Francisco Examiner*, October 24, 1897
18. "Lavigne Wins Strictly on His Merits," *San Francisco Chronicle*, October 30, 1897
19. "A Popular Victory," *Boston Post*, October 30, 1897
20. "Eddie Graney Will Act As Referee," *San Francisco Chronicle*, October 27, 1897

21. "Lavigne Wins Strictly on His Merits," *San Francisco Chronicle*, October 30, 1897
22. Ibid
23. George Lavigne, "When Fights Were Fights," *Los Angeles Times*, February 26, 1928
24. "Lavigne Forced Walcott to Quit," *National Police Gazette*, October 28, 1919
25. "Lavigne Victor," *San Francisco Examiner*, October, 29, 1897
26. "Walloped the Freak," *Saginaw News*, October 30, 1897
27. George Lavigne, "When Fights Were Fights," *Los Angeles Times*, February 26, 1928
28. "Lavigne Wins Strictly on His Merits," *San Francisco Chronicle*, October 30, 1897
29. George Lavigne, "When Fights Were Fights," *Los Angeles Times*, February 26, 1928
30. "Walloped the Freak," *Saginaw News*, October 30, 1897
31. George Lavigne, "When Fights Were Fights," *Los Angeles Times*, February 26, 1928
32. Jack Kofoed, "The Saginaw Kid," *Fight Stories*, February, 1931, Volume 3, No. 9
33. "About the Poolrooms," *San Francisco Examiner*, October 31, 1897
34. "Talks of His Victory," *San Francisco Examiner*, October 31, 1897
35. "Lavigne Wins Strictly on His Merits," *San Francisco Chronicle*, October 30, 1897
36. Ibid
37. "Wanted a Knock-Out," *San Francisco Examiner*, October 31, 1897
38. "Refused a Contest," *Saginaw Evening News*, November 3, 1897
39. "About the Poolrooms," *San Francisco Examiner*, October 31, 1897
40. "Talks of His Victory," *San Francisco Examiner*, October 31, 1897
41. International Boxing Hall of Fame write-up on Walcott in Old Timers section
42. Jim Amato, "Burying the Demon," *www.myboxingfans.com* , December 17, 2008
43. "Kid Lavigne Is Right," *National Police Gazette*, December, 1925
44. George Lavigne, "When Fights Were Fights," *Los Angeles Times*, February 26, 1928
45. Ibid
46. "The Governor and the Fight," *Grand Rapids Press*, November 1, 1905, p. 4

Chapter 22

1. Jack Kofoed, "The Saginaw Kid," *Fight Stories*, February, 1931 Volume 3, No. 9
2. "Lavigne a Boxer," *Detroit Free Press*, February 4, 1898
3. "Two Champions Met," *Detroit Free Press*, February 3, 1898
4. "Lavigne a Boxer," *Detroit Free Press*, February 4, 1898
5. "Fought to a Draw," *Chicago Daily Tribune*, March 18, 1898
6. "Was a Great Battle," *Saginaw Evening News*, March 18, 1898
7. "Fought to a Draw," *Oregonian*, March 18, 1898
8. "Was a Great Battle," *Saginaw Evening News*, March 18, 1898
9. Ibid
10. "Fought to a Draw," *Chicago Daily Tribune*, March 18, 1898
11. *Milwaukee Evening Wisconsin*, March 24, 1898
12. "Will They Meet Again," *Detroit Free Press*, March 20, 1898
13. Jack Kofoed, "The Saginaw Kid," *Fight Stories*, February, 1931 Volume 3, No. 9
14. *Sioux City Journal*, March 20, 1898
15. George Lavigne, *Los Angeles Times*, March 4, 1928
16. "Will They Meet Again," *Detroit Free Press*, March 20, 1898
17. *Republican News* (Hamilton, Ohio), March 22, 1898
18. *Detroit Free Press, April 3, 1898*
19. *Morning Star* (Sandusky, Ohio), April 19, 1898
20. *Sioux City Journal*, April 3, 1898
21. "Lavigne and Daly Draw," *Chicago Daily Tribune*, April 12, 1898
22. George Lavigne, *Los Angeles Times*, March 4, 1928
23. Tracy Callis, Bobby Dobbs' Ring Record, Cyber Boxing Zone Website, *www.cyberboxingzone.com*
24. "Two Black Eyes For Kid Lavigne, *World,* June 10, 1898
25. John Laflin Ring Record biography comments from BoxRec Website, *www.boxrec.com*
26. "Police Gazette Makes Matches," *National Police Gazette,* July 6, 1898

Chapter 23

1. James J. Corbett, "Corbett and McCoy Describe Their Work," *St. Louis Republic,* August 14, 1898, page 8
2. Kid McCoy's Ring Record, Cyber Boxing Zone Website, *www.cyberboxingzone.com*
3. *Landmark* (Statesville, North Carolina), August 12, 1898
4. "Erne's Bout," *Boston Daily Globe,* November 28, 1896 page 2

5. Arthur Daley, "Champion of Another Era," *New York Times*, October 26, 1945 page 14
6. "New Boxing Club," *Syracuse Sunday Herald*, September 11, 1898 page 15
7. *Milwaukee Evening Wisconsin*, September 2, 1898
8. "It Didn't Take Place," *Titusville Herald*, September 13, 1898 page 2
9. *San Diego Evening Tribune*, September 28, 1898, p. 4
10. "Erne Got a Draw," *Syracuse Evening Herald*, September 29, 1898
11. "Lavigne and Erne Fought a Draw," *World*, September 29, 1898
12. "Kid Lavigne Fights a Draw with Frank Erne," *Mirror of Life*, October 12, 1898
13. "Erne Got a Draw," *Syracuse Evening Herald*, September 29, 1898
14. "Kid's Narrow Escape," *Detroit Free Press*, September 29, 1898
15. *Milwaukee Evening Wisconsin*, September 29, 1898
16. George Lavigne, "When Fights Were Fights," *Los Angeles Times*, March 4, 1928
17. Jack Kofoed, "The Saginaw Kid," *Fight Stories*, February, 1931, Volume 3 Number 9
18. Bo Needham, "In the Squared Circle," *Detroit Free Press*, June 25, 1899
19. *Milwaukee Evening Wisconsin*, March 7, 1902
20. George Lavigne, "When Fights Were Fights," *Los Angeles Times*, March 4, 1928
21. "Lavigne Ahead In The Betting," *San Francisco Chronicle*, November 25, 1898
22. "Kid Lavigne Is Ready For Tracey," *San Francisco Chronicle*, November 24, 1898
23. Ibid
24. *Oakland Tribune*, November 23, 1898
25. Jack Kofoed, "The Saginaw Kid," *Fight Stories*, February, 1931, Volume 3 Number 9
26. "Good Fighters Slow To Get Started," *California Evening News*, November 2, 1918, page 5
27. "Lavigne Wins From Tracey," *San Francisco Chronicle*, November 26, 1898
28. Ibid
29. "Lavigne Bests Tracey," *Washington Post*, November 26, 1898, page 9
30. "Lavigne Wins From Tracey," *San Francisco Chronicle*, November 26, 1898
31. *National Police Gazette*, December 24, 1898

Chapter 24

1. "Kid Lavigne Got Fresh," *Sandusky Star,* January 4, 1999, p.4
2. "Tommy Ryan, "Pugilism Should Boom," *New York Herald,* January 1, 1899
3. Stewart H. Holbrook, "Mysterious Billy Smith," *The American Mercury,* July 1949, p. 107
4. Murray Greig, *Goin' the Distance,* (Toronto, McMillan Canada, 1996) p. 62
5. Tracy Callis, "Tommy Ryan Profile," Cyber Boxing Zone Website, *www.cyberboxingzone.com*
6. Stewart H. Holbrook, "Mysterious Billy Smith," *The American Mercury,* July 1949, p. 108
7. Ron Jackson, "The Dirtiest Fighter Ever," *www.supersport.com/boxing,* December 31, 2003
8. *Salt Lake Tribune,* September 5, 1896
9. Charles Francis, "Mysterious Billy Smith," *www.Scribd.com*
10. "Men of the Mitts," *Detroit Free Press,* February 5, 1899, Page B8
11. George Lavigne, "When Fights Were Fights," *Los Angeles Times,* March 11, 1928
12. "Lavigne Won Prize Ring Fame," *Saginaw News,* January 25, 1948
13. "Billy Lavigne Saved His Brother From a Knockout," *San Francisco Call,* March 11, 1899
14. "Smith's Bout," *Boston Daily Globe,* March 11, 1899
15. George Lavigne, "When Fights Were Fights," *Los Angeles Times,* March 11, 1928
16. "Champion Lavigne Tastes of the Bitters of Defeat," *San Francisco Chronicle,* March 12, 1899
17. Ibid
18. "Billy Lavigne Saved His Brother From a Knockout," *San Francisco Call,* March 11, 1899
19. "Champion Lavigne Tastes of the Bitters of Defeat," *San Francisco Chronicle,* March 12, 1899
20. Ibid
21. "Billy Lavigne Saved His Brother From a Knockout," *San Francisco Call,* March 11, 1899
22. Ibid
23. Ibid
24. "Champion Lavigne Tastes of the Bitters of Defeat," *San Francisco Chronicle,* March 12, 1899
25. "Billy Lavigne Saved His Brother From a Knockout," *San Francisco Call,* March 11, 1899

26. *Milwaukee Evening Wisconsin*, March 30, 1899
27. George Lavigne, "When Fights Were Fights," *Los Angeles Times*, March 11, 1928
28. "Ringside Gossip," *Police News*, March 1899

Chapter 25

1. *Milwaukee Evening Wisconsin*, March 25, 1899
2. *Police News*, April 1899
3. Ibid
4. *Sandusky Star*, May 4, 1899
5. *Louisville Courier Journal*, June 24, 1899
6. "Champion Will Train at Oceanic," *Detroit Free Press*, May 28, 1899
7. "In the Squared Circle," *Detroit Free Press*, June 25, 1899
8. Ibid
9. "Erne Lowers the Colors of Kid Lavigne," *San Francisco Call*, July 4, 1899
10. "Fought a Game Fight," *Saginaw Evening News*, July 4, 1899
11. "Lavigne Defeated by Frank Erne," *New York World*, July 4, 1899
12. "Fought a Game Fight," *Saginaw Evening News*, July 4, 1899
13. "Lavigne Defeated by Frank Erne," *New York World*, July 4, 1899
14. "Erne Lowers the Colors of Kid Lavigne," *San Francisco Call*, July 4, 1899
15. Ibid
16. "Fighting Frank Erne Made Ring History," *National Police Gazette*, July, 1951
17. "Erne Defeats Kid Lavigne," *Chicago Tribune*, July 4, 1899
18. "In the Boxers Corner," *Detroit Free Press*, July 16, 1899
19. "Erne the Champion," *Fort Wayne News*, July 4, 1899
20. "In the Boxers Corner," *Detroit Free Press*, July 16, 1899
21. Ibid
22. George Lavigne, "When Fights Were Fights," *Los Angeles Times*, March 11, 1928
23. "Lavigne Lost to Erne," *Detroit Free Press*, July 4, 1899
24. Sam Austin, "How Erne's Skill Discounted Lavigne's Aggressiveness," *National Police Gazette*, July 22, 1899 p. 11
25. Ibid
26. *London Daily Mail*, July 5, 1899
27. "In the Boxers Corner," *Detroit Free Press*, July 16, 1899
28. Arthur Daley, "Champions of Another Era," *New York Times*, October 26, 1945

29. *National Police Gazette,* July 1899
30. "In the Boxers Corner," *Detroit Free Press,* July 16, 1899

Chapter 26

1. *Sandusky Star,* July, 8, 1899
2. *Milwaukee Evening Wisconsin,* July 24, 1899
3. Sam Austin, *National Police Gazette,* September 2, 1899
4. *Sandusky Star,* August 3, 1899
5. Sam Austin, *National Police Gazette,* September 2, 1899
6. *Sandusky Star,* August 29, 1899
7. *Milwaukee Evening Wisconsin,* July 24, 1899
8. *Milwaukee Evening Wisconsin,* September 2, 1899
9. Ibid
10. "Kid Lavigne and McFadden," *World* (New York), October 6, 1899
11. "Lavigne Knocked Out by George McFadden," *World* (New York), October 7, 1899
12. "And The End At Last," *Saginaw Evening News,* October 7, 1899
13. "Lavigne Knocked Out by George McFadden," *World* (New York), October 7, 1899
14. "McFadden Whips Lavigne," *New York Times,* October 7, 1899
15. "Lavigne Is Knocked Out By McFadden," *San Francisco Call,* October 7, 1899
16. *Sandusky Star,* October 11, 1899
17. "McFadden Whips Lavigne," *New York Times,* October 7, 1899
18. George Lavigne, "When Fights Were Fights," *Los Angeles Times,* March 11, 1928
19. "And The End At Last," *Saginaw Evening News,* October 7, 1899
20. "Kid Lavigne Was No Match For George McFadden," *National Police Gazette,* October 28, 1899
21. *Milwaukee Evening Wisconsin,* October 14, 1899
22. *Racine Daily Journal,* October 14, 1899
23. *Racine Daily Journal,* November 28, 1899

Chapter 27

1. *Mansfield News,* January 1, 1900
2. *Boston Daily Globe,* January 12, 1900
3. *Mansfield News (Ohio),* January 24, 1900
4. "History of Savate – Part 1," *www.martialinfo.com*

5. "A Brief History of Savate," http://www.srcf.ucam.org/cuscs/savate.html
6. *New York World,* January 23, 1900
7. *Boston Daily Globe,* May 29, 1900
8. *Mansfield News,* May 1, 1900
9. *Saginaw News,* February 1900
10. *Milwaukee Evening Wisconsin,* June 26, 1900
11. *Milwaukee Evening Wisconsin,* October 18, 1900
12. William White, "Addiction Treatment Programs 1840-1950," www.williamwhitepapers.com
13. *National Police Gazette,* November 3, 1900
14. *Racine Daily Journal,* November 3, 1900
15. *Milwaukee Evening Wisconsin,* October 18, 1900
16. *National Police Gazette,* December 8, 1900
17. *Oshkosh Daily Northwestern,* January 31, 1901
18. *Racine Daily Journal,* March 30, 1901
19. *Trenton Times,* December 28, 1900
20. *National Police Gazette,* December 8, 1900
21. *Encyclopedia of Chicago,* (Chicago, University of Chicago Press, 2004) p. 89
22. Kelly Nicholson, *Hitters, Dancers and Ring Magicians,* (Jefferson, NC and London, McFarland, 2011) p. 102
23. *Oshkosh Daily Northwestern,* April 15, 1901
24. *Oshkosh Daily Northwestern,* August 3, 1901
25. *Trenton Times,* August 3, 1901
26. *Oshkosh Daily Northwestern,* October 4, 1901
27. *Brooklyn Daily Eagle,* October 2, 1901

Chapter 28

1. *Oakland Tribune,* October 9, 1901
2. "Australian Boxer Will Soon Fight," *San Francisco Call,* November 30, 1901
3. Barry Deskins, Aurelio Herrera Ring Record, Cyber Boxing Zone Website, www.cyberboxingzone.com
4. *Oakland Tribune,* December 6, 1901
5. *San Francisco Call,* December 7, 1901
6. *Oakland Tribune,* December 6, 1901
7. *Oakland Tribune,* December 11, 1901
8. *San Francisco Chronicle,* December 12, 1901
9. *Oakland Tribune,* December 13, 1901

10. *San Francisco Call,* December 13, 1901
11. *Los Angeles Times* December 13, 1901
12. Ibid
13. *Illustrated Police News,* December 1901
14. *Oakland Tribune,* December 13, 1901
15. *Illustrated Police News,* December 1901
16. *San Francisco Chronicle,* December 13, 1901
17. Sam Austin, *National Police Gazette,* January 11, 1902
18. Lou Houseman, *Denver Republican,* December 22, 1901
19. Tracy Callis, Tim Hegarty Ring Record, Cyber Boxing Zone Website, *www.cyberboxingzone.com*

Chapter 29

1. *Trenton Times,* December 20, 1901
2. *Trenton Times,* December 23, 1901
3. *Milwaukee Evening Wisconsin,* January 4, 1902
4. *Oakland Tribune,* February 13, 1902
5. *Fort Wayne Journal-Gazette,* February 3, 1902
6. *Oshkosh Daily Northwestern,* January 31, 1902
7. George Lavigne, "When Fights Were Fights," *Los Angeles Times,* March 11, 1928
8. *San Francisco Chronicle,* May 30, 1902
9. *San Francisco Call,* May 30, 1902
10. Ibid
11. *San Francisco Chronicle,* May 30, 1902
12. *San Francisco Call,* May 30, 1902
13. Ibid
14. *San Francisco Chronicle,* May 30, 1902
15. Ibid
16. *San Francisco Call,* May 30, 1902
17. *Oakland Tribune,* May 31, 1902
18. *San Francisco Chronicle,* May 30, 1902
19. *Saginaw News,* January 25, 1948
20. *Milwaukee Evening Wisconsin,* March 14, 1912
21. *Republic,* April 19, 1921, page 10
22. *San Francisco Call,* November 15, 1913
23. George Lavigne, "When Fights Were Fights," *Los Angeles Times,* March 11, 1928
24. *Oakland Tribune,* May 31, 1902

Chapter 30

1. *Brooklyn Eagle,* June 14, 1902, page 10
2. *Oakland Tribune,* July 3, 1902
3. *Davenport Daily Republican,* July 20, 1902
4. *National Police Gazette,* September 6, 1902
5. *National Police Gazette,* September 20, 1902
6. *Milwaukee Evening Wisconsin,* January 8, 1903
7. Information taken from a Wikipedia list of London's Gentlemen's Clubs
8. *Racine Daily Journal,* August 30, 1905
9. Jack Kofoed, "The Saginaw Kid," *Fight Stories,* February, 1931, pages 80 and 81
10. *National Police Gazette,* March, 1904
11. *Boston Daily Globe,* June 10, 1905
12. "Kid Lavigne Gives George The Big Chance," *Republic,* April 19, 1921, page 10
13. Unknown source – 1904 quote taken from Antiquities of the Prize Ring Archive
14. *Chicago Examiner,* December 17, 1911
15. *Boston Daily Globe,* April 23, 1901
16. *Milwaukee Free Press,* September 3, 1905
17. *Milwaukee Evening Wisconsin,* August 30, 1905
18. *Milwaukee Evening Wisconsin,* October 1, 1905

Chapter 31

1. *Washington Post,* December 8, 1905
2. *Fort Wayne Journal-Gazette,* April 29, 1906
3. George Lavigne, "When Fights Were Fights," *Los Angeles Times,* March 5, 1928
4. *National Police Gazette,* May 1906
5. Box Rec Ring Record of Mike Ward, www.boxrec.com
6. "Back in the Ring," *Salt Lake Tribune,* December 23, 1906
7. Ibid
8. Box Rec obituary information on Young Erne, www.boxrec.com
9. Box Rec obituary information on Young Erne, www.boxrec.com
10. *Louisville Courier Journal,* January 6, 1907
11. Ibid
12. "Lavigne Passes to Oblivion," *Los Angeles Herald,* February 2, 1907
13. Ibid

14. "Pitiful Showing Made by Lavigne," *Saginaw Courier Herald*, January 20, 1907
15. Ibid
16. "Lavigne Passes to Oblivion," *Los Angeles Herald*, February 2, 1907

Chapter 32

1. *Washington Post*, May 15, 1907
2. *Seattle Daily Times*, April 29, 1907 page 10
3. *Milwaukee Evening Wisconsin*, February 2, 1908
4. "Champion Fighters Have Nearly Always Been White," *Oakland Tribune*, January 14, 1908
5. *San Antonio Daily Express*, August 27, 1908
6. "Alabama Kid Again Scraps," *San Antonio Light*, March 23, 1909
7. "Alabama Kid Again Scraps," *San Antonio Light*, April 6, 1909
8. "Bert Davis Had Kid Lavigne in Helpless Condition," *Lowell Sun*, May 17, 1909
9. Ibid
10. *Williamsport Daily Gazette and Bulletin*, May 24, 1909
11. "Kid Lavigne Is Globe Trotter," *Los Angeles Herald*, May 29, 1908

Chapter 33

1. "Kid Lavigne Boxes Exhibition With Nelson," *Denver Post*, December 18, 1909 page 6
2. *Grand Forks Daily Herald*, December 29, 1909
3. *Milwaukee Evening Wisconsin*, December 17, 1910
4. *Denver Post*, December 21, 1910 page 10
5. *Milwaukee Free Press*, August 18, 1911
6. *Milwaukee Evening Wisconsin*, February 20, 1912
7. *Denver Post*, February 26, 1912 page 8
8. *Lima Daily News*, February 12, 1912
9. *Springfield Daily News*, February 28, 1912
10. Ibid
11. "In The Wake Of The Rosin," *Cleveland Plain Dealer*, April 14, 1912
12. "Kid Lavigne Is Insane," *Abilene Daily Reporter*, July 24, 1912
13. "Kid Lavigne Off To The Bughouse," *Fort Worth Star-Telegram*, July 24, 1912 page 8
14. "Prize Fighter Drink Victim," *Milwaukee Free Press*, June 30, 1912

15. "Kid Lavigne Once Great Boxer All In And Wreck," *Denver Post*, July 23, 1912
16. "Mrs. Lavigne Puts Famous 'Kid' Away," *Los Angeles Examiner*, July 16, 1912
17. "Somebody Must Be Insane But 'Kid' Lavigne Isn't The Person," *Detroit Free Press*, June 30, 1912, page 17
18. "Ex-Champion Has New White Hope," *Milwaukee Free Press*, September 17, 1912
19. "Bouts in Many Cities Hold The Fans," *San Francisco Call*, December 17, 1912
20. "Lavigne Not Insane," *Jersey Journal*, December 26, 1912

Chapter 34

1. "Tom O'Rourke Calls Roosevelt To Aid," *New York Times*, February 14, 1913
2. *Boxing*, February 22, 1913
3. Ibid
4. Tad Dorgan, "Tad's Tid Bits," *New Castle News*, January 4, 1923, page 16
5. "Congalton Seeking Aid," *Muscatine Iowa Journal*, May 21, 1913
6. "Lavigne To Teach Boxing," *Milwaukee Evening Wisconsin*, December 20, 1912
7. "Kid Lavigne, 46 Today, Is Playing On Very Hard Luck," *Trenton Evening Times*, December 6, 1915
8. "Friends to Dig for ex-Champion George Lavigne," *Milwaukee Free Press*, December 17, 1915
9. "Prominent Boxers in Kid Lavigne Benefit," *Wilkes-Barre Times*, December 21, 1915, page 19
10. "Small Sum For Lavigne," *New York Times*, December 22, 1915
11. Otto Floto, *Denver Post*, December 29, 1915, page 12
12. "Lavigne But Shadow Of His Former Self," *Milwaukee Free Press*, December 26, 1915
13. "Carl Morris and Arthur Pelkey Will Meet Here On February 11," *Tulsa World*, January 30, 1916, page 6
14. *Portsmouth Daily Times*, October 3, 1916
15. "Kid Lavigne in Jail," *Saginaw News*, September 22, 1916, page 3
16. "Kid Lavigne Declared Insane by Physicians," *Jackson Citizen Patriot*, April 14, 1920, page 9
17. "Lavigne Escapes Asylum," *Kalamazoo Gazette*, November 2, 1916, page 10

18. "George Lavigne Reforms and Punches Time Clock," *Plain Dealer*, November 19, 1917
19. "Lavigne Gets Good Job Working With Ford," *Elkhart Truth*, December 10, 1917, page 2
20. "Lavigne Working On Flivvers," *Salt Lake Telegram*, January 17, 1918, page 33
21. Amy Wilson, "Harry Bennett: Henry Ford's Chief Thug Targets UAW," *Automotive News*, June 16, 2003
22. "Lavigne Adjudged Insane Man," *Times-Picayune*, April 14, 1920, page 19
23. "Kid Lavigne Declared Insane by Physicians," *Jackson Citizen Patriot*, April 14, 1920, page 9
24. "Lost Bout Makes Fighter Insane," *Racine Journal-News*, May 3, 1920, page 14
25. "Kid Lavigne O.K. Again," *San Diego Evening Tribune*, August 14, 1920, page 22
26. Joe Vila, "Sam Fitzpatrick Now Critically Ill Was Great Manager, *Philadelphia Enquirer*, October 18, 1922, page 18
27. *Saginaw News*, November 28, 1922
28. *Trenton Evening Times*, October 26, 1921, page 17
29. Ibid
30. Jack Keene, "Sports Snapshots," *Nevada State Journal*, February 14, 1922, page 5
31. "Saginaw Kid Gets His Second Marriage License Within Three Weeks," *Boston Daily Globe*, November 28, 1923
32. *Chronicle Telegram (Ohio)*, December 13, 1923, page 6

Chapter 35

1. "Kid Lavigne, Once Champion, Nearly Forgotten By Fans," *Ludington Daily News*, February 18, 1925, page 6
2. Ibid
3. "There Was Only One Griffo Says Lavigne," *Plain Dealer*, December 8, 1927, page 24
4. "Saginaw Kid Answers Final Bell; Fans Mourn," *San Diego Evening Tribune*, March 10, 1928
5. John Philip Schuch, *Michigan's Old Inn*, (1946)
6. *Ludington Daily News*, November 2, 1928, page 6
7. Thomas J. Young and Laurence A. French, "The 'Greatest' Boxers of All Time Heuristics and Biases Among Boxing Historians," *Perceptual and Motor Skills*, 87, no. 3, (1988): page 1310
8. *Baltimore American*, August 15, 1910

9. Tracy Callis, Benny Leonard's Ring Record, Cyber Boxing Zone Website, *www.cyberboxingzone.com*
10. Mike Casey, "Benny Leonard: Golden Talent of a Golden Age," *East Side Boxing.com*, January 15, 2009
11. *Sandusky Star Journal*, November 21, 1925 page 9
12. George K. Franklin, "George 'Kid' Lavigne," *Boxing Illustrated*, September 1959, p. 25
13. *Racine Journal-News*, March 25, 1918, page 7
14. Robert Edgren, "Two Ring Feats of Lavigne Made Him 'Stand Out' as Greatest of Lightweights," *New York Evening World*, 1913
15. Otto Floto, "Are Not Far Amiss In Giving Lavigne Laurels," *Denver Post*, December 18, 1915
16. *Oakland Tribune*, May 19, 1911
17. Tad Dorgan, "Fights We Can't Forget," *San Antonio Light*, August 3, 1926, page 9
18. George K. Franklin, "George 'Kid' Lavigne," *Boxing Illustrated*, September 1959, p. 25
19. Sam Austin, *Police Gazette*, August 8, 1903
20. George K. Franklin, "George 'Kid' Lavigne," *Boxing Illustrated*, September 1959, p. 25
21. Nat C. Goodwin, *New Castle News (PA)*, March 22, 1902
22. George K. Franklin, "George 'Kid' Lavigne," *Boxing Illustrated*, September 1959, p. 25
23. Harry Tuthill, "Lavigne King in Days when Fights Were Fierce," *Detroit Times*, March 11, 1928
24. Tom O'Rourke, George Underwood, "'Greatest Fight I Ever Saw' When Lavigne Met Walcott" (Unknown newspaper of 1920)
25. Michael "Dad" Butler, *Detroit Times*, March 11, 1928
26. *Casa Grande (AZ) Dispatch*, November 8, 1912
27. *New York Evening Telegram*, April 4, 1912 page 10
28. "Jim Corbett Discusses the Big Fighting Men, *Ogden Standard*, February 4, 1908
29. Nat Fleischer, *Trenton Evening Times*, August 4, 1926, page 14
30. Jack McAuliffe, *San Mateo Times*, May 15, 1928, page 5
31. Joe "Buck" Kelly, *Wilkes-Barre Times*, June 12, 1916 page 14
32. *San Francisco Call*, November 15, 1913
33. Jack Skelly, *Baltimore American*, June 25, 1919, page 2
34. Eddie Hanlon, *Salt Lake Telegram*, February 18, 1917, page 27
35. George Underwood, "Kid Lavigne's Bout With Everhardt Recounted," *Detroit Free Press*, August 21, 1921, page 21
36. *Washington Post*, September 25, 1904

37. George K. Franklin, "George 'Kid' Lavigne," *Boxing Illustrated*, September 1959, p. 61
38. Larry Gustin, "New Facts About Kid Lavigne," *Boxing Illustrated*, March 1964, page 68
39. B. H. Benton, "He Stands The Shadow Of A Mighty Name," Unpublished letter, probably 1920

Postscript

1. Nat Fleischer, *Jack McAuliffe The Napoleon of the Prize Ring*, (Ring Magazine Press, 1944) page 2
2. Frank Butler, *A History of Boxing in Britain*, (London: Arthur Barker Limited, 1972) page 159
3. *Detroit Free Press*, March 1, 1896
4. Nat Fleischer, *Jack McAuliffe The Napoleon of the Prize Ring*, (Ring Magazine Press, 1944) page 63
5. Gerald Suster, *Lightning Strikes – The Lives and Times of Boxing's Lightweight Heroes*, (U.K.: Robson Press Ltd, 1996) page 13
6. John V. Grombach, *The Saga of Sock*, (New York: A. S. Barnes and Company, 1949) page 112
7. "Eager To Fight," *Los Angeles Times*, April 13, 1896, page 3

BIBLIOGRAPHY

Books

American Lumberman; the Personal History and Public and Business Achievements of Eminent Lumberman of the United States. Chicago: American Lumberman, 1905

Arnold, Peter. *History of Boxing.* Chartwell Books, Inc., 1985

Aycock, Colleen and Scott, Mark. *Joe Gans – A Biography of the First African American World Boxing Champion.* North Carolina and London: McFarland and Company, 2008

Boxing's Book of Records to June 30, 1914, Published by *Boxing*

Boddy, Kasia. *Boxing A Cultural History.* Reaktion Books, 2009

Butler, Frank. *A History of Boxing in Britain.* London: Arthur Barker Limited, 1972

Deghy, Guy. *Noble and Manly: The History of the National Sporting Club.* London: Hutchinson, 1956

Douglas, Francis Archibald Kelhead. *The Sporting Queensberry's.* London: Hutchinson, 1942

Edwards, Billy. *Legendary Boxers of the Golden Age.* Chartwell Books, Inc., 1990

Encyclopedia of Chicago. Chicago: University of Chicago Press, 2004

Fleischer, Nat. *Jack McAuliffe: The Napoleon of the Prize Ring.* Ring Magazine Press, 1944

Fleischer, Nat. *The Three Colored Aces: Story of George Dixon, Joe Gans, Joe Walcott and Several Contemporaries volume 3 of Black Dynamite: The Story of the Negro in the Prize Ring from 1782-1938.* New York: Ring Athletic Library, 1938

Fleischer, Nat. *Young Griffo: The Will-O'-The-Wisp Of The Roped Square.* Ring Magazine, 1928

Gorn, Elliot J. *The Manly Art: Bare-Knuckle Prize Fighting in America.* Ithaca and London: Cornell University Press, 1986

Greig, Murray. *Goin' the Distance.* Toronto: McMillan Canada, 1996

Grombach, John V. *The Saga of Sock: A Complete Story of Boxing.* New York: A. S. Barnes and Company, 1949

Haldane, R. A. *Champions and Challengers – One Hundred Years of Queensberry Boxing.* London: Stanley Paul, 1967

Heinz, W. C. *The Fireside Book of Boxing,* Simon and Shuster, 1961

Holbrook, Stuart H. *Holy Old Mackinaw: A Natural History of the American Lumberjack.* Ballantine Books, 1971

Isenberg, Michael T. *John L. Sullivan And His America.* Urbana and Chicago: University of Illinois Press, 1988

Johnston, Alexander. *Ten and Out! The Complete Story of the Prize Ring in America.* New York: Ives Washburn, 1947

Kahn, Roger. *A Flame of Pure Fire: Jack Dempsey and the Roaring 20's.* Mariner Books, 2000

Kilar, Jeremy W. *Michigan's Lumbertowns, Lumberman and Laborers in Saginaw, Bay City, and Muskegon, 1870-1905.* Wayne State University Press, 1990

Kilar, Jeremy W. and Bloomfield, Ronald. *Bay City Logbook.* St. Louis: G. Bradley, 1996

Lamarre, Jean. *The French Canadians of Michigan.* Great Lakes Books, 2003

Lears, Jackson. *The Rebirth of a Nation: The Making of Modern America, 1877-1920.* Harper Perennial, 2010

Liebling, A. J. *The Sweet Science.* New York: North Point Press, 2004

Nicholson, Kelly. *Hitters, Dancers, and Ring Magicians.* North Carolina and London: McFarland and Company, 2011

Pollack, Adam J. *John L. Sullivan: The Career of the First Gloved Heavyweight Champion.* North Carolina and London: McFarland and Company, 2004

Reel, Guy. *The National Police Gazette and the Making of the Modern American Man 1879-1906.* Palgrave Macmillan, 2006

Roberts, James B. and Skutt, Alexander. *The Boxing Register: International Boxing Hall of Fame Official Record Book.* Ithaca, NY: McBook Press, 2002

Roberts, Randy. *Jack Dempsey: The Manassas Mauler.* Baton Rouge: Louisiana State University Press, 1984

Rodriguez, Robert G. *The Regulation of Boxing,* North Carolina and London: McFarland and Company, 2009

Sammons, Jeffrey T. *Beyond the Ring: The Role of Boxing in American Society.* Urbana: University of Illinois Press, 1990

Schuch, John Philip. *Michigan's Old Inn.* Saginaw, Hartwell Printing Company, 1946

Silver, Mike. *The Arc of Boxing: The Rise and Decline of the Sweet Science.* North Carolina and London: McFarland and Company, 2008

Stillman, Marshall. *Great Fighters and Boxers – Psychology of the Ring.* New York: Marshall Stillman Association, 1920

Streible, Dan. *Fight Pictures: A History of Boxing and Early Cinema.* Berkeley: University of California Press, 2008

Suster, Gerald. *Lightning Strikes – The Lives and Times of Boxing's Lightweight Heroes.* U.K.: Robson Press Ltd, 1996

Periodicals

American Mercury, Arena, Automotive News, Boxing, Boxing Annual, Boxiana Review, Boxing Collectors' News, Boxing Digest, Boxing and Wrestling, Boxing Illustrated Wrestling News, Famous Fights, Fight Comics, Fight Stories, IBRO Journal, Perceptual and Motor Skills, The Queensberry Rules, The Ring, Sport Story, True Magazine Boxing Yearbook, World Boxing

Newspapers

Abilene Daily Reporter, Anaconda Standard, Baltimore American, Bay City Times, Beloit Daily News, Boston Daily Globe, Boston Herald, Boston Post, Brooklyn Daily Eagle, California Evening News, Canton Ohio Repository, Casa Grande Dispatch, Centralia Enterprise and Tribune, Chicago Dispatch, Chicago Examiner, Chicago Tribune, Chronicle Telegram (Elyria, Ohio), Daily Evening Herald (Oskaloosa, Iowa), Daily Iowa Capital (Des Moines), Dallas Morning News, Davenport Daily Republican, Decatur Daily Review, Decatur Morning Herald Dispatch, Denver Post, Denver Republican, Detroit Free Press, Detroit Times, Elkhart Truth, Fort Wayne Journal-Gazette, Fort Wayne News and Sentinel, Fort Worth Star Telegram, Grand Forks Daily Herald, Grand Rapids Press, Jackson Citizen Patriot, Kalamazoo Gazette, Illustrated Police News, Landmark (Statesville, North Carolina), Lima Daily News, Logansport Pharos, London Daily Mail, Los Angeles Herald, Los Angeles Times, Louisville Courier Journal, Lowell Sun, Ludington Daily News, Mansfield News, Milwaukee Evening Wisconsin, Milwaukee Free Press, Mirror of Life (London), Morning Star (Sandusky, Ohio), Muscatine Iowa Journal, National Police Gazette, Nevada State Journal, Newark Daily Advocate, New Castle News, New Jersey Journal, New Orleans Daily Item, New York Herald, New York Illustrated News, New York Sun, New York Times, New York World, Oakland Tribune, Ogden Standard, Oshkosh Daily Northwestern, Philadelphia Enquirer, Philadelphia Evening Bulletin, Philadelphia Item, Philadelphia Record, Plain Dealer (Cleveland, Ohio),

Portland Oregonian, Portsmouth Daily Times, Racine Daily Journal, Racine Journal-News, Republic (Columbus, Indiana), Republican News (Ohio), Saginaw Courier Herald, Saginaw News, Saginaw Evening News, Saint Louis Republic, Salt Lake Telegram, Salt Lake Tribune, San Antonio Daily Express, San Antonio Light, San Diego Evening Tribune, Sandusky Star, San Francisco Bulletin, San Francisco Call, San Francisco Chronicle, San Francisco Examiner, San Francisco Post, San Francisco Report, San Mateo Times, Seattle Daily Times, Sioux City Journal, Sporting Life (United Kingdom), Sporting Review (United Kingdom), Sportsman (United Kingdom), Springfield Daily News, St. Louis Republic, Syracuse Daily Sentinel, Syracuse Standard, Syracuse Sunday Herald, Tacoma Daily News, Times-Picayune (New Orleans, Louisiana), Titusville Herald, Trenton Times, Tulsa World, Washington Post, Waterloo Daily Courier, Watertown Daily Times, Wilkes-Barre Times, Williamsport Daily Gazette and Bulletin

Websites

www.aboutbillythekid.com – material on Billy the Kid
www.acadian-home.org – material on the Carignan Regiment
www.ancestry.com – material on the Fille de Roi
www.antekprizering.com – an assortment of materials and pictures
www.bay-journal.com – material on early Bay City and logging
www.boxrec.com – material on boxers records and photographs
www.britannica.com – article by Jeffrey T. Sammons, "Boxing's Legal Status"
www.common-place.org – article by Melissa Haley, "Storm of Blows"
www.coxcorner.com
www.cyberboxingzone.com – material on boxers' records and photographs
www.eastsideboxing.com
www.fightsrec.com – material on boxers' records
www.genealogybank.com – access to historical newspapers
www.ibhof.com – biographies of several boxers
www.martialinfo.com – material on the history of Savate
www.myboxingfans.com – article by Jim Amato, "Burying the Demon"
www.newspaperarchive.com – access to historical newspapers
www.scribd.com – article by Charles Smith, "Mysterious Billy Smith"
www.shootingtimes.com – article by Jim Wilson, "The Truth About Billy the Kid"
www.supersport.com – article by Ron Jackson, "The Dirtiest Fighter Ever"
www.theboxinghistorian.com
www.williamwhitepapers.com – paper by William White, "Addiction Treatment Programs 1840-1950"

INDEX

Numbers in *bold italics* indicate pages with photographs

Aaron, Barney 47
Abbott, Stanton 80, 166, 175, 189, 224
Acme Athletic Club, Oakland 281, 284, 289, 290, 312
Active Athletic Association, New Jersey 117
Alabama Kid 315
Albany, New York (and C.A.C. Smith) 37
Al Carroll's Roadhouse, Grand Rapids, Michigan 57
Alexander, Ted 119, 126, 205, 236, 285
Ali, Muhammad ix, 117, 407
American French Genealogical Society viii, 14
Angle, Jack (referee) 151, 155
Antiquities of the Prize Ring, *see also* Shaffer, Harry 2, 10,
Arbeiter Hall, Saginaw 77
Armstrong, Billy 200, 205
Ash, Kid "The Pork Chops King" (Albert Laurey) 278
Attell, Abe "The Little Hebrew" 309, 344
Auditorium (venue in Detroit) 71
Auditorium Athletic Club, New Orleans 100, *102*

Austin, Sam G. (writer/referee) *see also Police Gazette* 231, 259, 260, 263, 286, 300, 301, 307, 346
Aycock, Collen (historian/writer) viii, 403

Baer, Max ix
Baldwin, Caleb 47
Baltimore Sun 47
Banks (area in Bay City) 25
bare-knuckle fighting 35, 47, 50, 88, 92, 96, 354, 404
Batchelor, Henry A. 33, 34, *40*
Battery B Armory, Chicago 75
Battle Creek, Michigan 263, 314
Bay City, Michigan vii, 1, 2, 24, *25*, 26, 30, 31, 33, 34, 39, 58, 59, 68, 279, 361, 362, 370, 404, 406
Bay City Logbook 24, 39, 404
Bay City Times 24, 69, 405
Breckwith, Lon 229
Bell, Dick 135
belladonna 295. 296, 298
benefit (fund raiser) 57, 62, 69, 72, 105, 107, 133, 134, 186, 221, 301, 321, 329, 330, 341, 342, 361, 362, 366
Bennett, Jack 224
Bennett, Harry 333, 334

407

Benton, Benjamin H. "Rob Roy" (manager/writer) 143, 350; on Burge fight 144, 147, 150, 151, 153, 154, 155, 156, 157; description of Wolcott 123; on Wolcott fight 128, 129, 132
Benton Harbor, Michigan 6, 7
Bernstein, Joe "Pride of the Bowery" 307
Bettinson, A. H. 148
"Billy the Kid" (William H. Bonney) 178
Bishop, Biddy (trainer) 200, 345, 346, 348
Bittle, Sam 353, 354
Black, Harry 171
Blanken's Six Mile House, San Francisco *199*, 200, 236, 245, 283, 289
Blunt, Bill (writer) 202
Bohemian Club of New York 171, 175
Bolingbroke Club, London 252
Bonney, William H. "Billy the Kid" 178, 179
Bordwell's Opera House 44, **45**
Boston Daily Globe 83, 167, 172, 176, 184, 185, 190, 191, 192, 194, 228, 246, 271, 273, 301, 302, 405
Boston Herald 57, 81
Boston, Massachusetts 36, 79, 80, 84, 121, 134, 210, 241, 253, 362, 363, 366, 405
Boston Post 204, 405
Boucher, Billy 58, 361
Boucher, Pierre 17
Bowen, Andy "The Louisiana Tornado" 53, 93, **96**, 96-107, 109, 133, 162, 169, 214, 302, 307, 332, 348, 354, 363
Bowen, Mathilde (wife of Andy) 102, 103
Bowen, Joe (promoter) 307
Bowery (New York) 122, 193, 221, 307

Bowker, Joe 301, 302
Boxing 209, 327
Boxing Illustrated 346
Box Rec 2, 308, 317, 354, 356
brain fever 299, 357
Brannagan, Patrick "Scotty" 47
Breckwith, Lon 229
Brisbane, Arthur 333
Britt, Jimmy **291**-298, 300, 301, 306, 313, 347, 349, 365
Britt, Willus 291
Broad, Ned "Kid" (William M. Thomas) 288, 289
Broadway Athletic Club, New York **264**, 269
Broughton, Jack 46, 47, **88**, 89, 90, 159
Brooklyn Daily Eagle 280, 298, 405
Burel, Jeanne (ancestor) 19, 369
Burge, Dick "Iron Man" iii, 53, 54, 80, 134, 136, 137, 138, 141-156, *142*, 168, 170, 189, 192, 235, 272, 284, 345, 346, 348, 351, 355, 356, 363; challenge to the world 133; fight with Carney 142; "Iron Man" of England 141, 142; on Lavigne's power 345; McAuliffe refuses to fight 134, 343; physical comparison to Lavigne 145; refuses to fight Billy Smith 43; rematch attempts 224, 225, 252, 253; trouble making weight for title bout 147-149
Burge, Jim "Iron Bark" 64, **65**, 66, 96, 100, 292, 295, 362
Burke, "Texas" Jack 93, 97
Burns, Jim (referee) 213
Burns, Oregon x
Burns, Tommy 163, 279, 335
Burt, Wellington 33
Butler, Eddie "Terror of the Midwest" 242, 243
Butler, Frank (writer) 87, 354, 403
Butler, Michael "Dad" (trainer) 144, 147, **148**, 151, 154, 346

Cahill, Frank P. 178
Callahan, Tim 278, 280, 309
Callis, Tracy (historian/writer) viii, 75, 84, 109, 221, 242, 331, 344
Canton Ohio Repository 367, 405
Carignan-Saliéres Regiment 18, 406
Carney, Jem 51, *52*, 53, 142, 143, 145, 151, 343, 354, 355, 356
Carnival of Champions 99
Carpentier, George "The Orchard Man" 187, 284, 296, 301
Carroll, Jimmy 92
Carson, Nevada 240
Casey, Mike (historian/writer) 344
Casseux, Michel 272
Causer, George 192
Centralia Enterprise and Tribune (Illinois) 194, 405
Cereghin, Bill 210
cestus 90
Chambers, Arthur *49*, 50, 352
Chambers, John Graham *see also* Marquess of Queensberry 89, 90
Charbrier, Ferdinand 301
Charlemont, Charles 272, **273**
Charlement, Joseph (father of Charles) 272
Charles, Ezzard ix
Cherry, Bob 43
Cherry, Joe 305
Cherry, Jack 43, 360
Cherry Valley, Illinois 326, 366
Chiarini's Nouveau Cirque, Paris 301
Chicago Athletic Association 147, 160
Chicago Daily Tribune 71, 76, 100, 101, 105, 119, 135, 139, 201, 215, 217, 220, 258, 362-364, 405
Choynski, Joe 59, 60, 61, 123, 191, 209
chronic traumatic encephalopathy 324
Chronicle Telegram (Ohio) 338, 405
Clark, Dr. F. P. (Sanitarium) 298, 299
Clark, "Professor" John 50

Clemens, Christian *see also* Mt.Clemens 211
Cleveland, Ohio 108, 214, 218, 271, 274, 275, 276, 296, 364, 367
Cleveland Central Armory 215, **216**
Cleveland Plain Dealer 323, 406
Collins, Scott "Bright Eyes" 109
Collins, Tim 49
Collyer, Sam 47, 48, 49
Columbian Athletic Club, Roby, Indiana 73, 74
Coney Island, New York 82, 84, 110, 193, 196, 224, 227, 231, 336
Congalton, Edward (trainer) 328
Connolly, Eddie 108, 183, **188**-191, 215, 279, 284, 363
Connors, Dan 43, 44, 360
Considine, George 101, 199, 213, 217, 288
Constentino, Lucille LeBlanc 17
Cook, Funny 151
Cooke, Captain 241
Coppelberger, Burt 334
Corbett, "Gentleman" Jim 53, 59, 92, 97, 105, 123, 199, 222, 226, 227, 229, 231, 259, 308, 329, 345, 347, 356
Corbett, Young II (William J. Rothwell) 279, 288, 307, 308, 309, 319
corkscrew punch *see also* McCoy, Charles "Kid" 315
Corri, Eugene (referee) 94
Cotton, Joe 205
Courtmarsh, Joe 59, 65
Creedon, Dan 123
Croll's Gardens, California 202
Crowhurst, Burt (referee) 191, 192, 310
Cuoco, Dan (historian/writer) viii, 9
Curtiss, Dick 47
Cuthbertson, Jim (father of John) 31, 32
Cuthbertson, John (historian/writer) vii, 31, 32

Cyber Boxing Zone 2, 75, 84, 170, 282, 354, 364, 365, 406

Dacey, Bill 51
Daily Evening Herald (Iowa)
Daily Iowa Capital 170, 405
Daly, "Wilmington" Jack (Cornelius T. Moriarity) **214**, 214-220, 229, 240, 364
Dallas Morning News 110, 405
Dally, Harry "The Australian Butterfly" 63
Dana, Illinois 70, 71, 108, 362
Danforth, Tommy 59, 84
Davis, Bert 314, 316, 317
Decatur Morning Herald Dispatch 181, 183, 405
Deghy, Guy (historian/writer) 159, 401
Dempsey, Jack "Manassas Mauler" ix, 5, 6, 7, 164, 187, 284, 296, 404
Dempsey, Jack "The Nonpareil" (John Edward Kelly) 35, 50, 59, 259, 352; fight with "Mysterious" Billy Smith 243, 244; as fight trainer 99; and LaBlanche pivot punch 61; middleweight title **51**, 52, 356 ; and the origin of trunks 92; as referee 63, 64; as second to Jack McAuliffe 52
Denver Post 153, 319, 320, 322, 324, 330, 365, 366, 405
Detroit, Michigan iv, 2, 33, 35, 36, 58, 67, 71, 72, 114, 188, 199, 210-213, 263, 274, 303-306, 309, 315, 318-322, 327, 328, 331, 332, 335, 338, 339, 341, 349, 361, 362, 364, 365, 366, 370.
Detroit Athletic Club 305, 308
Detroit Free Press 72, 108, 117, 125, 134, 135, 136, 144, 172, 174, 213, 218, 233, 244, 254, 256, 258, 260, 325, 355, 364, 405
Detroit Times 80, 362, 405
Dewey, Bertha Christine 78, 370

Dime, Jimmy 108, 189
dementia pugilistica 324
dissipation 1, 177, 196, 211, 233, 258, 262, 324, 343, 348, 349, 357, 358
Dixon, George "Little Chocolate" 81, 84, 110, 121, 122, 126, 131, 205, 228, 229, 279, 300, 307, 319, 340, 366, 380, 403
Dobbs, Robert "Bobby" 38, **53,** 121, 220, 221, 226, 235, 253, 264, 272, 278
Dr. F. P. Clark's Sanitarium, Oakland 298, 299
Dr. Jekyll 135, 332
Dolsenville (area in Bay City) 25
Donovan, Mike 289, 290
D'Or, Louis 302
Dorgan, Tad (writer) 61, 328, 345
Dorman, John 317
Dougherty, Jack (manager) 180, 182, 193
Douglas, John Sholto, *see also* Marquess of Queensberry 90
Dowling, Martin 135, 224
Driscoll, Jerry 272, 273
Drujon, Julia (first wife of Kid Lavigne - also Drugon) 303, 370
Duggan, Tommy 147
Duke of Cumberland 89
Duffy, John (referee) 100, 101, 104

Eaton, Sam 58, 59, 361
Edgren, Robert (writer) 65, 127, 132, 141, 142, 156, 327, 333
Edison, Thomas A. 81, 114, 290
Edwards, Billy 47, **48,** 49, 352
Elkhart Truth 333, 405
Elliot, Red 43, 360
Elms, Joe 126
Empire Athletic Club, New York 114, 117, 125, 132
Erne, Frank 53, 114, **228**, 240, 263, 272, 275, 276, 277, 284, 289, 290, 291, 296, 301, 329, 333, 336, 364 ; first Lavigne fight

224-235; second Lavigne fight 254-260, 265, 334, 349
Erne, "Young" (Hugh Frank Clavin) 308-311, *309*
Ernst, Billy 118
Everhardt, Jack "The Louisiana Tiger" 97, **109, 111,** 116, 133, 176, 183, 184, 186, 215, 238, 255, 279, 345, 351, 355; first Lavigne fight 109-112, 348, 363; second Lavigne fight 168-175, 363

Ferns, Rube 244, 261, 290
Fights Rec 2, 354
Fight Stories Magazine 211, 405
Fille du Roi 19, 406
finish-fight 57, 65, 70, 73, 76, 92, 93, 94, 144, 219, 228
Fitzgerald, Willie "The Fighting Harp" 309
Fitzpatrick, Sam "The Australian Comet" (manager) 101, 103, 107, 116, **125,** 126, 127, 128, 133, 138, **148,** 149, 152, 153, 156, 157, 166, **169,** 171, 172, 174, 175, 178, 182, 186, 192, 198, 200, 203, 235, 252, 265, 266, 269, 307, 313, 329, 348; becomes Lavigne's manager 81, 264, 265, 305; and Jack Daly 214, 215, 217-219; death 35; and Young Griffo 194, **195,** 196; negotiates Burge bout 143, 144; negotiates first Walcott bout 124, 125; and Jack Johnson 62; recalls treatment in England 145, 146; splits with Lavigne 197, 276, 308; and Tommy Ryan 127;
Fitzsimmons, Bob 51, 59, 114, 115, 116, 123, 199, 212, 226, 239, 243, 308, 329, 340, 343, 347, 356
Fleischer, Nat (historian/writer) 46, 94, 98, 122, 179, 187, 194, 209, 215, 235, 319, 342, 343, 344, 346, 347, 354, 355, 356, 365, 403

Flemming, John 143, 145, 146, 151
Floto, Otto (writer) 330
Ford, Henry 113, 114, 332, 333, 334
Ford plant, Highland Park 333, 334, 338, 340, 349
Forest Lawn Cemetery, Saginaw 303, 313, 335, *341*
Fort Wayne Journal-Gazette 290, 306, 405
Fort Wayne News and Sentinel 258, 405
Fort Worth Star-Telegram 323, 405
Fox, Richard K. *see also Police Gazette* 36, 133, 171, 187, 221, 336
Franey, Jim 214
Franklin, George (writer) 113, 346, 349
Frawley Law 164
Frazier, Billy 51, 352, 353
Freeman, Ollie 43
French-Canadian 38, 67, 156
Frenchtown (area in Bay City) 25, 26
Fulljames, George 50
Furey, Barney 281

Gaffney, Billy 71, 72, 362
Gahbell, M. 272
Gallagher, Billy 243
Galento, Tony "Two-Ton" ix
Galvin, Bat 99
Gans, Joe "The Old Master" 54, 121, 183, 215, 220, 234, 235, 240, 261, 265, 266, 275-278, 280, 290, 291, **306,** 307, 314, 328, 337, 340, 342-347, 349
Gardner, Billy 289
Garrard, Frank 214
Gatling Gun iii, 72, 74, 117
Gayety Theatre, Detroit 306
Genslinger, Charlie (promoter) 171
Gibbs, George "Young" 275
Gilfeather, Tommy 285
Gilmore, Harry 37, 51, 69, 353, 354

gloves; early padding 38, 84, 91, 92; and injuries 59, 92; inspection of 139, 151, 180, 246; invention of 90; Lavigne's first pair 38, 39, 313; and Marquess of Queensberry rules 90, 92, 161; skin tight (hard) 35, 47, 48, 52, 90; weight of 48, 56, 57, 71, 76, 77, 84, *91*, 139, 151, 162, 164
Godfrey, George "Old Chocolate" 36, 335
Goldman, Herbert G. (historian/writer) 46, 356
Goodman, Abe "Kid" 309
Goodwin, Nat C. (writer) 346
Gorman, Paddy (trainer) 171, 234
Gorn, Elliot J. (historian/writer) 92, 404
Graney, Ed (referee) 203, 205, 207
Grand Central Palace, New York 133
Grand Forks Daily Herald 319, 365, 405
Grand Rapids, Michigan 57, 307, 361
Grand Trunk Railroad 24
Gray, William 231
Graziano, "Rocky" (Thomas Rocco Barbella) ix
Greater New York Athletic Club 192, 231, 233
Grebb, Harry "The Pittsburgh Windmill" 339
Green Springs Sanitarium and Water Cure 274, 275, 321
Greig, Murray (writer) 241, 404
Griffin, Johnny T. "The Braintree Lad" 79, *84*, 85, 96, 110, 189, 363
Griffo, "Young" (Albert Griffiths) iii, 73, *74*, 79-82, 84, 101, 108, 109, 116, 121, 126, 128, 166, 167, 169, 175, *195*, 196, 207, 215, 227, 264, 307, 343, 344, 362, 363, 403 ; death 340; drinking problems 54, 75, 173;

first defeat 75; first fight with Lavigne 75, 76; incarcerations 118, 194; lack of training 75, 196; physical description of 117, 119; quitting on "Philadelphia" Tommy Ryan 195, 197; robbed of win over McAuliffe 98, 355; second fight with Lavigne 117-120, 168
Griguerre, Edward 336
Grombach, John (historian/writer) 93, 356, 404

Hadley, "Professor" Charles 37
Haley, Melissa (historian/writer) 98, 161, 406
Haley, Patsy 347
Hall, Jim 59, 100, 101, 105, 110
Hally, Father Thomas 341
Hammam Baths 203, 271
Handler, Jimmy 80, 114, *115*, 116, 179, 180, 351, 363
Hanlon, "Cute" Eddie 347
Harlem Athletic Club 329
Harrison, Billy 62, 63
Harris, Dooney 168
Harris, Sam (manager) 290, 336
Harvey, Charlie 330
Hawkins, Dal 240, 254, 269, 275
Hawthorne Athletic Club, New York 229, 231, 254
Hayes, John 69, 362,
Hays, Bill 93
Hearns, Tim 240
Hegarty, Tim 282-288, *283*, 290, 291, 296, 365
Hennessey, Billy 80, 363
Herdling, George P. 222, 223
Herford, Al (manager) 235, 237
Herget, John *see also* Mitchell, Young 197, 236
Herrera, Aurelio 282, 309
Hill, Jack 285
Holbrook, Stuart H. (historian/writer) 23, 242, 404

Horton Law 162, 163, 171, 180, 181, 229, 230
Hot Springs, Arkansas 213, 214, 219, 364
Houseman, Lou (writer/promoter) 277, 286
Howard, Robert E. (writer) 350, 351
Hughes, John 225
Humprhies, Joe (manager) 118
Hurley, John B. 221, 336
Hurst, Tim (referee) 85, 110, 112, 118, 120, 126, 128, 131, 167, 347

Illustrated Police News 74, 114, 116, 124, 180, 181, 182, 193, 202, 241, 251, 253, 285, 405
Indiana Militia 74, 117
insane 298, 299, 321, 323-326, 332, 334, 349
International Boxing Research Organization (IBRO) viii, 9, 407
Isenberg, Michael T. (historian/author) 158, 159, 160

Jackson Citizen Patriot 334, 405
Jackson, Peter 59, 209, 335
Jeffries, Jim 123, 124, 163, 239, 240, 296, 347
Johnson, Billy 313
Johnson, Charley 184
Johnson, Jack ix, 35, 62, 123, 163, 214, 296, 335
Johnson, Pikie 22, 44, 361
Johnston, Alexander (writer) 48, 50, 52, 97, 107, 131, 132, 404
Jones, Deacon 63
Jones, Harrington (writer) 317
Jones, Harry 63, 64, 362
Jordan, Ben 299, 300
Jordan, Billy 205

Kahn, Roger (historian/writer) 7, 404
Kalamazoo Gazette 332, 405

Kattel, George 326, 366
Kelly, Joe "Buck" (referee) 347
Kelly, "Honest" John (referee) 171, 173, 174, 255, 257
Kelly, John Edward *see also* Dempsey, Jack "The Nonpareil" 50
Kelly, Paddy 366
Kelly, Sammy 171
Kelly, Ted 125
Kid Lavigne's Triangle Café 304, 321, 329
Kilar, Jeremy (historian/writer) viii, 37, 404
Kinetograph, *see also* Edison, Thomas 81
Kinney, Butch 57, 361
Kitchen, Jack (referee) 285
Kofoed, Jack (writer) 175, 180, 211, 218, 233, 234, 237

LaBlanche, George "The Marine" 50, *61*, 65, 109, 215
Laflin, Professor J. M. 223, 224
La France Hall, Bay City, Michigan 58
Lamarre, Jean (historian/writer) viii, 404
LaMotta, Jake ix
Landmark (North Carolina) 227, 405
Laudanum 298
Lavigne, Agnes (Dufort – mother of George) 19, 20, 24, 26, 30, 33, 34, 39, *169*, 188, 299, 303, 321, 335, 369
Lavigne, Agnes Marie (sister of George) 33, 321, 370
Lavigne, Andre Poutre dit (ancestor) 16, 18, 19, 369
Lavigne, Eleanor Emma (author's mother) v, 5-9, 11, 13, 16, 17
Lavigne, Dennis (infant brother of George) 370
Lavigne, Eugene (author's great uncle) 16
Lavigne, Flora (M. Morrison-Davey, second wife of Kid Lavigne) *337*, 338, 341, 370

413

Lavigne, Frank (brother of George) 274, 370
Lavigne, George Henry "Kid" *32, 40, 82, 99, 119, 125, 137, 148, 154, 169, 201, 204, 230, 245, 253, 255, 280, 331, 337*; abstinence from alcohol 262-264, 275, 277, 312, 321-323; American title 53, 107, 134, 162; ancestry iii, 1, 2, 13-19 ; arrests xi, 1, 43, 58, 71, 101, 108, 120,161, 194, 239, 274, 275, 303, 321, 322, 324, 331, 332 ; birth 26, 84; boxing style xi, 43, 44, 66, 71, 73, 83, 85, 116, 123, 126, 153, 167, 173, 180, 185, 199, 200, 203, 220, 236, 237, 238, 259, 324, 327, 335, 344, 345; Burge fight 141-157, 189, 252; childhood/adolescence 38; death 340, 351; and death of Andy Bowen 101-105, 162; Daly fights 214-220; drinking problems 43, 135, 177, 188, 193, 194, 196, 197, 200, 210, 211, 218, 220, 222, 224, 229, 233, 245, 254, 258, 259, 262, 269, 286, 322, 323, 324, 331; Erne fights 228-234, 254-261; Everhardt fights 109-112, 168-175; and fight fixes 203, 204, 207, 208, 209, 327, 328; and fight managers 59, 62, 65, 80, 81, 197, 226,252, 265, 276, 278, 328; fighting heavier foes 42, 69, 80, 81, 96, 126, 139, 143, 148, 149, 167, 170, 176, 184, 191, 193, 198, 213, 214, 215, 224, 235, 236, 245, 264, 289, 355; first "Kid" 42, 179; and "Gentleman" Jim Corbett 226, 227, 231, 308; and Henry Ford 113, 114, 332-334; as greatest (gamest) lightweight 105, 126, 155, 156, 207, 208, 249, ,255, 259, 268, 297, 314, 322, 324, 328, 346, 347; Griffo fights 73-76, 81, 109, 117-120, 194-196, 340; injuries 66, 67, 80, 209, 210, 223, 227, 234, 251, 258, 261,269, 276, 277, 290, 294; insane 298, 322-326, 331, 332, 334; marriages 273, 274, 303, 337, 338; misidentified with other Kid Lavignes 263, 313, 314-317; on fighting Joe Gans 234, 235, 306, 343; nickname origin 42, 179; non-boxing jobs held 23, 34, 59, 304, 329; and Paris boxing school 300, 301; physical description 60, 63,65, 83, 99, 110, 119, 141, 146, 284, 330; and Savate 271-273; Smith fights 72, 244-252, 254; and John L. Sullivan 128, 129, 177, 186, 213, 221, 224, 249, 329, 346; world title 107, 155
Lavigne, Henry (author's grandfather) 8, 10, 16, 17
Lavigne, Ida (infant sister of George) 370
Lavigne, Jean Baptiste (father of George) 13, 14, 17, 19, 20, 24, 25, 30, 33, 335, 340, 369
Lavigne, Jean Baptiste (infant brother of George) 14, 20, 370
Lavigne, Jacques (ancestor) 15, 369
Lavigne, James (brother of George) 299, 321, 370
Lavigne, Jochin (infant brother of George) 370
Lavigne, John Baptiste (brother of George) 63, 335, 370
Lavigne, Joseph Marie (ancestor) 15, 16, 369
Lavigne, Joseph Procul (infant brother of George) 20, 370
Lavigne, Julia (first wife of Kid Lavigne) *see also* Drujon, Julia 324, 325, 332-335, 337, 370

Lavigne, "Boston" Kid 281, 314
Lavigne, Marie Louise (infant sister of George) 20, 370
Lavigne, William "Billy" (brother of George) 24, 35, 43, 63, 70, 76, 102, *169,* 179, *201,* 203, 210, 214, 220, 237, 269, 281, 286, 345; birth 20; as club manager 271, 276, 281, 289, 312, 343; death 312, 313; as fighter 37, 38, 39, 57, 69, 72, 105, 202, 226, 227, 360, 361, 362; manager of the Kid 41, 42, 55 56, 59, 197, 198, 215, 218, 225, 226, 231, 234, 235, 244, 246, 248, 249, 250, 252, *253,* 265, 276, 278, 293, 294, 298 ; marriage 78
Lavigno II, "The Mexican Kid Lavigne" 317
Lawler, Jim 285
Layton, Billy 103, 214, 215, 364
Lecour, Charles 272
Leeds, Horace 169, 175, 224
Lenox Athletic Club, New York 253
Leon, Casper "The Sicilian Swordfish" 126, 171
Leonard, Benny (Benjamin Leiner) 329, 337, 342, 344, 349
Leonard, Mike "The Fashion Plate" 81
Levinsky, King "Kingfish" *v*
Lewis, Harry 307
Lewis, Jimmy 59, 361
Lewis, Joe (manager) 80, 81
Lewis, John 38
Lewis Law 163
Lewis, Willie 210
Liebling, A. J. (historian/writer) 149, 404
Loftus, Johhny 309
Logansport Pharos (Indiana) 170, 221, 405
London Daily Mail 259, 405
London, England iii, 53, 64, 141, 143, 144, 145, 147, 156, 157, 166, 252, 253, 254, 274, 299, 301, 327, 328, 356, 363
London Prize Ring rules 46-50, 89, 90, 92, 93, 94, 224, 352
London Sporting Life 152, 155
Lonsdale, Lord 145
Los Angeles Herald 310, 311, 317, 405
Los Angeles Times 38, 145, 210, 269, 282, 285, 362, 365, 405
Louisville, Kentucky 213, 219, 276, 290, 309, 364
Lowell Sun 316, 405
Ludington Daily News 339, 341, 405
Ludington, Michigan 59, 72, 362

Maber, Billy "Shadow" 244
Madden, Billy (manager) 136
Madden, Mike 93
Madison Square Garden, New York 122, 135, *138,* 166, 209
Major, Pete 43
Malone, Mike 51
Manistee, Michigan 45, 57, 59, 361, 366
Mansfield News 43, 271, 272, 273, 405
Marciano, "Rocky" (Rocco Francis Marchegiano) ix, x, 124
Marlboro Athletic Club, New York 175
Marquess of Queensberry, *see also* Douglas, John Sholto xi, 90
Marquess of Queensberry rules; *see also* John Graham Chambers 1, 46, 47, 56, 97, 356, 361
Marshall, Jerry 81, 82, 83, 96, 108, 126, 355, 363
Maspeth, Long Island 125, 132, 208, 345, 347, 348
Masterson, Bat 110
Matthews, Matty 244
"mauser" punch *see also* Sullivan, Dave 290
McAuliffe, Jack "Napoleon of the Prize Ring" 38, 51, 54, 69, 92, 94, 97, 98, 104, 107, 121, 122, 124, *134*-140, *137,* 142, 144,

176, 186, 187, 213, 221, 229, 313, 329, 336, 343, 344, 347, 352-356, 363, 403
McCaffrey, Dominick (referee) 82, 83
McCarty, Luther 330
McConnell, Frank 214
McCoy, Charles "Kid" (Norman Selby) 35, 80, 124, 179, 215, 217, 226, 227, 229, 231, 239, 286
McDonald, Jim (referee) 236, 238, 246, 247, 250
McDonald, Stephen "Young" 164
McEnery, Samuel D. 162
McFadden, Dennis "Kid" 239
McFadden, George "Elbows" 179, 240, 254, 264-269, *266*, 275, 278, 281, 284, 288, 364
McFarland, Packey 309
McGannon, Dan 151
McGovern, "Terrible" Terry *260*, 275-279, 282, 288, 290, 291, 307, 308, 336, 340
McGrath, Tim 236
McGuigan, Jack (manager) 310
McKeever, Charles 166, *167*, 168, 170, 175, 178, 182, 184, 185, 186, 191, 215, 224, 363
McNally, Morris viii, 41, 42, 58, 360, 361
McPartland, "Billy Kid" 178-181, *179*, 183, 185, 186, 188, 191, 193, 215, 217, 221, 229, 330, 363, 367
McVey, Jack 222, 223
Melbourne, Michigan 33, 34
Mechanics Pavilion, San Francisco 197, *198*, 205
Menton, Jack 45, 361
Mexico iv, 312, 314
Michigan's Old Inn 40, 405
Milwaukee Evening Wisconsin 70, 71, 73, 74, 75, 85, 95, 96, 108, 136, 139, 170, 175, 220, 225, 229, 233, 252, 262, 274, 289, 296, 304, 313, 328, 363, 366, 405
Milwaukee Free Press 303, 322, 323, 325, 329, 366, 405
Miner's Theatre, New York 122
Mirror of Life (London) 143, 144, 147, 197, 233, 405
Miske, Billy 7
Mitchell, Charley 72, 362
Mitchell, Jimmy 353
Mitchell, Young (John L. Herget) 197, 207,
Moneghan, Johnny 47
Montreal 13, 15, 19
Montreal Athletic Club 224
Moore, Maxwell (referee) 98, 355
Moran, Owen 320
Morris, Carl 330, 331
Morrisette, Margaret L. Dumont 337, 370
Mount Clemens, Michigan 188, 211, 274
Muldoon, Bill (manager) 35
Mr. Hyde 135, 192, 193, 220, 274, 303, 324
Murphy, "Torpedo" Billy 79, 81, 84, *221*
Murphy, Martin 101
Myer, Billy "The Streator Cyclone" 69, 97, 107
Myer, Eddie (brother of Billy) 69, 71, 105, 108, 362, 363

National Athletic Club, Philadelphia 309
National Club of San Francisco 197, 204
National Sporting Club of London 46, 94, 136, 138, 143, *150*, 171, 300, 302
Nee, Paddy 305
Needham, Danny 62, 63, 362
Nelson, Art 325
Nelson, Jimmy 136
Nelson, "Fighting" Dick (Richard Christensen) 318, 319, *320*, 365

Nelson, Oscar "Battling" 296, 306, *318*, 319, 320, 323, 365, 366
Nevada State Journal 336, 405
Newark Daily Advocate 52, 405
New Jersey 114, 117, 220, 226, 254, 265
New Jersey Journal 110, 115, 405
New Orleans, Louisiana 38, 74, 96-99, 101, 104, 107, 109, 160-163, 169, 221, 243, 356, 363
New Orleans Times-Picayune 99, 406
New York; and benefit for Lavigne 133, 134; as center of boxing 160; and Dowling Saloon incident 135; and legalization of prizefighting 162-165, 171; and McAuliffe anointing Lavigne 186, 187; and Metropolitan Hotel incident 222, 224; and police involvement 167, 171, 180; and trolley accident 227, 234
New York Athletic Club 328
New York Clipper 47
New York Herald 168, 239, 405
New York Illustrated News 116, 405
New York State Athletic Commission 35, 314
New York Times 82, 101, 103, 228, 261, 267, 268, 327, 330, 405
New York World 128, 150, 154, 166, 172, 174, 181, 190, 191, 222, 256, 257, 273, 405
Nicholson, Kelly (historian/writer) viii, 404
Nickless, Harry 145
Nonpareil Athletic Club, Louisville 276, 281

Oakland Tribune 236, 282, 283, 284, 289, 299, 314, 405
O'Brien, Billy 58, 361
O'Brien, Dick 79, 80, 123, 125, 272, 362
O'Brien, Jack 58, 371
O'Brien, "New York" Jack 289, 290

Occidental Club of San Francisco 197, 198, 204, 207
O'Donnell, Jack 229
O'Donnell, Steve 151
Old Man Putman's Roadhouse, Saginaw 56
Olympic Club of Birmingham, England 192
Olympic Club of New Orleans 97, 109, 160, 162
Ordway, Dr. Aaron P. 143, 147
Oregon State University 147
O'Rourke, Tom (manager) 121-124, 126, 129, *130*, 131, 132, 197, 198, 205-210, 327, 328, 346
Oshkosh Daily Northwestern 277, 288

Pacific Athletic Club, San Francisco 59, 62-64, 141
Palace Theatre, Manistee, Michigan 57
Paris, France iv, 271-276, 288, 298-301, 303, 308, 321, 323, 325, 332, 333, 365, 367
Park Rink, Saginaw 69, 72, 362
parlor style boxing 172, 237, 359
Pastime Athletic Club, Portland, Oregon 63
Pelican Club 300, 301, 356
Pelkey, Arthur (Pelletier) 330, 331
Philadelphia 166, 169, 176, 185, 194, 197, 198, 219, 302, 304, 308, 363, 364, 365
Philadelphia Arena 220
Philadelphia Enquirer 405
Philadelphia Evening Bulletin 177, 184, 185, 405
Philadelphia Item 83, 405
Philadelphia Record 182, 184, 185, 191, 192, 196, 405
"Philadelphia" lightweight 169, 170, 175, 215
Pitts and Cranage mill 25, 26, 33
"pivot" punch *see also* LaBlanche, George 50, 65, 109, 215

Police Gazette see also Sam F. Austin and Richard K. Fox viii, 23, 36, 70, 77, 80, 96, 98, 108, 120, 125, 131, 171, 173, 174, 187, 188, 206, 210, 221, 224, 231, 238, 258, 259, 261, 263, 269, 275, 276, 277, 282, 286, 299, 300, 307, 318, 336, 346, 354, 404, 405
Pollack, Adam J. (historian/writer) 160, 161, 404
Port Huron, Michigan 24, 33, 35, 36, 37
Portland Oregonian 63, 64, 216, 406
Portsmouth Daily Times 331, 406
Priest, Jimmy 42, 360
Providence, Rhode Island 80
Purity Crusades 159

Quaker City Athletic Club, Philadelphia 175, 184, 191, 194

Racine Daily Journal 269, 275, 277, 366, 405
Racine Journal News 334, 406
Ralph, Bob 42, 360
Randall, Jack 47
Republican News (Ohio) 218, 406
Reno, Nevada 163
Reynolds, George 301, 367
Rickard, Tex (promoter) 5, 6
Ring, Clark 149
Ring Magazine 9, 10, 122, 200, 350, 351, 365, 403
Ripley, Robert L. (writer) *331*
Ritchie, Willie 309, 329
road cane 336, 359
Roberts, Billy 42, 360
Roberts, Jack 301, *302*, 365
Roberts, James 165, 404
Roberts, Randy 164
Roche, Billy (manager) 191, 278, *279*, 280, 281, 288, 289, 299
Roche, Dick (referee) 182
Rochette, Charles *62*, 63, 141, 362
Rockne, Knute 5, 6. 147

Rodriguez, Robert G. (historian/writer) 165, 404
Roosevelt, Teddy 163, 165
Root, Jack 286
Rucker, Ed 219, 364
Ryan, "Australian" Jimmy 243
Ryan, "Philadelphia" Tommy 194, 197
Ryan, Tommy (Joseph Youngs) 51, 67, *68*, 69, 80, 110, 124, 126, 127, 134, 144, 200, *201*, 215, 236, 239, 240, 244, 270, 363

Sage, Bob "The Battling Barrister" 339, 340
Saginaw, Michigan; benefits for Lavigne 69, 72; early fight scene 23, 31, 32, 42, 43, 44, 212, 213. 305; history 25, 26, 39, 40, *41*, 75; Lavigne family migration to 24
Saginaw Armory 105
Saginaw Athletic Club 305
Saginaw Auditorium 42
Saginaw County Sports Hall of Fame vii, 351
Saginaw Courier Herald 310, 406
Saginaw Evening News 43, 57. 58, 69, 106, 198, 199, 216, 217, 266, 369, 406
Saginaw News 39, 43, 55, 56, 129, 187, 206, 207, 208, 274, 295, 298, 325, 331, 406
Saginaw River 23, 24, 26, 58
St. Joseph's Catholic Church, Bay City *25*, 30
St. Joseph's Sanatorium, Dearborn 323, 325, 334
St. Louis (steamship) 144, 157
St. Louis Republic 226
St. Mary, Billy 32, 212, 255
St. Polycarpe, Quebec 19, 24, 369, 370
Salt Lake Tribune 308, 406
Sammons, Jeffrey T. (historian/writer) 159, 160, 162, 404, 406

San Antonio Daily Express 314, 406
San Antonio Light 315, 406
San Diego Evening Tribune 341, 406
Sandusky Morning Star (Ohio) 219, 239, 264, 268
San Francisco; as center of boxing 160, 163
San Francisco Bulletin 199, 406
San Francisco Chronicle 60, 63, 64, 204, 206, 236, 237, 248, 250, 284, 286, 292, 293, 362, 364, 406
San Francisco Examiner 2, 202, 203, 206, 368, 406
San Francisco Morning Call 60, 185, 200, 246, 247, 249, 257, 267, 282, 292, 298, 326, 361, 366, 406
San Francisco Olympic Club 160
San Francisco Post 189, 406
Sarnia, Ontario 24
Savate 272, 273, 300, 303, 406
Savoie, Thomas Francois de 18
Schroeder, Stephen (writer) 57
Schuch, John Philip (writer) 57, 405
Schutte, Bill (historian/writer) vii, 8-11
Seaside Athletic Club, Brooklyn 82, 110, *111*
Second Regiment Armory, Chicago 75
Second Ward School, Bay City 34
Shaffer, Harry (historian/writer) vii, 2, 10, 11
shanty boys 27, 30, 37, 39, 40
Sharkey, "Sailor" Tom 123, 124, 239, 240
Shaughnessy, Martin 67, 68, 69, 362
Sheridan, Mickey *321*, 366
Sholtreau, Ed (also Sheltraw) 279, *280*, 365
Siddons, George (Ambrose Smith) 55, *56*, 57, 58, 63, 76, 153, 227, 344, 361
Siler, George (referee) 76, 108, 347
Silver, Mike (historian/writer) viii, 342, 405
Simms, Artie 279-281
Sioux City Journal 219, 406
Skelly, Jack 114, 347
Skutt, Alexander (historian/writer) 165, 404
Slater bill 164
Smith, Al 326
Smith, Alfred E. 165
Smith, Billy 302
Smith, "Mysterious" Billy 80, 124, 142, 143, 209, 234, 240, 241, *242, 245,* 261, 279, 313, 362, 364, 406, ; birth 241; bouts with Wolcott 245; defeat of Lavigne 245-253; early exhibition with Lavigne 72; fight with coalminer 242, 243; fight with "Nonpareil" Jack Dempsey 243, 244; nickname origin 241, 242; welterweight title 244
Smith, Charles A. C. "Black Thunderbolt" 35, *36*, 37, 43, 59, 360
Smith, "Denver" Ed 168
Smith, Eddie (referee) 292, 294
Smith, Jem 142, 145
Smith, Solly (Soloman Garcia Smith) 75-*78*, 81, 84, 110, 126, 135, 205, 227, 307, 362
Soto, Joe 59-63, 76, 81, 107, 153, 267, 344, 345, 362
Sporting Life (London) 149, 151, 152, 155, 363, 406
Sporting Review (London) 112, 406
Sportsman (London) 151, 155, 406
Springfield Daily News (Massachusetts) 322, 406
Spring Valley, Illinois 242
Stevenson, George 88
Stewart, Jack "Scotch Giant" 35, 36, 37
Stone, Jig 253
Sullivan, Dave 279, 288, 290
Sullivan, Jerry "Horsebite" 79, 80, 83

Sullivan, John L. "Boston Strong Boy" 35, 59, 119, 134, 158, 160, 184, 213, 223, 224, 304, 328, 329, 340, 346, 348, 404; begs referee to stop Lavigne/Wolcott bout 128, 129, 249, 348; draws the color line 36, 335; and drinking problem 97, 98, 177, 194; and Lavigne's championship belt 186, 187, 221; loss to Corbett 53, 97, 98, 356; praise for Lavigne 346; predicts Lavigne as champion 62, 63
Sullivan, "Kid" (Harry Sheehy) 305, 307
Sullivan, Mike (referee) 65, 66
Sullivan, "Spike" (William Clothiers) 224, 225, 240, 253, 288
Suster, Gerald (historian/writer) 356, 405
Syracuse Daily Sentinel 193, 406
Syracuse Standard 186, 406
Syracuse Sunday Herald 67, 214, 229, 232, 406

Tacoma Daily News 73, 75, 406
Tany, Jack (historian/writer) vii
Tattersall Athletic Club *see also* Houseman, Lou 277
Tendler, Lew 337
Thompson, Lachie 145
Tittabawasee River 26
Titusville Herald (Pennsylvania) 230, 406
Tracey, "Smiling" Tom **235**-239, 240, 364
Trenton Evening News 329
Trenton Times 271, 278, 288, 406
Tunney, Gene ix
Tuthill, Harry (trainer/manager) 346

Unholz, Boer 323
University of Detroit 147

Valentine, Arthur 107, 108, 116, 118, 166
Van Court, De Witt 236
Van Heest, Johnny 75, 215
Vaudeville 187, 213, 296, 300, 313
Veiock, Jack (writer) 296
Vesely, Robert "Mr. V." ix

Walcott, "Jersey" Joe x
Walcott, Joe "Barbados Demon" 80, 122, **123**, 144, 152, 153, 174, 183, 189, **205**, 218, 219, 235, 236, **241**, 284, 307, 328, 346, 348, 351, 355, 403; battle at Maspeth with Lavigne 53, 125-133, 249, 347, 363; birth 121; death 209; description of 122, 124, 126; famous quote by 123; fighting style 123; nicknames 116, 124; second Lavigne fight 197-211, 236, 258, 291, 349, 364; welterweight title 209, 210
Walker, Arthur 236
Walker, James J. "Jimmy" *see also* Walker Law 165, 209
Walker Law 165, 315
Ward, Mike 307
Warren, Tommy 42, 55
Washington Avenue Rink, Bay City 69
Washington Post 101, 120, 146, 152, 176, 180, 182, 217, 237, 305, 312, 348, 406
Waterloo Daily Courier (Iowa) 193, 406
Watts, Jim 219, 364
Weir, Ike "The Belfast Spider" 55, 75, 84
Welsh, Freddy 329
Weston, Stan (writer) 117, 118
White, Billy 42, 360
White, Charlie 171
White, Tommy 75
Whitney, Chubb 366
Whitney, David Jr. 33, 34
Willard, Jess ix, 164, 330

Williams, Frank "Captain" 104
Williams, Tom 145
Williamsport Daily Gazette 316, 406
Wolgast, Ad "The Michigan Wildcat" 313, 320, 321, *323*, 345, 365, 366
Woodward's Pavilion, San Francisco 235, 240, *241*, 292, 297

X-ray, *see also* Edison, Thomas A. 290

Yosemite Athletic Club, San Francisco 289

Zale, Tony ix
Ziegler, Owen 136, 166, 169, 175, *176*, 177, 180, 183, 184, 191, 192, 193, 215, 224, 231, 240, 330, 355, 363, 364

ABOUT THE AUTHOR

Lauren Chouinard comes by his love of sports naturally. His mother, Kid Lavigne's second cousin a few times removed, was a diehard sports fan, and Lauren was raised on Chicago's south side, just a few blocks from the home of Cassius Clay, now known as Muhammad Ali. Lauren earned a bachelor's degree in history from Illinois State University, where he helped found its rugby team. In 1978 he moved to Eugene, Ore., to open Pacific Nautilus, a health and fitness club. Lauren worked in municipal government for 27 years, retiring as the City of Eugene's human resource director in 2008. He also wrote *Get Off Your But*, a practical guide to getting in shape while overcoming excuses that prevent a healthier lifestyle. Lauren belongs to the International Boxing Research Organization and lives in Eugene with his wife, Carrie.

For more on George "Kid" Lavigne visit:
www.KidLavigne.com.

Lightning Source UK Ltd.
Milton Keynes UK
UKHW010929271119
354284UK00003B/1084/P